Norfolk Record Society
Volume LXXXIV for 2020

The COTTAGE of H.Repton Esqr. HARE-STREET, ESSEX.

'The Cottage of H. Repton Esqr., Hare-Street, Essex',
published in *Peacock's Polite Repository* (1800, p. 10),
an engraving from a drawing by Repton
(The Bodleian Library, University of Oxford, MS. Eng. misc. g.72, p. 10,
reproduced by kind permission)

Humphry Repton
and his family

Correspondence, 1805–1816

Heather Falvey

General Editor
Anthony Howe

Norfolk Record Society
Volume LXXXIV
2020

First published in 2020
by the Norfolk Record Society

ISBN 978-0-9957736-3-9

Typeset by Carnegie Book Production, Lancaster
Printed and bound by Short Run Press, Exeter

Contents

Maps and illustrations

Acknowledgements

As I am primarily an early modern historian, the early nineteenth century was, and to a great extent still is, a mystery to me but I was drawn to the life and work of Humphry Repton through my role as Secretary of the Hertfordshire Record Society. I was involved in the publication, in 2011, of *Humphry Repton's Red Books of Panshanger and Tewin Water, Hertfordshire, 1799–1800* (HRS volume XXVII). During that project I learned of the collection of letters written between various members of Repton's family that is now owned by The Huntington Library, San Marino, California. Dr Steve Hindle, W. M. Keck Foundation Director of Research at the Huntington, suggested that I apply for a scholarship to visit the library and work on the letters. Usually when applying for a scholarship you ask your PhD supervisor to be one of your referees, but, as in his former academic incarnation Steve had been my supervisor, that was not an option. I am therefore very grateful to Profs Richard Hoyle and Bernard Capp and to Dr Samantha Williams for writing letters of recommendation for my scholarship; and to Steve for suggesting that I apply. Due to our connection he was not allowed to consider my application, so I thank the selection committee for their positive decision.

In June and July 2013 I worked in the Huntington Library, transcribing and photographing the letters. For a variety of reasons, not least academic commitments and activities for various historical societies, this edition has taken a long time to complete; and, of course, over 200 letters needed to be read and re-read, annotated and, in many cases, assigned dates. Putting them into chronological order has been a challenge: whenever I thought I had cracked it, a phrase or comment in another letter seemed to suggest a possible change in the order. The order published here is my best interpretation. Furthermore, just days before submitting the final text I obtained from the Huntington a photograph of the endorsement to one of the letters: my own photograph was too faint to read and I felt that simply saying 'illegible' was inappropriate in that case. Although still very faint, the words were legible in the new photo and cast light on one of the many conundrums concerning Humphry Repton. I gratefully acknowledge the permission of The Huntington Library, San Marino, California, to publish the text of the letters and the photographs used as illustrations.

I have received a great deal of advice from Humphry Repton specialists. In particular I would like to thank Prof Stephen Daniels who has been very supportive of my work and unfailingly helpful in offering suggestions, answering very many questions and endorsing my findings. He also very kindly invited me to participate in a 'Repton round-table' at the Paul Mellon Centre, Bedford Square, on 30 January 2019, where I met many Repton scholars, all of whom were very welcoming and expressed great interest in this project.

As the letters were accumulated by Repton's son William, a solicitor practising in Aylsham, I approached the Norfolk Record Society with regard to publishing the letters, and I am very grateful to the Society for agreeing to do so and to Anthony Howe, the General Editor for 'modern' volumes, for his advice and for identifying quite a number of the people mentioned by the correspondents. I have received help from many other people, including staff at the Huntington Library, the Avery Architectural Library, the Norfolk Record Office, the Norfolk Heritage Centre, the Essex Record Office and The National Archives, and Martin Grier, General Secretary of the British Postmark Society. During 2018 various counties' Gardens Trusts published books to celebrate the bicentenary of Repton's death. The Hertfordshire and Norfolk volumes have been particularly useful, and I have enjoyed discussions with Sue Flood, Anne Rowe and Tom Williamson. I am also very grateful to Maggie Vaughan-Lewis, whom I just happened to meet in the NRO in March 2015. When I explained my research interests she very kindly gave me a copy of *Aylsham: A Nest of Norfolk Lawyers*, which she and her husband, William, had recently published. It certainly enabled me to identify many people mentioned in the letters written from Aylsham and Maggie also responded promptly to various subsequent questions. I also thank Jane Walker for compiling the family tree and Andrew Macnair for supplying the maps. Finally thanks are due to the Bodleian Library, the University of Oxford, for supplying the image of Repton's Hare Street Cottage, the place where many of these letters were written.

I think that my husband Denis is pleased to be saying farewell to Humphry Repton and his family, but nevertheless he has been very supportive during the seven years that they have 'lived' with us. He enjoyed a visit to California once I had completed my scholarship and has also been on several short breaks in Norfolk when I needed to visit the NRO or NHC, or just wanted to visit Sheringham Park, perhaps the best preserved Repton landscape.

Croxley Green, March 2020

Abbreviations

A to Z of Regency London	*The A to Z of Regency London (Richard Horwood's Map, 3rd edn. 1813)*, introduction by P. Laxton (London, 1985)
Alumni Cantab.	J. A. Venn, compiler, *Alumni Cantabrigienses: A Biographical List of All Known Students, Graduates and Holders of Office at the University of Cambridge, from the Earliest Times to 1900*, part 2, *1752–1900*, 5 vols. (Cambridge, 1940–54)
Alumni Oxon.	J. Foster, *Alumni Oxonienses: The Members of the University of Oxford, 1715–1886*, 4 vols. (London, 1887–8)
Avery Library	Avery Architectural Library, Columbia University, New York
Aylsham	W. Vaughan-Lewis and M. Vaughan-Lewis, *Aylsham: A Nest of Norfolk Lawyers* (Itteringham, 2014)
Aylsham Directories	G. Gale and T. Mollard, eds., *Aylsham Directories, 1793 to 1937 (extracted from the directories for Aylsham Norfolk …)* (Aylsham, 2004)
Aylsham in 1821	T. Mollard, ed., *Aylsham in 1821. The population of the parish of Aylsham recorded by William Morris in May, 1821* (Aylsham, 1997)
BL	British Library, St Pancras
British Banking	J. Orbell and A. Turton, eds., *British Banking: a guide to historical records* (Aldershot, 2001)
Carter et al., *Repton*	G. Carter, P. Goode and K. Laurie, *Humphry Repton: Landscape Gardener 1752–1818* (Norwich & London, 1982)
CCEd ID	Clergy of the Church of England database (followed by individual's ID number) www.theclergydatabase.org.uk

Daniels, 'Cankerous blossom'	S. Daniels, 'Cankerous blossom: troubles in the later career of Humphry Repton documented in the Repton correspondence in the Huntington Library', *Journal of Garden History*, 6 (1986), pp. 146–61
Daniels, *Repton*	S. Daniels, *Humphry Repton: Landscape Gardening and the Geography of Georgian England* (New Haven and London, 1999)
Dictionary of land surveyors	S. Bendall, ed., *Dictionary of land surveyors and local map-makers of Great Britain and Ireland, 1530–1850* (2nd edition, 2 vols., London, 1997)
ERO	Essex Record Office
Fragments	H. Repton, *Fragments on the Theory and Practice of Landscape Gardening (including some Remarks on Grecian and Gothic Architecture)* (London, 1816)
Hist. Parl.	*The History of Parliament Online (Members 1790–1820)* (unless otherwise stated)
HL	The Huntington Library, San Marino, California
HM	Huntington Manuscript
LMA	London Metropolitan Archives
London Encyclopaedia	B. Weinreb and C. Hibbert, eds., *The London Encyclopaedia*, (London, 1983)
Loudon, *Landscape Gardening*	J. C. Loudon, *The Landscape Gardening and Landscape Architecture of the Late Humphry Repton Esq.* (London, 1840)
Memoirs	A. Gore and G. Carter, eds., *Humphry Repton's Memoirs* (Norwich, 2005)
NHC	Norfolk Heritage Centre, Norwich Millennium Library
Norwich Directory for 1811	*A concise history and directory of the City of Norwich for 1811: containing besides the lists, a variety of local information, useful and interesting to residents and strangers* (Norwich, 1810).
NRO	Norfolk Record Office
ODNB	*Oxford Dictionary of National Biography* (online version)
OED	*Oxford English Dictionary* (online version)
PA	Parliamentary Archives
Pigot's *Directory* (1823)	Pigot's *Directory: Middlesex & the Towns & Villages within 12 miles of London* (1823)

Polite Repository	W. Peacock, *Polite Repository*, (London, 1790 onwards) (annual publication)
Repton in Bucks	S. Rutherford, ed., *Humphry Repton in Buckinghamshire and beyond* (Buckinghamshire, 2018)
Repton in Herts	S. Flood and T. Williamson, eds., *Humphry Repton in Hertfordshire* (Hatfield, 2018)
Repton in Kent	(Kent Gardens Trust), *Humphry Repton in Kent* (Eynsford, 2018)
Repton in London	(London Parks and Gardens Trust), *Repton in London: The gardens and landscapes of Humphry Repton (1752–1818) in the London Boroughs* (London, 2018)
Repton in Norfolk	S. Bate, R. Savage and T. Williamson, eds., *Humphry Repton in Norfolk* (Aylsham, 2018)
Repton in Sussex	S. Batty, ed., *Humphry Repton in Sussex* (Sussex, 2018)
Repton in the West Midlands	D. Whitehead and J. Bradney, 'In the enemy's quarters': *Humphry Repton in the West Midlands* (Hereford, 2018)
Repton in Yorkshire	P. Eyres and K. Lynch, *On The Spot: The Yorkshire Red Books of Humphry Repton, Landscape Gardener* (Huddersfield, 2018)
Rogger, *Landscapes*	A. Rogger, *Landscapes of Taste, The Art of Humphry Repton's Red Books* (Oxford, 2007)
Sail and Storm	S. Spooner, ed., *Sail and Storm: The Aylsham Navigation* (Aylsham, 2012)
SRO (Bury)	Suffolk Record Office, Bury St Edmunds branch
Stroud, *Repton*	D. Stroud, *Humphry Repton* (London, 1962)
Temple, 'Repton, illustrator'	N. Temple, 'Humphry Repton, Illustrator, and William Peacock's "Polite Repository" 1790–1811', *Garden History*, 16: 2 (Autumn 1988), pp. 161–73
TNA	The National Archives, Kew
Universal Directory (1790)	*The Universal British directory of trade and commerce; Comprehending lists of the inhabitants of London, Westminster, and borough of Southwark; and of all the Cities, Towns and principal Villages in England Wales...* (London, 1790)
VCH	*The Victoria County History*

Repton family tree

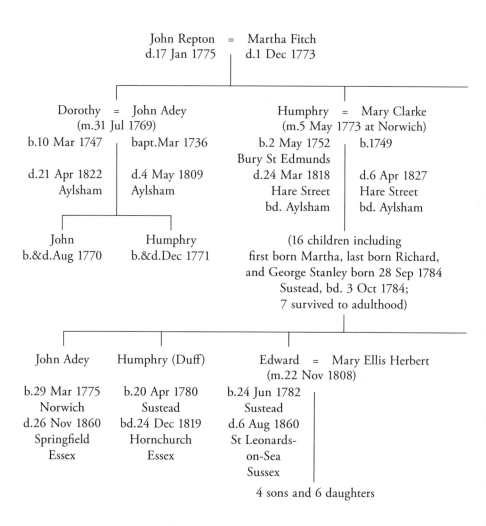

John Repton = Martha Fitch
d.17 Jan 1775 | d.1 Dec 1773

Dorothy = John Adey
(m.31 Jul 1769)
b.10 Mar 1747 | bapt.Mar 1736

d.21 Apr 1822 | d.4 May 1809
Aylsham | Aylsham

Humphry = Mary Clarke
(m.5 May 1773 at Norwich)
b.2 May 1752 | b.1749
Bury St Edmunds
d.24 Mar 1818 | d.6 Apr 1827
Hare Street | Hare Street
bd. Aylsham | bd. Aylsham

John
b.&d.Aug 1770

Humphry
b.&d.Dec 1771

(16 children including
first born Martha, last born Richard,
and George Stanley born 28 Sep 1784
Sustead, bd. 3 Oct 1784;
7 survived to adulthood)

John Adey

b.29 Mar 1775
Norwich
d.26 Nov 1860
Springfield
Essex

Humphry (Duff)

b.20 Apr 1780
Sustead
bd.24 Dec 1819
Hornchurch
Essex

Edward = Mary Ellis Herbert
(m.22 Nov 1808)
b.24 Jun 1782
Sustead
d.6 Aug 1860
St Leonards-
on-Sea
Sussex

4 sons and 6 daughters

Key: b. = born, bapt. = baptised, bd. = buried, d. = died, m. = married
References for the dates given above are in the biographies in the Introduction

John = Elizabeth Knight
(m.May 1799)

b.25 Aug 1753   b.1778

d.14 Jun 1809   d.24 Feb 1848
Oxnead

Elizabeth (Eliza)
bapt.18 Oct 1801

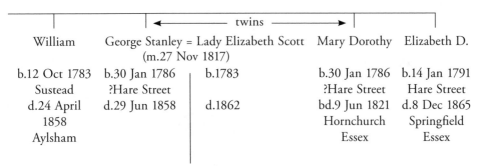

		twins		
William	George Stanley = Lady Elizabeth Scott		Mary Dorothy	Elizabeth D.
	(m.27 Nov 1817)			
b.12 Oct 1783	b.30 Jan 1786	b.1783	b.30 Jan 1786	b.14 Jan 1791
Sustead	?Hare Street		?Hare Street	Hare Street
d.24 April	d.29 Jun 1858	d.1862	bd.9 Jun 1821	d.8 Dec 1865
1858			Hornchurch	Springfield
Aylsham			Essex	Essex

1 son and 2 or more daughters

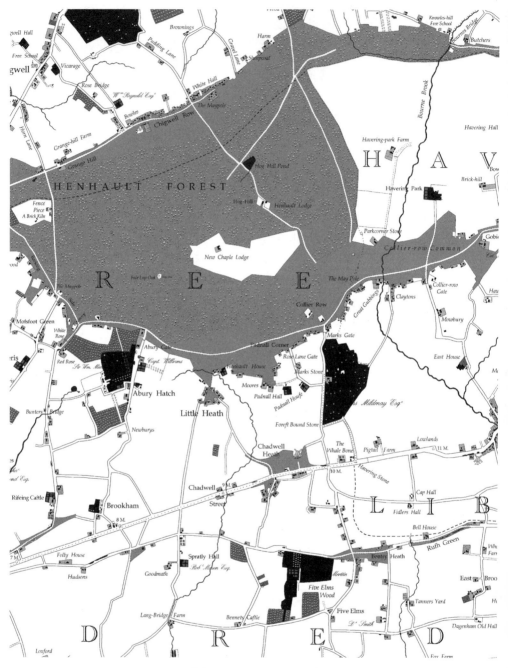

Map of the Hare Street area of Essex
for detail of Hare Street see overleaf
(digitally redrawn by Andrew Macnair from John Chapman and Peter André,
A Map of the County of Essex (1777))

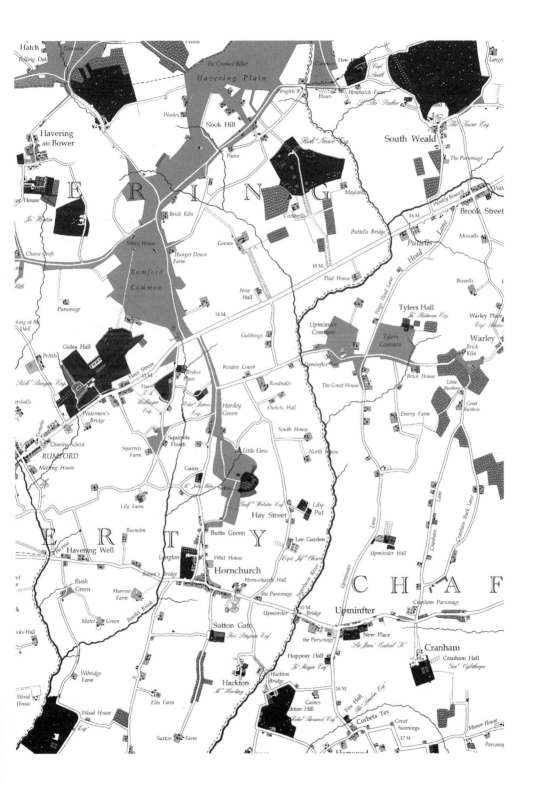

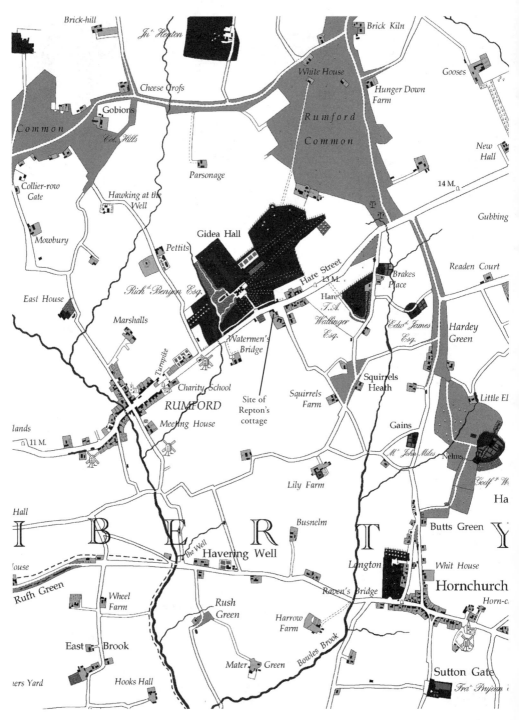

Detail of the Hare Street area of Essex, showing the site of Repton's cottage

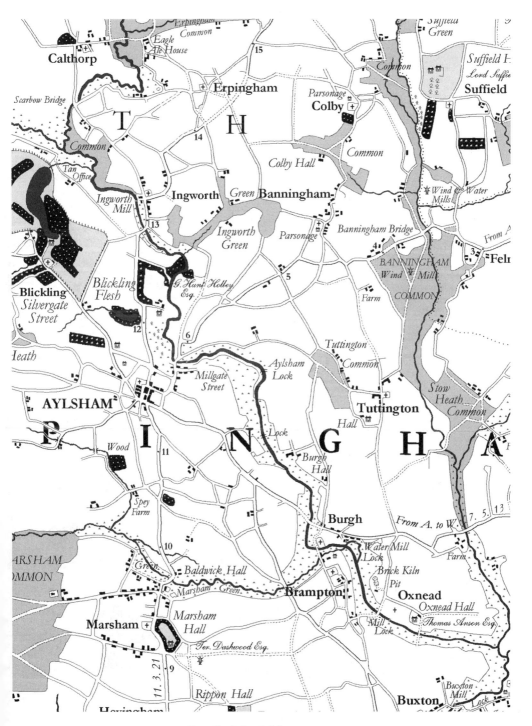

Detail of the Aylsham area

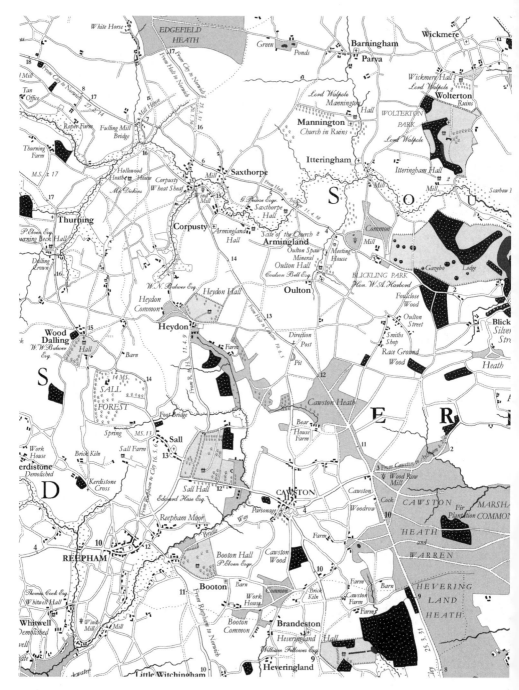

Map of the Aylsham area of Norfolk
for detail of Aylsham see previous page
(digitally redrawn by Andrew Macnair from William Faden, *Map of Norfolk* (1797))

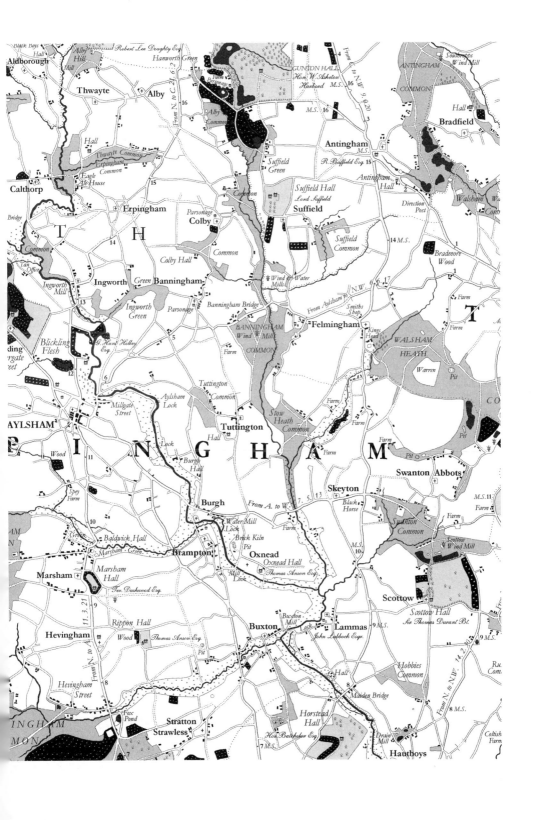

Introduction

I have alterd my intention – was going to write to George but thought I had better stop till I meet his letter at Uley to morrow. Then I thought of writing to Duff [Humphry junior] – but he never writes to any body, so I will tell you all [at Aylsham] where I am – & what I have been doing.

(Humphry Repton to his son William, 25 September 1807)[1]

The letters published here, many addressed to William Repton at Aylsham, were acquired by the Huntington Library in 1974.[2] Since then only three publications have made more than passing reference to the letters and have used them as evidence for Humphry Repton's life and career. The first was *Humphry Repton: Landscape Gardener 1752–1818*, the catalogue compiled by George Carter, Patrick Goode and Kedrun Laurie to accompany the Repton exhibition held in Norwich, and then in London, in late 1982 and early 1983; in 'Cankerous blossom: troubles in the later career of Humphry Repton documented in the Repton correspondence in the Huntington Library', an article published in 1986, Stephen Daniels considered some of the letters in detail; and in his 1999 monograph, *Humphry Repton: Landscape Gardening and the Geography of Georgian England*, Daniels used many extracts from the letters.

The life and work of Humphry Repton are of interest to scholars and readers from a wide variety of historical sub-disciplines because his activities made an impact not only on architecture, gardens and the landscape but also on individuals, localities and Georgian society more generally. His surviving letters, manuscripts and published works of

---

1 Letter 20. According to the Gloucestershire Gardens Trust, this is the only mention of Repton going to Uley. The likely property in question was known as Stour's Hill.

2 For details of the collection's provenance, see below, pp. 44–45.

various types are housed in numerous repositories in both the UK and the USA, ranging from county record offices, through university and research libraries, to private collections.[3] Historians have drawn on these documents to reconstruct different aspects of Repton's contribution to the English landscape and Georgian society. Interest in Repton continues unabated, as witnessed by the number of books about him published in 2018, the bi-centenary of his death.[4]

Whereas Repton's landscape design books (the majority known as Red Books from their red leather covers), his other designs and his published printed works display his public side, as do his memoirs;[5] by contrast, the letters written by him held at the Huntington Library and published here provide a different view. They shed light on some of his private thoughts and attitudes, at times somewhat negative, written as they were towards the end of his life, which, although successful in terms of renown, had been rather less successful financially. Daniels cautions that Repton was conscious that his family members constituted an audience to whom his letters were addressed, just as much as polite society to whom his published works were addressed, and so in that sense his letters were 'as conventional as his published writings'.[6] Nevertheless, commencing in late 1806 and continuing until 1816, the letters written by Repton himself provide insights not only into his later life, but also, amongst other topics, his opinions on the changing nature of local society, the impact of the war with France and the introduction of income tax. Although the bulk of the letters were written during a period when he was infirm and had more time for reflection, he was not always pessimistic.

It must be emphasised, however, that the letters in this collection were not only written by Humphry Repton, for commencing in June 1805 there are letters, or postscripts, from all of his immediate family. Humphry and his wife Mary, together with their two daughters, Mary and Elizabeth, lived at Hare Street (Essex); three sons, Humphry, Edward and George, lived away from home, generally in London; William lived in Aylsham with his aunt Dorothy Adey née Repton, and her husband John, whose legal practice William eventually took over; the eldest son, John (known as John Adey Repton, who was profoundly deaf), seems to have

---

3 See, for example, the bibliographies of his manuscripts and printed books in Daniels, *Repton* and Carter et al., *Repton*.

4 Several of the 2018 publications referred to one or more of these letters, but not always accurately.

5 *Memoirs*, an edited transcript of BL, Add. MSS 62112.

6 Daniels, 'Cankerous blossom', p. 158.

lived at Hare Street but stayed frequently at Aylsham. The letters reveal a close-knit family concerned about each other's well-being and gossiping about friends and acquaintances in Norfolk and Essex, such that they disclose much about local society in and around Aylsham and Hare Street. Generally the letters are affectionate and convey strong familial ties, the latter particularly obvious in times of crisis, for example, in bereavement, when the legal matter of 'Shalder's deed' required attention, and when Edward's impending marriage apparently threatened to divide the family. There are also a number of business letters addressed to William and his draft replies to various clients and acquaintances, mostly in Norfolk, which shine a valuable light on the work of an early nineteenth-century country attorney.

The family's closeness is clear from frequent visits by the sons to Hare Street, and by all family members to Aylsham. Hare Street was only 13 miles from London and Romford only 12.[7] Pigot's *Directory* for 1823 indicates the frequency of coach services to Romford: coaches left the White Hart for London daily at 8.00 a.m. and 9.00 a.m., and at 2.30 p.m., and also travelled in the opposite direction.[8] For members of the family travelling to Aylsham, the Mail coach left The Swan in Romford for Norwich every evening at 10.00 p.m., or there was a coach at 6.45 a.m. every morning also from The Swan to Norwich. Indeed 'the village of Hare Street was busy with traffic. Stage-coaches to London from throughout East Anglia passed Repton's front door, chaises and carriages too'.[9]

This particular collection of letters does not reveal a great deal about Repton's ideas and practices with regard to landscape gardening, for these letters were not written to clients and so are unlike those outlining a current or future project, such as the numerous letters sent to the duke of Bedford, or to his steward, William Adam.[10] Some of the letters in this collection are, nevertheless, important because they reveal details how Repton worked on a practical level. From their contents it is clear that his was a family business and that family members frequently accompanied him on his professional visits, both before and after he was seriously injured in a carriage accident in January 1811.[11] Some of the letters do, however, mention later commissions; others indicate return visits to places where he been employed several

---

7 The 12- and 13-mile markers are indicated on the 1805 Ordnance Survey map.

8 Pigot's *Directory* (1823), p. 64.

9 Daniels, *Repton*, p. 59.

10 Such letters are held by the Bedfordshire Archive Service in the Woburn Estate Papers, and the Devon Record Office, in the Bedford MSS, Repton papers.

11 *Memoirs*, p. 23.

years earlier; and a handful indicate (possible) commissions not recorded anywhere else.[12]

The remainder of this introduction has a three-fold purpose: firstly, to highlight what the letters disclose about Repton's life and professional activities; secondly, by considering the early career of William Repton, to outline the place of the Aylsham family members in the wider society of Norfolk at the time; thirdly to provide biographies of the other members of the Repton family, many of whom have been largely overlooked, or misrepresented, in the numerous works on Repton himself.

Humphry Repton in the Huntington letters

Humphry Repton was born on at Bury St Edmunds on 2 May 1752[13] and baptised at St James's, Bury, on 5 May.[14] Some other details of his life, such as his marriage and the births of his children, are given below in the family members' biographies. After being educated at school in Bury, Norwich and near Rotterdam, when Repton was 16 he was apprenticed to a textile merchant in Norwich.[15] After his apprenticeship his father John set him up in business also in Norwich, but following severe losses, in 1778 Humphry bought a small country estate at Sustead, where he lived 'as a gentleman amateur, doing a little farming, some sketching and writing'.[16] During this time he became friendly with William Windham, lord of the manor of Sustead and one of Norfolk's leading landowners and politicians. In 1783 he was briefly Windham's private secretary in Dublin and in the 1784 election was his political agent.[17] Also in 1784 Repton went to Bath where he invested time and most of his remaining capital in a venture with John Palmer to reform the mail-coach system: the scheme was successful financially for Palmer but Repton received no recognition for his contribution.[18] Repton moved his growing family from Sustead to a rented cottage in Hare Street, possibly in early 1785 and certainly by July 1786 when the twins George and Mary were baptised at Romford parish

---

12 Some of these latter are discussed below, pp. 13–16.

13 *Memoirs*, p. 9. In Letter 160 Repton notes 2 May as his birthday; in several publications it has been given erroneously as 21 April 1752.

14 Stroud, *Repton*, p. 15.

15 *Memoirs*, pp. 9–11; Carter et al., *Repton*, p. 5.

16 Daniels, *Repton*, p. 30.

17 T. Williamson, *Polite Landscapes: Gardens and Society in Eighteenth-Century England* (Stroud, 1995), p. 142.

18 Daniels, *Repton*, p. 32.

church.[19] Although he described his new home as his 'humble Cottage', it was in fact a smart, detached roadside villa.[20] (*See the frontispiece.*) Initially he tried to 'make a career in writing and drawing for publication'.[21] Then, as he announced in his memoirs, 'Anno dom: 1788, Now at the age of thirty-six I commence a new career': that of landscape gardening.[22] The aspects of this new phase of his life best illuminated by the Huntington letters concern his status and family relationships, his methods of working, his later ill-health, some of his hitherto unknown commissions, and his will.

Repton's 'social position is hard to particularise'.[23] On the one hand, his father was a Collector of Excise, and, as already noted, had apprenticed his elder son to a merchant; but on the other hand in his will Repton senior identified himself as 'gentleman' and bequeathed Humphry, subject to a number of conditions, landed property in Stoke by Clare (Suffolk), Lichfield (Staffs.), Dickleburgh and Aylsham.[24] At his own death Humphry possessed real estate in Norfolk, Suffolk and Essex, and in the cities of Norwich and Lichfield.[25] Furthermore, as a Norfolk landowner, on 11 March 1807 he received an invitation to become a justice of the peace of that county, which he declined.[26] In theory, if he were a gentleman he should have been able to support himself and his family using the income from his land; in fact, he was unable to do so. Indeed several of the letters here refer to annual interest of £35 due on a loan made to Repton by the M.P. and banker Claude Scott.[27] Furthermore, although the professions of three of his sons – a clergyman, a civil office holder and a solicitor – were those typical of younger sons of a gentleman, the missing figure – who indicated gentlemanly status – was the

---

19 The date of the family's removal to Hare Street has been reported variously, ranging from soon after October 1783 to around 1786. (Stroud, *Repton*, p. 25; Daniels, *Repton*, p. 33) The earlier date is belied by baptismal records at Sustead. Stephen Daniels has recently received details of a letter written by Repton from Hare Street in May 1785 concerning the mail coach business (private communication).

20 *Fragments*, p. 235.

21 Daniels, *Repton*, p. 34.

22 *Memoirs*, p. 25. Several published biographies discuss Repton's successful landscaping career, for example, Daniels' biography of Repton in the *ODNB*; Daniels, *Repton*, which covers his life, and especially his work, in great detail; Carter et al., *Repton*; Stroud, *Repton*; *Repton in Norfolk*, pp. 15–27.

23 Carter et al., *Repton*, p. 5.

24 NRO, NCC will register Bloss 21, will of John Repton, gentleman, of Norwich, 1775. See also *Aylsham*, p. 178.

25 TNA, PROB 11/1609/222, the will of Humphry Repton of Harestreet, proved 16 October 1818; none of the properties were identified by name or specific location.

26 Letter 9.

27 See, for example, Letter 134.

eldest son with no profession but who lived off the income from his father's estate. His eldest and youngest sons were architects.[28] It seems, however, that his sons considered themselves to be gentlemen: in April 1809 Dorothy, writing to William, reported that his brother John had said 'that all his Brothers were <u>real Gentlemen</u> but Brother William more a Gentleman than any'.[29] So the Reptons' social status remained ambiguous. That his large family could be financially burdensome to Repton comes across in several letters, particularly because his own financial situation was somewhat precarious. Indeed, in the very first letter, written in 1805, Edward observed to William:

> I think it has been the misfortune, with all the rest of us except yourself – to have been too much together, and now while we should be shifting for ourselves, we are all still a burden and expence to my poor Father, who, I am sorry to say, has not a vast deal of employment abroad …[30]

Given that Repton provided advice, produced plans and drawings for, and was paid by, clients, he was a professional man. Perhaps the term that best describes his status is 'genteel'.[31] He was certainly a member of Georgian polite society. His own view is revealed in his 'extraordinary Letter to Mr Repington of Tamworth', wherein he sought confirmation that the surname 'Repton' was the contraction of an 'ancient', that is, long-established family name.[32] In cultural, or even moral, terms Repton's views on gentility are expressed in his memoirs, where he described many of his clients, mostly anonymously, having households wherein there was a 'prevalence of feelings of reverence for what is good'.[33] He also reported, with obvious approval, the definition of a gentleman expressed by Will Woollands, his neighbour, the Hare Street wheelwright: 'one who ain't proud, and likes to do good to everybody, and was always kind'.[34] Repton's disapproval of the ungentlemanly conduct of the two Hare Street landlords, John Coape

---

28 R. Muir, *Gentlemen of Uncertain Fortune: how younger sons made their way in Jane Austen's England* (New Haven and London, 2019) The other professions that Muir highlights are medicine, banking and commerce, the navy, the army and India; he does not mention architects at all.

29 Letter 71.

30 Letter 1.

31 A. Vickery, *The Gentleman's Daughter: Women's Lives in Georgian England* (New Haven and London, 1998), p. 1.

32 William's endorsement to Letter 84.

33 *Memoirs*, p. 130.

34 *Memoirs*, p. 69.

and Alexander Black, in ejecting tenants, including Woollands, is clearly expressed in a letter of September 1812.[35]

As a landscape gardener offering suggestions for estate improvements – albeit improvement in an aesthetic rather than an economic sense – Repton rubbed shoulders with many of the great estate owners of his day, as well as some newly wealthy merchants and industrialists. While he was duly deferential to his social superiors, some of the letters published here indicate the personal nature of his relationship with some of his clients, not least from the very fact that he stayed in their homes when making a professional visit rather than at a local inn. For example, in December 1806 he was at Witley Court, Lord Foley's house at Great Witley (Worcs.): he was trying to write a letter to William while 'the Lady Foley, Lord Petersham, Lady Isabel & your Brother Reverend Edward are all singing at my elbow'.[36] Also when staying with the duke of Bedford in April 1809, Repton told his daughter Mary, 'We are very Comfortable here – the Young Marchioness a charming woman & makes the house cheerful & Comfortable'.[37] On the other hand, two letters written to William in late 1807 and early 1808 confirm just how sour Repton's relationship with William Windham had become. In the first Repton writes damningly of Windham's character and includes a spoof letter from the pugilist Bully Gully to Windham;[38] in the second he indicates that he and his son John had been producing some architectural designs for Felbrigg, Windham's house, but that the latter had subsequently called on the services of John Nash.[39]

The letters written by Repton, and by other correspondents, reveal a keen interest in the politics of the day, not only providing the latest news but also personal observations thereon; indeed many of Repton's clients were M.P.s. Furthermore, the proximity of Hare Street to London made events very immediate. An extreme example of this is Duff's letter, dated 11 April 1810, recounting how he had assisted a rioter who had been shot outside his door in Piccadilly on the previous Saturday night.[40] The next month his father was aware of continuing disorder, and demonstrations, on the streets of London, which could only be suppressed by the military.[41] The effects of war with France were felt keenly, not least the impact of income

---

35 Letter 163.
36 Letter 6.
37 Letter 68.
38 Letter 23.
39 Letter 24.
40 Letter 131.
41 Letter 134.

tax, which Repton could not, or would not, understand, as evidenced in several letters to William in his capacity as his father's business adviser.[42] On 10 April 1814 a brief letter was sent to William from Hare Street containing notes made by Duff from the previous day's newspapers on the abdication of Napoleon and the proclamation of Louis XVIII.[43] Very shortly afterwards Humphry senior wrote a 'sermon' giving thanks for the abdication. In the preface to the printed version, he noted that 'I have caused a few copies to be printed of a MS. which I put into the hands of a clergyman, and desired him to alter in any way that he thought would make it proper to be delivered from the pulpit, (on Sunday, the 17th of April, being the first Sunday after Easter, 1814)'. Perhaps that clergyman was his son Edward?[44]

Several of the letters convey information about Repton's working practices. In April 1800 his son John went into partnership with him and they worked closely on a number of project designs.[45] When he visited clients, however, he was frequently accompanied by at least one of his other sons, even though they each had their own profession, but William went only rarely.[46] Repton's clients knew this too. The most revealing letter about the family nature of his business is that written from Woburn on 5 April 1809 to his daughter Mary. On this occasion Repton was on his own. As well as mentioning various clients to her – in a manner that indicates that she knew perfectly well who they were – he reported that

I miss my boy Edward here & wish poor George could have come. The Duke ask'd me why I had not brought an Aid de Camp. I said John was gone to Norfolk & Edward married & he said 'where is Master Humphry?'.[47]

In general, after his initial visit to a client, Repton would produce a Red Book or an illustrated report indicating how that property and grounds might be improved. Unlike 'Capability' Brown, he was not a contractor who

---

42 See, for example, Letters 6 and 134.

43 Letter 181.

44 [Humphry Repton], *The Work of Twenty Years Brought to a Crisis in Twenty Days! Addressed to the Fashionable World, at the West End of the Town* (Essex Press: Printed by T. Robinson, Romford, for T. Hookham, Jun. & Co. Old Bond Street, London, 1814) The only known copy is held in the NHC.

45 Carter et al., *Repton*, p. 129.

46 Further details in the individual biographies.

47 Letter 68.

employed a team of labourers or headed a group of experts. The design on paper, rather than on the ground, was his product.[48] He might, however, be called back to give further advice and supervise the transformation of a landscape: several of the letters give instances of this.[49] For example, in the letter from Woburn quoted above he reported, 'It is bitter cold weather here – but I potter about after the different workmen & come in to drop at 6. & dine at 7 – or later'.[50]

Several of the letters also indicate the precarious nature of his business. It was essential that he viewed a client's property in order to make his recommendations and so he travelled many miles, but such activity was very much dependant on the weather. For example, in December 1806, his wife told his sister, 'I thank God dear H is well and hearty again but I had rather he had not been obliged to go this long Journey into Worcestershire at this Season'; however, he had told her, 'if he had given it up till the Spring he should have lost the Job' and that, she acknowledged, 'woud have been a bad thing'.[51]

After Repton's accident in 1811 his daughter Mary accompanied him on visits, some of which were to distant sites. Indeed, on 16 November 1812 he told those at Aylsham 'You will rejoice to know that Mary & I are safely returnd after a journey together of 32 days in which we traveld 466 miles'.[52] In early July 1814 he told William that he was not in as much pain and was preparing to go on a long journey for business which would take in Norfolk, Bristol and Devon, after a short trip into Kent. He explained 'I mean to travel as I always do with a son or Daughter in my own Carriage – which I suppose I can do for about 60 Guineas & I am to have 200 Guineas for the Visit'. On this occasion his companion would be his daughter: 'so if I am able to bear [the long journey] perhaps I may vary the scene to myself & Mary & not make a bad fortnights work'.[53] There is no definite indication that Elizabeth ever accompanied her father on business but his comment about travelling with a son or daughter suggests that she might have done. Repton's wife Mary senior 'never accompanied her husband on professional engagements'. In general she remained at Hare Street, although she did travel to Aylsham and to Bath.[54]

48 Williamson, *Polite Landscapes*, p. 144.
49 Daniels, *Repton*, p. 38.
50 Letter 68.
51 Letter 5.
52 Letter 164.
53 Letter 188.
54 Daniels, *Repton*, p. 39.

A study of middle-class families from 1780 to 1850 has discussed 'women's contribution to the enterprise'.[55] Wives played a pivotal role in small businesses by providing vital support systems. Furthermore as the nineteenth century progressed, it was not just wives but all female relatives who might prove to be a 'hidden investment'.[56] It is clear that Mary senior played an important part in Repton's business, as did their two daughters, and it was at Hare Street that the female Reptons provided their main contribution to Repton's 'enterprise'.[57] Mary junior was an accomplished watercolourist and it seems that Elizabeth was competent at drawing: in 1814 her aunt commented that 'd begins to be expert at Profiles', such that she sat two guests down 'and went to work upon their faces in an instant'.[58] Aside from ensuring the smooth running of the household, it seems that Mary senior undertook 'various secretarial tasks', the main one being to 'forward letters to clients' houses or to post offices *en route*' for Repton to collect as he travelled.[59] The reformed postal system increased the speed of post and linked not only major cities but also, by 1815, most small towns across the country.[60] Postal charges, however, were increasingly expensive because the government increased prices to raise revenue for the war.[61] To circumvent this, whenever possible the Reptons took advantage of the franking privileges of clients who held public office or were members of parliament. Indeed many of the letters here mention being able to get a frank (or not), and those that did have the relevant frank on the outside.[62] The females' duties when Humphry was working at home were somewhat different: he needed to be entertained. On 7 March 1810 Mary senior told Dorothy, 'My dear H has been at home this last fortnight very hard at work drawing and making Books and we are kept in constant employ of reading to him'.[63]

It seems likely that before 1812 Repton had an office somewhere in Romford. In September 1812 he told William 'we have removed all our papers &c &c – from the office to a room hired next door at Ward's', perhaps in the premises of Alfred Ward, attorney, which were in the

---

55 L. Davidoff and C. Hall, *Family Fortunes: Men and Women of the English Middle Class 1780–1850* (London, 2nd edn., 2002), pp. 279–89.
56 Davidoff and Hall, *Family Fortunes*, p. 279.
57 Davidoff and Hall, *Family Fortunes*, p. 279.
58 Letter 175.
59 Daniels, *Repton*, p. 39.
60 Daniels, *Repton*, p. 28.
61 Daniels, *Repton*, p. 38.
62 See below on the postal system at the time, pp. 52–54.
63 Letter 117.

Market Place, Romford.[64] In his 'library' in the Hare Street house he had a large cupboard divided into 'pigeonholes', individually numbered for each client.[65] The only office employee mentioned in the letters is 'our ingenious draftsman Frederick': Frederick Mackenzie (1788–1854), a pupil of John Adey Repton.[66]

In general Humphry Repton enjoyed good health, until he sustained severe injuries on the night of 29 January 1811; thereafter many of the letters refer to consultations with doctors in various locations. He had accompanied his daughters to a ball given by Sir Thomas (Barrett) Lennard at Belhus, in the parish of South Ockendon.[67] On the way home, their carriage overturned 'owing to an accumulation of snow on the road' and he received a spinal injury 'from which he never entirely recovered'. The account in his memoirs states that '[f]or many weeks this accident confined him to his bed, deprived of all power of motion'.[68] By contrast, in the first letter here written after the accident, on 19 February 1811, Dorothy indicates that after three weeks he was moving around the Hare Street house.[69] Five days later, Repton himself gave William a brief report of his progress, and managed to make a joke likening his sore elbow to a ham bone being scraped of its meat.[70] As time went on both Dorothy and Mary senior reported on Repton's health. Although he now had far fewer commissions, he continued to visit clients, sometimes making use of a wheeled chair. These visits included several to the duke of Bedford's Devon properties.[71] In his book *Fragments on the Theory and Practice of Landscape Gardening*, Fragment XXIX, 'Concerning the luxuries of a garden', Repton discusses, amongst other things, how a garden might be enjoyed 'when the power of walking fails', noting, from experience, how a gravel path caused intolerable shaking and rattling to anyone in a 'Bath chair with wheels'.[72] The accident

---

64 Letter 163; Pigot's *Directory* (1823), p. 63. The office may have originally been used for Repton's mail coach business.

65 *Memoirs*, pp. 88, 90.

66 Letter 24. Mackenzie first exhibited at the Royal Academy in 1804 when he was sixteen. He later became a noted architectural illustrator. (Carter et al., *Repton*, p. 16; *ODNB*, Mackenzie, Frederick (c.1787–1854).)

67 Repton had given professional advice to Sir Thomas previously: there is an illustration of 'Bel-House, Essex, Sir Thos. Barrett Lennard' for January in the 1807 issue of Peacock's *Polite Repository*.

68 *Memoirs*, p. 23.

69 Letter 152.

70 Letter 153.

71 For details, see Daniels, *Repton*, pp. 186–90.

72 *Fragments*, pp. 177–83.

also resulted in the loss of his 'accustomed exercise', which in turn caused him to suffer from *angina pectoris*.[73]

One of the letters suggests that he was also going deaf. While staying at the New Inn, Ventnor, on the Isle of Wight, in September 1811 he wrote for his daughter Mary a 49-line poem entitled 'On deafness'.[74] In it he expressed regret for loss of hearing but counted the blessings of the other four senses and of not being distracted by roaring waves or others' conversation. The poem was enclosed in a letter to Mary that Repton sent from Rochester on 23 October. William endorsed it: 'My father's letter to Mary with very good Poetry on his deafness &c'.[75] The poem makes a virtue of deafness and is particularly poignant as his companion on that visit to the Isle was his deaf son John.

The last four letters in the Huntington archive written by Repton, dated between 22 May 1815 and 23 April 1816, are somewhat melancholy. They indicate increasing money troubles and portray a man depressed by his lack of mobility, which is scarcely surprising given the miles travelled to sites, and distances walked over them, during the course of his career. Nevertheless, in March 1816 he had two local commissions, one in Essex, the other in Middlesex.[76] In that same letter he hinted that William had been looking into housing his parents with Samuel Taylor, the Aylsham surgeon, whose house was also in the Market Place. Repton observed that 'this would be incumbering you & Dee as much as living with you – & burying me before I am dead'. But it is clear that he had already been considering Aylsham as his final resting place, for in January 1815 he had written to the vicar of Aylsham about his chosen plot in the churchyard;[77] and in May he asked William whether he had secured his 'retreat', that is, his burial place.[78] His constant love for his family and devotion to his wife, and hers to him, are the most positive features of these last letters, when there are changes for the worse all around at Hare Street, including empty houses and a closed inn. On 23 April 1816, he wrote: 'I was glad to enjoy a Walk by myself to day – moving too slow for my dear skipping girls – so I have been sauntering half way to the bridge – sitting & sunning against Black's pales – then walking into the Unicorn Yard & viewing all the premises – empty – untenanted

---

73 *Memoirs*, p. 23.

74 Letter 158.

75 The addressee is 'Miss Repton, Aylsham, Norfolk', which explains why a letter addressed to Mary Repton survives in this particular collection.

76 Letter 198.

77 Daniels, *Repton*, p. 101.

78 Letter 195.

& dilapidated'.[79] On the morning of 24 March 1818 he died at his home in Hare Street, probably from a heart attack.[80] He was buried in Aylsham churchyard, on the south side of the church, where there is a memorial inscribed with a verse that he had written for that purpose.[81]

Repton's personal wealth at death, as recorded in the Probate Act Book of the Prerogative Court of Canterbury, was only £800.[82] While in general terms this was not a small sum for the times, it pales into insignificance when compared with the recorded wealth at death of some of his fellow professionals: his own son George about £9,000; 'Capability' Brown over £10,000; and the land surveyor Nathaniel Kent over £24,000.[83] From this point of view, Repton's seemingly continual complaining about a lack of cash appears to have had some foundation.

Commissions indicated in the letters

Whereas most of Repton's work is known about from his Red Books, letters in clients' archives and discussions in his publications, others have been deduced from illustrations by him that appeared in the almanac the *Polite Repository*.[84] Since the letters published here were sent between family members, they frequently reveal his whereabouts. Some provide confirmation of some of those deductions; others indicate initial work undertaken earlier than previously thought, such as at Sheringham;[85] yet more reveal otherwise unknown professional visits. Some of these latter have been noticed by other scholars, for example, Bedwell Park (Herts)[86] owned by Sir Culling Smith and Canons Park, Stanmore (formerly Middx) owned by Sir Thomas Plummer;[87] but a few have not. Three Repton commissions revealed in these letters are discussed in more detail below.

One also has to be careful not to jump to conclusions regarding possible 'new' Repton commissions mentioned in these letters. Henry (or Harry)

79 Letter 200.

80 *Memoirs*, p. 23.

81 The verse is recorded in *Memoirs*, p. 24; for his will see below, pp. 17–18.

82 TNA, PROB 8/211, Askew & Abbot, October 1818. (The Act Book is unpaginated.)

83 *ODNB*, Repton, George Stanley (1786–1858); Brown, Lancelot [known as Capability Brown] (bap. 1716, d.1783); Kent, Nathaniel (1737–1810).

84 See, Carter et al., *Repton*, pp. 139–44; Temple, 'Repton, illustrator'.

85 On 11 December 1812 Repton said of Sheringham, 'Now I have made 2 most striking views of the Place with the House proposed & the hill with Situation for a Column or obelisk will render it very appropriate'. (Letter 168.)

86 Letter 26; Daniels, *Repton*, p. 260.

87 Letter 198; Daniels, *Repton*, p. 262.

Botham, a client of Adey & Repton, was also a friend of the family. In three letters written in March and April 1814 Dorothy Adey spoke of a forthcoming visit to Haselwood (Hazelwood), Botham's home at Abbots Langley (Herts).[88] Botham was 'determined to build an impressive country seat for himself'. The estate that he purchased was originally 43 acres. He and his wife had 'a very fine house' built and eventually created an estate of 72 acres by purchasing some adjoining land from the earl of Essex.[89] While it is tempting to speculate that this is a previously unknown Repton site – indeed the earl of Essex had been a client of Repton[90] – the proposed visit to Hazelwood was by Dorothy and Mary junior, not Humphry senior. Similarly, on 3 July 1814 Humphry mentioned going to 'visit a job near Crayford & return next day by Woolwich & Wanstead'.[91] Whereas he *was* engaged at Wanstead House (Essex), the reference to Woolwich indicates a journey across the Thames via the ferry there.

i) Auberies at Bulmer (Essex) near Sudbury (Suffolk)

In December 1806 Mary senior told Dorothy that Repton had decided against going to Mr Greenwood's near Sudbury until the spring as it was too cold.[92] Charles Greenwood had recently purchased the property of Auberies at Bulmer, on 25 September 1806, so was clearly keen to engage Repton there. On 12 March 1810 Repton told William that he 'returned last night from Sudbury where [he] went to meet Mr Greenwood'.[93] That an illustration of 'Auberries, Suffolk. Seat of Chas. Greenwood Esqr.' was published in 1811 edition of the *Polite Repository* indicates that Repton had indeed advised Mr Greenwood. From these letters it is clear that Repton subsequently returned there in April 1814.[94] On that occasion he was accompanied by Dorothy, as John had declined to go with him, which is fortunate for historians because Dorothy provided details that John would never have given. As well as reporting on the attentiveness of Repton's client in providing 'a very excellent dinner', she made it clear that Repton was actually advising on work being done on site. On Good Friday, Dorothy, Mr Greenwood and his niece had gone to church while Repton 'was engag'd with the Laborours'.[95]

---

88   Letters 176, 177 and 182.
89   S. Hastie, *Abbots Langley: A Hertfordshire Village* (Abbots Langley, 1993), p. 45.
90   *Repton in Hertfordshire*, pp. 234–40.
91   Letter 188.
92   Letter 5.
93   Letter 119.
94   Letter 179.
95   Letter 180.

ii) Summerhill, near Tonbridge (Kent)

On 25 April 1810, Edward reported to William that their father and Duff would be arriving at Crayford the next day, having been at Tonbridge.[96] There is no indication whom they had been visiting but, in the light of two later letters and evidence from the diarist Joseph Farington, it is possible that they had visited Summerhill, near Tonbridge, the home of William Francis Woodgate. Farington indicated that, prior to his own visit in July 1810, Repton has been there. He noted 'Repton's indifference abt. seeing places where he was not employed. At Summer Hill it was proposed to him to walk abt. the grounds, which he declined, saying "He had seen fine places enough, & after all was best contented with his own situation which was by the road side"'.[97] Nevertheless, in 1811 an illustration 'after Humphry Repton' of 'The Entrance of Somerhill, Kent – Seat of W. Woodgate Esq' appeared Peacock's *Polite Repository*. Furthermore on 15 December 1812, Humphry senior told William that 'I have just heard that the Tunbridge Bank faild – by which I loose £200 which Major Woodgate ought to have paid long ago'.[98] That sum represents nearly four times his standard charge of 50 guineas for a consultation, strongly suggesting a commission, which had not been paid for.[99] In a later letter the outstanding amount was said to be £119 5s.[100]

iii) Mickleham (Surrey)

On 3 October 1815, Repton told William 'I rub on with some few concerns having lately been to one at Mickleham in Surry & got 25 Guineas'.[101] No one has been able to identify this property, or its owner, but apart from this letter, it is known about from two letters from Humphry Repton to Sir Harry Fetherstonhaugh at Uppark (Sussex), dated 3 and 8 October 1815, that is, concurrent with this letter to William.[102] In one of the Uppark letters he explained:

> I have been giving my opinion respecting a spot – with relation to a future residence in one of the very few beautiful scenes, which a high-road

---

96 Letter 133.

97 Daniels, *Repton*, p. 37, quoting K. Cave, ed., *The Diary of Joseph Farington*, vol. 10, *July 1809–1810* (New Haven and London), p. 370.

98 Letter 169.

99 There is nothing about Woodgate in Daniels, *Repton*, Carter et al., *Repton*, or *Repton in Kent*.

100 Letter 197.

101 Letter 197.

102 Daniels, *Repton*, p. 267.

commands – it is at Mickleham – in that vale of the blind and sleepy and fanciful River Mole ...[103]

It is possible that the client was Richard Sharp, former M.P. for Castle Rising, who had residences at Park Lane (Middx) and Fredley Farm, Mickleham.[104] Sharp had been mentioned by Dorothy in a letter written in March 1808.[105] While this identification might seem a long-shot, a published description Sharp's property at Mickleham is suggestive of a Reptonian site. Fredley Farm lay almost opposite Juniper Hall, in the valley of the river Mole, just off the main Dorking road.[106] A tiny cottage property with a few meagre outbuildings when Sharp took it over, he later arranged for a number of alterations and extensions to be carried out. A description, written in the early twentieth century, emphasises the view from the house:

> ... a well-built cottage some 200 years old, surrounded by fine trees, fields and small woods – or plantations – of great beauty. The ground fell rapidly from the terrace, on which the larger house was subsequently built, and the view is surely one of the most perfect of its kind in Southern England. The fore-ground of sloping lawn with an immense cedar leads to the 'shrubberies' of yew, juniper, choisia, kalmia, lilac and all manner of flowering plants growing among silver birches, Scotch firs and chestnuts. On either side of the house – curiously undulating lawns, the one bounded by cedars, the other by huge beech trees form the foreground for a distant view of Dorking spire, with the chalk slopes of Box Hill on the left and the wooded heights of Ranmore and Leith Hill on the right.[107]

---

103 M. Meade-Fetherstonhaugh and O. Warner, *Uppark and its people* (2nd edn., London, 1995), p. 88.

104 *Hist. Parl.*, Sharp, Richard (1759–1835).

105 Letter 34.

106 This is clearly marked on the map of the Mole at Mickleham in *VCH Surrey*, vol. 3, p. 302.

107 D. J. Knapman, *Conversation Sharp: the biography of a London Gentleman Richard Sharp (1759–1835) in letters, prose and verse* (Dorchester, 2003), p. 266. The Hon. Mrs Hills wrote the description.

Humphry Repton's will

In most respects Repton's will, made on 14 July 1814, is not particularly remarkable.[108] He appointed all five of his sons as his executors; he possessed (unspecified) real estate in Norfolk, Suffolk and Essex, and in Norwich and Lichfield; he made provision for his widow and for each of his children. There was, however, one very specific bequest to his eldest son of 'all my printed books, maps, sketches and drawings and prints for his own use, benefit and disposal, And all my written books and Manuscripts of every description', including 208 pages of his memoirs, to be published by John, with the consent of his co-executors.[109] Internal evidence indicates that the will was written at Aylsham.

On 3 July 1814 he wrote from Hare Street to William regarding the renewal of the lease of his cottage at Hare Street, saying that he was about to travel to Kent and 'immediately afterwards into Norfolk', intending to be at Aylsham at the end of the week.[110] The witnesses to his will were his sister Dorothy Adey, Leonard Shelford and Arnold Wallinger.[111] All three witnesses were connected with William's practice at Aylsham. Dorothy's connection is obvious, but those of Shelford and Wallinger have not been previously recognised: both young men were serving 5-year apprenticeships with William as articled clerks, part of their training to become solicitors.

Shelford's father, also Leonard (d.1813), had been rector of North Tuddenham, about 15 miles from Aylsham. He had wanted his son to become a solicitor, although he had died before his son's apprenticeship began: the articles of agreement, dated 17 July 1813, were made between Leonard and his widowed mother, Ellen, on one side and William on the other.[112] In fact, he went on to be called to the bar (Middle Temple) in 1827. His *ODNB* entry states that, with regard to his initial legal training, Leonard 'served his articles with William Repton of Aylsham, Norfolk'.[113] Indeed

---

108 TNA, PROB 11/1609/222.

109 In fact John did not do so, but the second part of them was eventually published in 2005.

110 Letter 188.

111 In the letters the surname is spelled as both Wallinger and Wallenger; Wallinger is the modern form.

112 TNA, KB 105, Piece 24 (Court of King's Bench: Plea Side: Affidavits of Due Execution of Articles of Clerkship, Series I).

113 *ODNB*, Shelford, Leonard (1795–1864). This was not mentioned in the detailed discussion of William Repton's practice at Aylsham in *Aylsham*, chapter 13.

writing to William from Hare Street in March 1814 Dorothy mentioned Leonard twice, both times in connection with the arrival of William's new clerk, Arnold Wallinger. Firstly, on 17 March she spoke of Leonard being in London and meeting the new clerk.[114] Secondly, on 28 March 1814, she reported that 'young Arnold' had arrived at Hare Street with his mother.[115] Dorothy had 'expected from the Girls' account to have seen a grubb of a school boy, but he is a tall gentlemanly looking young man, and eer long will be as tall as Leonard'. She continued, 'Remember me to [Leonard], and I have no doubt but he will very soon be much pleas'd with his junior Clerk', thus indicating not only that Leonard was progressing through the practice, being now 19 or 20 years old, but also that Dorothy approved of the forthcoming addition to William's practice.

Arnold was the son of William Wallinger and his wife Elizabeth, who had lived at Hare Street and so were known to the Repton family. By the time the articles of agreement relating to Arnold's apprenticeship were drawn up, on 25 June 1814, his father had died and he and his mother were living at Montague Square, London.[116] Thus, less than a month after commencing work with William, Arnold served as a witness to Humphry Repton's will. Also within this collection is a letter written in London on 11 April 1815, from Arnold to William.[117] In it he reports on various tasks that he had undertaken and on meeting with 'Mr Repton' (Humphry senior) who was visiting a doctor there. It is striking that William and his father were happy for these two young men, together with Dorothy, to witness Humphry's will; and it is to William that we now turn our attention.

William Repton (1783–1858) and his place in society in and around Aylsham

William was born while Mary and Humphry lived at Sustead. His baptism took place privately on 14 October 1783, two days after his birth, and he was 'Received into the Church' on 20 November.[118] He was probably apprenticed to John Adey at his successful solicitor's practice in the Market

---

114 Letter 176.
115 Letter 177.
116 TNA, KB 105, Piece 25.
117 Letter 194.
118 NRO, PD 393/3, Sustead Baptisms 1783 and 1784. The Sustead Register states clearly that William was born on 12 October 1783 and baptised privately on 14 October. The memorial stone in Aylsham churchyard incorrectly states that he was born on 14 October 1783.

Place, Aylsham, in the mid-1790s.[119] John and Dorothy Adey had no children of their own, two sons having died in infancy.[120] In his memoirs Repton stated that 'William had been adopted by my sister's husband'.[121] This was not an adoption in the modern legal sense, rather he was treated like a son and followed in John Adey's footsteps. William became an articled clerk in 1799.[122] He was probably made a partner round about his 21st birthday in 1804.[123]

As it was William who amassed this collection, as well as his family connections, the letters disclose much about his activities as a leading local solicitor. In 1846, Sir George Stephen, an attorney and solicitor, stated that 'It is quite impossible to define within a narrow compass the nature of a solicitor's business: it extends to anything, it extends to everything: law, I should say, forms about the least part of the duty of a solicitor in a large practice'.[124] William was practising at a time of great economic and social change in the country as a whole and when the profession and role of country attorneys was expanding; indeed 'country attorneys, whether operating singly or in networks, effected aspects of the change' in the period.[125] Such men 'proved indispensable to their landholding clients; besides practising law, they collected rents and fines, held manorial courts, and clerked for enclosure, fen drainage and turnpike commissions'.[126] These letters provide evidence of William doing all of these things for his Norfolk clients, apart from clerking for fen drainage. In March 1808, for example, 'Cooper the Turnpike Man' called into the office of Adey & Repton for his pay of £17 due from the justices.[127] During much of John Adey's lengthy final illness in 1809 William was in London overseeing the passage of the

---

119 *Aylsham*, p. 183.

120 On a stone inside in the church of St Michael and All Angels, Aylsham, it is recorded that 'On the 3rd of August 1770, and the 18th December 1771, were Interr'd here Two Infants, Son's[*sic*] of JOHN ADEY of Aylsham'.

121 *Memoirs*, p. 75.

122 TNA, CP 71, piece 2 (Court of Common Pleas: Registers of Articles of Clerkship and Affidavits of Due Execution).

123 *Aylsham*, p. 183

124 Giving evidence before the Select Committee on Legal Education; quoted in R. Robson, *The Attorney in eighteenth-century England* (Cambridge, 1959), p. 84.

125 A. J. Schmidt, 'Lawyer professionalism in rural England: changes in routine and rewards in the early nineteenth century', *Lincolnshire History and Archaeology*, 32 (1997), pp. 25–39, p. 25.

126 A. J. Schmidt, 'The Smiths of Horbling: country attorneys', *Huntington Library Quarterly*, 54 (1991), pp. 143–76, p. 143.

127 Letter 32.

Sheringham enclosure bill. The letters here confirm that he was engaged in promoting a number of other Norfolk enclosures: in January 1809 he was at a Holt enclosure meeting;[128] in April 1809 he had to attend a meeting in relation to the Tivetshall enclosure;[129] in April 1810 he was about to call a meeting of the claimants in the Swanton Abbott, Buxton and Lamas enclosure;[130] and in March 1814 he was promoting the enclosure bill for Skeyton, Burgh next Aylsham and Tuttington.[131] Country attorneys were also often 'money scriveners – money lenders and investment brokers – to a local society that was sorely in need of cash and necessary banking services'.[132] There is no evidence of such activity in this archive, although it is clear that William was financially astute and that his father, who appears rather naïve in relation to money, consulted him about matters relating to income tax and banking.[133]

Dorothy Adey was a prolific letter-writer, some of her letters giving insights into the organisation and concerns of her husband's and nephew's legal practice. Unlike her sister-in-law Mary Repton, Dorothy was not usually involved in the day-to-day business since there were clerks and workers, including Francis Barnes and George Ives, and servants for that.[134] It is clear, however, that she was able to keep the Aylsham solicitors' practice running when necessary, as in March 1808 and in April 1809, when William was absent on business, mostly in London, during periods when John Adey was ill, and dying. On these occasions Dorothy was acting as William's 'agent at home'.[135] His absences generated a number of letters, especially when minor crises arose, such as local representatives failing to carry out allotted tasks. Her letters therefore identify some of the people with whom the business of Adey & Repton came into contact, and also disclose some of William's professional activities. The letters indicate that Dorothy knew the background to the various matters that she had to deal with; however, her attention was distracted by her husband's ill health and so her requests for advice have an air of panic about them. These letters also illuminate the

---

128 Letter 62.

129 Letter 73.

130 Letter 129.

131 Letter 174.

132 Schmidt, 'The Smiths of Horbling', p. 143. See also, Robson, *Attorney*, pp. 112, 115.

133 The documents under the reference HM 40952 are numerous cancelled cheques relating to William's business.

134 For Barnes and Ives see, for example, Letter 25.

135 S. T. Damiano, 'Agents at home: wives, lawyers, and financial competence in eighteenth-century New England port cities', *Early American Studies*, 13 (2015), pp. 808–35.

parts played by various members of the Adeys' household in the care of the sick and dying man. After John Adey's death on 4 May 1809 William and Dorothy received a number of letters of condolence, all of which indicate the high esteem in which he had been held. All of the letters in this collection written by Dorothy in the years after her husband's death were written to William at Aylsham while she was away from home, usually staying at Hare Street, and so after May 1809 there are no details of how she assisted the practice during his subsequent absences.

William became steward of many of the manorial courts that Adey had managed. Some of the letters, however, reveal that other manorial lords had been asked to 'give' William their courts. These particular letters seeking advancement were mostly written by his father, perhaps at William's prompting. The responses elicited were mostly negative, in that the particular landowner had made other arrangements, but one in particular shows the regard in which William himself was held. John Wodehouse, first baron Wodehouse, having regretfully refused Humphry's request, went on: 'I am aware that There is no Professional Gentleman in the county whose Character stands higher than that of your Son, and it is impossible that anything can be more pleasing than his manners'.[136]

Indeed, it appears that William was well-regarded in Norfolk and seems to have been noted for his discretion. A number of the draft letters (office copies) indicate the nature of some of his local business and social relationships. For example, John Johnson Gay invited William to dinner and then to the Holt Assembly on 18 December 1809 and also to another dinner on 22 December.[137] In June 1810, John Steward, mayor of Norwich, was concerned to know the rank of a particular member of the Walpole family and where he came in order of precedence compared with other guests invited to 'the Country Table' at the Guild Day dinner in St Andrew's Hall. Not only was William able to give advice on this but he himself was to attend in the company of the gentleman in question.[138] The following month the second earl of Orford, another member of the Walpole family, asked William whether a report that Lord Suffield was dangerously ill had any foundation and asked him not to mention his enquiry to anyone.[139] In August 1810 John Thurston Mott, one of Humphry Repton's clients, invited William and Dorothy to a ball at his house at Barningham.[140] In

---

136 Letter 82.
137 Letter 108.
138 Letter 136.
139 Letter 140.
140 Letter 142.

complete contrast, in September 1809, William wrote an obsequious note to Colonel Harbord at Blickling apologising for being caught trespassing unintentionally on his land while out shooting with one of his brothers.[141]

Other letters confirm that William was on visiting and social terms with Norfolk landowners, despite, or perhaps because of, his professional position. The Anson family was particularly important in this respect. There were several earlier connections between the Reptons and Ansons. In March 1773 John Repton, Humphry's father, took on a lease from Thomas Anson of Shugborough (Staffs) of the old Paston estate at Oxnead Hall, which Humphry's brother John subsequently farmed, managing it for his siblings.[142] In addition John Adey and the Anson family had many connections in and around Lichfield and later William conducted business for the Ansons at their Shugborough estate in Staffordshire.[143] The key local connections were the Revd Charles Anson, rector of Lyng, and his brother the Revd Henry Anson, instituted to the living of Oxnead with Buxton in 1804, but other members of the family were present in Norfolk from time to time and several wrote fulsome letters of condolence on John Adey's death.

Although only the fourth son, it was William to whom family members turned in times of difficulty or crisis. Three instances will suffice. Firstly, there was trouble over conveying 'the St George Estate, formerly Captain Clarke's', to Mr John Shalders. This property in the parish of St George Colegate, Norwich, had been in the occupation of Jacob Shalders.[144] Originally it had been left by Samuel Clarke, warehouseman of Norwich, to his niece Mary (Clarke) Repton, then to her husband and to their children and then, failing such issue, to Clarke's other niece Elizabeth Marsh and her children. In 1797 legal moves were commenced whereby the property would be sold to Jacob Shalders and his heirs. A condition of the sale was that the Repton children, on their attaining the age of 21, 'would execute all reasonable conveyances or otherwise enter into a bond for guaranteeing the title of the said property to Jacob Shalders and his heirs & assigns'. This matter is mentioned in letters written in March and April 1810, at which time Elizabeth Repton was only 19. James Marsh, a lawyer and one of the sons of the late Elizabeth Marsh, was pushing for the matter to be settled. George questioned whether this could be done before their

---

141 Letter 106.
142 *Aylsham*, p. 177.
143 The Aylsham-Lichfield connections have been reconstructed diagrammatically in Vaughan-Lewis and Vaughan-Lewis, *Aylsham*, p. 168.
144 Details from NRO, AYL 835, Copy conveyance Marsh and Repton to Shalders of property in parish of St George Colegate, Norwich, 1814.

sister Elizabeth was 21,[145] but nevertheless he and Duff eventually signed the document sent by Marsh.[146] It is unclear why he was trying to close the matter in 1810; in the event it was not concluded until 1814, when Elizabeth came of age.[147] Secondly, the family asked William for advice on behalf of others. In April 1814 Repton raised 'the Case of Sally' with him.[148] Sally, mentioned in earlier letters, seems to have been a servant of some kind in the Hare Street house.[149] She was the widow of James Gibbs, who had died intestate and had had two sons by a former marriage. His mother was claiming his goods for the boys. Repton asked William for advice on Sally's rights, enquiring 'Would a letter from you as her attorney be of use?'. Given the nature of this archive we have no way of knowing the outcome of the matter, or even whether William did intervene on Sally's behalf. Thirdly, the penultimate letter in the collection is a draft from William to Baxter & Bowler, probably his agents in London, regarding two claims for unpaid bills against his father, the second of which is revealing about Repton's travelling arrangements. In December 1809 Edward had written to William to say that the 'Yorkshire Journey was a profitable one', a journey on which he had accompanied his father, and possibly John and George as well.[150] In 1816 a claim had been received from Holditch, a coachmaker in Long Acre, London, for the hire of a 'Chariot' in 1809, for which there was an outstanding charge of £7 16s. William noted that the hire was 'for Yorkshire Itinerary &c at per week with option to purchase'.[151] It was not clear to William whether his father had paid the outstanding account: he may have confounded 'this case with some other Coachmaker as was continually hiring Carriages from diff' persons in Longacre'.[152] Furthermore his 'Memory [was] bad under present infirmities'. William was asking Baxter & Bowler for advice 'bearing in mind [he was a] lawyer not fond of going to law', although he did wonder whether the Statute of Limitations might apply in this case.

William seems to have been a fair employer. In February 1811, Mileham, one of his clerks, had become involved with the wife of Mr Smith of

---

145 Letter 126.

146 Letter 132.

147 NRO, AYL 835.

148 Letter 183.

149 Letters 174 and 177.

150 Letter 110.

151 Letter 199. For Repton's visit(s) to Oulton Hall and Armley, see *Repton in Yorkshire*, pp. 95–136.

152 Long Acre had been a centre of coachbuilding since the mid-seventeenth century.

Aylsham.[153] George indicated that William had given Mileham a lecture and dismissed him. John's attitude, reported by Dorothy, may reveal John's view of women in general, or of Mileham's attractiveness to women: 'John says "poor Mileham. I pity Mileham, woman seduc'd him I know, they always do, I wish William had not turn'd him away"'. Dorothy herself suggested that the townspeople had dealt very harshly with Mileham but suspected that there was more to the matter than met the eye. She commented that 'if all the men in the Town were refus'd a Bed in a private or publick house because they had sin'd in this way, we shou'd have a pretty parcel of them in the Market'.[154] But it seems that William relented and offered work Mileham in Norwich on his behalf;[155] and ultimately took him back since he was probably the Harry Mileham who received a bequest in William's will.[156]

William never married. He died at Aylsham on 24 April 1858 and was buried with his parents in the churchyard.

Other Repton family members

Mary Repton née Clarke (1749–1827)

Humphry Repton married Mary Clarke in Norwich on 5 May 1773.[157] They had known each other for more than three years but his father had objected to his marrying before he was 21. Initially they lived in Norwich. Their firstborn, Martha, was born on 5 March 1774 and baptised at St Giles' the following day but she did not survive.[158] In all they had sixteen children, of whom seven lived to adulthood. That the loss of the little ones affected them is clear from a comment Humphry made in 1812 when Lord Erskine lost a child: 'poor Erskine's last born infant walk'd off with a Spasm last night, just as ours have done – hiccupd – turnd yellow – & gave a kick'.[159] Mary and Humphry were married for nearly 45 years. These letters confirm

153 It is not possible to identify this man: there are several Smiths in the Aylsham directories for 1793 and 1822. (*Aylsham Directories*)

154 Letter 152.

155 Letter 153.

156 NRO, AYL 1157, which includes a detailed abstract of his will.

157 The biography given in the Introduction to *Memoirs*, says they married on 3 May; this is incorrect. See Letter 186, where, in the postscript, Mary says it is her 41st wedding anniversary on 5 May, when there will be a family party.

158 NRO, AYL 80, Repton family pedigree; NRO, AT Norwich city parishes 1773 (1773–4), St Giles.

159 Letter 163.

that theirs was a companionable relationship. The letters written by Mary, and also by Dorothy Adey, from Hare Street give much information about local Essex society.

Occasionally, whether from Mary herself or from her children, letters mention the state of her health; on the other hand, on several occasions correspondents failed to go into details about their parents' health because they knew that their letters were read by them before being posted. So, for example, in December 1810 George complained to William: 'I am anxious about my poor Mother, who I fear is not so well as she should be – but that I cannot learn for certain, as all my sisters' letters are seen by her'.[160] Her last communication here, written on 23 April 1816, indicates that she was not in the best of health, but was keeping busy:

> Though I am such a poor Creature, and can but just coast about, I am allways employd, with work, what with making gowns, patch work, and mending old Rags, which is the only thing I am good for …[161]

In fact, outliving her husband by more than nine years, she died on 6 April 1827 and was buried at Aylsham on 15 April.[162]

Dorothy Adey née Repton (1747–1822)

Dorothy was born on 10 March 1747.[163] Of the eleven children born to her parents, Dorothy was the eldest of the three who survived to adulthood. She married John Adey on 31 July 1769.[164] Their two infant sons were buried in Aylsham church, John in August 1770 and Humphry in December 1771.[165] Her letters provide details of business and inhabitants not only in Aylsham but also elsewhere in Norfolk. For example on 29 March 1808 she referred to Stephenson and Matchett, printers and booksellers, and also Kerrison's bank, both in Norwich, and discussed the price of sugar charged by various traders, including Clover's, the shop situated next door but one to Adey & Repton.[166]

---

160 Letter 146.
161 Letter 200.
162 Date of death given on memorial stone in the churchyard; date of burial in Bishop's Transcripts, Archdeaconry of Norwich 1827, A-C, p. 60, Aylsham burials (image on Ancestry).
163 Stroud, *Repton*, p. 15 states that Dorothy was born in 1747; this would agree with Dorothy's own statement that she was 67 on her birthday in 1814. (Letter 175)
164 *Aylsham*, p. 174.
165 *Aylsham*, p. 176, and memorial in the church.
166 Letter 37.

After her husband's death in 1809 Dorothy frequently visited Hare Street and all of the letters from her during the period 1811 to 1814 were written from there. She died at Aylsham on 21 April 1822.[167]

John Repton of Oxnead (1753–1809)

The younger brother of Dorothy and Humphry, John was born on 25 August 1753.[168] In March 1773 his father leased the old Paston estate at Oxnead Hall from Thomas Anson of Shugborough and John took over the 453 acre farm.[169] He was obviously a successful farmer. In his *General view of the agriculture of the county of Norfolk*, Arthur Young mentioned a number of times the good farming methods practised at Oxnead by 'Mr Repton' not only in terms of tillage but also animal husbandry, animal feed and keeping accounts. For example, he described in detail how John prepared potatoes and turnips as feed, 'the cattle licking it up with great avidity, and doing perfectly well on this food'.[170] Furthermore 'Mr Repton, at Oxnead, favoured me, from his books, kept with uncommon accuracy and care, with an account of his [barley] crops' from 1773 to 1800.[171]

John married Elizabeth Knight in May 1799 and they had one daughter, Elizabeth, known in the family as Eliza, baptised on 18 October 1801.[172] John was aware that his wife was unpopular locally. Writing to Humphry he mentioned various invitations that they had received but that he had declined, nevertheless 'my dear Girl you see has Friends in this County'.[173] Indeed, it is clear from the letters that various members of the family looked down on 'Mrs John'. For example, just after his brother's death, Repton remarked to William, 'What a Melancholy reflection that we cannot look back on any part of poor John's conduct that is not influenced & embitterd by his dotage for this low woman'.[174] Humphry rather cruelly 'mimicked' Elizabeth in some of his letters; indeed in a mock epitaph for John's tomb, he wrote:

---

167 *Aylsham*, p. 177.

168 As recorded on his planned monument. (Letter 128)

169 Copy of a lease is NRO, AYL 91/2; cited in *Aylsham*, p. 177.

170 The Secretary of the Board (Arthur Young), *General view of the agriculture of the county of Norfolk, drawn up for the consideration of the Board of Agriculture and Internal Improvement* (London, 1804), p. 348.

171 *General view of … Norfolk*, p. 252.

172 *Aylsham*, p. 177.

173 Appendix 1, HM 40930.

174 Letter 101.

> Our poor Brother John
> For ever is gone
> Bequeathing his foolish wife Bess
> She long buckled his Shoes
> Then slipd on the Noose
> And he Married – "He coon't du no less".[175]

John died on 14 June 1809. The family continued to see Elizabeth and Eliza, who both stayed at Hare Street from time to time.[176]

Repton's children

At the beginning of Repton's published memoirs the modern editors included the 'Biographical Notice of the Late Humphry Repton, Esq.' previously printed by J. C. Loudon in his collection of Repton's works.[177] This 'notice' was 'furnished by one of Mr Repton's family'.[178] Although unidentified it is obvious that this family member had access to the whole of Repton's memoirs as the notice includes extracts from the now lost first section. They also added some illuminating notes to the surviving second section. At the end of the notice, the author provided brief details of then surviving Repton children – four sons and one daughter – indicating that it was written after Mary junior's death in June 1821. This has caused confusion amongst subsequent writers because the death of Humphry junior in December 1819 meant that his younger brothers were identified in the 'notice' as Repton's second, third and fourth sons, rather than third, fourth and fifth.

John Adey Repton (1775–1860)[179]

John Adey Repton was baptised at St Giles, Norwich, on 1 April 1775, having been born on 29 March.[180] He was the oldest of the seven Repton siblings who survived to adulthood, and was the last of them to die. He was profoundly deaf, probably from birth. According to his obituary, at 'an early age' he attended the grammar-school at Aylsham, 'where he was taught to

---

175 Letter 101.
176 See, for example, Letter 161.
177 *Memoirs*, pp. 9–24; Loudon, *Landscape Gardening*.
178 *Memoirs*, p. 7.
179 A biography of John Adey Repton appears as a supplement to that of his father in the *ODNB* and details of his work have been recorded in, for example, Carter et al., *Repton*, pp. 129–31.
180 NRO, PD 192/3, St Giles, Norwich, baptisms, p. 55.

read, write and cypher, but received no instruction in grammar or in classical literature, probably from the difficulty the master found in teaching a deaf boy'.[181] At the age of 14 he became a pupil of the architect William Wilkins, then practising in Norwich. After seven years with Wilkins, in 1796 John moved to London to be apprenticed to John Nash, who had become his father's partner. His father's association with Nash ended acrimoniously in about 1800[182] and in April 1800 John went into partnership with his father.[183] In 1803 he was elected a fellow the Society of Antiquaries and contributed many articles on antiquities and archaeology to *Archaeologia*, the Society's journal. It has even been suggested that John was 'by inclination more of an amateur antiquarian than a professional architect'.[184]

Within this edited collection there are two postscripts and one letter written by John; all three reveal something of his character and his interests. The first was added to a letter from their father, written at Hare Street to William following the latter's absence from the family home at Christmas 1808. Between chatty notes from Edward and their sister Mary, John simply said: 'This Postscript is much shorter <but> I don't know what to say – but my Love to Uncle & Aunt Adey & hope they are well – & also to all the pretty girls at Aylsham'.[185] Writing on his birthday in 1814, John's postscript to William said: 'I wish you could borrow the letters of Oliver Cromwell from Mr Sewell to shew to the Society of Antiquaries – I will take great care of them & return them by you'.[186] The letter from John to William, written on 17 February 1810 from the Maid's Head, Norwich, is similarly brief, regretting that he would be going directly to Hare Street rather than returning to Aylsham, where he had left his portmanteau. He asked for his luggage to be sent on and for him to be remembered to Mr Charles and Mr Henry Anson and to Mr Lubbock and 'his Lovely Daughter'.[187] Thus two out of three of his missives indicate that John had an eye for the ladies, but he never married.

A letter from his father to William, written in 1808, mentioned some possible work on behalf of William Windham at Felbrigg and enclosed a

---

181 *Gentleman's Magazine* (January 1861), pp. 107–8.
182 Daniels, *Repton*, p. 135.
183 Carter et al., *Repton*, p. 129.
184 S. Daniels, 'Voices from the grave', *Landscapes of Memory: Landscapes of Humphry Repton*, special edition of *Garden Museum Journal*, 36 (Winter 2018/19), pp. 12–25, p. 18.
185 Letter 57.
186 Letter 178. NRO, AYL 1223, Index made by William Repton [n.d. *c.*1811] of clients and landholders includes William Sewell. Neither these letters of Cromwell nor their current whereabouts have been identified.
187 Letter 113.

design drawn up by their draughtsman Frederick for the entrance hall and the library in Gothic style.[188] The drawing was to be returned because it 'forms part of a Collection John is making for his great Work on Gothic Architecture'. John's 'great Work' was never published.[189] The final letter in this collection indicates that Humphry and John were still collaborating on projects: Parliament had launched a prestigious architectural competition to commemorate Wellington's victory at Waterloo and they had submitted a design.[190]

Due to his infirmity, John stayed with his aunt when working for clients in the Aylsham area, which is probably the reason for the survival for the first of the two letters in the collection addressed to him. This letter, from his father, dated 26 July 1807, includes a drawing of a staircase rail (*see illustration on p. 75*) and mentions one commission that they were working on for John Thurston Mott at Barningham Hall and a second, for 'Mr Harbord', that was proving troublesome.[191] The only direct evidence of work by the Reptons for Mr Harbord of Gunton Hall are drawings dated 1816: this letter suggests much earlier contact.[192] Furthermore it is one of the few letters that mentions 'Stannard': Joseph Stannard and Joseph junior were local contractors and architects who had been brought in to oversee the work at Barningham Hall, and who also supplied some new windows for the Adeys' house in the Market Place at Aylsham.[193]

The second letter to John, dated January 1809, was from George, written while at Nash's home, East Cowes Castle on the Isle of Wight. He provided a very detailed critique of initial plans that John had drawn up for the entry that the two brothers planned to submit for the competition to design new public buildings in Parliament Square.[194] Ultimately they gained first prize in that competition. That this particularly detailed letter ended up in Aylsham is explained by a brief note on the address panel: their father had sent it to Dorothy 'to see what a clever boy George is'. Once John had acted upon it he must have left it at Hare Street and it was then sent on to Aylsham.

In December 1810 George told William that 'John & I have now some Designs before the Governors of Bethlem Hospital, which he very

---

188 Letter 24.
189 Stephen Daniels has noticed that some of John's 'great work' seems to have found its way into his father's final publication, *Fragments* (personal communication).
190 Letter 200.
191 Letter 11.
192 *Repton in Norfolk*, pp. 155–7.
193 Letter 71.
194 Letter 58.

unwillingly consented to join in, though at a time he was not doing any thing else'.[195] George's frustration with John is obvious, but nevertheless he seems to be suggesting that a joint entry was preferable; in fact they gained second prize for their design for the New Bethlehem Hospital.[196]

Although John's severe deafness did not prevent him becoming an accomplished architect, at times his disability caused problems or embarrassment for those with whom he worked. The most striking and explicit example comes in a letter from his father to William, dated 9 February 1810, asking him to attend a meeting between John and John Thurston Mott because he could not be present: 'from his not hearing distinctly all that is said – he is often apt to mistake & make answers which may commit him, for tho he means always right – he sometimes says what is better not said'.[197]

John's antiquarian interests are briefly noted in this volume, particularly his attending meetings of the Society of Antiquaries. In March 1807, his father told William: 'I have been with dear John to the Antiquarian & Royal Society to night & introduced him to many persons, which pleases him poor fellow'.[198] Indeed John's interest in the curious ensured that these letters record one rather obscure early nineteenth-century phenomenon. In June 1809 he and his mother had been staying in Aylsham after the death of John Adey. On their way home they saw the famous 'pedestrian' Captain Barclay walking on Newmarket Heath.[199] Mary was not keen to stop but 'dear John said he woud certainly see him. "God bless my soul, many people would give 10 Guineas to see him and we are so near and not see him wou'd be a shame"'.[200] Her account is quite detailed even though they only watched Barclay walk for about 10 minutes. There are reports of his activities in various issues of *Sporting Magazine*, but Mary's eyewitness account of 'this wonderful man' is strikingly spontaneous.

John lived with his mother at Hare Street until her death in 1827. Thereafter he and his younger sister Elizabeth lived at Springfield near Chelmsford, where he died on 26 November 1860, aged 85.[201]

---

195   Letter 146.
196   Carter et al., *Repton*, p. 133.
197   Letter 112.
198   Letter 9.
199   *ODNB*, Allardice, Robert Barclay [known as Captain Barclay] (1779–1854).
200   Letter 102.
201   Obituary in *Gentleman's Magazine*, January 1861, p. 107. This says he was 86 when he died, but if born on 29 March 1775 he must have been 85.

Humphry Repton junior (1780–1819)

Written just after its acquisition by the Huntington Library, a summary of this collection noted that there were thirteen letters 'from the second son Humphry junior, about whom nothing has been known before'.[202] He was born at Sustead on 20 April 1780 and baptised the same day.[203] He was known within the family as Duff, to distinguish him from his father.[204] He attended Eton but did not complete his schooling there, because, as his father recalled, 'I had taken this son from Eton at the age of nearly 17 in the expectation of forming him for my own profession, and with this in view frequently made him the companion of my visits'.[205] Indeed, on a visit to Holwood, the property of William Pitt the younger, Pitt observed that Duff was completing his education by accompanying his father: 'Your mode of finishing your education by travelling with your father, reading in his carriage, seeing and improving all the finest places in England … must be one of the most desirable situations for a young man'.[206] In fact, he did not follow in his father's footsteps, but, as has already been noted, he did continue to accompany his father on professional visits.

Repton was not afraid to seek preferment both for himself and for his sons. In early 1806, not long before his death, Pitt the younger appointed Duff to a clerkship in the Audit Office.[207] In Duff's first letter here he explains to William how the office was organised and how he was 'in fact at the head of this Office as Mr [Francis Percival] Eliot's adviser – tho' they have unjustly given the title & the Salary to an old gentleman 70 years old who will make his place a sinecure'.[208] Nevertheless, he gradually rose through that office.[209] Although the Audit Office was situated in Somerset House, Duff's first office was nearby at Adelphi, an imposing riverside development designed and built by John, Robert, James and William Nash.[210] In October 1806 he was temporarily lodging at 'the best hotel in

---

202 J. F. Preston, 'Intramuralia (the Repton letters)', *Huntington Library Quarterly*, 38:4 (August 1975), pp. 372–3, p. 373.

203 NRO PD 393/3, Sustead parish register, 1783–1808, p. 6.

204 Carter et al., *Repton*, p. 26, states that John, the eldest son, was 'known within the family as Duff', but William's endorsements on Humphry junior's letters clearly identify him as Duff.

205 *Memoirs*, p. 60.

206 *Memoirs*, p. 60.

207 *Memoirs*, p. 60. Pitt died on 23 January 1806. (*ODNB*, Pitt, William [known as Pitt the younger] (1759–1806).)

208 Letter 3.

209 *Memoirs*, p. 60, note 36.

210 *London Encyclopaedia*, pp. 6–7.

London – the Tavistock in Covent Garden' but the next week was moving to 184 Piccadilly. This particular letter also illustrates the connections that Repton's sons were able to make through their father's professional association with landowners and politicians: Duff mentioned the duke of Portland, Lord Sidmouth and Mr Pitt.[211]

That the London-based family members were frequently at Hare Street at weekends is obvious from many of the letters. On 10 August 1810, Duff told his aunt Dorothy, 'I always read your letters with the greatest pleasure whether addressed to me or to the circle at Harestreet where I see them every week'.[212] Indeed, on 30 October 1817, writing to his publishers to ask why he had not yet received their remarks on his manuscript, Repton suggested that they send them 'tomorrow or any Saturday Morning before 11 oClock – by addressing your parcel (sealed) to my son, H Repton Esquire junior, Office of Audit, Somerset House, Who always comes down on a Saturday'.[213]

Humphry junior seems to have been a personable fellow, such that not long after taking up his post in the Audit Office, Claude Scott, one of his father's clients, made him a gift of perpetual admission to Drury Lane Theatre in return for 'some little official service render'd him'.[214] This was renewed in 1808, although Scott did request some information in return.[215] That this gift was used is demonstrated in a letter from Dorothy to William in 1814, when referring to obtaining seats for performances by Kean in May.[216] Duff also played cricket: in September 1810 he was happy to avail himself of Mr Eliot's 'invitation to make cricket matches at Richmond & Hampton Court'; although in this instance there was an ulterior motive as the report by Bankes's Committee on the Audit Office had just been published and Mr Eliot, his superior, used these matches as cover for meetings of office staff.[217]

Based in London and well-connected, Duff was able to supply the family with up-to-date news, whether social or political, and it is this aspect of his letters which is the most striking. Some of them convey news of events almost as they occurred. For example, in addition to the shooting in

---

211 Letter 3.
212 Letter 143.
213 NHC, Colman Collection, ac. no. 37410 (M569/RE).
214 Letter 9.
215 Letter 52.
216 Letter 185.
217 Letter 144. Stephen Daniels has found that Duff's cricketing career involved 8 first class matches, his average for 14 innings was 4.75 runs: a 'duff' cricketing career (personal communication).

Piccadilly in April 1810 mentioned above, in October 1810 he reported on the death of Nathaniel Kent, his account coming from Kent's clerk 'with tears in his eyes'.[218] With regard to political events, he sent news of the war from London newspapers and, for example, on 5 January 1811 he sent details of the division in the House of Commons over the Regency Bill on 1 January.[219] But perhaps the most surprising political item is the 13-stanza poem that he sent to William on 28 November 1808.[220] As William noted in the endorsement, the poem concerns the 'Staffordshire County Meeting' held in Stafford earlier that month. Information about this meeting can be gleaned from the *Staffordshire Advertiser*, a weekly newspaper, published on a Saturday. The *Staffordshire Advertiser* of 29 October 1808 printed a letter, signed on behalf various individuals, requesting the High Sheriff to call a meeting on 11 November 1808 of the

> Noblemen, Gentlemen, Clergy, and others, Freeholders of the County of Stafford, to consider the propriety of petitioning his Majesty, that he will be graciously pleased to assemble his Parliament, in order to [allow] a constitutional and effectual investigation into the causes which led to the late Convention, concluded by the Officers commanding his Majesty's Forces in Portugal.[221]

A report of the meeting was printed on 12 November.[222] In the issue of 19 November Thomas, Lord Anson, gave his opinion on the proceedings.[223] On 26 November a satirical poem and various letters were published disagreeing over the paper's reports and comments on the meeting.[224] However, the poem published in the *Staffordshire Advertiser* on 26 November was *not* the poem that Duff sent to William on 28 November. 'His' poem *was* published in that newspaper, but not until 3 December, nearly a week after the date of Duff's letter.[225] That Duff had seen this poem in advance

218 Letter 145.
219 Letter 148.
220 Letter 53.
221 *Staffordshire Advertiser*, 29 October 1808, p. 4, column 4. See also *Staffordshire Advertiser*, 5 November 1808, p. 1, column 1, where the notice of the meeting is reprinted.
222 *Staffordshire Advertiser*, 12 November 1808, p. 4, column 1.
223 *Staffordshire Advertiser*, 19 November 1808, p. 1, columns 1 and 2. He had been M.P. for Lichfield from 1789 until 17 February 1806, when he was elevated to the peerage as Viscount Anson. (*Hist. Parl.*, Anson, Thomas (1767–1818).)
224 *Staffordshire Advertiser*, 26 November 1808, p. 3, column 1 for the poem and p. 4 columns 1 to 4 for letters.
225 *Staffordshire Advertiser*, 3 December 1808, p. 3, column 1.

of its publication, and had sent it to the family, strongly suggests that he had acquired it through a Staffordshire acquaintance whom he had met in London, probably a member of Lord Anson's family, who, as noted above, were well-known to the Reptons through connections in both Staffordshire and Norfolk.

Some of the letters convey Duff's sense of humour. Thus, he added a comment to the poem of 'Seven doughty knights' noting that they were 'doughty in Staffordshire', 'not Doughty in Norfolk', referring to Mr Robert Lee Doughty of Hanworth (d.1819), a client and friend of his father and also a client of Adey & Repton.[226] Writing to his aunt in October 1810, Duff said, 'I hope William will give my <u>best respects</u> to all friends at Hadisco – for a <u>grimmer</u> set I never encountered': a pun on the name of the Grimmer family, lords of the manor of Hadiscoe.[227]

Duff's erudition is also clear in several of his letters. In one he quoted from several writers in classical Rome[228] and it was he who supplied the Latin quotation for their uncle John Repton's monument.[229] The original editor of his father's memoirs noted that Humphry junior was 'a man of considerable talent contributing articles to the *Quarterly Review*'.[230] His name is not to be found among those contributors to the *Quarterly Review* identified from 1809 to 1821, although seventeen of its articles remain unattributed.[231] On the other hand, it is possible that the journal to which Duff had contributed was misidentified.

Duff died unmarried at the young age of 39, less than two years after his father, 'from brain fever caught by sitting on a stage coach one intensely cold night, after being much heated by running'.[232] It seems likely that he had been running to catch the evening coach to Hare Street, perhaps on his way home for Christmas, for he was buried at St Andrew's, Hornchurch, on 24 December 1819, although his abode was given as George Street, Marylebone.[233]

---

226 Hanworth was probably Repton's second commission after he became a professional landscape designer. (*Repton in Norfolk*, pp. 45–9.)
227 Letter 145.
228 Letter 53.
229 Letter 128.
230 *Memoirs*, p. 60, note 36.
231 J. B. Cutmore, *Contributors to The Quarterly Review: a history, 1809–25* (London, 2008). Appendix A is a list of all articles and their contributors.
232 *Memoirs*, p. 60, note 36.
233 ERO, D/P 115/1/12, Hornchurch St Andrew burials 1813–1848, p. 40.

Edward Repton (1782–1860)

As Edward was a clergyman there are some biographical details for him in the Church of England Clergy Database.[234] These are, however, incomplete (and even erroneous). The letters in this collection, both from himself and from other family members, reveal something of his character and of the precarious nature of the career of a Georgian clergyman who did not have quite enough influential connections to provide him with lucrative appointments.[235] In 'The Mitre', the poem that his father dedicated to him, Repton encouraged Edward to 'Labour – study – watch and pray' in order to secure advancement.[236]

Edward was born at Sustead on 24 June 1782 and baptised the following day.[237] His father recalled in his memoirs how Edward's education had been advanced by no less a person than Henry Addington, Speaker of the House of Commons from 1789 to 1801. He explained that Addington 'proposed to me that I should send one of my sons to Winchester where he had some interest with the Warden (now bishop of Gloucester); … the foundation of [Edward's] future career was laid by the unsolicited patronage of him to whom I am proud to acknowledge an obligation'.[238] Edward subsequently attended Magdalen College, Oxford, where he became BA and MA, before being ordained deacon on 1 September 1805. This collection opens with a letter from Edward to William written at Magdalen on 5 June 1805. The letter chattily brought William up to date with family news, but, as noted above, also hinted at uncertainty for his own future and bemoaned the burdens of family life that weighed on their father. He also mentioned his future wife, Mary Herbert, indicating that their acquaintance dated from at least 1805; subsequent letters reveal his family's anxieties over their relationship.

His first appointment was as curate at Ardingly, near East Grinstead (Sussex). By July 1807 he had become disillusioned with the place: 'I am now tired of Sussex Dirt, unpolished clowns, and squalling Brats – and want a situation, where there is more politeness, and less misery among the poorer sort – whose poverty I can't relieve'.[239] He did not, however, take up

---

234 CCEd Person ID: 21309

235 Dorothy Stroud also gives some details of his family and later life. (Stroud, *Repton*, p. 162.)

236 Poem no. 5 in the collection at the Avery Library. (MS ref 3233, microfilm reference: MICROFOR F a4379.)

237 NRO, PD 393/3, Sustead parish register, 1783–1808, p. 6. The entry appears on the same page as that for Humphry junior.

238 *Memoirs*, p. 41.

239 Letter 10.

his next appointment – at Crayford (Kent) – until sometime in 1808, and certainly by 13 October 1808, when Duff wrote about his being there.[240] One of their father's designs was for a new workhouse at Crayford. Fragment XXXV, 'Concerning Houses of Industry', takes the form of a letter to Edward describing the layout of the new building 'with all proper attention to the Comforts of the Poor'.[241] The design was not taken up.

In January 1813 Edward wrote to William, indicating that he was about to leave Crayford.[242] The outline of his career in the CCEd seems to be incomplete: there, his next recorded appointment after Crayford is in 1817 as rector of Miningsby (Lincs). In 1820 he was appointed chaplain of the chapel of St Philip Regent Street, in the parish of Westminster St James. The letter to William shows that he had another (minor) appointment in London in early 1813 and also that he was contemplating teaching a few pupils, either in their own homes or in his home, but without boarding with him. He had had pupils at Crayford, including a member of the Wallinger family.

The letters reveal some of Edward's various other non-parochial clerical roles. In 1808 he was selected to give the series of 'Boyle's Lectures'. In a codicil to his will, dated 28 July 1691, the famous scientist and devout Anglican Robert Boyle left £50 per year to be an annual salary for 'some learned Divine or preaching Minister … to preach Eight Sermons in the year, for proving the Christian Religion against notorious Infidels …'. They were to be preached on the first Monday of eight specified months. On the evening of Monday 5 September 1808 Repton told Dorothy 'We are all returned from London where we have been to hear Dear Edwards first Boyles Lecture at Bow Church'.[243] Edward hurriedly published that lecture.[244] In the preface he explained that he had taken this hasty action because he knew from experience that the lectures were poorly attended and wished to encourage potential listeners to attend the rest of the series.[245] Indeed his father noted that 'the Congregation [was] very thin'.[246] Edward's

---

240 Letter 50.
241 *Fragments*, pp. 227–30, preceded by a drawing of the proposed building. See also Daniels, *Repton*, pp. 57–8.
242 Letter 170.
243 Letter 48.
244 *The Works of Creation, A Series of Discourses for Boyle's lecture, No. 1. Being the First Sermon of the series delivered at St. Mary Le Bow Church, Cheapside, On Monday 5th of September 1808*, By the Rev. Edward Repton, A.M. of Magdalen College, Oxford, Curate of Crayford, in Kent. This includes the codicil to Boyle's will.
245 *The Works of Creation*, p. viii.
246 Letter 48.

innovation in publishing the first lecture in order to attract a larger congregation met with disapproval. On 13 October 1808 Duff told William that 'George says Lord Sidmouth objected to Edward having published his sermon against which he stated many arguments'.[247] He also preached the series of Boyle's Lectures in 1809 and 1810.[248]

A number of Edward's letters to William were in pursuit of 'livings' or clerical appointments: William's role as a country attorney in Norfolk meant that he was in contact with people who held advowsons, that is, the right to appoint to livings. One example of William's exertions on Edward's behalf will suffice. In July 1810 he had heard of the death of John Corbould, the incumbent of Bawdeswell and Eccles (on Sea, with Hempstead), livings in the patronage of Sir John Lombe. William asked Thomas Coke of Holkham to recommend Edward to Sir John, writing glowingly, but with some exaggeration, when he said 'I think if I am not mistaken Edward has the honor to be one of the Duke of Bedford's Chaplains'.[249] In fact, Coke declined to intervene on Edward's behalf because he had recently obtained two other livings from Sir John for other supplicants.[250]

In 1815, when the appointment to a living in Lancashire, valued at £1,000 per annum, was likely to become available, the tone of Edward's letter to William was almost frantic because he thought that he or Dorothy might know the Dowager Lady Suffield, who held the patronage.[251] Robert Stephens (or Stevens), who had been appointed originally had declined subsequently as he was to become the Chaplain (to the Speaker) of the House of Commons.[252] Edward thought he was worthy of the valuable Lancashire position: 'now as I have no small share of Vanity – I wan't her Ladyship be acquainted with my Merits'. In fact the current incumbent, Robert Walker, did not die until 1818. Eventually Edward himself was Chaplain to the Speaker from 1832 to 1833.[253]

---

247 50, HM 40925/1.

248 J. R. Bloxam, *A register of the presidents, fellows, demies, instructors in grammar and in music, chaplains, clerks, choristers, and other members of Saint Mary Magdalen College in the University of Oxford, from the foundation of the College to the present time*, vol. 7 (Oxford, 1881), p. 143.

249 Letter 137.

250 Letter 138.

251 Letter 193.

252 The Chaplain to the Speaker of the House of Commons served for no more than three years. Robert Stevens was the 49th Chaplain. He was appointed by Speaker Abbott in 1815; continued by Speaker Manners Sutton in 1817; and replaced by Christopher Wordsworth in 1818.

253 D. Gray, *Chaplain to Mr Speaker: the religious life of the House of Commons* (London,

Within the collection is a series of letters concerning the proposed marriage of Edward to Mary Ellis Herbert, which was causing consternation amongst the family. These letters shed light on their marriage and its circumstances: an earlier publication simply recorded the marriage, stating that 'Nothing more seems to be known of [Mary] than that she produced in due course a family of ten children'.[254] The disquiet caused by Edward's affection for Mary arose mainly from the precarious situation of her father, Joseph Herbert: he was president of the Council of Montserrat in the far-distant West Indies; his financial affairs were in disarray, such that he had no means to provide a dowry for Mary; and he was threatening to take his daughter (and her sister) back to the West Indies as the surest way to break the longstanding attachment with Edward.[255] Close reading of letters exchanged in October 1808 also reveals that various family members felt that the marriage would break up the close-knit family: Mary would be subtracting Edward rather than adding herself. William related to Edward their father's views that Mr Herbert's promises of financial support were untenable and that their father would not consent to the marriage because the 'chance of [Edward's] happiness is so desperate'.[256] Duff's letter to William explained that Edward had heard some tall stories from Mary and one of her aunts about life in Montserrat such that Edward had determined to marry her to prevent her going there.[257] Edward's letter to his own father laid out his reasons and feelings and requested his consent.[258] The *Gentleman's Magazine* reported the marriage of the Revd Edward Repton to Mary Ellis [Herbert] at Leyton (Essex) on 22 November 1808.[259] Mary's 'Aunt Ellis' lived at Leyton, about 9 miles from Hare Street. From Edward's letter to William after the wedding it is unclear which family members had attended but their sister Mary was currently staying with the newly weds in Crayford.[260]

During the time of these letters it appears that five children were born to Edward and Mary: the very last letter mentions five children, although only the eldest two, Edward and Georgiana are ever named; another child

1991), pp. 18–21; the second part of book comprises biographies of Speaker's Chaplains 1660–1991.

254 Stroud, *Repton*, p. 162.
255 Letter 45.
256 Letter 49.
257 Letter 50.
258 Letter 51.
259 *Gentleman's Magazine*, November 1808, p. 1039.
260 Letter 56.

had been born not long before January 1813.[261] The family seems to have had great affection for them. Writing from Hare Street on 5 January 1811, Duff told William 'The dear little Reptonini & Reptonina are both well & by their "squalling" enliven our little Circle'.[262] The only letter from Edward's wife in the collection relates to giving, or withholding, a reference for a former nurse of their children.[263] Eventually Edward and Mary had four sons and six daughters.[264] He died, aged 78, at St Leonards-on-Sea, on 6 August 1860, when a Canon of Westminster. He left about £16,000.[265]

George Stanley Repton (1786–1858)

A George Stanley Repton, son of Humphry and Mary, was born at Sustead on 28 September 1784, privately baptised two days later and buried on 3 October 1784.[266] Dorothy Stroud stated that the twins George Stanley and Mary Dorothy were born on 30 January 1786;[267] however, it was not until 14 July 1786 that they were baptised at the parish church of St Edward the Confessor, Romford.[268] As he was a successful architect in his own right, George has an individual biography in the *ODNB*, so the following concentrates on what can be learned from these particular letters. In 1802 George succeeded his brother John as a pupil of the London architect John Nash.[269] Indeed, the first letter from George in this collection was written on 31 July 1807 at Nash's office at 29 Dover Street, and is characteristic of him.[270] He had ordered a seal for William from Halfhide, of Halfhide, Barnes & Co., Coventry Street, and was sending him sketches of it. (*See illustration on p. 76.*) He was, unfortunately, too busy to spend a week or two at Aylsham any time soon. He had recently heard from Edward (and his future wife Mary) and there was currently very little 'Public news'.

While working for Nash, George divided his time between Nash's homes (and offices) on the Isle of Wight and in London. Like his siblings he accompanied his father when he could but he had to juggle such excursions

261 Letters 200, 174 and 170 respectively.
262 Letter 148.
263 Letter 173.
264 *Memoirs*, p. 41, note 14.
265 Stroud, *Repton*, p. 164.
266 NRO, PD 393, Sustead Archdeacon's transcript, Easter 1784 to Easter 1785.
267 Stroud, *Repton*, p. 25; archival reference not given.
268 The baptisms of George and Mary are recorded in ERO, D/P 346/1/3, St Edward the Confessor, Romford.
269 *ODNB*, Repton, George Stanley (1786–1858).
270 Letter 12.

with his main employment. In July 1809 he told William that their father wanted to know if he could accompany him, but 'I am so uncertain what are my plans that I can scarcely answer him – for I am daily expecting a summons from Nash to go to the Isle of Wight'.[271] Animosity between Repton senior and Nash continued. In 1812 a disagreement had arisen between George and his father over work at Sheringham. Dorothy reported to William that: 'He and his Father have talk'd over the Sherringham concern and they part friends, but George said this morning "reverse it Aunt Adey, what wou'd my Father have said if Mr Nash and I had taken a concern from him"'.[272] This suggests that Nash and George had had hopes of working at Sheringham but that the owner, Abbot Upcher, had preferred Repton senior (and his son John).[273] Some of George's letters mention architectural work, such as the plans for buildings at Westminster, already noted above. In December 1810 and January 1811 he was in correspondence with William about the competition for plans for the new Lunatic Asylum to be built at Norwich.[274]

George undertook to design the (small) monument for their uncle, John Repton, to be erected in Oxnead church. There are several letters about this from July 1809 to April 1810, both to ensure the correct wording for the memorial and because there was some discussion as to the extent to which John's wife should be involved in the planning. The family had little respect for 'Mrs John' and George was keen that there should not be space on his uncle's monument for any other names, presumably meaning hers. One of these letters contains a sketch.[275] The bill for the monument was only to be paid once George had verified it.[276] In fact, a letter from the mason, Samuel Adson, to William, dated 8 January 1812, indicates that the account, dated 13 June 1810, which came to £26 1s 10d, was still unpaid. Adson had sent the account before 'but having never heard from you I thought my letter might not have come to hand. I mentioned it to Mr G.S. Repton and he was surprised it was not paid and desired me to write'.[277]

There are some similarities between the letters of Duff and George, who seem to have been close. Writing in December 1810, George was unsure when

271 Letter 103.
272 Letter 162.
273 For the work at Sheringham, see *Repton in Norfolk*, pp. 144–54.
274 Letters 146 and 147.
275 See in particular Letters 103 (with sketch), 122 and 128.
276 Letter 147.
277 NRO, AYL 438 (bundle of papers labelled 'John Repton's Extors'), letter to William from Samuel Adson, Fitzroy Square Statuary, New Road, Fitzroy Square, London, enclosing 'the account of the Marble Monument for the Memory of John Repton Esq.'.

he would leave the Isle of Wight: 'it in some degree depends upon whether I go to Glocestershire, where my noble client appears to be again <u>nibbling</u>'. Given the family's liking for puns, it is highly likely that his 'noble client' was William FitzHardinge Berkeley, first earl Fitzhardinge, who owned the manor of North Nibley in Gloucestershire.[278] George's letters, like Duff's, were often chatty, imparting news of the family at Hare Street to those at Aylsham. On 28 August 1809 he reported that his father, who was away on business in the West Country, was 'highly pleased with a letter he had received from the Duke of Bedford asking his advice about the Buildings and Grounds at Tavistock Abbey'.[279] In fact the plans for preserving the remains of the abbey, landscaping the grounds and building various amenities were drawn up by Humphry senior, John and George.[280] When in London, like Duff, he was in a position to send the family political news. That he was well-informed, and well-read, is clear from his comments in March 1810 on reports of William Windham's speeches in *Cobbett's Weekly Political Register*, when Windham had been complaining in parliament about newspaper reporters.[281] George summarised the arguments and offered to send William the relevant newspapers. Duff continued the discussion, speaking against Cobbett's writing a few weeks later.[282]

George was the only other of the Repton siblings to marry. His marriage caused a scandal at the time: in 1817 he eloped with Lady Elizabeth Scott (1783–1862), eldest daughter of the first earl of Eldon, the Lord Chancellor. They were married, without his blessing, by special licence, on 27 November 1817 at St George's, Hanover Square, London.[283] George continued as an architect and many of his drawings, if not the actual buildings that he designed, have survived.[284] He had retired by 1845 and died, aged 72, on 29 June 1858 at his home, 27 New Norfolk Street, Park Lane, London.

Mary Dorothy Repton (1786–1821)
Mary was the twin of George. Both Mary and her sister Elizabeth are 'present' in the letters but little is known about them. There is, however, a

---

278 Letter 146.
279 Letter 105. The commissioning letter from the sixth duke of Bedford was dated 12 August 1809. (Carter et al., *Repton*, p. 151.)
280 Daniels, *Repton*, p. 184; the sketch is on p. 185.
281 Letter 116. See the footnotes to that letter for details of the various issues of *Cobbett's Weekly Political Register*.
282 Letter 126.
283 *ODNB*, Repton, George Stanley (1786–1858).
284 *ODNB*; Carter et al., *Repton*, p. 133.

surviving unsigned sketch of Mary.[285] There are only four pieces of writing from Mary in this collection, three short and one longer. The latter, written to William in March 1811, chattily informed him about the family's doings at Hare Street and included a sketch of a fishing rod, by her father, as John wanted William to bring John's 'fishing poles' from Norfolk.[286]

Mary was an accomplished artist in watercolours. Five of her watercolours and wash drawings survive in an album in the Colman Collection at the NHC.[287] There are also at least five more in the Avery Architectural Library, Columbia University, New York.[288] It has been suggested that, as well as John, Mary assisted their father in plant drawing and, after Repton's carriage accident in 1811, also in 'broader landscape compositions'.[289] That she travelled with her father to assist him in his business has already been noted. It is also clear that she was known to some of Repton's clients. Writing from Rochester on 23 October 1811 to Mary, who was staying at Aylsham, he reported: 'You will be pleased, my dear Girl, to hear that Lord Darnley, Your favorite, has behaved uncommonly handsome' by sending a draft for £100; and 'A letter from Lord Sheffield wonders I have not brought my daughter to Sheffield Place'. Furthermore he wanted her to accompany him soon: 'I think I have an engagement early next month for Gosfield near Hedingham & Clare &c – can't I contrive to fetch you – or meet you at Bury or Sudbury – write & say'.[290]

Despite the disquiet caused by Edward's marriage to Mary Herbert, Repton did expect his own daughters to marry. Not long after Edward's marriage he told Mary senior that 'we must bear the loss of our dear Edward', but there were enough of them in the family to be happy; which they would be 'till our Mary & our dee find out those they can love better than us'.[291] In the event, neither daughter married. Mary died at Hare Street and was buried on 9 June 1821, at St Andrew's, Hornchurch.[292]

---

285 Reproduced in Stroud, *Repton*, p. 158.

286 Letter 154 and illustration.

287 Carter et al., *Repton*, p. 170. Two of her pictures, one a floral arrangement, the other of Penshurst (Kent), have been reproduced in Daniels, *Repton*, pp. 39, 40.

288 In the Avery Library's catalogue the drawings have been misattributed to Mary (Clarke) Repton. (http://clio.columbia.edu/catalog/157397)

289 Daniels, *Repton*, p. 4.

290 Letter 159.

291 Letter 67.

292 ERO, D/P 115/1/12, Hornchurch St Andrew burials 1813–1848, p. 47.

Elizabeth D. Repton (1791–1865)

Elizabeth was born at Hare Street on 14 January 1791 and was baptized 'Elizabeth D. Repton' at Romford parish church six months later, on 15 July 1791.[293] She was the youngest of the surviving adult Reptons, although the family 'pedigree' indicates that the sixteenth, and last, child of Humphry and Mary had been named Richard.[294] It has frequently been assumed that 'D.' stood for 'Dorothy',[295] but none of the surviving official or legal records relating to Elizabeth expand 'D.' to 'Dorothy'. On the same page of the Romford baptismal register the baptisms of 'Elizabeth Mary' (Masters) and 'Elizabeth Charlotte' (Dixon) are recorded, so the use of 'D.' was not a question of space limiting the second name to an initial. Similarly, in the will of her brother William the executors were named as William Henry Scott and Elizabeth D. Repton.[296] In her own will she was named as Elizabeth D. Repton, late of the parish of Springfield, Essex, spinster.[297] While it might *seem* likely that her middle name was Dorothy, there is absolutely no firm evidence for it, and much to confirm the reason why in these letters she was often referred to, or called herself, 'd', 'dee', 'Dee' or 'D'.

Six of the letters have postscripts from Elizabeth, the most substantial written in late April 1814. She thanked William for fabric, which he had sent for his sister to make into dresses, that had arrived while Elizabeth was in London; Mary was still there having gone to a fair at Wandsworth with friends. Like all of the siblings, Elizabeth expressed concern for their father's welfare. At that time he had no formal commissions: 'it is sad to see him wandering about the garden all day without employment or amusement except his book' (*Fragments*).[298]

As already noted, after 1827 Elizabeth and her brother John lived together at Springfield. She died there on 8 December 1865.[299]

---

293 ERO, D/P 346/1/3, St Edward the Confessor, Romford.

294 NRO, AYL 80, Repton family pedigree.

295 See for example, *Aylsham*, p. 188, where it is stated that one of William's executors was his sister 'Elizabeth Dorothy Repton'.

296 NRO, AYL 1157, papers relating to will of William Repton, will dated 26 February 1855.

297 NRO, AYL 847, probate copy of the will of Elizabeth D. Repton.

298 Letter 183.

299 Principal Probate Registry, *Calendar of the Grants of Probate and Letters of Administration made in the Probate Registries of the High Court of Justice in England*, p. 209, Wills 1866.

Ƨ∕Ɔ

In 1815 Humphry Repton told his old friend and client Sir Harry Fetherstonhaugh that 'In the busiest days of my life I have found relief from professional pursuits in the employment of my pen, and I shall leave a large mass to my executors to prove that leisure was irksome to me at all times …'.[300] This volume makes more readily accessible a small portion of that mass, but considerably more of the letters in the collection in the Huntington Library were written by members of his family, all of whom supported him in his professional pursuits. Moreover their letters reveal the importance that they attached to their correspondence both in terms of keeping each other informed of their activities and of providing each other with help and guidance. The composition of 'fireside party' at Aylsham and at Hare Street varied as family members travelled to and fro, but regardless of who was present the reading of these letters was 'enlivening' and conveyed, as Dorothy said, 'the united love of our fireside'.[301]

The Repton letters at the Huntington Library

Provenance
The Aylsham papers held at the Norfolk Record Office are a rich source for historians of the county as the collection consists of the papers of Adey, Repton & Scott, Aylsham solicitors, and their clients.[302] These papers were deposited anonymously at the NRO over a number of years, from March 1969 onwards.[303] The collection in the Huntington Library is from the same source. Sold at Sotheby's, London, on 25 March 1974, the papers formed lot 272, described as 'Repton, (Humphry, 1752–1818, landscape-gardener) Important archive of about 230 original letters and papers by or concerning him and his family'. The only provenance given is that the items in the lot were 'The Property of a Gentleman': most likely the same person as the anonymous NRO depositor.[304] Sotheby's *Catalogue* describes the letters as 'uninhibited', 'constituting a lively and spontaneous record of

---

300 Meade-Fetherstonhaugh and Warner, *Uppark*, p. 72.

301 Quotations from Letters 184, 53 and 175 respectively.

302 NRO, reference AYL. Indeed, the original document transcribed in *The Notebook of Robert Doughty, 1662–1665*, ed. James Rosenheim (NRS vol. LIV) is in that archive.

303 Information via email correspondence with the NRO, 1 May 2019.

304 One suspects that these items were dealt with separately because they were likely to make a considerable amount of money at sale. The NRO received one of its AYL deposits a few weeks before, on 14 February 1974.

[Repton's] day-to-day life, his financial and domestic affairs, the execution of his various commissions, his personal relationships ... and containing intimate passages of self-revelation'.[305] Although the sale catalogue focusses on the letters written by Repton himself, it gives a fairly detailed breakdown of the various correspondents.

Following its acquisition from Sotheby's by the Huntington Library, this archive, which had been accumulated by William Repton at Aylsham, was also described in some detail by Jean Preston in the *Huntington Library Quarterly*.[306] The most significant items are just over 200 letters, more than 100 of which were addressed to William; 55 of the letters were written by Humphry, of which 42 were addressed to William, the others mostly to various members of the family. As well as family letters there are also several letters from William's legal clients and his draft replies. The rest of the archive comprises a large number of cheques drawn by William; three vellum documents dating from 1769 and 1770 concerning the marriage settlement of Dorothy Repton, Humphry's sister, upon her marriage with John Adey; a legal document drawn up for John Botham on 3 June 1746; and an undated pedigree of the Paston family of Oxnead. It seems likely that, prior to its acquisition in 1974, for most, if not all, of the period since William's death in 1858 the collection had lain unnoticed in No. 1 Market Place, Aylsham, the building where he had lived and practised.

Rather than ordering the letters by their call number, this edition orders them by date, whether actual or surmised.[307] Arranging them chronologically, rather than alphabetically by author, as the originals are in the Huntington archive, has two particular benefits. Firstly, items separated in the archive have been reunited; and secondly, a clear picture emerges of the family, their local society and their connections as time passed, as well as of Repton's wider activities over the eleven years covered by the letters.

---

305 Sotheby & Co., *Catalogue of Valuable Printed Books, Autograph Letters and Historical Documents comprising The Property of Sir Christopher Chancellor, the Property of Lady Pooley, The Property of P. J. McKie, esq., The Property of P. W. Ford, esq., the Property of the Jewish Museum and other properties* (Day of Sale: Monday, 25th March, 1974, at 10.30 a.m. precisely), p. 60.
306 Preston, 'Intramuralia', pp. 372–3. My analysis of the numbers of letters from the various correspondents differs slightly from Preston's.
307 See below, 'Numbering the letters'.

Dating the letters and identifying the correspondents

William endorsed many, but not all, of the letters as to content, date and correspondent; some have postmarks of varying legibility. Some of the unendorsed letters are undated or only give the day of the week. With the assistance of Cheney's *Handbook of Dates*,[308] and of the related contents of the letters themselves, it has been possible to ascertain with accuracy the dates of nearly all of these loosely dated letters.

The Huntington Library's cataloguer assigned each letter to one particular correspondent; close reading of the letters, however, reveals that other family members had added postscripts or even filled whole pages, partly to make maximum use of the expense of the post. The correspondence is, therefore, more representative of the family than might first appear. By far the most 'chatty' correspondents were Dorothy Adey and her sister-in-law Mary, but there are letters and/or postscripts from all seven Repton children. There are also ten letters from John Repton, Dorothy and Humphry's younger brother.[309]

In some instances several letters apparently from the same author, written in fairly quick succession, were catalogued together under one number. Close reading has shown either that the writer is not necessarily the same for every letter or that one of the letters does not fit the dating sequence. Where the latter are undated, or loosely dated, it is from their contents that their place in the archive's sequence had been ascertained.

Occasionally the writer refers to an enclosure of some kind, perhaps another letter or a drawing. Some of these enclosures are missing from the archive. The recipient may have been asked them to forward them to someone else, and did so; others have been found under a separate reference number, assigned because the writer was a different person. Furthermore, identifying the year in which a programme for the Three Choirs Festival was printed (and sent to a family member) has helped to date one particular letter.[310]

---

308 C. R. Cheney, ed., *Handbook of Dates for Students of English History* (London, 1991).
309 Four of them have been miscatalogued by the Huntington Library as being from John Adey Repton. Six of John Repton's letters are published in Appendix 1 as they have proved impossible to date.
310 Letters 20 and 21.

Numbering the letters

The letters have been published here in date order. The Huntington Library cataloguer assigned reference numbers in alphabetical order of writer (but beginning with the letters written by Humphry Repton senior), and then in what they considered to be date order. Thus the order in which the letters have been published here is somewhat different. In this edition each letter has been assigned a number, from 1 to 200; placed at the end of the letter is the Huntington Library's 5-figure reference number HM 40xxx as noted on the archive folder for each letter. Appendix 2 is a concordance of the letter numbers assigned here and the Huntington Library references, together with the writer, recipient and date; it also lists the other items from Adey & Repton's practice held at the Huntington.

Many of the letters were catalogued individually, but some catalogue numbers were assigned to groups of letters, for example, many of those from Dorothy Adey. In this edition, such letters have been separated out and assigned individual numbers, not least because they are not chronologically sequential: the original HM number has had a subsidiary number added, e.g. HM 40xxx/1. These subsidiary numbers are *not* present on the originals which are in no particular order in their archive folder.

Naming the correspondents

In the letter headings it has been necessary to distinguish between people with the same or similar names.

Humphry Repton = the landscape gardener

Humphry Repton junior = second son of Humphry and Mary (Clarke) Repton

John Repton = brother of Humphry Repton

John Adey = brother-in-law of Humphry Repton, husband of Dorothy

John Adey Repton = eldest son of Humphry and Mary (Clarke) Repton

Mary (Clarke) Repton = wife of Humphry and mother of his children, i.e. she was neé Clarke

Mary Repton = daughter of Humphry and Mary (Clarke) Repton

Mary (Herbert) Repton = Mary Repton neé Herbert, wife of Edward Repton

In the letters themselves, 'Dee' occurs: usually this is Dorothy Adey neé Repton, sister of Humphry and wife of John Adey; however, occasionally this is referring to Elizabeth Repton, the younger daughter of Humphry and Mary. Elizabeth is also referred to as 'D', 'dee' or 'd'. This caused some confusion to the Huntington Library cataloguer.[311] Where necessary in the letters this has been clarified, for example d: [Elizabeth]; Dee [Dorothy].

Place names

Original spellings of place names have been retained, e.g. Hare Street is often spelled Harestreet; Romford may be Rumford.

The transcription

One of the key points about the layout of the original letters is that the writer was maximising their use of the space on the page. To save space only occasionally did the writer start a new paragraph when they moved on to a new subject. Most of the letters comprise a sheet of paper about 15 inches (38 cm) by 9 inches (23 cm) that has been folded in half, thus making four sides of 7½ inches (19 cm) by 9 inches.[312] The writer began on the side with the fold on the left, continued on the left-hand side of the open double page, then the right-hand side of the double page, and then on the 'flaps' on the fourth side. The flaps comprise roughly the top and bottom quarters of the back page. These were then folded over towards the first page, the address of the recipient written in the middle of the central panel of the back page, and then the two sides folded inwards and sealed. In the middle of the third side of the letter (the right-hand side of the double page), the writer often left a margin of an inch or so on either side, to allow for the seal being broken upon opening. A few of the letters are damaged at this point. Some of the letters have text written upside-down on the first page above, or even through the writer's address and date. For example, when writing her long letter to William on 26 May 1808, his mother added various sentences in any available space, so that below William's address she added the instruction 'turn it'.[313] (*See illustration of Letter 45, HM 40934.*) One of the few notes by John Adey Repton was written at the top of a letter from his aunt on 29 March 1814.[314] (*See illustration of Letter 178, HM 40881.*)

---

311 See Elizabeth's biography above, where her name is discussed.
312 Thanks to Lisa Caprino, Reference Services Assistant at the HL, for measuring a 'typical' letter for me.
313 Letter 45.
314 Letter 178.

Folio breaks [*fb*] have been indicated. Some paragraphing has been added to break up the continuous text and thus aid the reader.

Most of the original capitalisation has been retained and some capitalisation has been added. Humphry Repton's individual style of punctuation, which includes many dashes, has been retained; Edward's was similar. Some punctuation has been supplied as some of the letters, especially Dorothy's, are particularly 'breathless'.

Unless otherwise stated the text has been transcribed in full with the original spelling. Although spelling is somewhat erratic, in general [*sic*] has only been used where the meaning is otherwise unclear.

The address from which each letter was written is given in the form supplied by the writer; if not stated by the writer, but given in William Repton's endorsement, or surmised, it has been supplied in [ ]. Occasionally the address of correspondent was included at end of the letter, this has been moved to the beginning but identified as such in a footnote.

The date of each letter has been reproduced as given by the writer; where the date has not been stated, but is given in William's endorsement, or surmised, it has been supplied in [ ]. Within the text days of the week and months of the year have been silently expanded.

Christian names within the letters have been expanded silently. For example, Edwd is now Edward; Wm William; Humpy Humphry. In the valediction the signature or name of the writer was not always given in full; the name has been left as in the original. Similarly names on the address panel have been left as written.

The valediction itself was frequently heavily abbreviated and simply continued on from the main text. For the sake of clarity it has been moved onto a separate line and expanded silently. For example, yrs affec'ly (and variants) has been rendered as 'Yours affectionately'; yr affec'te (and variants) has been rendered as 'Your affectionate'; G B Y is now 'God bless you'; hmbl' obed' s'vt (and variants) is 'humble obedient servant'.

Single quotation marks have added by editor (thus, 'words') where reported speech in the letters is not enclosed in quotation marks by the writer; compared with "words" which are reported speech as indicated in double quotation marks by the writer.

In view of the family's obsession with postage costs, all marks regarding postage have been noted thus:

B st or *b st* (capitalized if at start of line) followed by letters and numbers = black stamp, either rectangular with the place of posting or round with the date. These stamps are in varying condition; some are not wholly legible.

R st or *r st*: followed by letters and numbers = red stamp, either with the place of posting or with the date. Again, these are in varying condition, not always wholly legible. All franked letters have red stamps.

Cross Post is written in full; it was always written by hand

charge: followed by a number indicates the postal charge noted by the address[315]

All endorsements are by William Repton unless otherwise stated.

All postscripts have been added after the signature, although frequently written randomly in margins and on adjacent folios.

In the footnotes cross references to other letters are expressed as the number of the letter published here. Corresponding HM reference numbers will be found in Appendix 2.

Editorial Conventions

* *   Insertions by the writer are enclosed thus: *inserted words*
< >   Deletions by the writer are enclosed thus: <deleted words>
Folio breaks noted thus: [*fb*]
[?]widow – doubt about the transcription of a word.
[*italics*] editorial explanation inserted
Some writers contracted words, most have been expanded thus: rec[eip]t; a few have been retained where their meaning is clear, such as wou'd, cou'd.
Book titles and Latin phrases within the letters have been *italicised*.

The Postal System in England *c.*1805–1816

In 1801 London's Penny Post system became the Two-Penny Post, in 1805 all rates went up by a penny, and again in 1812.[316] The rate paid for post also varied according to the number of miles a letter was sent. In 1812 the charges for a single letter ranged from 4d for under 15 miles, through 9d for 80–120 miles, to 1s for 200–300 miles, and over 300 miles an additional 1d for every 100 miles more.[317] Letters were also charged according to their size: a single letter consisted of one sheet of paper under one ounce in weight; a double letter was two sheets of paper (or a cover and one enclosure)

---

315 See below for an explanation of the contemporary postal system.
316 F. Staff, *The Penny Post, 1680–1918* (Cambridge, 1993), p. 71.
317 Staff, *The Penny Post*, p. 72.

under one ounce in weight; a treble letter was originally three sheets of paper (or a cover and two enclosures) under one ounce but from 1784 it was any letter of more than two sheets under an ounce.[318] Charges for a double letter were twice that of a single letter; for a treble letter three times.[319] Frequently there is a figure scrawled across the address on a letter; this is the amount of postage due for that letter. The final letter here, sent by Repton and his wife to William and Dorothy in April 1816 has been endorsed by Repton 'Single sheet'; the charge written by the address is 9, i.e. 9d.[320] In March 1814 Dorothy sent to William a letter from Edward's wife together with one from herself. The matter was deemed urgent so she sent them together but explained 'I wish the enclos'd had been sent at once to you, because, I have no means of sending it but making you pay a double letter'. The charge written over the address is 1/6, i.e. 1s 6d (18d).[321] On some letters the charge is illegible or unclear.

Many of those letters that have an address panel have been stamped in black with the place of posting and a number; for example, RUMFORD 12, EAST GRINSTEAD 29 and AYLSHAM 132.[322] (*See illustration of Letter 178, HM 40881.*) There is also frequently a round ink stamp with a letter and the date in shortened form. These stamps are either in black or red ink. Analysis shows that all of the letters with black round stamps were posted in London and have the letters A to C on them; those with red stamps were posted outside London and have the letters B to E on them.[323] The black stamp indicates that the postal charge had been paid by the sender, the red stamp indicates that the charge was to be paid by the recipient.[324] For example, a letter written by Duff from London to Aylsham on 13 October 1808 has the black stamp C OC14 808, indicating

---

318 O. R. Sanford and D. Salt, *British Postal rates, 1635 to 1839* (Beckenham, 1990), p. xi.

319 Sanford. and Salt, *British postal rates*, p. 21; charges for letters weighing over an ounce were four times that for a single letter.

320 Letter 200.

321 Letter 174.

322 For example, Letters 178, 10 and 93 respectively. The number relates to the number of miles from London.

323 'In 1787 after a period with an experimental double-ring type [ink stamp], that shown in Figure 2 [in the publication] came into use. Later varieties had a letter on the left inside the outer ring, or outside it at the top to distinguish the different handstamps in use on the same day. At the Chief Office, owing to the times of arrival and departure of the coaches, incoming mails were usually dealt with on the morning duty and outgoing mails on the evening duty.' (R. C. Alcock and F. C. Holland, *British Postmarks: A Short History and Guide* (revised edn.,1977), p. 14.)

324 Information from Martin Grier, General Secretary, British Postmark Society.

that it was posted from London the following day.[325] On the other hand, a letter written from Aylsham by Dorothy Adey to William in London on 4 May 1809, on the afternoon of her husband's death, has the black stamp AYLSHAM 132 and the red stamp B May 6 1809, indicating that it was posted in Aylsham two days later.[326]

A number of the letters in the collection have 'Cross Post' written on them by hand. In 1696 the first official cross post was set up between Exeter and Bristol; from 1735 a complete network of new cross posts was developed by Ralph Allen. A cross post in England and Wales was a route between two post roads which did not pass through London; but, between two post towns not on the same post road, however near, letters could only circulate through London. Initially, whenever a letter passed through London it was charged twice, once for distance from its place of origin to London and a second time for the distance from London to its destination. An Act of 1784 provided that all letters within England and Wales should be charged only once for the total distance they were carried from the place of origin to the destination.[327] Those letters here endorsed 'Cross Post' were sent from Romford to Aylsham, or vice versa, without going through London. For example, the letter written by Duff from Hare Street to William at Aylsham on 27 November 1808.[328] (*See illustration of Letter 53, HM 40925/3.*) In a similar manner, on a letter sent by Dorothy from Aylsham to William when he was staying at the White Swan, Long Stratton, she wrote 'Short post', indicating that the letter was to go directly there from Aylsham.[329]

One way to avoid paying postal charges was to put letters into a basket of goods that was being transported by coach. For example, on 9 May 1814 Dorothy, writing from Hare Street, told William that the previous day Duff 'prevented my putting a line to you into the basket of Linnen I sent by a Coach Yesterday to Izzy [at Aylsham]', because Duff was expecting William to arrive at Hare Street soon, but since he had not arrived, she had posted it 'and therefore you will pay 9d for what if written yesterday wou'd have been basket free'.[330]

Another way to circumvent postal charges was to take advantage of the franking system, abuse of which was rife. The privilege of franking letters free of postage had been conferred on members of both Houses of Parliament

---

325 Letter 50.
326 Letter 79.
327 Sanford and Salt, *British Postal rates*, p. xiii.
328 Letter 53.
329 Letter 93.
330 Letter 186.

in 1656. Peers and members of the Commons would make presents to their friends of a few 'franks' – letter sheets bearing their signatures.[331] Within this collection there are seven franked letters from family members, and several others written by M.P.s or aristocrats. The franked letters have a red stamp with the date, a crown and lion, together with the name or signature of the person providing the frank and the date of posting handwritten.[332] Some of those who provided the franks were people with whom Repton was staying – such as Lord Henry Fitzgerald, uncle of his hostess, Lady Foley at Witley Court,[333] and Lord Tavistock.[334] At other times the frank might be from a former client: in March 1807, writing from London, Repton told William 'I will try to send this free tomorrow' and subsequently obtained a frank from John Fuller of Rose Hill (Sussex), a Sussex M.P., whom he had provided with a Red Book in 1806.[335] That M.P.s might be persuaded to frank a number of letters for the Repton family is demonstrated in a letter, dated 6 July 1812, from Dorothy at Hare Street to William in Aylsham. Charles Callis, Lord Western, had visited Repton's house the previous day and

> your Father and George employ'd him in franking for them, and tho I fancy'd I shou'd like one to you I did not like to trouble him further, but George said "Mrs A: has left a good Brother of mine at home, she writes to every day, pray let her next history go free", so free it will come and a day or two earlier than I intended.[336]

If a letter was taken late to the post office, it might be accepted upon pre-payment of a late fee. At post towns throughout the country the postmaster could accept late fee letters if he so wished, but there was no obligation on him to do so. If he did, the fee, which was his perk, had to be one penny.[337] If a letter missed that day's mail coach, it would be stamped TOO LATE.[338] On Sunday 10 March 1811, Dorothy told William how she had gone to the Romford post office to enquire about a letter being said to be too late: the post mistress was 'quite crumpy'.[339]

---

331 Staff, *The Penny Post*, p. 73.
332 The frank had to clearly state date and signature/name of privileged person.
333 Letter 17.
334 Letter 68.
335 Letter 9.
336 Letter 162; this particular frank has not survived on the letter.
337 Sanford and Salt, *British postal rates*, p. 43.
338 See, for example, Letter 102.
339 Letter 155; 'crumpy' means 'brittle, or crisp'(*OED*).

The family sent numerous letters, not only business letters sent by William and his father, but also personal letters necessary to keep each other informed of their welfare and activities in a period long before telephones. One wonders whether their interest in, not so to say obsession with, postal charges relates to Repton's earlier financially unsuccessful foray into the mail coach business. At the end of each transcript has been noted the address of the recipient; any endorsement by William; the various ink stamps; and, where applicable, 'Cross Post' or the amount of the postage due.

Details of the organisation of the post in Aylsham and in Romford in 1793 are available from the *Universal British Directory*. Just before the time of the Reptons' letters the directory entries explain the system that was available to them. At Aylsham 'The post goes out every Sunday, Wednesday, and Friday at 11 in the morning; and comes in every Tuesday, Thursday, and Saturday, about 2 in the afternoon'.[340] At Romford

the principal inn is the Cock and Bell, Isaac Palmer, which is the post-office. The bag to London goes by Norwich mail early in the morning: letters to be put in for London by ten o'clock the preceding evening. All letters for the country as far as Norwich must be put in by eight o'clock in the evening, and go by mail without going to the general post-office: postage to London 2d.[341]

---

340 *Aylsham Directories*, p. 1.
341 Reproduced in H. Feldman, *Letter receivers of London, 1652–1857: a history of their offices and handstamps within the general, penny and twopenny posts* (Bristol, 1998), vol. 2, entry R11: Romford Twopenny Post Office.

Letters

1. Edward Repton to William Repton

Magdalen College, Oxford, June 6th 1805

Dear William

It is not often that I have occasion or opportunity to trouble you, and now this will not reach you this fortnight or 3 weeks – but I cannot allow your friend Pittman,[1] to return and speak of all the wonders of this fine place – without interrupting your deep researches with a little chat – I like your friend, he seems to be a good natured Young Man, without affectation – and with some of the Aylsham simplicity, for as yet fuss, finery, and fashion have not al-[*fb*]together invaded that little nook – I was sorry to be from home, when you came to London – all at Harestreet were loud in your praises, and did not like to lose you again – but alas! I think it has been the misfortune, with all the rest of us except yourself – to have been too much together, and now while we should be shifting for ourselves, we are all still a burden and expence to my poor father, who, I am sorry to say, has not a vast deal of employment abroad, to make hi<m>s return to home quite easy and satisfactory.[2] – I shall take Orders in or before September,[3] but where I am to dwell or what is to become of me, I cannot at present determine – I

---

1 Samuel Pitman (1781–1853) was appointed curate at Oulton, on 22 September 1805, having been curate at Bintree since 25 September 1803. On 26 September 1806, he married Barbara Bell, only child of Coulson Bell of Oulton Hall; the couple lived at Oulton Hall, about four miles from Aylsham; later J.P. and Deputy Lieutenant for Norfolk. (CCEd Person ID: 114441; *Alumni Cantab.*)

2 Stephen Daniels' chart of Repton's new consultations from 1788 to 1818, based on exactly datable first visits either from his account book (up to 1791) or known Red Books, shows only one commission in 1804 and three in 1805. (Daniels, *Repton*, p. 40.)

3 Edward was ordained deacon on 1 September 1805 and priest on 21 December 1806. (CCEd Person ID: 21309.)

think [*fb*] I shall look out for a Curacy in or near London – for I should by no means like to be banished to a distance from home.

Duff is still in his twopenny-halfpenny Office at Somerset house,[4] he has Friends who promise him much; but I doubt all friendships – George is with Nash still[5] – and a great favorite, what will be his fate – we know not. – It gives me pleasure to hear from Pittman – that you are much respected and beloved by those who know you. – Mott[6] is with us at present, I gave him a hint about his Courts, but he says that Hewit[7] is his Agent, and he has [no] reason to find fault with him, but in case of any change, I hope he will think of you – Pittman [*fb*] tells me Mr Adey[8] is considerably better – long may he enjoy his health and be a comfort to poor Mrs A[9] – who would greatly feel his loss – I shall remain here till the latter end of this month, and quit this place, I hope, for ever, I mean as a residence – I shall have great pleasure in coming to see my friends here – but not to reside for a constancy.

My father was here yesterday[10] – quite well, but fagged – and Mr Herbert,[11] on his return from Cheltenham – where he has been to try the waters which did not agree with him, he is very weak and ill, from the effects of the yellow fever. My Mother, Mary &c – are all well – Love to all, and believe me,

Your affectionate ER

Pittman is going I have not time to read this over

---

4 Humphry junior worked in the Audit Office, at that time situtated in Somerset House. (See Letter 3.)

5 John Nash (1752–1835), architect. Humphry Repton and Nash worked together from 1795, and John Adey Repton joined Nash's office then. The partnership between Repton senior and Nash ended acrimoniously in 1800. John Adey Repton had by then left the office, but his place was taken about 1802 by George Repton, who remained with Nash until about 1820. By 1800 Nash was on his way to becoming one of the most successful domestic architects in England. (*ODNB*)

6 John Thurston Mott (c.1785–1847) of Barningham Hall, which had passed to him at the age of three, on his father's death. (*Repton in Norfolk*, p. 117.) Mott matriculated at Magdalen College, Oxford, on 19 March 1803, aged 18; he was created MA on 5 July 1805. (*Alumni Oxon.*)

7 Not identified.

8 John Adey, Humphry Repton's brother-in-law.

9 Dorothy Adey (neé Repton). See her biography on pp. 25–26.

10 Repton had provided Magdalen College, Oxford, with a Red Book in 1800. (Daniels, *Repton*, p. 265.)

11 Edward's future father-in-law, the Hon. Joseph Herbert (1758–1836), President of the Council of Montserrat in the West Indies. According to Letter 51, in 1808 Edward had been cherishing hopes of marrying Mary Herbert for six years.

Address: W. Repton Esqr, Aylsham, Norfolk, by favor of the Revd
S. Pittman
Endorsed: 6ᵗʰ June 1805   Edwd Repton Esqr   from Oxford
HM 40908

**2. William Repton to Dr Lachlan MacLean;[12] Dr MacLean to Humphry
Repton's tenant in Suffolk; Adey & Repton, solicitors, to the same tenant**
(all drafts)

Aylsham, 6 July 1805

Dear Sir

My father <by a L[ett]re> has <directed> ordered me to send you notices
to be served on his Tenant at Stoke to yield up the possession of his Cottage
&c at Michaelmas next *(in consequence of some intimituation you have
fav[oure]d him with, on the subject) together with a* <together with a
L[ett]re> Lawyers Lettre to <ser> the Tenant requiring the payment of all
arrears of Rent <to you which are>*now* due   Both which are to be made
use of as you shall see occasion – <But unless these the>*I apprehend **the**
possession cannot be obtained at Mich[aelm]as* next <unless the> without
six months previous Notice unless the Tenant has entered into a written
agreem[en]t to quit <at> on receiving *notice of a shorter date* <3 months
notice I fear the notice will be of but little avail & in that case the notices
sho'd be drawn pursuan framed in all respects pursuant to such agreement>
    As there is no immediate opportunity of obtaining my fa[the]r's signature
to the notices I think they *had* better be signed by the person who has
usually given discharges for the Rent. Be so good as to let such P[er]son
insert the Tenant's name in the blank left for that purpose & examine the
2 notices to enable him to prove *in case it should be necessary hereafter
<that> the one **which** he shall hold is exactly similar to* the other*
<that> which shall* <that they are> have been served on the Tenant <exactly
similar in case it should be necessary> I <sho'd> hope these proceedings will
be sufficient to attain our object without having recourse to more arbitrary
measures as I *do not* believe <it to be for my [?]person> my father has any
intention of <of> distressing the tenant if poverty be his only fault – <*By

---

12 Dr, later Sir, Lachlan MacLean (1761–1843), physician, of Sudbury, Suffolk; seventh
son of Dr MacLean of the Isle of Skye, a noted Hanoverian in 1745. Here MacLean is acting
as Repton's agent, but see later letter regarding consultation on medical matters (e.g. Letters
168, 179 and 190).

acting herein as you shall think most conducive to*> By acting herein as
you shall think <best for> *most conducive* to my father's interest you will
much oblige both him &

<D >Sir, Your very obedient humble servant

WR

Mr & Mrs Adey desire *to add* <their> Comp[limen]ts <may be> to
yourself & Mrs Maclean

Dr MacLean to Humphry Repton's tenant

<M> Sir

<As Agent for Mr Humphry Repton your Landlord> I hereby give you
notice to quit and deliver up on the 11ᵗʰ day of October – next the possession
of *all & singular* the Mess[uag]es *Tenem[en]ts or Cottages* <or Dwelling
house together with all and singular the farm> Lands, Heredit[amen]ts &
prem[is]es with the appurt[enance]s which you now hold of <Mr> Humphry
Repton Esqr your Landlord situate in the parish of Stoke in the County of
Suffolk.¹³

Dated the [blank] day of [blank] 1805

Yours &c

Agent for the s[ai]d Humphry Repton

To Mr [blank]

Or whom else it may concern

Adey & Repton, solicitors,¹⁴ to Humphry Repton's tenant

Aylsham, Norfolk, 6 July 1805

Sir

<You are desired> We are directed to apply to you for payment of
<all> *the* arrears of Rent due to your Landlord Mr H. Repton – for the
Cottage & Land which you hold under him at Stoke – <and are> <*and we
request*> *& are* desired to inform you that unless the same shall be paid
to Dr Maclean or some person whom he shall appoint, within 14 days we

---

13 Repton's mother Martha was a member of the Fitch family of Stoke by Clare (Suffolk).
(*Aylsham*, p. 170.)

14 The solicitors' practice of John Adey and William Repton was acting for Humphry
Repton in this matter.

shall be under the necessity of taking such Steps for <recove> enforcing the paym[en]t as the Law will allow.

    <Sir> Your humble servants

    Adey & Repton

    Att[or]nies at Law

Endorsed: 6 July 1805   Letters to Dr Maclean & The Stoke Tenant
HM 40954/1

3. Humphry Repton junior to William Repton

Adelphi,[15] October 24[th] 1806

My dear William

    I have been prevented writing to you till this time by the dilatoriness of the Exchequer people who have been keeping holidays – but have this day paid at Williams & Moffats[16] £50 for you on Sir R. Kerrisons Acc[oun]t[17] – with many thanks for the accommodation.

    Tell Mrs Adey that I have got a receipt for her from her friend Mrs Tennant[18] who wished to know whether her stays fitted – but I told [her] I was not in the secret.

---

15 Although the Audit Office, where Humphry junior worked, was situated in Somerset House, from this it appears that his own office was nearby at Adelphi, an imposing riverside development designed and built by John, Robert, James and William Nash. (*London Encyclopaedia*, pp. 6–7.)

16 The private bank of Williams & Moffat was established as Raymond, Vere, Lowe & Fletcher in Cornhill, City of London, in 1771 and subsequently moved to Birchin Lane nearby. The bank operated under many names including Williams, Son & Drury from 1792 and Williams, Son, Moffat, Burgess & Lane from 1812. (*British Banking*, pp. 539–40.)

17 i.e. Kerrison's Bank, Norwich. This private bank was formed in 1768 as Allday & Co and was known subsequently as Allday & Kerrison by 1776, as Kerrison & Kerrison by 1804 and later as Kerrison & Sons. It also traded as the Norwich Bank. (*British Banking*, p. 302.) Sir Roger Kerrison (1740–1808) was the son of Roger Kerrison of Seething. He was sheriff of Norfolk in 1774, and mayor of Norwich in 1778. For 30 years he was Receiver-General for taxes in Norfolk. His bank's premises were at the Back-of-the-Inns, Norwich. As high sheriff of Norfolk in 1800, he presented to King George III the county's address on his wonderful escape from assassination and was knighted on that occasion. His firm was made bankrupt at the time of his death. He had property at Thorpe, Carrow Abbey and Brooke Hall. All were sold on his bankruptcy. He died on 6 May 1808 in Norwich. (Details from NRO catalogue, person search 'Roger Kerrison'.)

18 Not identified.

We have been in what Mr Eliot[19] calls an intermitting state ever since I left [*fb*] you – & have not yet begun business tho' he expected it on the first of October – I remain exactly in *statu quo* – except that Mallet[20] being promoted as Secretary with 1000 *per ann*[*um*] I am in fact at the head of this Office as Mr Eliot's adviser – tho' they have unjustly given the title & the Salary to an old gentleman 70 years old[21] who will make his place a sinecure.

Tell me when we are likely to meet: I have been living ever since I left you at the best hotel in London – [*fb*] the Tavistock in Covent Garden,[22] but shall remove next Wednesday to No 184 Piccadilly – where I have a large bow window – commanding at one view all the kingdoms of the earth and the glory thereof[23] – & being exactly opposite to your uncle the Duke of Portland[24] – I can dine with him you know without the fatigue of getting into a hackney coach – I wrote a respectful letter to Lord Sidmouth[25] complaining of injustice in not being promoted – & our establishment has since been returned to the Treasury for revision, but I have learned to expect nothing that I may not be dissappointed. [*fb*] My father says that having been promoted by Mr Pitt's favor I am lucky to keep what I have got – but on that point we differ – Mr Pitt has however made me independant of all

---

19 Francis Perceval Eliot (1755–1818), writer on finance and army officer. Following his army career, in 1806 he was appointed a commissioner of audit. His financial writings were mainly on currency and banking. (*ODNB*)

20 John Lewis Mallet (1775–1861) was appointed through Pitt's influence to a clerkship in the Audit Office in 1800 and rose to be secretary to the Board of Audit. He was the father of Sir Louis Mallet (1823–1890). (*ODNB* entry for Louis Mallet.)

21 This 'old gentleman of 70 years old' has not been identified.

22 The Tavistock Hotel, 4–10 Great Piazza, Covent Garden. The last of Inigo Jones's houses in the Piazza, the Tavistock was demolished in 1928. It had 200 bedrooms. The great dining room occupied the whole of the first floor. (*London Encyclopedia*, p. 856.)

23 Quotation from Matthew, ch. 4, v. 8.

24 William Henry Cavendish Bentinck, third duke of Portland (1738–1809), twice prime minister. (*ODNB*) He was not, of course, William's uncle, but Repton had advised on improvements at Welbeck Abbey (Notts). (See Daniels, *Repton*, pp. 154–66.) He provided two 'Red' Books, the first, dated 4 January 1790, was actually brown, the second, dated 14 May 1793, was red. (Rogger, *Landscapes*, pp. 200, 203.) Burlington House, Portland's London property, was in Piccadilly; for his property of Bulstrode (Bucks), see Letter 17.

25 Henry Addington, first viscount Sidmouth (1757–1844), politician; prime minister (1801–4). (*ODNB*). The Repton family seem to have had a good relationship with Sidmouth, mentioned in several of the letters. Repton advised on the landscaping of Sidmouth's property White Lodge, Richmond (Surrey). There is no Red Book but three watercolours by him are in the possession of Sidmouth's descendants. (Carter et al., *Repton*, p. 162.)

the world & I shall make my happiness depend on myself.[26] Love to all & tell them with how much pleasure I <lov> remember their hospitality in Norfolk.

ever yours

H Repton

Address: William Repton Esq., Aylsham

B st: B OC 25 806

Endorsed: 24 Octo'r 1806   Hu Repton Jun Esqr [*various mathematical calculations*]

HM 40923

4. Revd Richard George Robinson[27] to John Adey

Lichfield, October 30th 1806

Sir

The Revd Richard Buckeridge[28] told me lately, that the last time he saw you, you enquir'd after Mrs Boyd,[29] a blind widow lady, who resided in Lichfield. As I suppose your reason for making the enquiry was, the gentleman being your client, part of whose estate was charg'd with an annuity, which was her only subsistence, I think it proper to acquaint you, that she died suddenly on the 17th of last month. I and my wife were almost the only persons who took any notice of her. I, therefore, in conjunction with a reputable tradesman here, with whose aunt she had been acquainted, gave directions for her funeral, took an inventory of the few effects she had, for she was in lodgings, and examined her papers, in order to find out her nearest relation; which her maid servant told us she believed to be a niece, with whom she had had no intercourse for 20 years.

26 William Pitt the younger (1759–1806), prime minister. Repton advised Pitt regarding his property at Holwood (Kent) and met him on several occasions. (*Memoirs*, pp. 56–61.) Regarding Humphry junior's relationship with Pitt, see his biography in the Introduction, and *Memoirs*, pp. 60, 75.

27 Revd Richard George Robinson was vicar of Harborne (29/05/1772–11/07/1825) and of Barrow with Twyford (27/06/1803–30/09/1825), both in the diocese of Coventry and Lichfield. (CCEd Person ID: 19485.)

28 Revd Richard Buckeridge (d.1824) held a number of appointments including priest vicar of the united prebends of Brewood and Adbaston (Lichfield cathedral) from 1789 and rector of Beighton from 1803. (CCEd Person ID: 9701.)

29 Not identified, but probably related to the Eliza Boyd who was Elizabeth Repton's godmother. (See Letter 172.)

I have discovered her place of residence, and am in daily expectation of hearing from her in order to [complete] the settling her affairs. There are letters from two Clergymen in Norfolk, of the name of Stoughton, her relations, one of whom is since dead, who I believe was rector of Wymondham.[30] Those from the rector of Sparham[31] make mention of his taking an early opportunity of speaking to Mr Day,[32] respecting a complaint she had made, that the latter had deducted too much [fb] from her annuity, on account of the tax upon income. I suppose her annuity ceased at her death, without Mr Day being liable to pay for any portion of the last half year.

Mrs Robinson and I spent the evening on Tuesday at Col. Patton's,[33] where we had the pleasure of meeting my old acquaintances, Mr and Mrs Sneyd of Belmont.[34] I have the pleasure also to tell you they are both well. I acquainted them that I should write to you soon, when they desired me to present their best regards to you and Mrs Adey, and to say, that they received Mrs Adey's letter at Cheltenham, that they are very glad to hear you are well, and that you will hear soon from Mrs Sneyd.

If you have anything material to communicate to me respecting Mr Day's transactions with the late Mrs Boyd, you will have the goodness to favor me with an early answer.

I am, Sir
Your most obedient servant
Rich Geo Robinson, Cler.

Address: John Adey Esq., Aylsham, Norfolk
R st: C Oct 31 1806; *b st*: LITCHFIELD 119   OCT 30 1806; *charge*: 8

---

30 The only CCEd entry for 'Stoughton' in the Norwich diocese in this period is that for James Stoughton (see following note). The recently deceased rector of Wymondham has not been identified; William Papillon was vicar of Wymondham from 3 November 1788 until his death on 26 September 1836. (P. Cattermole, ed., *Wymondham Abbey: a history of the monastery and parish church* (Wymondham, 2007), p. 224.)

31 James Stoughton was appointed rector of Sparham on 19 April 1792. (CCEd Person ID: 100326.)

32 According to William's endorsement, Mr Day of Horsford. (See, for example, NRO, MC 2403, Day of Horsford papers.)

33 Col. James Patton of Lichfield. In 1805 he commanded a battalion of 545 men in the Staffordshire Volunteers. (M. R. Hales, 'Civilian soldiers in Staffordshire, 1793–1823' (PhD thesis, Sheffield Hallam University, 1995), p. 100.)

34 The Sneyds of Belmont were related to John Adey: in January 1794 Mary Adey, John Adey's half-sister, had married John Sneyd of Belmont Hall, in the parish of Ipstone (Staffs). (*Aylsham*, p. 169.) Within the Huntington archive are three, virtually illegible, letters from Mary Sneyd. (See Appendix 1.)

Endorsed by John Adey: 30ᵗʰ October 1806   Revd Mr R. G. Robinson
Lichfield
Endorsed by William: About Mrs Boyd to whom Mr Day of Horsford pays
an Annuity
HM 40953/1

5. Mary (Clarke) Repton to Dorothy Adey

[Hare Street], Monday 8ᵗʰ [December 1806]³⁵

My dearest Dee

I doubt you wonder much at not hearing from me, but we are all quite well, or you may be assured I wou'd have written, but I was willing to wait to tell you <u>decidedly</u> whether we shoud come to you at Christmas and I am truly sorry that I am the person appointed to say that dear Humphry has given it up, to my great Mortification, he poor fellow has pointed out many reasons why he ought to defer it till the Summer, the first is that he thinks he shall not go to Mr Greenwoods near Sudbury³⁶ as he does not think of doing any thing till the Spring – in that case it will cost too much money – 2ᵈ it is such a cold time of the year that we shall all get ill and be to Nurse as poor Mary³⁷ was last year – 3ᵈ he is obliged to go to Ld Foleys³⁸ & set off this day and he thinks, and is almost sure that he cannot be back in time – That I believe to be the chief and most material reason why he has given *it* up – but the [fb] last words he said this morning when he went away "tell the dear Adeys to come to us, and I will get home to dinner on Christmas day" – now, my dear dee, if you Mr Adey and Dear William cou'd do that how happy it woud make us – I thank God dear H is well and hearty again but I had rather he had not been obliged to go this long Journey into Worcestershire at this Season, but he says if he had given it up till the Spring he should have lost the Job which woud have been a bad

---

35 8 December 1806 was a Monday, and later in the letter she mentions the recent death of Mr Basely, which occurred on 30 November 1806. Daniels dates this letter to 1807. (Daniels, 'Cankerous blossom'.)

36 Charles Greenwood of Sudbury (Suffolk). His property, known as Auberies, is pictured in the *Polite Repository* (1811). (Daniels, *Repton*, p. 266; Temple, 'Repton, illustrator, p. 173.) Repton eventually paid his first visited to Mr Greenwood in March 1810. (See Letter 119.)

37 Presumably referring to her daughter Mary.

38 Thomas Foley, third baron Foley (1780–1833), whose house was Witley Court (Worcs). (Daniels, *Repton*, p. 269.) Repton's work there is known from a letter dated 28 January 1807 (Herefordshire R.O.); see also the next letter in this collection. For his work there, see *Repton in the West Midlands*, pp. 88–9.

thing, therefore you come to us, we shall be together and it matters not <u>where</u> my dear Dee.

I have been looking at your last letter and am quite surprizdd[*sic*] to see the date, which is only Wednesday, but I hope it was last Wednesday. Friday Mary and I went with Humphry to Town, in his way to Mr Mannings[39] – and we brought Anna Wallinger[40] with us and H persuaded poor Mrs W[allinger] to come <back> back with him on the Saturday and she is now with us, poor thing, in great trouble. [*fb*] I told you that the Solicitor General[41] has given his decided opinion that it [*i.e. Hare Hall*] is little Johns, of course Mr Tucker[42] who supposed it to be his, is extreemly disappointed, as he is obliged to remove all his things and has been at a great expence after living there all the Summer – it is very mortifying it has been offerd to him to Rent it, but he will not give more than 300 a year not quite so much – it has been so much [?]blown upon and undervalued that it is most likely to stand empty. She poor woman will have nothing but the 3rd of what it let for [*damaged*] with nine Children, what is she to do[43] –

---

39 According to Daniels, 'Mr Manning's Villa' was The Darlands, Totteridge (then in Hertfordshire) and was depicted in *Polite Repository* (1808). (Daniels, *Repton*, p. 263.). However, it is not mentioned in the list of *Polite Repository* plates in Carter et al., *Repton*, pp. 141–5 or Temple, 'Repton, illustrator', pp. 172–3. Repton himself refers to 'Mr Manning's Villa at Totterige' in his *Designs for the Pavillon*[*sic*] *at Brighton* (1808), p. v, note 4. William Manning, as well as M.P. for various places, was a director and then governor of the Bank of England and a West India merchant; he was father of Cardinal Manning. (*Hist. Parl.*, Manning, William (1763–1835).) Darlands was part of the Copped Hall estate and the site now forms Darlands Lake Nature Reserve. According to London Gardens Online: 'From 1780 [the house] was occupied by William Manning whose wife Mary was involved in the redesign of the grounds probably with advice from Humphry Repton.' http://londongardensonline.org.uk/gardens-online-record.php?ID=BAR019 [accessed 15/4/2019]

40 Perhaps one of the daughters of John Wallinger II. (See note 43.)

41 Sir Samuel Romilly (1757–1818) (*ODNB*)

42 Mr Tucker was then living in Hare Hall.

43 John Arnold Wallinger, owner of Hare Hall, had died in 1792. He had three sons, John, William and Joseph. Although here I have dated this letter to 1806, rather than 1807 as suggested by Daniels, the details of the lawsuit given by Daniels are not invalidated. (Daniels, 'Cankerous blossom', p. 156.) After the death of John Wallinger senior (John I) in 1792 the landed and business interests of the family were divided between his first and second sons, causing the eldest son, also John (John II), financial difficulties. On John II's death in 1805 Hare Hall was put in trust and was subject to a legal wrangle. (Daniels, 'Cankerous blossom', p. 156.) The 'little John' mentioned by Mary Repton was the eldest son of John II, i.e. John III. 'Mrs Wallinger' mentioned here was Matilda, the widow of John II and mother of his nine young children. (A. Searle and C. Brazier, *A History of Hare Hall* (n.p., 1960), pp. 10–16.)

she [*damaged*] her best love to you, Mr A, and William – she desires me to say she had a letter from Mrs Joseph,[44] they are very well, have been at Dawlish and are now at Exeter – how are our dear friends at Oxnead.[45] I received a Hare yesterday from my Brother.[46] Will you give my best love and thanks to them – and some good kisses from us all to the dear Eliza and tell her when the Cuckoo has picked up all the dirt in the Roads, we *will* come and see her – [*fb*]

Poor Mrs Wallinger's troubles will never end I fear. she has just had a letter to say her little girl is very ill, and that Sir Samuel Romily and the Attorney *General*[47] disagree about Harehall. the first says it is Johns, the other that it is not, and may be sold, and is not to be let, only for one year, it must be put under the Lord Chancellors[48] care to decide it, poor thing she must leave me to morrow morning, and I hop'd she coud have staid till Thursday.

God bless you all. I wish we coud have met, and perhaps we still *may* do so sooner than we think of. pray God grant we may all meet well and happy is the sincere prayer of your affectionate

M Repton

I see by the papers Mr Basely[49] is dead.   what a fine Character they give him.

Address: Mrs Adey, Aylsham, Norfolk
B st: RUMFORD 12; Cross Post; *charge*: 8
Endorsed: Mrs Repton
HM 40933/1

---

44 Anna Maria Jordan married Joseph Wallinger in 1797.
45 John Repton and his family.
46 i.e. her brother-in-law, John Repton
47 Sir Arthur Piggott (1749–1819) was Attorney General in 1806–7. (*Hist. Parl.*)
48 At this time Thomas Erskine, first baron Erskine. See note to Letter 9.
49 John Greene Basely of St Saviour's, Norwich, born *c.*1740, died on 30 November 1806, buried on 5 December. (*The Norfolk Chronicle*, Saturday, 6 December 1806, issue 1917, p. 2.)

6. Humphry Repton to William Repton

Whitly Court, Sunday evening [14 December 1806][50]

Dear William

Having got a Cover – I must write tho Lady Foley,[51] Lord Petersham[52] – Lady Isabel[53] & your Brother Revd Edward are all singing at my elbow – – but I had two things to mention – 1st ab[ou]t Windham[54] – if I see him in Town may I not say what I think ab[ou]t the shabby agent[55] who expects interest on an Acc[oun]t – many people have own me money many years – but I never expect interest & think my self well off to get the Capital – in short let Adey set off against it the expenses of entertaining the Windhams & Lukins[56] for a series of years at only 20 or 30 £ *per annum.*

[*fb*] the next thing is – this – I delivrd my Income £400 – for which I paid £20 last year this year they rate me 800 for which I must pay 80£[57] – I appeald & stated two shedules – one of moneys rec[eive]d & 1 other of expenses belonging to my profession. <they> I also sent my Mem[oranda] Book & my Bankers Acc[ount] seald & desired the seals might not be broke open unless absolutely necessary – It seems they did not break open the

---

50 Dated by the previous letter, written on 8 December, where Mary (Clarke) Repton said that Repton was going to Lord Foley's.

51 Lady Cecilia Olivia Geraldine Fitzgerald (1786–1863), daughter of William, second duke of Leinster; married Thomas Foley 18 August 1806.

52 Charles Stanhope (1780–1851), styled Viscount Petersham, until on the death of his father in 1829 he became fourth earl of Harrington. (*ODNB*). In 1818 his sister Charlotte married Lady Foley's brother, Augustus Frederick, who was by then third duke of Leinster.

53 Perhaps Lady Foley's sister, Lady Isabella Charlotte (1784–1868).

54 William Windham (1750–1810), of Felbrigg, politician, formerly Repton's landlord at Sustead, and (formerly) a close friend. (*ODNB* and *Hist. Parl.*)

55 Probably referring to Windham's lawyer, Thomas Budd. (See Letter 39.)

56 William Windham's mother had been Sarah Lukin. (*ODNB* for Windham.)

57 Income Tax had been introduced by William Pitt the younger in the act of 1799, as a temporary measure, to fund the war against French forces under Napoleon. In 1803 Henry Addington's act was for a 'contribution of the profits arising from property, professions, trades and offices' (carefully avoiding the words 'income tax'). Income taxes were divided into five 'schedules': A (income from land and buildings), B (farming profits), C (public annuities), D (self-employment and other items not covered by A, B, C or E) and E (salaries, annuities and pensions). Although in opposition Pitt opposed Addington's innovations, he adopted them almost unchanged when he returned to office in 1805. Under Addington the rate was 5% but in 1806 Pitt returned it to the original rate of 10%. These changes are reflected in Repton's comments here. (Details from HMRC's website: https://web.archive.org/web/20100724033906/http://www.hmrc.gov.uk/history/taxhis1.htm, accessed 15/09/19.)

seals – but have returnd for answ'r that they see no reason to alter their charge – Now must I abide by this, or may I swear to my statement – or kick the Commissioners or bid them kiss my A... which that you may all do &c &c &c

[*fb*] this is the way Edward finished his sermon to day before this noble family – in the most splendid Chapel in all Europe – enrichd with Gold & Marble & Crimson Velvet – & painted Glass &c &c[58]

My Love to dear JA – & Dee &
the folks at Oxnead when you see em
Yours ever affectionately
HR

Monday morning

Edward says this Letter written after dinner is too jocular for a serious question to a Lawyer. therefore seriously – can I resist the surcharge & how is it to be done – or must I pay any thing Mr Bauvis[59] chuses to impose upon me

Endorsed: Dec'r 1806   Humphry Repton Esqr   Mr Windham   Income Tax   At Lord Foley's
HM 40844

7. John Thurston Mott[60] to Humphry Repton

Norwich, Monday Evening [January 1807]

Dear Sir

I am this Moment arrived here, with the intention of proceeding to Aylsham tomorrow Morning, if that day will suit you to go to Barningham; I should like very much to see you again at that place previous to your leaving Norfolk, as I have many things to say to you, and observations to make which cannot be done any where so well as upon the spot – Should more than [*fb*] one day be necessary for your attendance at Barningham I

---

58 In 1937 a disastrous fire ripped through Witley Court, 'destroying one of England's greatest country houses'. Edward had preached in the parish church of St Michael and All Angels, attached to Witley Court. Untouched by the fire, it survives as a 'delightful church with [an] amazing Italianate Baroque interior', (https://www.english-heritage.org.uk/visit/places/witley-court-and-gardens/things-to-do/).

59 Probably one of the income tax commissioners.

60 Erroneously catalogued as being from 'Thomas I. Mott'. For Repton's work at Mott's property Barningham Hall, see *Repton in Norfolk*, pp. 117–29.

can manage to stay with you till <Tuesday> *Wednesday* evening, when I must go to Holt – We can either sleep at Mr Guntons,[61] (who I am sure will be very glad to see us) tomorrow Evening, or return to Aylsham. Be so good as to return an answer by the Bearer of this Note. I shall direct this to Mr Adey also in case you should not be at home, and will thank him to [fb] have the goodness [to] forward it to you by a Man from Mrs Strains;[62] whom I will pay – With best Comp[limen]ts to all your Party I remain Sir

   Your obliged Humble Servant

   J T Mott

   [fb] I have got all the Plans, which I will bring with me.[63]

Address: To H. Repton Esqr Or John Adey Esqr, Aylsham
Endorsed: Jan'y 1807 Th. J Mott Esqr to Hy Repton Esq   app[rop]os to meet at Barningham
HM 40906

8. Dorothy Adey (instructions on her will)

Aylsham, 4th January 1807[64]

I give to my Sister Mary Repton of Harestreet all my Clothes and Linnen <and> *I mean* wearing apparel, desiring her to let William Repton have handkerch' stockings or any thing that may be useful to him, and the rest as she pleases to take herself or dispose of to my neices Mary & d: [Elizabeth], William to keep his dear Uncle's Hair Ring and my diamond one and give the others and all my little ornaments to his sisters except my Garnets which if my Neice Eliza lives to be seventeen years of Age I desire she may have and if she dies before that Age I give the Garnets to d: as Mary will have her mother's, five Guineas to my sister at Oxnead for a Ring, and five Guineas and the silver half pint Mug to my Nephew John Adey Repton. My Real and personal estate of <u>all kinds</u> or whatever else I may be possessed of I give to my dearest Nephew William Repton his Heirs and <Ass > *Assignees* Execetors[sic] and the more I die possess of for his sake the happier I shall be, D Adey

---

61 One branch of the Gunton family resided at Matlaske, near Barningham. (*Aylsham*, p. 243.)

62 In 1793, the proprietor of the King's Head, Alysham, was William Strain, so it appears that by this time his widow was running that establishment. (*Aylsham Directories*, p. 3.)

63 i.e. the plans for Barningham.

64 Address and date at the end in the original. Dorothy has definitely written 1807, so it has been placed here in the sequence.

if I have not been sufficiently explicit – I mean that the little I have to dispose of <may> may not go from my nephew William

Endorsed: 4 Jan'y 1809⁶⁵ Mrs Adey's Instr[ucti]ons for her Will
HM 40893

9. Humphry Repton to William Repton

[London], [12 March 1807]⁶⁶

Dear William

Under a Cover from Lord Erskine⁶⁷ I received this letter⁶⁸ and as I suppose you are my <u>solicitor</u> I beg you to do the needful but as I have no present intention of taking out my *dedimus*⁶⁹ it may be worth enquiring what expense will be incurred to me if any – because the Lord Chancellor said he should "whip in my name with a Cold seal" – if it must be heated afresh I may chance to burn my fingers – so make enquiry ab't it, & if I see Martin⁷⁰ I will ask him –

---

65 William has definitely written 1809.

66 Undated, but after the date of the letter from Lord Eskine on which Repton has written this letter, and before the date of the accompanying letter to William on a separate sheet, so it has been assigned to 12 March 1807.

67 Thomas Erskine, first baron Erskine, (1750–1823), lawyer and politician; Lord Chancellor in the Ministry of All Talents, 7 February 1806 – 1 April 1807. (*ODNB* and *Hist. Parl.*)

68 The letter follows immediately after this one.

69 *Dedimus potestatem* ('We have given power') A writ or commission issuing out of Chancery, empowering the persons named therein to perform certain acts, including to administer oaths of office to justices of the peace, etc. (https://thelawdictionary.org/dedimus-potestatem/) The following letter from the lord chancellor indicates that Repton was to become a justice of the peace in Norfolk, but he clearly wished to decline this. His property holding in Norfolk qualified him to be a justice: his father had purchased several properties in Aylsham, including 1 Market Place, where John and Dorothy Adey lived after their marriage, and also leased the estate at Oxnead Hall. In 1775 on the death of John Repton senior, the Aylsham property was split into equal thirds; in 1799 John Repton junior conveyed his third to his brother-in-law John Adey and his brother Humphry. (*Aylsham*, pp. 173–8.)

70 John Dayrell Martin, (1764–1814), gent., born in Barbados, only son of John Martin, late of Barbados, esquire, deceased. He was admitted to Lincoln's Inn on 29 May 1783 and articled to Stafford Baxter (q.v.) 7 June 1783. (*Lincoln's Inn Admission Register: 1420–1893*, vol. 1, p. 507.) He was later at Furnival's Inn, affiliated to Lincoln's Inn. In some letters referred to as 'Bro' Martin, suggesting Masonic connections. He was well-acquainted with Humphry Repton: he wrote two essays (nos. 21 and 27) that were

Tell Your Mother, if she be not departed – that I cannot go to Harestreet till I know she is there – & I have not business to keep me from home longer than the end of next week if so long – I am engaged to-morrow – & Sa[turda]y – & Monday & poor George & Duff count of[sic] spending Easter with us – Duff is a lucky fellow – Cl[aude] Scott[71] – for some little <u>official</u> service render'd him by Duff – has made over to him a perpetual admission to Drury lane Theatre, which to a Young man is a very acceptable Compliment.[72]

[fb] I have been obliged to exert some firmness in refusing to advance him money – which his brother George had been able to do – & thus the boys must help one another. I have been with dear John to the Ant[iquaria]n & Royal Society[73] to night & introduced him to many persons, which pleases him poor fellow – adieu – I will try to send this free tomorrow[74] – but if I have no more time, give my best love to all about you

H R

Address: H. Repton Esqr

Lord Chancellor, March 11th 1807
Mr Clerk of the Crown haveing received the Chancellors order to insert Mr Reptons name into the Commission of the Peace for the County of Norfolk, Mr R. will be pleased to direct his solicitor to apply to the Clerk of the Peace for that County requiring him to bring the Commission into the Crown office for the purpose of that insertion, and immediately after [fb] that is made Mr R's solicitor will be enabled to take out Mr R's *Dedimus* under which he will be entitled to act –

---

published in H. Repton, *Variety or a Collection of Essays written in the Year 1787* (London, 1788). See Carter et al., *Repton*, p. 172.

71 Claude Scott (1742–1830) M.P. and 'self-made entrepreneur in the corn trade'. (*Hist. Parl.*) The previous owner of his property at Sundridge Park, Bromley, had had a Red Book made for the site. Scott subsequently implemented all of Repton's recommendations. (*Repton in London*, pp. 90–4.)

72 This gift to Duff of perpetual admission to the theatre was renewed in 1808. (See Letter 52.)

73 In 1803 John Adey Repton was elected a fellow the Society of Antiquaries, and he wrote many items for the society's journal, *Archaeologia*. (*ODNB* entry within that for Humphry Repton) In 1780 the Society moved to new premises in Somerset House granted by George III, where it met until 1874, when it moved to Burlington House. (https://www.sal.org.uk/about-us/our-history/)

74 The letter does have a red stamp 'FREE', with 'From John Fuller' written underneath. (See note 81.)

[London, 13 March 1807][75]

Friday morning – quite well – John is gone to Tottenham[76] & goes home tomorrow. I do good by being in Town – have pick'd up some business – & some payments – so I rub on & am as happy as I can be away from you all.

I have been with Lord Harcourt[77] who sends his Comp[limen]ts to Mrs Repton – Adieu – let Mary write to [me] here from Camb[rid]ge – & if not flown *also* from Norfolk & say how dear J. A. goes on

Blessings on you all

I will not seal this till I have the Billmans bill[78] Lest I shou'd have any thing to add –

A report (only) of a battle on the 14th & that the French have left Warsaw _[79]

Duff goes with me to Chinerys[80] Sunday for Music & back next day –

Address: London March the thirteenth 1807, To Wm Repton Esq, Aylsham, Norfolk; Free John Fuller[81]
R st: FREE Mar 13 1807
Endorsed: 13th March 1807   Humy Repton Esqr   With the Lord Chancellor's Letter as to Commission of the Peace
HM 40845

---

75 Postscript to the above, on a separate sheet.

76 This visit may have been to Corridor House in Tottenham, the property of William Salte. (*Memoirs*, p. 121.) Repton's first visit there was in 1806. (Daniels, *Repton*, p. 262.) It is depicted in the *Polite Repository* (1808). (Carter et al., *Repton*, p. 144.) Or the visit may have been to the home of William Row. (See Letter 43.)

77 George Simon Harcourt, second earl Harcourt (d. 20 April 1809). The family home was at Nuneham Harcourt (Oxon.). Repton had worked at Nuneham before 1800 for Gen. the Hon. William Harcourt, who was George's younger brother (Daniels, *Repton*, p. 265; see also *ODNB* for William Harcourt, third earl Harcourt (1743–1830).)

78 Not clear, but 'Billmans bill' is most likely.

79 Referring to the French campaign in Poland and Russia, which resulted in the Treaty of Tilsit in July 1807.

80 Presumably Gillwell House, near Chingford (Essex) the home of W. Chinnery. (Daniels, *Repton*, p. 258; *Polite Repository* (1807).)

81 John Fuller (*c.*1756–1834) of Rose Hill, Sussex, one of the Sussex M.P.s 1801–1812. (*Hist. Parl.*) In 1806 Repton had provided Fuller with a Red Book. (See *Repton in Sussex*, pp. 96–105.)

10. Edward Repton to William Repton

Ardingly – East Grinstead, July – 11ᵗʰ – 1807[82]

Dear William

I am neither in want of a fresh Certificate nor of information about a Living, so that I cannot now be accused of the same selfinterested motives; which I am sorry were attributed to my former letter. But Mrs Adey, I believe, has never taken the trouble to acquaint herself with my Character and disposition – or if she has, I trust, she has drawn false conclusions – You, my dear William, I am sure, do not require fresh professions of my Affection, which, were we a little nearer, you would find to be as warm and sincere as the Love of those who see more of you – but distance does not lessen that strong attachment, which is, and I hope ever will be, the firm bond; and cement of our Family – I was [fb] led to hope that business would have brought you to London – and that, I might have shewn you my house – and my flowers – and my Hostess[83] – and my Ducks – and my whole establishment – and made you partake of all the little comforts which I enjoy here – but I believe it is the fate of Man never to be satisfied – I am now tired of Sussex Dirt, unpolished clowns, and squalling Brats – and want a situation, where there is more politeness, and less misery among the poorer sort – whose poverty I can't relieve. Mr Kent,[84] his Wife[85] and Daughter have been here, on a visit of a few days to Mrs Merry[86] – and it gave me the greatest pleasure to hear him talk of you – and your future prospects – I look upon Kent to *be* as solid and honest a Man, as is to be seen in a Century – and praise from him – is truly *"Laus a laudato Viro"*[87] – He talked of Uncle John and the compliments he received from [fb] the great

---

82 Daniels, *Repton*, p. 277, n. 168, dates this letter to 11 July 1809, but the original clearly says 1807.

83 Presumably Mrs Merry, who is mentioned later in the letter.

84 Nathaniel Kent (1737–1810), land agent and writer on agriculture; of Rippon Hall, Aylsham, 1770–1810; also of London, 1775–1810; his 'Office for Landed Property' was at Craigs Court, 1788–1810; advisor to William Pitt the younger on H. M. Forests 1788, to George III on model farms at Windsor and at Richmond (Surrey) 1790–1803. (*ODNB*; *Dictionary of land surveyors*, 2nd edn., vol. 2, p. 293, entry K88) See also P. Horn, 'An eighteenth century land agent: the career of Nathaniel Kent (1737–1810)', *Agricultural History Review*, 30:1 (1982), pp. 1–16.

85 In 1783 Nathaniel Kent married his second wife Armina, daughter of late Roger North esquire of Rougham, Norfolk.

86 An inhabitant of Ardingly known to the Repton family; see also Letter 150.

87 'Praise by a man who merits praise'.

Man of Norfolk[88] – and he mentioned a strange story of [?]Morey Hill's manuring his Land with the refuse of the London Hospitals[89] – which, for the credit of human nature, as well as of Norfolk farming – I hope is not true. I go tomorrow Evening to Brighton and shall return <of> on Monday – and in the middle of the week – I shall coach it to London as I am to take Mr Howlett's duty at the Foundling,[90] at his request on Sunday the 19th and probably before I return, I shall see them at Harestreet – Mary[91] had partly engaged to come to me, and I hope I shall be able to bring her back with me. She is a charming, good Girl, and every one who knows her must admire and love her – She won the hearts of all my few Neighbours last Year, and they are as earnest to see her here again – as I am – and I fear I shall have some difficulty in keeping her to myself, when they find she is with me – When you [*fb*] have leisure I shall be glad to hear from you, and learn the state of Mr Adey's health, to whom I beg you will give my kind Love – assure Mrs Adey also of my sincere affection – with whom – I fear, I am no favorite – but I trust if she knew me better, she would not find cause to Love me less.

Love to all at Oxnead – and believe me with great truth – my dear William

Your affectionate Brother Edward

If my friend [?]Surgison's[92] Petition succeeds you shall have my Rent free –

Address: William Repton Esq, Aylsham, Norfolk
R st: D [illeg] 1807; *b st*: EAST GRINSTEAD 29; *charge*: 9
Endorsed: 7th [*sic*] July 1807   The Revd Edward Repton
HM 40909

---

88 Perhaps referring to Thomas William Coke, first earl of Leicester of Holkham (1754–1842), politician and agriculturalist. (*ODNB*)

89 [?]Morey Hill cannot be identified. This method of manuring is not mentioned in either Kent's *General view of the agriculture of ... Norfolk, with observations on the means of improvement* (London, 1796) or his *Hints to gentlemen of landed property. To which are now first added, supplementary hints* (London, 1793 edition).

90 Presumably 'Mr Howlett' was the chaplain of the Foundling Hospital, London; cannot be identified through the CCEd.

91 Referring to his future wife, Mary Herbert.

92 Perhaps a friend from Oxford or a fellow clergyman; he cannot be identified in either *Alumni Oxon* or CCEd.

11. Humphry Repton to John Adey Repton

Harestreet near Romford, July 26 1807

Dear John

I wrote to you from Town yesterday – we must consider the staircase rail when we meet – that at the Speakers is very handsome of Cast Iron bronzed,[93] with a brass flat rail – it looks old. [*sketches of a staircase rail in cross-section and of staircase rail side on*] Let Stannard[94] do the windows with deal Mullions as Mr Mott particularly objected to the Casements in stone From Mr Harbord's[95] objection. Write & say when you think of returning but don't hurry yourself – if you wish to stop at Ely or Cambrg

HR   turn over

I have enclosed Mr Mott's letter – consider it & perhaps with Stannard you may do the thing he wishes – & answer it to Cromer – but the Contract shou'd be delivered to his Att[orne]y as soon as possible – & dont make any alterations that are not absolutely necessary or we shall never have done with it.

July 27

Hannah[96] coud not get a place last night so I have opened this & taken out Mr Motts letter in which he wishes to alter the position of the scullery & Housekeepers Room – which Stannard will explain.[97] Hannah has a parcel of Letters to bring on Wednesday night.

---

93 Probably in the speaker's house at Westminster. Charles Abbott, (1757–1829), speaker of the House of Commons (1802–1817) was a longstanding client of Repton's. (*ODNB*; *Hist. Parl.*) Regarding Repton's work at Westminster, see note to Letter 58.

94 Joseph Stannard (b. 12 March 1771; d. 7 December 1855) and Joseph Stannard junior (b. 5 May 1795; d. 29 June 1850) were local contractors and architects who had been brought in to oversee the work at Barningham Hall, the property of John Thurston Mott. (*Repton in Norfolk*, p. 121.) Joseph junior later produced surveys for glebe exchange, navigations, roads; he was Surveyor to Norfolk and Norwich Hospital; architect, builder, admitted freeman of Norwich 22 March 1817 as carpenter 1817; Norwich City Architect 1840. (*Dictionary of land surveyors*, vol. 2, p. 483, entry S450.)

95 The Harbord family lived at Gunton Hall, near Sustead. At this time the owner was Harbord Harbord, Baron Suffield (1734–1810). Direct evidence for Repton's involvement with the house and grounds comes from surviving drawings by Humphry and John dated 1816. (*Repton in Norfolk*, pp. 155–6.) 'Mr Harbord' might be either of Baron Suffield's surviving sons: Hon. William Assheton Harbord (1766–1821) or Hon. Edward Harbord (1781–1835). (*Hist. Parl.* for all three men.)

96 Not identified; perhaps a servant in the Hare Street house.

97 Sometime in 1807 John Adey Repton drew up a series of 'working plans' for the work at Barningham. These precise, architectural drawings, both plans and elevations, were

Address 1: J. Adey Repton Eq, Aylsham
Address 2: J. A. Repton Eq, Aylsham, (J Adeys Esq), Norfolk
B st: RUMFORD 12; Cross Post; *charge*: 8
Endorsed: 26 July 1807   Hy Repton Esq
HM 40839

1. Sketches of a stair rail by Humphry Repton, HM 40839

signed by Humphry and John and by Joseph Stannard senior and junior, and countersigned by John Mott. They have been reproduced in *Repton in Norfolk*, p. 123 and Appendix 2, pp. 195–7. Drawing 4 on p. 197 is 'Finishings for the Staircase and Billiards Room'; the staircase rail is not shown.

12. George Repton to William Repton

29 Dover Street, Piccadilly,[98] July 31ˢᵗ 1807

My dear William

I have ordered your seal of Halfhides,[99] it is to be like mine in form, and size, the letters engraved in the same manner, but the setting is to be different, and which he says will make the price one Guinea more than I paid for mine – It is to be like Duff's, which I believe at present is the most fashionable, and will have a greater quantity of gold and workmanship in it than mine – I send you the sort of thing it will be, which if you do not like, and will let me know, it will still be time for me to alter the setting of it – [*three sketches: a seal side on, in ink; seal face, in ink; seal side on, in pencil*]

2. Sketchs of three seals by George Repton, HM 40917

Thank Aunt Adey for her kind wish to see me at Aylsham and answer her that nothing would give me more pleasure [*fb*] than to pass a week or two in Norfolk which I am sorry I cannot, or indeed, do I at present see

---

98 In 1797–8, at the age of 46, John Nash built himself a handsome stuccoed house at 29 Dover Street, north of Piccadilly. (*ODNB*, Nash, John (1752–1835).) For many years in George worked in Nash's office in that house.

99 George Halfhide of Halfhide, Barnes & Co, leading seal engravers at 7 Coventry Street from 1800. (https://londonstreetviews.wordpress.com/2014/02/10/george-halfhide-seal-engraver/, accessed 15/09/19.)

any prospect of having it in my power – I heard from Dear Mary[100] and Edward yesterday they seem very happy at Ardingly and noticed by every body in their neighbourhood, your friend Mrs Merry told Mary she hoped to see more of her than when she was last at Ardingly

As to Public news there seems but little, and what little there is, very bad, every body are talking of the encreasing dangers of the Country, and every day doing less to counteract it[101] – our Public men as you will have observed are each accusing the other of having too great a share of <u>the good things</u> – the possession of which appear to be the principal object of both parties –[102]

Give my best love to Uncle & Aunt Adey and to all at Oxnead and believe me ever My dear William

Your very affectionate Brother George

I saw Duff last night, he tells me that he was written to Aunt Adey

Address: William Repton Esqre, Aylsham, Norfolk
B st: B JY 31 807; [*second b st illeg*]
Endorsed: 31ˢᵗ July 1807   Geo: S: Repton Esqr
HM 40917

13. Henry Smith[103] to William Repton

Ashby de la Zouch, 1ˢᵗ August 1807

Sir

Having Occasion to procure an Assignment of a Term[104] that was vested in the late Revd John Botham of Clifton[105] in Trust to attend the

---

100 Referring to Mary Herbert; but see Letters 49 to 51 where family members were not so accepting of Mary when Edward planned to marry her.

101 For example, *The Morning Chronicle* that day had little to report on the progress of the war: troops had embarked for an expedition but 'Nothing farther respecting the destination of the expeditions is yet publicly known'. Alexander, emperor of Russia, his brother Grand Duke Constantine and the Russian General Bennigsen had all become members of Napoleon's Legion of Honour. (*The Morning Chronicle*, Friday, July 31, 1807, Issue 11920, p. 2.) This followed the Treaty of Tilsit, which represented the zenith of Napoleon's power.

102 The Portland Ministry had been confirmed in power on 26 June, following the General Election of 1807. With the failure of an Opposition motion on the state of the nation, politics became largely quiescent. (A. D. Harvey, *Britain in the early nineteenth century* (London, 1978), pp. 204–5.)

103 A lawyer practising in Ashby de la Zouch, not otherwise identified.

104 i.e. term of a lease.

105 The Revd John Botham (1685–1739), rector of Clifton Campville (Staffs), was Harry Botham's grandfather. (CCEd Person ID: 40399) (See Letter 15.) HL, HM 40959, dated

Inheritance of an Estate lying in this Neighbourhood I shall esteem it as a Favour if you will have the Goodness to inform me who the Representative of the late Mr Botham is, And also of such further Particulars as may be necessary to enable me to prepare the Assig*n*ment – I shall with great Pleasure pay you for any Trouble you may have in this Business.

I am Sir, your very obedient & humble Servant
Henry Smith

Endorsed: 1ˢᵗ Augt 1807   Mr Hy Smith of Ashby de la Zouch   As to Assignm[en]t of a Term vested in Mr Botham
HM 40953/2

14. John Dayrell Martin to William Repton[106]

It seems to me that it wo'd be a breach of Trust in Messrs Adey & Martin to join in this conveyance. I repeatedly told Mr Daniel[107] he must send the Draft down to Mr Adey for his approbation before it was ingrossed.
S. S. Baxter[108]

Furnival's Inn
7ᵗʰ August 1807

My dear Sir

I was quite astonished at the receipt of your letter as I had not only never seen the Draft in question but had never heard a syllable of the business till I read your letter. I immediately shewd it Mr Baxter & I send you above a copy of his observation upon it. Mr Daniel it seems had laid the draft before him to peruse on behalf of Mr [George] Wyndham[109] & on Mr <u>Wyndhams</u> behalf <u>alone</u> he approved of the Draft. I am obliged by your precaution &

---

3 June 1746, is a deed relating to the settlement of 'Brook House', catalogued as 'by John Botham'. (See Appendix 2.) This John Botham was the son of the rector of Clifton. (See note to Letter 15.)

106 For Martin, see note to Letter 9. This letter relates to a legal issue that had arisen during an illness of John Adey. The first short section is a copy of a note from Stafford Baxter, followed by Martin's letter to William.

107 A partner in legal practice with Astley Thomas Maberley (q.v.).

108 Stafford Baxter (c.1748–1812) had been articled to Stafford Squire in 1765. 'Squire Stafford Baxter, Rob. Baxter & F. Murcott' had a legal practice at Furnival's Inn, Holborn. (*Universal Directory* (1790), p. 371.)

109 George Wyndham (1766–1810) lived at Cromer Hall. (Hindry Mason, *History of Norfolk*, p. 154.)

certainly shall act accordingly. It is [*fb*] something more than strange that Mr Daniel, who, in taking Mr Baxter the Draft, must have passed me in the office, sho'd not have thought it decent to mention the transaction to me as a party & a responsible party to the Deed. In truth I do not know how it happens that I am a Trustee; In your hands however & my good Mr Adey's I feel safe but wo'd wish that every care may be taken of us both as uninterested parties. Best regards to Mr & Mrs Adey

I am yours most sincerely

J. D. Martin[110]

Address: Wm Repton Esq, Aylsham, Norfolk

B st: A AU 7 807

Endorsed: 7ᵗʰ Augt 1807   Mr Martin   As to execution of a Deed respecting Estate in Berks: in which he & Mr Adey were Trustees for George Wyndham.

Marberly & Daniell[111] were concerned in town & Sewell & Blake[112] in the Country.

Mr Blake called on Mr Adey to execute this Deed at a time when he was scarcely capable of business. Mrs Adey wo'd not allow of his being troubled on the Subject & I was from home. On seeing the Deed it appeared to me to be improper for the Trustees to sign it & this L[ett]re is the result of my application to Martin on the subject.

HM 40953/3

---

110 There is a letter from Humphry Repton to 'J. D. Martin esquire, At Baxters, Furnival Inn, Holborn', dated 18 May 1812 at the NHC. (Colman Collection, Repton 'scrapbook'.)
111 Astley Thomas Maberley had a legal practice at 80 Hatton Garden, Holborn. (*Universal Directory* (1790), p. 383.)
112 Sewell & Blake were solicitors in Norwich. See, for example, NRO, MC 253/3-5, 678X7, letter from Sewell & Blake, Norwich, to Robert Cory, junior, solicitor, Great Yarmouth, 1815 (Papers relating to Lord Home's Estates in Norfolk).

15. Henry Botham[113] to Adey & Repton

Lamer Park,[114] August 18th 1807

Dear Sirs

I have delayed answering your Letter that I might write free of Postage[115] – My Father The Revd John Botham in his Will appointed Mrs Montagu his Executrix[116] – this Lady declining the Trust, my brother John Botham and myself acted as his administrators[117] – I am now the only remaining Representative of my Father[118] – and wish to sign the Deed in question whenever you forward it to me. If the Deed does not weigh above Privilege, you will please to send it under Cover to Lord Carleton, George Street – Hanover Square[119] – if it is too heavy I beg you will forward it Per Wheathamstead Coach, from the Golden Lion – St John Street.[120]

I am your very Obedient servant

Henry Botham

Messrs. Adey & Repton

Endorsed: 18 Aug't 1807   Henry Botham Esqr.   As to the late Mr B's Representatives
HM 40953/4

---

113 From later letters it is clear that Henry, or Harry, Botham was a friend of the Repton/Adey family, which presumably was why he had asked Henry Smith to contact Adey & Repton about his father's will. He subsequently purchased Hazelwood House in Abbots Langley (Herts), where Dorothy planned to visit him in 1814. (See Letter 176.)

114 In 1792 Humphry Repton had produced a Red Book for Lamer Park, near Wheathampstead (Herts), the home of Charles Drake Garrard. (Carter et al., *Repton*, p. 154; *Repton in Herts*, pp. 90–102.)

115 Charles Garrard was M.P. for Amersham (Bucks) from 1796 to Jan. 1805; his nephew William Drake took over this 'pocket borough' in 1805. (*Hist. Parl.*) There is no stamp or address on this letter at all, probably having been posted in an envelope, so the free frank has not survived.

116 John Botham (c.1710–1773), rector of Albury (Surrey) and vicar of Ealing (Middx). (CCEd Person ID: 40402.) In his will, dated 6 September 1765, he appointed as his executors John Knapton, esq., of Richmond (Surrey) and Elizabeth, wife of the Honourable Edward Montagu of Sandleford (Berks). (TNA, PROB11/992/390.)

117 By the time the will was granted probate on 26 November 1773, Knapton had died and Mrs Montagu had declined to act. In fact, only his son John Botham had been appointed administrator by the court.

118 i.e. his brother John had also died.

119 This was the London home of Hugh Carleton, viscount Carleton (1739–1826); he died there on 25 February 1826. (*ODNB*)

120 St John Street, London EC1, was the location of a number of coaching inns. (*London Encyclopaedia*, p. 723.)

16. Henry Smith to Adey & Repton

Ashby de la Zouch, 20 August 1807

Gent[lemen]

I received your Favor of the 5ᵗʰ inst[ant] for which please to accept my best thanks. I take the Liberty of troubling you with this to request that you will be so good as to furnish me with the necessary Information with as little delay as possible.

I am, Gent[lemen], Your very obedient Servant

Henry Smith

Endorsed: 20ᵗʰ Augt 1807   Mr Hy Smith for Information respect[in]g Mr Botham's Repres[entatives]
HM 40953/5

17. Humphry Repton to William Repton

[Witley Court, 30 August 1807]

Dear William

Having a power of franking – I write to say that I am now at Ld Foley's Whitley Court which I leave to-morrow & go p[er] Co[ach] from Worcester to Oxford on Monday – & on Tuesday to Bulstrode the D. of Portland[121] from thence to Mr Dupre's Wilton P[ar]k – Beaconsfield[122] – near – i.e. 2 miles from Bulstrode – but I fear I shall have no power of seeing you – the other day I dined at Adairs of Flixton[123] in Pall Mall when he told me Harry Negus was just dead[124] – so I bolted a letter at him that night to ask

---

121 Bulstrode (Bucks), estate of William Henry Cavendish-Bentinck (1738–1809), third duke of Portland. Repton first visited in 1790, as recorded in his account book. (Daniels, *Repton*, p. 256; Carter et al., *Repton*, p. 148.) Work for the third duke continued until 1803. (*Repton in Bucks*, pp. 84–91.)

122 James Du Pre of Wilton Park (Bucks). Daniels says that Repton visited before 1796, but Rutherford says that his work there was probably *c.*1803–5, and this return visit in 1807. (Daniels, *Repton*, p. 25; *Repton in Bucks*, pp. 151–5.) In his *Enquiry into the Changes of Taste* (p. 342), Repton referred to levelling the ground both at Wilton Park and Bulstrode.

123 Robert Shafto Adair of Flixton Hall, Flixton near Bungay (Suffolk); raised to baronet 30 June 1838. (*London Gazette*.)

124 Henry Negus owned the Hoveton estate in Hoveton St Peter and Neatishead. He was buried at Hoveton, aged 73, on 8 August 1807. His daughter Christobelle, widow of James Burroughes of Burlingham Hall, inherited Hoveton Hall on her father's death. (*Repton in Norfolk*, p. 139.)

him for his Courts, for You – but in a very polite letter [*fb*] he answerd me that Negus had been so long infirm he had long promised his Courts to a person in that immediate neighbourhood or from the general Character he had heard of Mr Wm Repton – he shou'd have required no other recommendation – & so it ended –

Pray have you heard from Windham – Am I at liberty to call on him to say all I feel inclined to do – on his Conduct to you & to myself in not answering my Leter – I do not like to make an Enemy but I have no partiality for a friend who is only half a one

[*fb*] Give my best Love to Dear John Adey & Dee. I suppose Duff will soon be of your party indeed he may now be at Aylsham – for he is one of the silent Dumb part of the family, yet he can talk & write to the purpose when urged to it. Ask him if he woud like to go with me to the Isle of Wight[125] these holidays & bear his share of extra <expp> expence – when I travel alone I go a Cheap way to work – Coach it – & shuffle on – &c &c

I sometimes wish you cou'd be of my party

God bless you, Yours ever HR

I will add a post script[126]

Address: Worcester August thirty 1807, William Repton Esq, Aylsham, Norfolk, Henry Fitzgerald[127]
R st: FREE Aug 31 1807
Endorsed: 30 Aug't 1807   Hump'y Repton Esq
HM 40846

18. Pipe & Blair[128] to John Adey; William's draft reply

Uttoxeter, 16 September 1807

Sir

You will no doubt recollect that abt the year 1798 you sold a Farm in

---

125 Drawings in the *Polite Repository* indicate six possible Repton commissions on the Isle, of which three were printed after 1807: 'Mr Mackenzie's Garden', Cowes (1810); Osborne, owned by B. P. Blachford (1810); Swainston, owned by Sir J. Barrington (1811). (Daniels, *Repton*, p. 261.)

126 Not added.

127 On this occasion Repton had obtained free postage via Lord Henry Fitzgerald (1761–1829), of Boyle Farm (Kent) and Thames Ditton (Surrey), M.P. for Co. Kildare. He was the uncle of Lady Foley. (*Hist. Parl.*; http://www.angelfire.com/realm/gotha/gotha/leinster.html.)

128 Lawyers in Uttoxeter.

Marchington Woodlands[129] in the Poss[essi]on of Sam. Collis to Messrs. Johnson of the Parish of Alvreton.[130]

A Descend[and]t of Edw[ar]d Holbrook (from whom the Estate was purchased in 17<u>46</u>) has recently claimed it, we cannot (for a moment) suppose that the Claim[an]t can have a shadow of a chance to recover the property, but it is <u>just possible</u> that the Claim may be made under some Limit[a]t[io]ns in an *hitherto suppressed* settlem[en]t which have very <u>lately</u> taken effect, & may not have been properly barred, we deemed it prudent to take the liberty of request[in]g you will give no information as to the Title <u>to any person whatever</u>; even tho <if case if> *the enquiry sho'd be made as if* on our behalf, as you will no doubt be well aware [fb] that as our Clients have the Deeds in poss[essi]on, they have every inform[atio]n respect of the Title you can give – Sho'd any enquiries be made of you, there can be no harm, & we shall be obliged to you to learn from the Claim[an]t how he makes out his Title, as sho'd he be mad<e> enough to risque an Eject[ion] we shall with the greater ease prepare a Defence –

We shall also be obliged to you to inform us whether Mr Edward Carr (the Conveyee in the Fine of Hillary Term 1782) is living as we have some tho[ugh]ts of taking a Convey[an]ce or Decl[arati]on of the Uses of the Fine executed by him

We are Sir, With much respect, Your much obliged servants

Pipe & Blair

Address: John Adey Esq., Aylsham, Norfolk
B st: UTTOXETER; *r st*: G PAID SEP 18 1807; *charge*: Paid

Gent[lemen]

My Uncle Mr Adey had directed me to say <in answer to> *that he is obliged to you for* your L[ett]re of the 16th <that he has> *which has of course* occasioned him <some> *much* surprise not unattended with regret, <that at this distance of> & that sho'd an opportunity occur of obtaining inform[atio]n <from the> upon the subject we will certainly avail ourselves of it

About a month ago *we received a L[ett]re from* Mr Henry Smith of Ashby de la Zouch stating that he found the late Revd Mr Botham

---

129 In March 1762 John Adey had mortgaged this property; it appears to have been sold in June 1770. (*Aylsham*, p. 179, n. 21, referring to NRO, AYL 1019, which are deeds of Adey property and Repton property in Hanbury, Lichfield, Aylsham, Stoke-by-Clare etc.) Marchington Woodlands was in Hanbury (Staffs); the premises were called Brookhouse, or Holbrooke House.
130 Probably Alfreton (Derbys).

was trustee of a Term of years to attend the Inherit[an]ce of an Est[at]e in his neighbourhood, & desiring to be informed who were his personal Representatives that an assignment might be taken to a new Trustee for a Purchaser.[131] This <I hope has> *may probably have* no reference to the Marchington Estate – but as it is an enquiry from your neighbourhood your Letter has naturally brought the circumstances to my recollection – & it is possible that the information *may be* <have> required *by Mr Smith* with a different view from that which <Mr Smith> *he* professes

Mr Edw'd Carr is still living & will I have no doubt join in any Conveyance which may be proper – & Mr Adey will of course be <glad to> ready to do any <thing> *Act* in his power <to secure the Title> *for the further assurance* of his Purchaser's *Title* <at their expence>.

I am, Gent[lemen], your most obedient humble servant

Endorsed: 16 Sept 1807   Messrs Pipe & Blair   As to Mr Adey's Title to Marchington Woodlands Estate.
HM 40953/6

19. Mary (Clarke) Repton to Dorothy Adey

[Hare Street], Wednesday [16 September 1807]

My dear Dee

John is this moment come from Town and has broght a newspaper containing the good news that Denmark has surrenderd[132] and we have possession of Copenhagen, all their <stree> Stores and Shipping with the loss of only one hundred men – if I am not the first to communicate this good news to you at Aylsham, I am sorry to have put you to the expence of postage, but was willing to try. God bless you all. I hope I am not too late for the post.

Your affectionate M Repton

Thank the dear Boys for a brace of Birds which I had to day – Kiss them and Mr Adey for me, love to Oxnead and kiss Eliza for me.

Address: Mrs Adey, Aylsham, Norfolk
B st: RUMFORD 12; Cross Post; *charge*: 8
Endorsed: Sept'r 1807   Mrs Repton   Taking of Copenhagen
HM 40933/2

---

131 See Letters 13 and 16.

132 Second battle of Copenhagen, 16 August to 5 September 1807; capitulation of Denmark signed 7 September. This was only reported in *The Times*, 2nd edition, 16 September.

20. Humphry Repton to William Repton

Hereford, [25 September 1807][133]

Dear <George> William

I have alterd my intention – was going to write to George but thought I had better stop till I meet his letter at Uley[134] to morrow. Then I thought of writing to Duff – but he never writes to any body, so I will tell you all where I am – & what I have been doing –

Sir John Cotterel, M.P. for the County[135] has kindly brought me to this place for the triennial Meeting of the 3 Choirs & gay doings we have had – Cathedral at ½ past 10 till 3, dinner at Town hall – D. of Norfolk.[136] Bishops & Barts & Foleys & M.P. & Dr *sine fine* – hurry to Dress for Music at night – from 7 till 11 – then I go to Bed – & the rest go to dancing – Ladies cover'd with Diamonds & Gents with Wax candle droppings [*fb*] But we have Linley[137] & Cramer[138] & Bartleman[139] & Sale[140] & Goss[141] & Vaughan[142] – & Miss Park[143] & Miss Tenant[144] that was – & the Band 100 Instruments & 100 Voices so I have had Music in plenty –

---

133 HL catalogue says 1809?, but this letter refers to the Three Choirs Festival for which Repton says he has sent Duff the 'bill of fare' (programme): that document can be dated to September 1807. The initial posting date on the programme is 'September Twenty Five'; this letter was probably written on the same day. The printed programme, sent by Duff to William on 28 September 1807, has been catalogued separately. (Letter 21.)

134 According to the Gloucestershire Gardens Trust, this is the only mention of Repton going to Uley. The likely property in question was known as Stour's Hill.

135 John Geers Cotterell (1757–1845), of Garnons (Herefordshire). (*Hist. Parl.*) Repton produced a Red Book for Garnons in 1791. (Daniels, *Repton*, p. 260.) For details of the work there, see *Repton in the West Midlands*, pp. 30–8.

136 Charles Howard, eleventh Duke of Norfolk (1746–1815).

137 Perhaps either Ozias Thurstan Linley (bapt. 1765, d.1831), composer and Church of England clergyman; or William Linley, (1771–1835), composer and author. (*ODNB* entry for their father Thomas Linley.)

138 Johann Baptist Cramer [John Baptist] (1771–1858), pianist and composer. (*ODNB*)

139 James Bartleman (1769–1821), singer. (*ODNB*)

140 Perhaps John Sale (1758–1827), singer and conductor. (*ODNB*)

141 John Jeremiah Goss (1770–1817), for many years principal alto at the Three Choirs.

142 Thomas Vaughan (1782–1843), singer, who 'sang at the Three Choirs festivals from 1805 to 1836'. (*ODNB*)

143 Maria Frances Parke (1772–1822) was principal soprano at the Three Choirs Festival in 1807. (*ODNB* entry for her father, John Parke (1745–1829).)

144 In 1806 Thomas Vaughan (1782–1843) married Miss Elizabeth Tennant, a soprano singer well known from 1797 in oratorio performances. After 9 or 10 years of married life they separated, and Mrs Vaughan was heard, as Mrs Tennant, at Drury Lane Theatre. (*ODNB* entry for Vaughan.)

but I send Duff the bill of fare. tell him the best thing was a dinner the first day with room <with> for 200 – & only 80 – given by the Conductor to the Performers – Catches Glees Songs &c &c till a late hour So we mix pleasure with business – & I only want Youth – or some of my Young Folks to enjoy it –

My Love to all at Aylsham – God bless them – Chaise waits & I leave this for a Cover

HM 40860

21. Humphry Repton junior to William Repton (printed item)

FIRST MORNING

OVERTURE – ESTHER

HANDEL'S DETTINGEN TE DEUM

"Holy, holy." – Miss PARKE.

After the Third Collect. – DUET, "Here shall soft Charity repair." – *Dr. Boyce*

Before the Sermon. – "My heart is inditing."

After the Sermon. – "CORNONATION ANTHEM."

FIRST EVENING

ACIS AND GALATEA

BETWEEN THE ACTS,

OVERTURE AND MARCH, "ZAUBERFLOTE." – Mozart

E. G. WRIGHT, PRINTER

Address 1: Hereford September Twenty Five Date of Year omitted.[*sic*]
J G Cotterell[145]
B st: HEREFORD 148
Address 2: William Repton Esqr., Aylsham, Norfolk[146]
R st: G SEP 28 1807; *charge*: [*illeg*]
Endorsed: 25 Sept'r 1807   Humy Repton Esq[147]
HM 40953/7

---

145 The programme was sent to Humphry junior using John Cotterell's franking privilege.
146 Initially this item had been sent by Repton to Humphry junior, who sent it on to William on 28 September; address 2 was written by Humphry junior.
147 William's endorsement refers to the date that his father sent the programme to Humphry junior.

FIRST MORNING.

OVERTURE—ESTHER.

HANDEL's DETTINGEN TE DEUM.

" Holy, holy."—Miss PARKE.

After the Third Collect.—DUET, " Here shall soft Charity repair."—*Dr. Boyce.*

Before the Sermon.—" My heart is inditing."

After the Sermon.—" CORONATION ANTHEM."

FIRST EVENING.

ACIS AND GALATEA.

BETWEEN THE ACTS,

OVERTURE AND MARCH, " ZAUBERFLOTE."—Mozart.

E. O. WRIGHT, PRINTER.

3. Printed programme for the first day of the Three Choirs Festival, 1807,
HM 40953/7

22. Humphry Repton junior to William Repton

Adelphi, 31ˢᵗ October 1807

My dear William

As I am obliged to send this letter to be franked immediately I have only time to return to you with many thanks £16 – which I shall be happy to hear you have received. Mr Davis was so cool not to say impertinent about your hat that I sent you one from Cunningham's which he assured me should be a good one. I hope it arrived safe & that you will like it – Mr Bannister says that he has not Mr Adey's measure, having made his breeches by another pair which were sent him for a pattern.[148] Mrs Adey's commission has been executed –

Mr Windham's friend Sir James Cockburn begins to smell powder & has been to Felbrigg to prepare for his examination by this Board next week – we have some facts against him which may possibly [fb] delay if not prevent his departure to his Government of Curacoa[sic][149] – but of this no more hereafter.

I must now conclude with my very best wishes to all around you,
Ever truly yours, H Repton

Address: William Repton Esqr, Aylsham
Endorsed: 31ˢᵗ Oct'r 1807   Hy Repton Jun'r Esq
HM 40924

23. Humphry Repton to William Repton

Harestreet near Romford, Christmas Eve 1807

Nothing Private
so you may read it out to our <u>own</u> family[150]

---

148 In 1790 John Cunningham was a hosier and hatter at 163 Piccadilly. (*Universal Directory*, p. 118). Davis and Bannister cannot be identified in this source.

149 The Dutch had owned Curacao but it was captured by the British in late 1806; a temporary governor had been appointed, who was subsequently replaced by 'a connection of the right hon. gent. Mr. Windham' (Sir James Cockburn). There was a debate in Parliament on the subject on 22 April 1807. (See https://api.parliament.uk/historic-hansard/commons/1807/apr/22/governor-of-curacoa, accessed 16/09/19.) Sir James Cockburn, ninth baronet (1771–1852), served as governor of Curacao until 1809, becoming governor of Bermuda 1811–12, 1814–16 and 1817–19. Duff's comments suggest that in October 1807 Cockburn was being investigated by the Audit Office.

150 A private letter for the family to hear and enjoy: it was derogatory towards William Windham.

Dear William

A merry Christmas to you all at Aylsham & Oxnead. I have so long felt myself in debt for your Long Letter that I am resolved not to let the *year* expire without <u>answering</u> it – or rather as there is nothing to answer – without <u>acknowledging</u> it –

It has been a rule with me this Life, my dear boy – Never to make an enemy – & particularly of a friend – tho' he may have behaved ill – W. W. [William Windham] has behaved ill – but I can feel for him – his necessities & not his will consented – he is hard run – he sees poverty & neglect are likely to be the fruit of all his ambition – & depend upon it – the <u>Talents</u>[151] as they are call'd are all like him men too clever to be useful – A Razor is neither so good as an ivory knife to cut paper – nor so good as a saw or an Axe to cut wood – in short it is only fit to shave with – & John Bull does not like to be shaved too close or too often – I have known W.W. from the earliest days when I cou'd discriminate Characters – & was always afraid of speaking my sentiments concerning him – because I never thought him, what the world supposed, a Man of <*illeg*> Parts – his Pride – his Vanity – & his dread of committing his supposed superiority – added to his Natural indecision [*fb*] totally incapacitated him from every useful or energetic effort – & the only thing I ever valued in him was his firmness & integrity – in these I have found myself mistaken of if he really possesses them – they are as useless to himself or others as his imagined Talents – they are the result of sophistry – not of upright principle – Speaking of his tergiversation with Lord. ––. lately – he said that W. "Never acted against his conviction of what was <u>right</u> but he had a power of reasoning himself into that conviction by the subtilty of his Logic" thus like the Devil in Milton – "he can make the worse appear the better reason".[152]

The same Noble Lord many years ago – in speaking of the difference between Pitt & W. – observed – that both cou'd in a manner intuitively see, every possible argument that cou'd be produced either for, or against any measure – but with this difference – that Pitt took them by weight – & W. by tale –[153]

<But> Now all this is only to introduce a Jeu d'Esprit which I cou'd not help writing, after the account James Marsh[154] sent me of W's – publickly

---

151 A reference to the ministry of 'All the Talents', a coalition formed by William Grenville, first baron Grenville, when he was appointed prime minister on 11 February 1806, following the death of Pitt the younger. (*Hist. Parl.*)

152 John Milton, *Paradise Lost*, Book II, lines 113–14.

153 Determined 'by counting individual objects or articles; by number; as distinguished from by weight, by measure'. (*OED*)

154 James Marsh was the son of Mary (Clarke) Repton's cousin, or cousin-in-law,

speaking in behalf of the Pugillist Mr Gully[155] at Norwich – which you may read but not print –

[fb] Copy of an Original Letter.
to a Right Hon[oura]ble Amateur of Boxing

Rt Hon Sir. I am embolden'd to put fist to paper by the hearty manner in which you stood up for me at N. We have both had sharp bouts & fought many good rounds

Nobody Nose better nor you, how to come round folks and you have kumd round yourself pratty often – & thoaf[sic] you were kick'd off the Stage last bout You may kum a bout again – & if so be you [damaged: ?do] I will be your second – for I cares as little as yourself – which side I takes – so I <illeg> snak *in* the Stakes. But as it may be sum time before we are calld out in Your way – you may be keeping your hand in in my way & I will take you for my bottle holder in my next set too – for I nose your bottom and I hope you nose mine – so no more from Yours till death gives the knock down blow to Bully Gully –

Address: William Repton Esq., Aylsham
Endorsed: 24 Dec' 1807   Hy Repton Esq.   Windham's Character
HM 40847

24. Humphry Repton to William Repton

Harestreet near Romford, January 10 1808

Dear William

When I heard that Mr Windham had sent for Nash – I coud not but feel that my Conduct concerning Felbrigg might have been misunderstood[156] –

Elizabeth Marsh, wife of Isaac Laughton Marsh of Norwich. James is described as the Repton children's 'cousin' in a conveyance dated 1814 (NRO, AYL 835, Copy conveyance Marsh and Repton to Shalders) He was an attorney, with premises in Bank Place, Norwich. (*Norwich Directory for 1811*, p. 109.)

155 John Gully (1783–1863), prize-fighter, racehorse owner, and politician. (*ODNB*). On '28 November 1807, John Gulley and Tom Cribb, the famous pugilists, gave an exhibition of sparring in the great room at the King's Head Inn, Norwich. Upwards of 200 persons were present, including the Right Hon. William Windham and the Hon. Edward Harbord.' (C. Mackie, *Norfolk Annals: A chronological record of remarkable events in the nineteenth century (Compiled from the files of the 'Norfolk Chronicle')*, vol. I, *1801–1850* (Norwich, 1901), p. 61.)

156 From what follows, it is clear that Repton and John had been producing some architectural designs for the house at Felbrigg; the Norfolk Gardens Trust has found no hard evidence that Repton advised on the park or gardens there. (*Repton in Norfolk*, p. 27.)

or that Mr Windham had thought his wishes neglected – If you can find an early & a fair opportunity – pray state the following facts –

John by his desire went to look at Felbrigg – & made a design for altering the skylight[157] – which I did not like & did not send – because it <did not> *was no* improve*ment* on the old one – which I supposed might be repaird – or renew'd without alteration.

From the manner in which Mr Windham mentioned the subject to me – I thought him not decided & therefore did not wish to tempt him to any expensive alteration of the skylight – & the Stair Case – otherwise I shou'd have suggested that as the Entrance Hall is Gothic & the Library Gothic – the Staircase connecting them shoud be Gothic also – Yet the Hall & Library are of that Pseudo Gothic Style which neither John nor I cou'd prevail on ourselves to imitate – and a more pure style wou'd be very expensive – However we amused ourselves with giving instructions to our ingenious draftsman *Frederick*[158] who made the design which [fb] I now send you – & which I must beg you to return as it forms part of a Collection <which> John is making for his great Work on Gothic Architecture[159] – & if you shew it Mr Windham – I beg you will explain that I do not advise any thing of the Kind to be adopted at Felbrigg – & only beg him to let it serve as my exculpation – if there be any necessary – I have now outlived too many old friends, to Suffer without regret *& some struggle* the abatement of any friendship which I do not feel that I have deserved to lose – & beleive me my dear William the Satisfaction I have felt in making friends, has never been embitterd by the sorrow of having lost any that were worth preserving –

I am ever Yours, H Repton

Return me the Gothic Sketch – the others you may put in the Fire as being useless[160]

But in comparing them together – take notice how nearly the same dimensions are preserved – and yet how much more lofty the Gothic appears (from the prevalence of perpendicular lines) – the Contrast is here very striking – & will perhaps deserve Mr Windhams attention as a Curious fact.

---

157 There is a drawing by John Adey Repton, entitled 'The staircase & sky light at Felbrigg in Norfolk', dated 1806, with overlay, in the Repton 'scrapbook'. (NHC, Colman Collection.)

158 Frederick Mackenzie (1788–1854), a pupil of John Adey Repton. (*ODNB*)

159 At the top of the page there is a contemporary pencilled note 'page 31'. This probably refers to a page in John Adey Repton's 'great Work on Gothic Architecture', which was never published. The (incomplete) manuscript may be that now in the Avery Library. (Carter et al., *Repton*, p. 130.)

160 The drawings have not survived in the HL archive, so perhaps William did return the Gothic sketch and burn the others.

Endorsed: 10ᵗʰ Jan'y 1808   Hy Repton Esq.   with Sketches for alterations at Felbrigg
HM 40848

25. Revd Richard Buckeridge to William Repton

Lichfield, January 24ᵗʰ 1808

Dear Sir

I transmit to you the <u>Form</u> of an aff[idavi]t, which, it appears, is *a* necessary Proof of the due execution of the <u>Grant</u> & <u>Memorial</u> prior to the Enrollment with the Clerk of the Peace – You will notice the observations of Mr S. Simpson in his Letter to Mr Adey (on the other side of this Sheet) upon the words <u>belonging to &c</u>. It certainly is an unusual way of describing Lands so situated, but I do not see any Reason to think that an objection can be taken to the <u>Grant</u> on that Acc[oun]t. If, however, <u>you</u>, or Mr Adey have any Doubts upon the Subject, it will, certainly, be advisable to have the Deeds <u>returned</u>, &, having substituted the words <u>situated in</u>, reexecuted – I sh'd reason, from the former Part of Mr S. Simpson's Letter th[a]t, if the Deeds are returned, there <u>is</u> a Mode of executing them w[hic]h will render an Aff[idavi]t <u>unnecessary</u>; but he had not described the form or Manner of doing it. I beg th[a]t you will not scruple to employ me when <u>this</u> or – <or> any other occasion, & that you will believe me to be

Dear Sir, with best Compliments to Mr & Mrs Adey,
Your faithful Humble Servant
Rich'd Buckeridge

Address: William Repton Esqre, Aylsham, Norfolk
Brown st: LITCHFIELD 119, JAN 25 1808; *charge*: 10
Endorsed: 24 Jan'y 1808   The Revd Rd Buckeridge   As to Annuity for a Vote

(enclosure) Stephen Simpson[161] to Revd Richard Buckeridge

Lichf[iel]d, 23ᵈ January 1808

Dear Sir

I send you a Draft of an Affid[avit] of the Exec[ution] of the Grant & Memorial, to save the trouble of the returning them to you. I think it would

---

161 Stephen Simpson, son of Charles, two of the four attorneys listed in Lichfield in 1793; both in turn its town clerk.

have been better if it *had* appeared on the face of them that the Lands are situated in the County of the City of Lichfield, instead of belonging to – though the fact is well known & easily proved <we> I only mention it for your consideration that if you think it worth while to alter the question the Writings may be returned.

If such a question were p[re]sented, it would easily be answerd by persons living there

I am, Dear Sir, Yours sincerely

Step' Simpson

[fb] [blank] of [blank] in the county of [blank] maketh Oath that he this Deponent was present & did see John Adey of Aylsham in the County of Norfolk Esqr Sign Seal & as his Act and Deed deliver a certain Indenture bearing date the 19th day of September in the Year of our Lord 1806 & made between the said John Adey of the one part & Wm Repton of the same Place Gent[lema]n Nephew of the said John Adey of the other Part purporting to be a Grant of an annuity yearly rent or sum of forty five Shillings by the said John Adey to the s'd Wm Repton & his Assignees for and during the Term of the Natural Life of him the s'd Wm Repton out of All those two Acres of Land be the same more or less of him the said John Adey – situate and being in a certain field late a Common or Leet field called Bole Botham belonging to the County of the City of Lichfield between the Land formerly of Sir Theophilus Biddulph & afterwards of Wm Moseley on the North side & the Land late of Joseph Adey & now Mary the Wife of John Sneyd Esqr[162] on the South side & abutting upon the road leading from the City of Lichfield aforesaid to Whittington & Freeford towards the West now in the Occupation of the Revd Rich'd Buckeridge or his Undertenants with the Rights Members & Appurt[enance]s. And that he this Deponent also saw the s[ai]d John Adey sign and Seal a Memorial of the said Grant bearing date the 20th day of September in the Year of our Lord 1806 directed to the Town Clerk of the City and County, of the City of Lichfield to which s'd Grant and also <to> the said Memorial this Deponent is a Subscribing Witness – And that the Names "Francis Barnes"[163] & "Geo Ives"[164] indorsed on the

---

162 Joseph Adey of Lichfield (1704–63) was the father, by two different wives, of John Adey and of Mary Sneyd née Adey. (*Aylsham*, p. 169.)

163 'Barnes' is mentioned frequently in the letters from Dorothy Adey; this document indicates that Francis Barnes was employed in some capacity by the practice of Adey & Repton of Aylsham. Francis Barnes was baptized at Aylsham on 7 Sept. 1790, son of Philip and Elizabeth; he married Elizabeth King at Aylsham on 17 Oct. 1811.

164 From this document it is clear that George Ives was also was employed in the practice

s[ai]d Memorial & Indenture as Witnesses thereto respectively are of the respective proper hands Writing of the s[ai]d [*blank*] & this Deponent respectively.

Endorsed: 23ᵈ Jan'y 1808   Step: Simpson Esq   With Draft of Aff[idav]it as to Annuity
HM 40953/8

26. Humphry Repton to William Repton

London, 25 February 1808

Dear William

You are a shabby fellow not to be decided when You come – an event of too much consequence to be left uncertain – George wont come to Harest[ree]t till Bro' Wm comes – Mary must go back to meet Bro' Wm – (for she is at Mrs Heatons[165]) – I dont know how to make my engag[emen]ts – not to miss of you – but know – that on Sunday next I cross over to Hartfordshire – to earn 20 Gui[nea]s & will be in London on Friday night if you write & say when You shall be in Town – & we will all go to Harest[ree]t together – so write to me there on Monday – or after that day to me at Sr Culling Smith, Bart,[166] Bedwell Park *(Hatfield)* Herts.[167]

Endorsed: 25 Feb'y 1808   Hy Repton Esq
HM 40849

---

of Adey & Repton of Aylsham. Dorothy Adey mentions 'George' in many of her letters written during John Adey's illnesses in 1808 and 1809, when William was absent in London on business. Various members of the Ives family are mentioned in *Sail and Storm* and in *Aylsham*.

165 A resident in the vicinity of Hare Street; not identified further. The surname recurs in later letters.

166 Sir Culling Smith (1731–1812) was the son of a merchant, possibly of Huguenot extraction, and his wife, sister and co-heiress of John Horne, governor of Bombay. In 1802 Smith was made baronet of Hadley (Middx), where he had family connections: his wife was sister of John Burrows, rector of Hadley. (*Repton in Herts*, p. 29, citing Debrett's, *Baronetage of England* (1832), p. 548.)

167 This is the principal documentary evidence for Repton's involvement at Bedwell Park, which Sir Culling had purchased from Samuel Whitbread II in 1807. Repton's stated fee of 20 guineas 'would imply several days' work, and almost certainly the production of a Red Book'. (*Repton in Herts*, p. 229.) Bedwell Park was depicted in the *Polite Repository* (1810) (Temple, 'Repton, illustrator', p. 172.)

27. Edward Repton to William Repton

Ardingly, March 5 1808

Dear William

It's a shabby piece of Paper to communicate my affection – but it will serve to tell you I shall be sincerely mortified – if you come to Town, and I not to see you – I went there this week purposely to meet you – but was disappointed – let me know therefore as soon as you are decided and at any <write> rate, write on Friday (I shall get it on Sunday) to say whether it will be immediately after the 13th as I am anxious to give my friends here as little trouble as I can – but shall make a point of being absent a fortnight to see you – and to see the most of you – Of course my Mother communicates all my changes, and prospects – of which, and our mutual successes and hopes we will converse as brothers when we meet –

Give my most affectionate Love to Mr and Mrs Adey and be assured of the sincere friendship and attachment of your Brother Edward

Address: William Repton Esqr, Aylsham, Norfolk
B st: EAST GRINSTEAD 29; *r st*: [*illeg*]; *charge*: 9
Endorsed: 5 March 1808   The Revd Edwd Repton
HM 40910/1

28. Humphry Repton to William Repton

Harestreet, Friday night [11 March 1808]

Oh William, William – you are a bad boy – here have I put off & put off my journey in the hope of seeing you next Sunday – & now I come home & find that you do not leave Aylsham till Thursday when I shall be on my road from Cambridge Northward – & do not return till Easter or after – I know not how we can see each other – which will be a great vexation to me – but I will tell you my route –
Monday 14 to London – to meet Edward – sleep St Martins lane[168]
Tuesday 15 with Edward to Crayford – sleep A Swans Bishops gate[169]
Wednesday 16 – in the fly to Cambridge –
Thursday 17 – some how or other in C. or Chaise Northward

---

168 Probably at Roberson's Hotel, which is mentioned in several later letters.
169 Presumably an inn; One Swan Yard and Two Swan Yard were in Bishopsgate. (*Regency London*, plate 15, grid Db.)

[*fb*] John goes somehow to Norwich on Monday or Tuesday next – & will perhaps see you before you leave Aylsham & will stay there during your absence – – but he must join me at Laxton[170] by 27th or 29th somehow –

I see no Chance of our meeting – unless you set off in time to catch me in London – & that will be uncertain – on Tuesday – or unless you & Mr Anson[171] like to come Via Cambridge on Wednesday & then we may spend a day together – for in that case I woud strain a point & stop all day Thursday at Cambridge to shew you the Lions[172] – but alas! I fear the Fates ordain it otherwise – & I know not when we shall meet – as my route from Laxton, must be [*fb*] in the Contrary direction to Norfolk – Woburn[173] the week before Easter – so we must move different ways – after all the pains I have taken to contrive a meeting – I wish I was going with John to see dear John Adey & Dee – but I must fill up my time in the North – while he is in Norfolk that we may meet & act together at Laxton Hall –

My Love, & believe me
ever Yours Fondly   HR

Your Mother says I have written a bothering letter about nothing at all at all – but I thought you might wish to know my motions – & I wish you hang'd for so badly contriving your Motions – but so it is – & it is so – & so it is very so – so –

Address: To Wm Repton Esq, Aylsham, Norfolk, or, Mr Adey [*monetary calculations probably in William's hand*]
B st: RUMFORD 10; Cross Post; *charge*: 8
Endorsed: 11th March 1808   Hy Repton Esq
HM 40850

---

170 Laxton Hall (Northants) home of George Freke Evans; Repton's first recorded visit there was in 1806. (Carter et al., *Repton*, p. 160.)

171 Either Henry or Charles Anson: letters later in this collection refer to both men. There were earlier connections between the Anson, Adey and Repton families. In particular in March 1773 John Repton, father of Dorothy, Humphry and John, took on a lease from Thomas Anson of Shugborough (Staffs) of the old Paston estate at Oxnead Hall, which John the younger farmed, managing it for his siblings. (*Aylsham*, p. 177.) Repton's manuscript poem 'Birds and Fishes' is dedicated to 'the Revd Charles and Henry Anson'. (Avery Library, MS 3233; microfilm MICROFOR F a4379.)

172 Not identified: either animals or architectural features.

173 Woburn Abbey (Beds); home of the sixth duke of Bedford. Repton visited frequently; he was employed there from 1804 until at least 1810; Red Book dated January 1805. (Carter et al., *Repton*, p. 147.)

29. Dorothy Adey to William Repton

[Aylsham, 18 March 1808]

My dear William

A letter from Mr Meux[174] to <u>me</u> is so intirely on business that I think I had better send it to you and Mr Adey begs you will call and settle it and tell Mr Meux if you please how unable your uncle is to write. You I dare say know the whole transaction but I myself perfectly remember Mr Meux always came over before Mr Adey went to hold the Wicklewood Court[175] to bring the interest and when he was too ill to come he sent. You left a letter to go to Thornage in the Study. I suppose you forgot to mention it so I sent it by the post tonight. George thought it was intended for the Holt Carrier but <u>single</u> was written on the outside so that must be for the post. I have a long letter from Lady Katherine[176] with a very circumstantial account of Ld Orford.[177] His complaint is a retention of urine, she says he has now no pain but I am not satisfied myself that he is as well as one coud wish, it snows very fast and has done so for three Hours. if you are not laid fast before you get to Thetford you will get on but it is bad road about Watton more heavy tho I believe than any thing else.

Love to all from all
Yours ever D Adey

Address: Wm Repton Esq., Harestreet near Romford, Essex
B st: AYLSHAM [*illeg*]; Cross Post; *charge*: [*illeg*]
Endorsed: 18th Mar 1808   Mrs Adey
HM 40886/1

---

174 Not identified but from what follows seems to have been connected with the manor of Wicklewood. A Mr Meux is also mentioned in a letter from John Repton (HM 40929/3 in Appendix 1).

175 Wicklewood, a village near Wymondham; copious (earlier) manorial records at NRO; enclosure award 1810.

176 Lady Katherine Walpole (d. 3 July 1831), fourth child and first daughter of the first earl of Orford.

177 The Honorable Horatio Walpole (1723–1809), of Wolterton, Norfolk, created first earl of Orford on 10 April 1806. (*Hist. Parl.*)

30. Dorothy Adey to William Repton

[Aylsham], Saturday [19 March 1808]

My dear William

A small parcel like the abstract of a Title or somthing, of about 7 or 8 sheets of paper a Man brought from Mr Stokes of Fakenham[178] yesterday morning it is directed to Messrs A & R and the man said he was order'd to take back an Answer to Mr Stokes. I told him you was in London and Mr Adey not well, but that I shou'd have an opportunity of sending it to you in a parcel the end of next week, so if I have no orders from you for its being sent sooner, Barnes shall take it with him. Mr Adey was exceedingly Bonny last night and play'd Loo with the Girls and John, to day he is not altogether so lively but considering the extreme coldness of the weather is as well as can be expected.

Yours ever affectionately   D A

Address: William Repton Esq, Messrs Bensons, House of Commons, London[179]
B st: AYLSHAM 125; *r st*: B Mar 21 1808; *charge*: 1/6
Endorsed: 19 March 1808   Mrs Adey
HM 40886/2

31. Dorothy Adey to William Repton

[Aylsham], Sunday afternoon [20 March 1808]

My dearest William

The enclos'd from Stokes[180] accounts for my sending the Blue parcel which for fear you may have left London I shall put an outward cover on to Messrs Bensons pay the carriage and [?]to [?]so lodge to him, and I will, at the same time, send three letters arriv'd to day. thanks for your scrap from Harestreet. I shall be heartily glad to hear as often from you as you can.

Yours ever affectionately D Adey

---

178 The NRO holds several letters from William Stokes of Fakenham, a lawyer or official of some kind. See, for example, NRO, WGN 1/4/121, 30 November 1802, William Stokes, Fakenham, to William Gunn, Irstead.

179 At this time William was at Westminster pursuing the Sheringham enclosure bill; 'Messrs Bensons' were probably solicitors.

180 'The enclos'd' has not survived in this collection.

Address: Wm Repton Esqr
Endorsed: 20 March 1808   Mrs Adey
HM 40886/3

32. Dorothy Adey to William Repton

[Aylsham], Monday evening [21 March 1808]

My dearest William

We look for a letter very anxiously you may easily believe. your last was written on Wednesday. from London I know we cou'd get none today, but from Harestreet we might, but we must wait patiently tomorrows arrival

I write to say Cooper the Turnpike Man[181] has been here to day for his Quarters pay seventeen pounds, I think he said, but I cannot pay him and he says he shall be in great distress for the want of his money, as he has been oblig'd to borrow to get on with his work and promised payment tomorrow to different people, and he begs of me to write to you and desire you will send him his pay, and he is to call on Friday morning for your answer so [*fb*] be so good to write and tell me what I am to say to him. Barnes was here in the Office with George[182] some time this morning. George says he look'd at the records and took the names down of those people who wou'd not pay their Church Rate and desired George wou'd go round to them all again and tell them if they did not pay before the Easter meeting he wou'd put them all in the spiritual Court.[183]

George ask'd Cubit[184] if Mr Woolmer Cubit[185] had given him a notice he left, and he said 'o yes you need not trouble yourself about that I have got it I promise you'.

The Blickling Corps are inspecting today and there is a Gala dinner.[186]

---

181 Eventually there was a turnpike road from Norwich to Cromer through Aylsham. At this time (1808) it only ran from Norwich to Aylsham. An act to develop the section from Norwich to Aylsham was passed in 1794; a second to extend the road to Cromer was passed in 1811. (*Sail and Storm*, p. 89.)

182 Francis Barnes and George Ives.

183 An 'office cause' could be brought in the church court against parishioners who failed to pay their church rates. See A. Tarver, *Church Court Records: an introduction for family and local historians* (Chichester, 1995), p. 31.

184 The father of Woolmer Cubit. (See Letter 35.)

185 Mr Woolmer Richard Cubit of Ingworth; in 1810 he married Mary Churchill of Erpingham.

186 Local volunteer corps were established during the Napoleonic Wars. (NRO, AYL 570–588.) For a general overview of volunteers, see A. Gee, *The British Volunteer Movement,*

Miss Churchill was invited, and goes with her father,[187] and Mrs Holley[188] is to be there, and Mrs Johnson Gay,[189] so I cannot help thinking, but I have not heard any body say so, that Johnson has join'd the [fb] the Heydon Volunteers to the Blickling

Your Uncle sent us his yesterdays paper containing, like poor Nelson's Victory good and bad news at the same time.[190] it will be right good news to hear you are well and your Bill[191] is going on well

God bless you

Yours affectionately D Adey

Address: William Repton Esqr, Mr Savills Hotle[*sic*], No. 202 Piccadilly, London
B st: AYLSHAM [*illeg*]; *r st*: B APR 6 1808; *charge*: 9
Endorsed: 21ˢᵗ March 1808   Mrs Adey
HM 40886/4

1794–1814 (Oxford, 2003); for the Norfolk volunteers, see R. Hindry Mason, *The history of Norfolk: from original records and other authorities preserved in public and private collections* (London, 1884), pp. 457–69. See Letter 35 regarding the Aylsham Volunteers and William Repton's commission.

187 Amongst many other appointments, the Revd Joseph Dixie Churchill was rector of Blicking (31/03/1802–05/10/1810). (CCEd Person ID: 48101.) It is possible that he was the father of the Miss Churchill mentioned here; in later letters Dorothy refers to 'Mr Churchill' and 'Sarah the second Miss Churchill' (b.1790), as well as to 'Miss Churchill'. Repton addressed one of his manuscript poems to 'the Churchills'. (Avery Library, MS 3233; microfilm MICROFOR F a4379.)

188 There were various members of the Holley family in and around Aylsham. (See *Aylsham*, chs. 10 and 18.) In June 1801 John Holley married as his third wife Sarah Addison, one of the daughters of Revd Leonard Addison of Saxthorpe. (*Aylsham*, p. 251.)

189 Mrs Martha Johnson Gay, wife of John Johnson Gay. (*Aylsham*, p. 238.) Johnson Gay (1782–1852) was the son of John Gay and his wife Frances, daughter and heiress of Richard Johnson, merchant. NRO, AYL 1223, an index made by William Repton [n.d. *c*.1811] of clients or landholders, perhaps in relation to various enclosures, includes: 'John Johnson Gay esq., Waborne, Waborne Priory, Bassingham, East Beckham, Beeston'. Letter 108 is a letter to William from J. J. Gay, written at Saxthorpe.

190 *The Norfolk Chronicle*, Saturday, 19 March 1808, issue 1982, published reports of the war and events in Europe, and also on p. 2 a report of the 'Agricultural Meeting' held on 11 March at the Angel Inn, Norwich, presided over by Thomas Wm. Coke esquire, President of the Norfolk Agricultural Society, at which Nathaniel Kent was presented with a 'magnificent Piece of Plate' in recognition for his services rendered to agriculture in the county.

191 The Sheringham enclosure bill.

33. Dorothy Adey to William Repton

[Aylsham], March 23rd [1808]

My dear William

Yesterday and to day I have look'd in vain for a letter from you as you promis'd <u>when you had seen Mr Benson</u> and I now only write to tell you that on Tuesday morning I gave the Post Boy to send by the Mail a Brown paper parcel directed to Mess'rs Bensons House of Commons and within a note requesting Mess'rs Bensons wou'd forward the enclos'd to you at Harestreet Romford Essex, if you was gone thither, the parcel <was> *to you* contain'd a Blue parcel from Stokes & three letters, one of them free Lilford[192] and a short one from me, and yesterday only one letter came, which I open'd without a thought (why I was <u>without thought</u> I will some time or other <u>satisfactorily</u> account for) it was from [fb] Amyott[193] and by what I cou'd understand seem'd to require being told to Roofe,[194] but I <u>have not said one word to any one</u> but put the Letter up again and drew my pen threw Aylsham Norfolk, and put Mess'rs Bensons House of Commons London, and I write today for fear you shou'd not have got either that or my parcel,[195] and to beg of you to say <u>as soon</u> as you get this if they have arriv'd safely

Barnes waits your orders and will set out the moment I hear from you that he is to do so. I am in hopes tomorrows post may bring a letter, if I shou'd be disappointed I am sure you will have the kindness to write <u>as soon as you get this</u> for a letter from you that your business goes on as pleasantly as you wish will be a comfort to know

God bless you, yours ever most affectionately D Adey

John leaves Aylsham tomorrow[196]

---

192 A letter sent free by Thomas Powys, second baron Lilford, brother-in-law of Robert Doughty (q.v.). NRO, AYL 44/2 includes a letter from T. Powys to his sister on her engagement to Doughty in 1775.

193 Thomas Amyot, esquire (1775–1850); born in Norwich, William Windham's election agent and private secretary and holder of Colonial Office appointments. (NRO catalogue description of COL 2/111.) At this time he was employed in an office in Downing Street.

194 James Roofe, carpenter, in Aylsham. NRO, AYL 1215 includes 'Roofe and Amyot Miscellaneous letters to William Repton 1786[sic] to 1809'. Roofe had been accused of fraud regarding excise payments. By 1814 James Roofe was also an auctioneer in Aylsham. (See Letters 176 and 177.)

195 NRO, AYL 1215 includes a letter addressed to William at Aylsham, redirected by Dorothy Adey to Mess'rs Benson, House of Commons. The letter is dated 21 March 1808, written at Downing Street by Thomas Amyot esq., 'as to James Roofe'.

196 William's brother John; see Dorothy's comment at the end of Letter 34.

Address: Wm Repton Esqr, Messrs Bensons, House of Commons, London
B st: AYLSHAM 125: *r st*: B Mar 25 1808; *charge*: 9
Endorsed: 23ᵈ March 1808   Mrs Adey
HM 40886/5

34. Dorothy Adey to William Repton

Aylsham, Thursday 24ᵗʰ [March 1808]

My dearest William

What I wrote to you of your Uncle playing Loo was most fortunate, for since then in no letter have I been able to mention him, now again I can do so with some degree of comfort, but he is still far from being even as well as usual. that night after my good account He never slept at all, but had a return and a very violent *one* of of[*sic*] Cold in the Head, and stomach, and feverish and delirious, <u>very much</u> so indeed, I sent to Taylor[197] and to your Uncle John, and your Brother Johns being here felt a comfort to me, I believe dear Soul he was perfectly aware of his own illness, for he hop'd I wou'd not write to bring you home, and nothing but an event I cou'd not help looking forward to with dread wou'd have suffer'd me to mention his extreme illness, I will not enlarge further, you know what a poor toad I am, and how I have of course suffer'd. dear Mr Charles Anson[198] came on Tuesday and therefore did not see him at the worst. Yesterday (Fairday)[199] I sat with him in the patchwork room and except to dinner never left him, at night Taylor administered your Mothers Recipe which had a glorious effect, this morning he had a Glorious natural motion, has din'd with us and is now in the next room with Uncle & Mrs John, Mr Charles and Nancy [*fb*] Holley[200] and Miss Churchill and tho it still takes three of us to get him up and down stairs, yet he mends every time, and <u>I do assure you</u> is I hope and trust getting on to be what he had been of late, tho still very <u>confused</u> and drowsy.

Now for business, first giving you a thousand thanks for your kind & long letter, I will direct this to Harestreet in consequence of what you say

---

197   Samuel Taylor, surgeon, of Market Place, Aylsham. (*Aylsham Directories*, p. 9.)

198   Revd Charles Anson (1770–1827), third son of George Adams (known as Anson from 1773) of Shugborough Hall (Staffs); rector of Lyng (1794–1827) and Mautby (1804–1827). Repton worked at Lyng Rectory before 1806. (Daniels, *Repton*, p. 264; Carter et al., *Repton*, p. 159; *Repton in Norfolk*, p. 133.)

199   Fairs were held at Aylsham on 23 March and the last Tuesday in September. (*Aylsham Directories*, p. 1.)

200   Nancy (b.1785), daughter of John and Elizabeth Holley. (*Aylsham*, pp. 250–1.)

of going thither, and give my love to your Dear Mother and tell her I cou'd not write to <u>her</u> no more than I cou'd to <u>you</u> but that I now will certainly write to her <u>on Saturday</u>. I have had George with me in the Study and found the notices which we have examin'd together, and he is to take a Horse and go with them tomorrow, Plumly lives at Southrepps,[201] we have found out, else He said a donkey wou'd have done. Mr Doughtys[202] steward he says was here yesterday to enquire if Notices had been served. as to Barnes I have consulted with Betty[203] and she advises my not seeing him till to morrow morning, so I suppose she thinks him not over sober this second fair night, but before I see him to morrow I will coppy from your letter the people he is to call upon, and I take it for granted you mean they shou'd sign their names at the <u>conclusion</u> of the printed Bill, and I will give him paper to make a memorandum of any answer he may receive.

I have sent Lady Catherines[204] note to Roofe. I have had Motts housekeeper and I told her [*fb*] [she] shou'd write to the High Sheriff[205] and when I <u>heard</u> from him I wou'd advance her more money, and I have written to him, and ought to have had an answer, but I have not. The George Wyndhams[206] came to breakfast yesterday and stai'd all day, but there was a good party of all my visitors together and they all excus'd me, so I knew no more of the Fair than if it had not been Fair Day, and I order'd all that came on Business to be shewn to George. he has not told me of any thing particular so I suppose there was nothing but what He coud Answer to, and he is gone home tonight so I cannot enquire. Mr Charles is reading the *Pilot*[207] in the other room. we think it is your sending and Uncle John says he likes what he has read and all took it in their heads they shou'd find some great news that you had been so good to give the earliest intelligence of. I wish you had seen Taylors inquisitive Face when I took it in the parlour. your account of Young Anson's promotion

201 Spurrell Plumbly of Southrepps, gent. See, for example, NRO, MC 2689, Spurrell Plumbly's letter of commission as Ensign in the Southrepps Volunteer Corps of Infantry, 4 September 1804.
202 Mr Robert Lee Doughty of Hanworth (d.1819). Hanworth was probably Repton's second commission after he became a professional landscape designer. (*Repton in Norfolk*, pp. 45–9.)
203 Not identified; perhaps Dorothy's housekeeper? In Letters 175 and 177 she refers to Betty Barn(e)s in relation to household matters.
204 Perhaps Lady Katherine Walpole.
205 In 1808 the High Sheriff of Norfolk was John Thurston Mott of Barningham, so it seems that there was some sort of disagreement between Dorothy and Mott's housekeeper.
206 George Wyndham married Marianne Bacon in 1799.
207 Probably *The Pilot*, a London newspaper that was first published in 1808.

was the <u>first</u> account to Mr Charles. He supposes he has letters gone to Lyng. all desir'd me when I left the parlour to give their fond love and dear Elisa said with great Glee, 'tell him I send my real love indeed'. God bless you and thank you again for your kindness I love to know what you are about and I am ever affectionately

Yours D Adey

Mr Charles is now come to look at the red book to see where Mr Sharp is member for[208]

[*fb*] no Major at home. John left us this morning. Charles Neale to be buried tomorrow.[209] Review of volunteers tomorrow

Address: Willm Repton Esqr, Harestreet near Romford, Essex
B st: AYLSHAM 125; Cross Post; *charge*: 8
Endorsed: 24ᵗʰ March 1808   Mrs Adey
HM 40886/6

35. Dorothy Adey to William Repton

[Aylsham], Saturday morning [26 March 1808][210]

My dear William

Your Uncle was rather a little fatigued at night and went to bed rather before ten, slept till 4 oclock when a little hack cough kept him from <u>sound</u> sleep, but he does not seem the worse today, and parted with all his friends with thanks for the time they had been with us, only Dear Nancy remains, but today or to morrow Sarah the second Miss Churchill comes to her, this I call and I trust you will think a very good account. George gave Cubits Notice to his Son, as the old Man was asleep[211] and Plumley was out and that notice he gave to <u>his</u> Wife,[212] I tell him you said serve them on the <u>people themselves</u> but he says, he knows if he only is able to prove the leaving <th> A notice at a persons house, is quite sufficient; however shou'd he be mistaken you will have plenty of time before the 5ᵗʰ of April

---

208 Richard Sharp (1759–1835), of Park Lane (Middx) and Fredley Farm, Mickleham (Surrey); M.P. for the pocket borough of Castle Rising from 1806 to 1812. (*Hist. Parl.*) For Sharp's Micklcham property as a possible Repton site, see the Introduction and Letter 197.

209 Charles Neale, peruke-maker, was buried at Aylsham on 25 March 1808, aged 63.

210 William endorsed the letter '2ⁿᵈ April 1808' but several people and matters mentioned herein suggest that the letter was written a week earlier.

211 See Letter 32.

212 See Letter 34.

to give fresh directions, He says Mrs Plumley told him her husband was Ex[ecut]or to G. Chapman.[213] George says he gets on with collecting the Rate very well, have you any idea of having him up to Town, you have not mentioned it. I told Barnes he must be prepard to set off on Monday by the Expidition[214] as you wanted him on Tuesday. <Why> 'Why Ma'm I was thinking if you please I wou'd go by the Bury Coach'. I said as you had told me the Expedition I rather wish'd him to go by that as perhaps that wou'd be in sooner, 'why as for the matter of that the Bury Coach will be off before the Expedition, and I [*fb*] had rather if it dont matter to Mr Repton go by the Bury Coach'.[215] I said no more, but I shall recommend the Coach you have orderd again when I see him tonight, and when he returns home I will add to this. He cou'd not set off yesterday till he had what he calls done soldiering,[216] but he was off about 2 oclock, and I made him go with me in the Studdy to look at the map, in order to take the direct road and put the names and places in such order on a sheet of paper he cou'd make no mistake

Mr Parmeter call'd yesterday to know if I cou'd tell him the date of your Commission, which I am sure I cou'd not, but he has given it in the

---

213 TNA, PROB 11/1464/223, will of George Chapman, gentleman, of Hanworth, dated 15 October 1805, probate granted 20 July 1807. The executors were his 'half-brother' John Cubitt, gentleman, of Ingworth and his brother-in-law 'Spurrel Plumbly', gentleman, of Southrepps.

214 'The Expedition, by Newmarket: A double-bodied coach, sets out from the White Swan, St Peter's, Norwich, every afternoon at three o'clock, to the White Horse, Fetter-lane, London; returns from the above Inn daily, at half past three o'clock; calls at the Bull, Bishop-gate-street, going out and coming in'. (*Norwich Directory* (1802), 'Coaches, Barges and Waggons, to and from Norwich'.)

215 'The Stage Coach, by Bury, sets out every Monday and Wednesday, at three in the afternoon, and on Saturday at half past three, from the Angel, in the Market-place, Norwich; and every Tuesday, Thursday, and Sunday, from the Swan with Two Necks, Lad-lane, London, at four in the afternoon.' (*Norwich Directory* (1802), 'Coaches, Barges and Waggons, to and from Norwich'.)

216 Drilling with the Aylsham Volunteers. On 22 July 1803 61 inhabitants of Aylsham offered to be enrolled as the 'Loyal Aylsham Volunteers'. This was the result of a meeting held on 14 July, with Dr Hugh Moises in the chair, at which they had resolved 'We will maintain and defend the Constitution and Government of the British Empire at the hazard of our lives against all enemies, foreign or domestic. We will be ready to act on the shortest notice within the military district in which we are situated; and in case our Sovereign's person should be endangered we will be ready to protect and defend his Majesty in any part of Great Britain. In case of insurrection or actual invasion, we will be subject to marshal law'. By 13 August 1803 there were 145 Aylsham volunteers and by 14 September there were 220. (Hindry Mason, *History of Norfolk*, pp. 460–1.)

same date as his own.[217] Masters[218] told him it was the wish of the new
Ld Leiu[tenan]t[219] to have all dates of Commission sent him. by the way
Mr Charles Anson tells us he is not what Marquis Townshend[220] was, that
he may be is very probable, but he has only been gazetted as Ld Leiu[tenan]t
of the Militia. We have been in a sad taking for Coals and thats a bad
business this cold weather. Mr Parmeter call'd over about that, to know if
a few from his own wou'd be of use, but your Uncle John was so good to
promise us a <u>Chaldron</u>[221] from Oxnead which I was to repay in the Summer
and Mr Parmeter was equally oblig'd with myself, however Aunt John
(<u>I fancy</u>), thought ½ a Chaldron was as well so she said when they return'd
they had not so many as they thought for, I was thankful for ½ a Chaldron,
but I have sent to Parmeter today to say I shall the sooner stand in want of
any that arrive at Aylsham, else he wou'd have thought we had a Chaldron
and supply'd others and we shou'd have been in a hobble again, and I also
said if they had any thing to send to the Young Ladies if they wou'd let me
have it on Sunday night I wou'd take care they have it safe so Barnes or you
can call as you like best.

You did not [say] [*fb*] if you had seen either of the Girls, but I dare say you
call'd, tell your dear Mother I have been talking with Charles this morning
and he says he has several little matters to settle with his Uncle and his mother
before he leaves them and that he cannot well get off before Wednesday and
talks of walking all the way, and when I said it wou'd be a long time before
he arriv'd at home, 'o! no', he said he cou'd walk it in two days. I told him he
wou'd be very wrong to attempt it, for he wou'd have to be nurs'd when he got
home. Your uncle John desired I wou'd remind you of his pills and when so
near my needle man pray bring as <under> follows Q[ua]rter Hundred of best

---

217 In 1803 William Repton and Robert Parmeter had been made Captains of the
Aylsham Light Infantry Corps. The company assembled for drill practice every Sunday
(and some week days) between harvest and December. This was Robert Parmeter of Burgh,
who owned the mills in Millgate and Ingworth. (*Aylsham*, p. 183.) His son, Robert William
(1795–1880), became a solicitor, being articled for 5 years in 1813 to Matthew Kingsbury
of Bungay, an attorney at the courts of Common Pleas and King's Bench. Once qualified,
he joined Robert Copeman's legal practice in Aylsham. (*Aylsham*, p. 271.)
218 Not identified.
219 William Assheton Harbord, second baron Suffield (1766–1821), was Lord Lieutenant
of Norfolk from 11 March 1808 to 1 August 1821. His military positions included
Lieutenant Commander of the Blickling Rifle Volunteers (1803).
220 George Townshend, first marquess Townshend, was Lord Lieutenant of Norfolk from
24 February 1792 to 14 September 1807.
221 A London chaldron of coals was 36 bushels, the weight of which was 3,156 lbs
avoirdupois. (*OED*)

curv'd needles[222] of No 1, 1 Quarter of hundred No 2, one of No. 3 & No 4, & No 5, and <u>half</u> a hundred that is <u>two</u> Quarters of No. 6, No 7 and No 8, in the whole eleven little papers you will have, and they will cost eleven Groats or eleven sixpences and remember me a Leather purse when you see <Morroco> *Morocco* things at a window, as to what I mention'd of extravagance I leave intirely to your own <u>better judgement</u> and shall be <u>perfectly Content</u> without Forks, and in their lein have such a toast rack as Edw'd purchas'd for his mother at Birmingham. Lubbock[223] had very heavy new forks the day I last din'd there, and Martin said they were one Guinea a fork, but if you think we shall be thought wrong to have such things if they cost but 2 a Gu[ine]a I had rather go without

Ever yours affectionately, my dear William, D Adey

PS ½ past 8 Barnes now home. nine names you gave me to get signed, five have, Freestone wou'd not because nobody but Eliz' Cook had, but when Barnes had more names if he went again he wou'd. Dysons so small a concern he shou'd not trouble himself about it, But Barnes has all the answers to send you but it is right I shou'd tell you William Robinson is in London, his direction John Bollands Esqr 25 Mark Lane London,[224] so you may if you like find him there, and if I hear nothing from you to the contrary on Tuesday Morning Barnes will certainly be at wherever the Expedition goes to in Town, and if he finds <u>no directions from you</u> there I shall tell him to enquire for you at No: 202 Piccadilly. Uncle coughs a good deal tonight is otherwise vastly well.

Yours ever DA

[*fb*]Uncle wou'd have me to put Mama's name on the outside that if may be sent you if you are gone to Town

Address: William Repton Esqr or Mrs Repton, Harestreet near Romford, Essex
B st: AYLSHAM 125; Cross Post; *charge*: 8
Endorsed: 2nd April 1808[225]   Mrs Adey
HM 40886/7

---

222 Small curved needles are used for awkward seams; larger ones for upholstery.
223 William Lubbock (1746–1823) was one of the executors John Repton, Humphry's brother. See Letter 89, note by John Repton regarding his will. Lubbock's 'seat' or 'villa' was at Lamas, near Oxnead. (Matchett and Stephenson, *Norfolk and Norwich remembrancer* (1822), p. 253.) His elder brother John (1744–1816), London banker, became baronet in 1806; his title was inherited by William's son, Sir John William Lubbock (1773–1840).
224 *Regency London*, plate 15, square Dd. John Bolland (?1742–1829), of Clapham (Surrey), hop merchant; M.P. for Bletchingley 1814–18. (*Hist. Parl.*)
225 As noted above, this endorsement seems to be wrong; the letter was probably written on 26 March.

36. Dorothy Adey to William Repton

[Aylsham], Sunday afternoon [27 March 1808]

My dear William

I sent so much chat to Harestreet last night that I have little to say by Barnes. Your uncle cough'd a good deal the first part of the night & slept sound the latter and is as well as usual to day, one thing I am sure you will be glad to hear ever since his illness he had lik'd the taste of port wine and had not mix'd any thing with it for these last three days –

This morning a man of the name of Green call'd to say he had purchas'd a bit of Land of some man at Marsham and you promis'd he shou'd have a title above a fortnight agon and the man he purchas'd of is very ill and he begs me to write and ask if it is not done and if it is if you will let him have it tho you are not at home and he is to call next Sunday to hear what you say

The Toll Keeper was here to pay his Rent which he says is due. I told him I cou'd take any money and give a rec[eip]t if he chose it but he said no he shou'd wait for your return. I fancy too John & George Holley[226] wait for your return for we have seen nothing of them so I suppose [fb] when Nancy[227] wrote that you was going to Town they thought there wou'd be nothing for them till your return and they wait for that. I wish you wou'd lay out somewhere about a pound or a Guinea for me (which I will honestly pay you again) or any less sum that you can buy for *Nancy* <for> some pretty little ornament of a Broach or what you like, for she is very good to me beside working hard at my Gown border day after day and I don't think it wou'd be amiss to give her some little thing. I mention a Guinea because I do not mean to spend more but as much less as you can get something not trumpery for

7 o clock a thousand thousand thanks to you my dearest William for your most kind letter and now that all my troubles I trust are at an end I feel more happy than otherwise that you was out of the way of seeing your dear uncle unwell, and me distress'd. I dare not read him the whole of your kindness for fear he shou'd know I was more uncomfortable than I hope he thinks I was. I have no idea what it was occasion'd the illness. he coughed as I told you without ceasing one whole night and I thought the drowsiness when he got up was occasion'd by a Teaspoonful of paregorick[228] I gave

---

226 Revd George Hunt Holley (1787–1836), son of John and Elizabeth Holley. (*Aylsham*, pp. 250–1.)
227 Nancy Holley
228 A pain-relieving or soothing medicinal preparation, especially an opiate. (*OED*)

him about 3 o clock but Taylor said no it was not, he had only miss'd evacuation <u>one</u> day. Taylor however gave a pill of Electuary[229] but it had no effect and tho' he said there was no hardness or necessity yet when dear Mr Adey told us he had been more dizzy than usual, we all agreed to have your Fathers new injection administered and it had not only a good [fb] effect in half an hour but <u>every</u> day since he has had a regular motion, and in short is going on quite as well as usual except that he certainly has a cough but not a bad one and this cold weather it will not I doubt leave him but he is not abroad now at all more than we often see him, nay less so I think, and when I was frightened He talk'd for ever some nonsense or other, and so angry with me for not answering but I wont think of it. Thank God it is over and I hope we shall see no more of it.

<Miss> Sarah Churchill came today to stay a few days and her sister is at home. Mr Charles Anson is so good to say if I write to him on Saturday he will either come for a day or two to Aylsham or will meet us at Oxnead if the weather shou'd be warm and Mr Adey be dispos'd to go there, but I think I shall not feel inclin'd to leave my own house till you and I meet again. Your Uncle is vastly pleas'd with Ld Walpoles[230] attention and I am sure you will not doubt but I am delighted. I wrote on Friday and I wrote last night, so that you have heard every day and I will not now write to you tomorrow but to your dear Mother and to you I will write again on Tuesday and direct to 202. Mr Charles said he was sure that number was Savills[231]

Farewell dear William a thousand thanks for your kindness to me. George says he goes on very well with his Role and has paid his Bills as he goes on. I had a note from Mr Parmeter thanking me for the offer of conveying a letter but one had he said been mis sent from the Girls and he was obligd to [fb] write last night to convince them all was well at home. what a dear snug Repton party, how I shou'd have liked to see you all. My kind love to all

Yours ever affectionately D Adey

I have a letter from the High Sheriff[232] to say he will call on me on

229 A medicinal conserve or paste, consisting of a powder or other ingredient mixed with honey, preserve, or syrup of some kind. (OED)

230 Horatio Walpole, second earl of Orford (1752–1822); he was the Hon. Horatio Walpole 1752–1806; Lord Walpole 1806–1809; M.P. for Kings Lynn 1784–1809. (Hist. Parl.)

231 William was staying at Savill's Hotel, 202 Piccadilly, London; see the address on Letter 38.

232 John Thurston Mott.

Tuesday or Wednesday and Mrs Brett[233] writes that Mr B Partridge goes to Cromer this week to <u>give</u> <u>away</u> his two neices.[234] I have a letter from your dear Father <he> rather fidgetty that I have not written to him to Babworth[235] but I did not write to him for the same cause I was silent to you and to your Mother and now that we are so well I do not know where to direct to Mr Evans.[236] John will tell him how well he left his Uncle on Thursday morn, but if any of the <u>Brethren</u> have a leisure moment I wish they wou'd say how perfectly Mr Adey is recover'd

Thanks for News and send another or two. Uncle Adey says this no letters to send you. I sent Lady Katherines to Roofe

Endorsed: 27 Mar 1808   Mrs Adey
HM 40886/8

37. Dorothy Adey to William Repton

[Aylsham], Tuesday Morning [29 March 1808]

Dearest William

I wrote to your Mother last night but your Uncle being <u>less himself</u> than was altogether comfortable to me I cou'd not write in spirits. he had a most charming nights rest, a natural motion this morning, and has not yet (two o clock it is now) been once what he was almost the whole of yesterday, so that I will write most happily. the sun has been so tempting that there was no keeping him out of the Garden and with the old Blue great Coat on I hope the two walks he has had has done him no harm. I have left him upstairs for the first time today and will write on business

This letter came in a parcel this morning to Nancy and enclos'd in it the two Papers <u>you sent</u> sign'd by George Holley and witness'd by Elizabeth Smith, I have lock'd them up safely and desir'd Nancy who writes to

---

233 Susanna Brett, a friend of the family. She stayed at Oxnead during John Repton's final illness. (See Letter 46.)

234 A reference to the forthcoming marriage of John Thurston Mott to Sophia Partridge, youngest daughter of the late Henry Partridge, esquire (and perhaps the marriage of another of her sisters). John and Sophia were married at Cromer on 12 April 1808 (*Gentleman's Magazine*, April 1808, p. 364.)

235 Babworth was the home of the Hon. John Bridgman Simpson. Repton's first visit to Babworth (Notts) was in 1790; Red Book dated 1790. (Rogger, *Landscapes of Taste*, p. 200.) This letter implies a return visit.

236 Perhaps referring to George Freke Evans of Laxton (Northants). A letter from Repton to Evans, dated 16 February 1806, gives his terms. (Carter et al., *Repton*, p. 160.)

Martha[237] tomorrow, will say, I have sent her Brother's letter to <u>you in Town and I think it is very probable you may write to him from thence</u>, so I shall keep the Draft you gave me and you if you like can send him one from Town for the two Legacys (but dont forget to keep the 5£) and say if I shou'd send George *Ives to* Town to old Burr[238] with the discharge and let George *I mean our George Ives* take his money off his hands. A Man call'd this morning with an Acc[oun]t from Stephenson and Matchett,[239] which I have taken care of. And Austin Bulwer[240] call'd and woul'd fain have given me the amount of your Bill but I told him I had had no rec[eip]t left with me for it; he said he wou'd give it me without a Rec[eip]t, however as it was a check of Kerrisons[241] I saw, that He wou'd have fill'd up, I thought it might as well <have> be<en> left till you return'd, if it had been Cash I might have been tempted not to have let it gone out of the House, not that I want money my dear William, I don't mean so, for I <u>have</u> <u>plenty</u>. by the way I have bought sugar of Clover[242] only 1£.14s.0 because your Uncle John bought a great deal. Lubbock has told him it will be very dear, somthing about its being us'd instead of malt, and John talk'd of laying out ten pounds in it. I only bought two loaves having one of the last parcel still in the house, and why I trouble you at all on the subject is, that if it shou'd really be in a fair way as to become as dear again [*fb*] as it now is it wou'd perhaps be worth your while to consult with your Mother where she has hers from and buy a stock and send down by the waggon – Clovers' at 1s a lb is better Mrs John says than what she buys at Norwich for 14d and she thinks about as Good as Lubbocks large London stock at 11d without the Carriage.

---

237 Martha (b.1784), daughter of John and Elizabeth Holley. (*Aylsham*, pp. 250–1.)

238 Perhaps Edmund Burr, gentleman of Burgh next Aylsham; he made his will in April 1808 and died in 1810. (Information from Maggie Vaughan-Lewis.)

239 Matchett and Stephenson were printers and booksellers, situated in the Market Place, Norwich. They published *The Norfolk and Norwich remembrancer, and vade mecum …* (the first edition is undated but was produced soon after 1801; the second edition was published in 1822). Their book provides the names of many Norfolk house-owners.

240 Augustine Earle Bulwer (1762–1831), amongst other appointments, rector of Heydon from 1786 until his death. (CCEd Person ID: 94820.)

241 Kerrison & Sons Bank, Norwich.

242 In 1793 Thomas Clover was an Aylsham shopkeeper; his premises were situated in the Market Place next door but one to John Adey's house. (*Aylsham Directories*, p. 2.) In 1822 the proprietor was said to be John Wright Clover and his business was listed as that of grocer, linen draper and woollen draper. (*Aylsham Directories*, p. 8.) He was also listed as being the sub-distributer of the Stamp Office. (p. 9.) In Repton's painting of Aylsham's market place looking south, the cream-coloured property, back right, has a sign over the door saying 'Clover'. (See the picture on the back jacket.)

8 o clock no letters by post today or any arriv'd since the last so sent. I shall write tomorrow or Thursday to Harestreet as I think on Saturday you will most probably be there to receive *it* but I will direct to your Agent and if you are not there and there is business in it – he will forward it to you in Town. Miss Sarah Churchill is our visitor now. she and Nancy drink Tea with Miss Shaw[243] tomorrow. the girls both very p'shaw for both girls had rather be at [damaged] home. Your uncle has held most charmingly well all day, sends his kind love to you and is sure you will write when the Bill has pass'd quietly in the Committee.

Yours ever affectionately   D Adey

Mr Thurston came to day to call with Mr Churchill.   He liv'd near Mrs Broome at Exeter and brought her Love to me.

Address: William Repton Esq, Aylsham, Norfolk
Endorsed: 29 Mar 1808   Mrs Adey
HM 40886/9

38. Dorothy Adey to William Repton

[Aylsham], Tuesday evening [5 April 1808]

My dearest William

I call'd myself on Mrs Ellis to ask if I sent your letters to London unopen'd if they wou'd have any additional charge upon them.[244] she says yes, most certainly, that it was a case she had before now written to the post office upon, that when a letter came to a place directed to a person who had been staying in the Town and had left it for any other place, only one postage need be paid, but to a person living in a Town a letter *sent* to that person at any other place must pay postage to both –

Burr is not in Town today and I don't see what I can do in the business, because if you recollect I told you in mentioning this business to you before, that I had desired Nancy to write home and say that I had kept the Discharges for the Legacies and sent Mr George Holley's letter to you, to you in London and [fb] I had no doubt but you wou'd write to him from thence. Collyer[245] told us this morning he had had a letter from Mr Holley,

243 Samuel Shaw (b.1764), attorney, occupied the property (later) known as 'Parmeters' in Cromer Road, Aylsham. He had two sisters, Sarah (b.1762) and Isabella (b.1763). (*Aylsham*, pp. 273, 275.)
244 Probably Mrs Ellis, Aylsham post mistress. The name of the post master or mistress was not given in 1793; in 1822 it was Elizabeth Nobbs. (*Aylsham Directories*, pp. 1, 6.)
245 Revd John Bedingfield Collyer was curate in Aylsham from 1804 to 1816 (CCEd

and thought he wou'd be over this week, I shall not know what to do when he comes, for I took it for Granted <u>that you wou'd send George</u> *Holley* a draft on Kerrisson for both Legacies *from London*. I you know have only one for <u>James Holley's</u>[246] <u>payment</u>, and as you dont say if you have done so or not, I shall be puzled to know if I [?]owt to give the draft or not.   however if Holley shou'd come to morrow, He will of course stay a day or two, and on Friday I can have your answer to this with direction what to do. I sent to the [Black] Boys[247] for Burr but he is not in Town, and Neale[248] who went saw his neighbour Postle[249] who said Mr Burr was to be at Aylsham to morrow, and he wou'd tell him to call, so if he does call I will take his money and give him the discharge.

Cubit has acknowledg'd having had his notice but Plumleys <u>I told you</u> was given to Plumleys Wife – I am sorry you have an objection to George's <giv> writing notices for he has written several – Murrell[250] (Mathew Read[251] tells Neale) went thro Aylsham to Norwich today, but he suppose will return tonight so I have left [fb] orders at the Black Boys if he calls there to send him and I will give him the parcel you have sent –

Your dear Uncle had been very sadly for these last two nights, and I dread his having another coughing tonight. I dont think it can be call'd a <u>Cold</u> but a sort of spas'm and nervous.[252] it began the night before last as soon as he went to bed, and we were up 2 hours with him, last night or rather this morning it began at 2 o clock and did not continue much above an hour, but it is dreadful and <u>alarming</u> whilst it lasts, he throws of phlegm <u>when he can</u> but appears to us as if he had not strength to get rid of it. he is very much frightend himself when it comes on, and told the Girls today He felt at one time during the fit as if he must go off. Thank

---

Person ID: 112308). He and his wife Catherine had various children baptised at Wroxham and a daughter, Elizabeth, at Aylsham in October 1809. (*Aylsham*, p. 200.)

246 James Hunt Holley (1770–1829) of Salthouse and Blickling. (*Aylsham*, pp. 142, 252–6.)

247 The Black Boys Inn, Market Square, Alysham.

248 Presumably a relative of the recently deceased Charles Neale.

249 The Burr and Postle families lived in Burgh next Aylsham. In 1822 Edmund Burr married Mary Postle, both of Burgh. (NRO, ANW 24/97/18, marriage licence bond, 7 June 1822.)

250 Thomas Murrell esquire was residing in Aylsham in 1793 (*Aylsham Directories*, p. 2.) He rented the property known as 'The Manor' (or, 'Great Edmonds') from 1788 to 1791. (*Aylsham*, p. 209.)

251 Mathew Read was a watch-maker in Aylsham. (*Aylsham Directories*, p. 3.)

252 The term 'nervous' is also used to describe Lord Suffield's illness, which is mentioned below.

God he is perfectly himself not any hurrying, but has been very weak and feeble all this day, and wou'd not come down till dinner was on the table for fear any body shou'd come in. he is rather brisk'd up again to night, and that you may be sure gives me life. Mr Churchill says to day that from my description Ld Suffield[253] is exactly [*fb*] in the same way, and those about him are in continual fear, that Dr Lubbock[254] calls it nervous. I have not sent to Taylor, last time I mean the first time that he was attack'd, Taylor gave him some medicine with a great deal of Nitre in it and we were all sure it made him low and did harm. He has this moment ask'd me for Camphor Julip so that I doubt dear soul he feels frightend again. I pray God keep it off to night. I mean to get him if I can eat a sausage for supper. last night he wou'd not touch a bit of any thing and I do think an empty stomach makes him worse and about 3 o clock this morning Izzy gave him a bason of Mutton Broth and it soon stop'd and he fell asleep. if you was to come home to day or in a day or two you wou'd see his dear Face hollow and thin, but he gets up again in four and twenty hours his looks, and I hope before we meet I shall get him in good plight and you will wonder what I have been afraid of, but I tell you how he is really.

Yours ever DA

Address: Wm Repton Esqr, Mr Savills Hotle[*sic*], No. 202 Piccadilly, London
B st: AYLSHAM 125; *r st*: B APR 7 1808; *charge*: 9
Endorsed: 5 April 1808   Mrs Adey
HM 40886/10

39. Dorothy Adey to Mary (Clarke) Repton

[Aylsham], Thursday [7 April 1808]

My dear Mary,

William by all means ought to see the enclos'd and as I think he may possibly leave on Saturday I will direct it to you. being directed to Mr Adey it must be a double letter at any rate, and as it was directed to my husband I open'd it, if it had been to dear William I wou'd not, as he does not approve my doing so, but I am glad I have done so now for in every

253 Harbord Harbord, first baron Suffield (1734–1810), of Gunton Hall.
254 Richard Lubbock M.D., 76 St Giles' Broad Street. (*Norwich Directory* (1802), list of physicians.)

thing that relates to Windham and his Lawyer Budd[255] I am sure we must be doubly diligent

Tell dear William too if you please that John [?]Wood was here this morning to make an oath before a master in Chancery of the serving Hicks[256] with some notice out of Chancery, and I told him to go to Mr Copeman[257] with my Comp[limen]ts and I would be oblig'd to him to do what was necessary, and Mr Repton wou'd settle with him at his return, as Mr Adey was not well enough to come down stairs. I am sorry to say this last was fact – he had another dreadful attack of coughing. he came down to his breakfast about eleven, and has been very still and free from cough ever since. I long dear Mary for a further and a better account of your dear husband. John Repton sent me a letter he had had from him that bespoke him most sadly out of spirits. I long for him to get home for your good nursing and I trust you will have the Comfort to send me a good account. I have this moment Williams letter by Roofe – tell him the will of M:L:D:[258] was not in the parcel but we found it in papers close by there. <we> I have told George to put down on a sheet of paper what is written on the outside of all the parchments he delivers so that William will know what He parts with, and I shall send George to Norwich by [?]Bearoys coach on Saturday.[259]

Mr Parmeter has twice enquired for William, he has business he says on the Carpet for him, I did not enquire what, but I suppose some sessions Cause. the two Girls[260] I find have left their London friends on account of the illness of Mrs Fenning and are gone to Camberwell. The poor Mother told me today she began sadly to wish for them, but as they had been at the expence of giving them pleasure she hop'd they wou'd not come home on her Account – she said they wrote her word you had been so kind to

255 Thomas Hayward Budd (1779–1829) (see http://www.buddfamilytree.uk/thomas_hayward_budd.html) Budd's higher valuations of Windham's properties led to Nathaniel Kent losing Windham's business in 1807. (P. Horn, 'An eighteenth century land agent: the career of Nathaniel Kent (1737–1810)', *Agricultural History Review*, 30:1 (1982), pp. 1–16, p. 11.) By 1807 Budd was living at 23/24 Bernard Street, Russell Square and was a partner at the law firm Clarke, Budd, Burroughs & Hayes. BL, Add MS 37919, vol. 3, contains many letters from Budd to Windham.

256 Perhaps John Hicks who was acting as William Windham's accountant in 1805. (*Aylsham*, p. 176.)

257 Robert Copeman (*c.*1771–1845) the attorney and banker of West Lodge, Aylsham. (*Aylsham*, p. 161; *Aylsham Directories*, p. 7.)

258 Not identified.

259 The name of the coach is unclear. In 1822 two coaches set out from the New Inn, Aylsham, to Norwich every day except Sunday. (*Aylsham Directories*, p. 9.)

260 Presumably two of Mr Parmeter's daughters.

each of them to pass a day or two with you on their return home, and she was sure it was too great a favor to be over look'd. she was ever desirous they shou'd visit where it would be flattering to them to be receiv'd so I think if you like it they will be glad to pass a few days with you. they are right <u>good girls</u>.

tell dear William we are very sorry he kicks his heels in the House of Lords in vain. I am sorry too he misses his visit at Fulham. pray d: [Elizabeth] to send me by William two pots of Lesly's [*fb*] pomatum[261] and settle my sundry account with him if you please and he will pay her for Pomatum. I hope Dear fellow he has not forgot my needles for my stock is nearly out[262] but he has so much on his mind it will be no wonder if he shou'd *forget*. <he> *his* uncle *John* always talks of the pills he is to bring. he will shortly you tell me bring himself. that I shall be right of glad indeed but I am quite easy and content that he shou'd not come home one moment sooner on my account than his business necessarilly wou'd bring him for so seldom as he sees all his friends it wou'd be cruel to wish him home. Arden[263] is just come in and sends best love to him and the girls send love and Mr Adey send love and my love to you all.

Yours affectionately D Adey

Address: Mrs Repton, Harestreet near Romford, Essex
B st: AYLSHAM 125; Cross Post; *charge*: [*illeg*]
Endorsed: 7ᵗʰ April 1808   Mrs Adey
HM 40884

40. Dorothy Adey to William Repton

[Aylsham], Saturday ½ past 8 [9 April 1808]

With all my heart and soul, my dearest William, do I congratulate you on the completion of your business. I have dreaded day after day what wou'd be the consequence supposing you <u>not</u> to have finish'd in Town, and yet that I might have had a necessity for you here, for ever since my Tuesdays letter my spirits have been all agitated and yet bad and alarmingly bad as your

---

261 Pomatum was an ointment for the skin or hair (*OED*); same as pomade, which was originally a scented grease or ointment applied to the skin as a perfume, cosmetic, or salve. In later use a scented ointment or oil used to dress the hair (*OED*). Lesly's pomatum was, presumably, a proprietory brand.

262 See Letter 35.

263 Perhaps Francis Edward Arden, who had married Rachel Pinckard in Blickling in 1803. (*Aylsham*, p. 255.)

dearest Uncle since that time has <u>often</u> been, yet he has also been at times <u>very</u> tolerably well. he certainly grows very much weaker, and you will if his cough continues I dare say think him more so than I do, it is not the cough like your dear Fathers, or like a Consumptive one, all he raises is <u>Froth</u> and Phlegm, his mouth is almost always full of spittle, somtimes he goes several Hours without what we call a Coughing Fit and then it comes as you have seen him in the Parlour and lasts from beginning to end generally [*fb*] three Quarters of an hour and when it is over he is quite exhasted, he has been out and in the Garden three seperate times <u>this morning</u>, but has never reach'd further than the Green house and in again, eat a very good dinner, and was more cheerful after than I have seen him for some time, but a violent fit of coughing came, he wou'd go upstairs, this was at ½ past 4. I left him with Izzy, his mouth so fill'd with spittle he cou'd not open it and quite vapour'd and low. Your letter came at five, and I went up and read it to him, and told him it was comfortable indeed to be well over, and he burst out into an hysterical sob and cry'd heartily. I let it take its course, and when he ceas'd, he said 'when is good friday? I shall be glad to see him'. I told him only five days to come but that if he was uneasy I cou'd have you any day that he wish'd,[264] but that you had been so long without seeing all your dear friends at Harestreet that much as I wish'd to have the comfort of your company I wou'd not for the world bring you home one day sooner, nay I shou'd rather say stay a day longer if you can, 'no' he said 'let him come when he has fix'd', and then cryd again.

Izzy has persuaded me to come down and leave him to get a sleep and she says he will then come down refresh'd, but he told me he had rather be excus'd coming down again. He will not let me send to Taylor, and without you was here I do not propose sending to Lubbock, if he was to go through the Town He shou'd see him because I think his [*fb*] Cough is nervous, and spasms. I have seen nothing of them from Oxnead since Monday. I said he was often <u>very ill</u> and I was alarm'd and shou'd your Brother I know will come when you.[265] he *Mr Adey* sent for me this minute & I have been up. he desired <u>I wou'd not</u> bring you home before your time, he hop'd he shou'd do again, and if I liked it I might send to Taylor. I have sent but he is out of Town. I will not seal this till supper time, and without I write and say I wish you to come <u>do not leave Harestreet</u> If we go on much the same I will write again on Monday night. If he grows worse I will write tomorrow. it is past six. George went off at 8 this morning and is not home yet, I ask'd

---

264 In 1808 Good Friday was on 15 April.
265 Unclear, possibly meaning she will let them know if he takes a turn for the worse.

Roofe if he had wrote to you. He said he shou'd from Norwich but he was only going there for the money.

½ *past* 7 o clock God love his dear Heart he came smiling into the room to Tell [us] 'Here's the dying Man all alive again Girls'. 'I am glad of it sir', says Nancy. 'We will keep you alive I warrant *you*', says Sarah Churchill. he is gone up now with Izzy – I hope for a Motion. he has had none yet to day but he is not at all bad in that way, has never miss'd two days together. I went to call Izzy and when I came back he was telling the Girls the story of "Get your little nose with the tongs".[266] what a change to what he was two hours agon, but I tell you exactly as he is. I have written two letters and not said a word because I was not alone, and I have almost a mind now he so well not to send this, but it shall go, and you know me exactly my dear William and how I feel, beside my rest is so sadly broke night after night, that that always knocks me up, it is near eight and no George. he now is come and I have been to him and am in a new alarm for fear of the draft not getting to you safely, he cou'd not get it till ½ past three from [?]Leavet & Co and when he carried his letter to the post office He was too late, but they told him if he paid a penny it wou'd go and he did pay a penny. I hope you *will* have it safe.

8 oclock. Taylor has been in, he says it is like all your uncles complaints feebleness and nervous, that he will give nothing to night but will [*fb*] bring him a nervous mixture to morrow, that he knows will be of use. I said he had never slept so well as two nights, that he had eat Sauceage & Pottatoes. 'by all means' Taylor says 'give him sauceage & pottato again', so I have orderd some. he had desir'd me to read what I am writing, so you may be sure I have made out a very different letter to what I really write, and he says 'As you have told him I have been poorly today with my cough, pray give my love to him and tell him I am better to night than I have been all day and that I shall be very glad to see him on Friday'. I hope I shall hear a good account of your dear Father. George says he saw the Oxnead party at Norwich. they were all going to the play. God bless you my dear William. I am happy again now, when I am most unhappy my first thoughts fly to you. You are all and every thing to

your ever affectionate D Adey

I sent the two Girls to the Coterie[267] last night at Mr Hollys. Mr Churchill was so good to take them there and <brough> bring them back. I am glad you have sent to George Holly

---

266 Not identified.
267 A social gathering or meeting.

Address: William Repton Esq, Harestreet near Romford, Essex
B st: AYLSHAM 125; Cross Post; *charge*: 8
Endorsed: 9 April 1808   Mrs Adey
HM 40886/11

41. Dorothy Adey to William Repton

[Aylsham], Monday Morning [11 April 1808]

All Well

My dear William your dear Uncle is so very charmingly that as Mr
Holley is going to Norwich today I must tell you so a day sooner than I
intended. O dear if he goes on as he has done yesterday and last night you
will think I have been alarm'd for <u>nothing</u>. never mind that I dont care.
pray God you may see him as he now is and John Holly is in a hurry so I
only say Cooper[268] has been with Kerrisson, he wou'd not pay without a
note from you. the man appeard distressed to death for Money, beg'd hard
for 10£. I really cou'd not give him so much but I ventured to let him have
5£ [*fb*] and [?]work his rent.

George says the Draft was on Kett[269] that he sent – it was indors'd on
the Back to Mr Doughty.

the Marsham man was here again yesterd[ay][270] very angry the writings
were not done, thinks the man will die before they are

pray call at Chamberlains and try your luck with a Cheese,[271] we are
intirely without. Mott they say married this morning.[272] God love you<e>.
Be happy as I have been these last four & twenty hours

ever yours Affectionately D A

I shall not now write to night

[*fb*] now George says the Draft *was* from Kett and <u>on</u> Hodgesons &
Co London.[273]

---

268 The 'Turnpike Man'. (See Letter 32.)
269 The private bank of Kett, Hatfield & Back was formed in 1792; it was known as
Kett & Back from 1810; and as Tompson, Barclay & Ives from 1820 to 1832 when it was
acquired by Gurneys, Birkbeck & Martin of Norwich. It was also known as the Norfolk
General Bank. (*British Banking*, p. 504.)
270 See Letter 36.
271 In 1790 William Chamberlain was trading as a cheesemonger at 204 Shadwell,
London. (*Universal Directory*, (1790) p. 100.)
272 In fact the marriage of John Thurston Mott took place the next day.
273 It has not been possible to identify Hodgeson & Co, London, in either *British
Banking*, or in F. G. H. Price, *A handbook of London bankers...* (London, 1809–1). No bank
has 'Hodgeson' (or Rodgeson) in their name.

Address: William Repton Esqr, Harestreet near Romford, Essex
B st: NORWICH 117; Cross Post; *charge*: 8
Endorsed: 11ᵗʰ April 1808   Mrs Adey
HM 40886/12

42. Joseph Constantine Stadler[274] to Humphry Repton

15 Villiers Street,[275] April 13ᵗʰ 1808

Dear Sir

His Royal Highness the Prince of Wales[276] having been pleased to grant permission that the Book of Plans for the Pavillon[*sic*] at Brighton should be published, and I having undertaken to engrave and and[*sic*] publish the same, in the best manner I am able, and as before verbally agreed, I hereby agree in writing, that I will at my own expence and risque engrave all the plates for the said work, and make the Copy as nearly as possible a facsimile of the Original: that after Deducting the expences of paper – printing and Coloring the Plates, letterpress &c. the profits shall be shared equally between yourself and me. – I also agree and am willing, to take all the hazard upon myself in Case the work should not succeed, and guarantee you from all or any lost by the same.

I am Dear Sir, your very humble servant

J. C. Stadler

To H. Repton Esqr.

Address 1: To Mr Repton, Harestreet near Romford, Essex
B st: B AP 13 808
Addrees 2: [*another wrapper*] Mr Repton, Solicitor, Aylsham
B st: NORWICH 110; *charge*: [?]4
Endorsed: April 1808   Stadler's Offer & agreem't for publishing my father's Work of Brighton Pavilion &c[277]
HM 40945

---

274 Joseph Constantine Stadler (fl.1780–1812), émigré from Saxony, employed as an engraver by the leading print publisher John Boydell. (*ODNB* entry for Ackermann, Rudolph (1764–1834).)

275 *Regency London*, plate 23, square Ca.

276 The future George IV (1762–1830), Prince Regent, 1811–1820; the Royal Pavilion at Brighton was built as his fashionable seaside retreat.

277 In 1808 J. C. Stadler published *Designs for the Pavillon*[*sic*] *at Brighton ...* by H. Repton. With the assistance of ... J. A. Repton and G. S. Repton.

43. Humphry Repton to William Repton

[London, 13 April 1808][278]

Dear Wm

Stadler shewed me the Copy of the letter which I cou'd not find at Harestreet – & which <he> I dictated to him to write – he has now sent me another Copy[279] – if you think this is a sufficient agreement – it will do – but if you think not – or that it should extend to H[ei]rs Ex[ecut]ors Ad[ministra]tors & Assignees – &c – put it into shape & he will sign it – but it must not exceed what I myself seem to have proposed originally.

Give my Love to John – tell him I call'd at the A&S Room & there will be no meeting to-morrow being Maunday Thursday – nor the Thursday following being Easter week.[280]

Love to all – particularly Mamma & Girls &c

HR

[fb] Love to Mary – I have seen the Chess board. it looks beautifully – but the man says if he packs it up before it has been finish'd a week – it will take harm – & the last coat is hardly hard enough for the last polish – but it shall be done the beginning of next week & I will bring it home with me so poor William will not see it – poor fellow[281]

I saw Mr Row & promised to visit his House[282] but whether to night or tomorrow I cannot yet tell as Duff's linnen is at the Wash – Adieu.

Dear George – you must help John to hunt for the plan you did for Brighton[283] – Stadler has not got it – & it must be some where –

HM 40851

---

278 Letter 42, dated 13 April 1808, relates to the content of this letter. Since this undated letter was written on the day before Maundy Thursday and must have been written in 1808, its date is also 13 April, the day before Maundy Thursday 1808.

279 The previous letter.

280 Meetings of the Society of Antiquaries.

281 In pencil, different hand: oh! oh!

282 At Tottenham before 1850, 'Cottages on the south side of Page Green were replaced c.1806 by the residence of William Row, set in 12 acres of grounds laid out by Humphry Repton and considered one of the finest in the parish. Row also bought a neighbouring villa at the eastern end of Page Green, built at about the same date and later called the Hurst'. (*VCH Middlesex*, vol. 5, p. 316.) Row's 'Villa at Tottenham' was depicted in the *Polite Repository* (1810). (Temple, 'Repton, illustrator', p. 172.)

283 Three of George's 'impeccably drawn' architectural notebooks have survived, including the one for the Brighton Pavilion. His 'Pavillion Notebook' is dated 1805 and runs to about 1818. It is held at the Royal Pavillion Art Gallery, Brighton. (Carter et al., *Repton*, p. 133.)

44. John Repton to Dorothy Adey

[Oxnead, April 1808]

My Dear Dee

I find to Morrow is my Sheep Shearing Day and therefore wish to be at home – I considered at coming away. my good William stayd from the Meet[in]g of the Clergy on my Acco[un]t. by all means dine with them *William* by old [?]Uncle. The Churchwardens of Aylsham (time out of mind) have had that honour. The Churchwarden of Oxnead (once stole in) and offended all the rest of the Churchwardens in the Deanery – (God love you) Bess[284] will take her Tea with you and bring Miss Eliza home and I may look at you before all Them returning to Ling. If not God bless him

Love to Mr. B & Miss B[285]

Yours

JR

Inclosed are Parish Papers[286]

to Young Ives pay his & their [?]Fees <u>William</u> or <u>Izzy</u>

Address: Mrs Adey, Aylsham
Endorsed: April 1808   Mr John Repton   About dining at the Generals[287]
HM 40929/1[288]

45. Mary (Clarke) Repton to William Repton

[Hare Street, 26 May 1808]

My dearest William

I ought before this to have thanked you and dear Aunt Adey both for your long letters, that gave <u>me</u> so much pleasure – which made <u>us</u> all happy to hear how well you succeeded in all your Causes, particularly that of Baseys,[289] on

---

284 John Repton's wife, Elizabeth.
285 Not identified.
286 Not found.
287 Meaning a general meeting of the churchwardens in the Deanery of Ingworth.
288 This is the first of three letters by John Repton catalogued under in HM 40929. HM 40929/2 is Letter 59; HM 40929/3 has been placed in Appendix 1 as it is impossible to date.
289 Robert Beasey (*c.*1765–1839), his wife Sarah and family had a property in the Market Square, Aylsham, from 1803. Initially he was a cordwainer but he also became a mail cart contractor running between Aylsham and Norwich (via St Faiths). (Information from M. Vaughan-Lewis.) In these letters his name appears as Basey, Beasy and Beasey, and he is

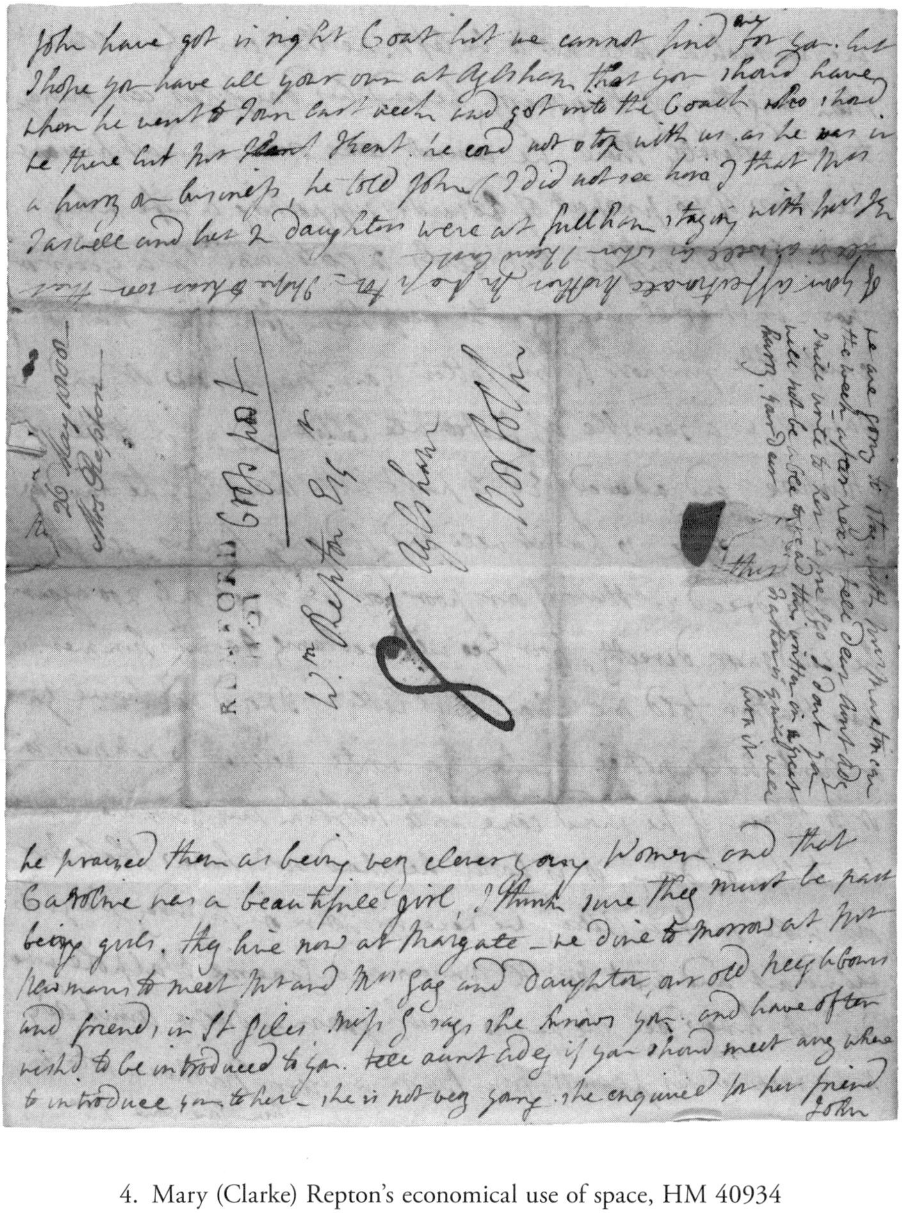
John have got is right Coat but we cannot find any for you. but
I hope you have all your own at Aylsham that you should have
them he went to Town last week and got into the Coach who should
be there but Mr Trent he could not stop with us. as he was in
a hurry on business, he told John (I did not see him) that Mrs
Jarwell and her 2 daughters were at fullham staying with Mrs

he praised them as being very clever young Women and that
Caroline was a beautifull girl, I think sure they must be past
being girls. they live now at Margate — we dine to morrow at Mrs
Newmans to meet Mr and Mrs Gay and daughter, our old neighbours
and friends in St Giles Miss G says she knows you and have often
wished to be introduced to you. tell aunt Adey if you should meet any where
to introduce you to her — she is not very young. she enquired for her friend
John

4. Mary (Clarke) Repton's economical use of space, HM 40934

this account as well yours – our gentry in the Kitchen were all much surpriz'd that he was acquitted, it was not what they at all expected – as Charles said they talked so much against the poor fellow when he was at Aylsham – but I told them they ought not to mind what is said of people behind their backs, people *when* in trouble have always *their* enemies in abundance, who endeavour to catch up every thing they can to degrade them – You did not say what your Cause was about at Walsingham, I hope you *are* as success full in that, as the others. dont forget to let us know. The smelts you were so good as to send us, arrived in Charming order. Beautiful and very good. Your dear [fb] Father was at home and enjoyd *them* exceedingly. We drank your health, not forgetting dear Uncle and Aunt Adey – You were so very bountifull in your present that we sent our Neighbour Page²⁹⁰ (who loves good eating) a score of Smelts – which delighted and pleased so much that a couple of tame Rabbits came the next [day] to us – and very nice they were –

Your Father sent the Rent to Mr Sterry²⁹¹ and return'd a receipt with the Balance, so that is all right – I have examind every where for the papers you mention and can not find them, I forgot to ask Duff, perhaps you might leave them in his Rooms –

the Herberts²⁹² left in this day fortnight. Mary had a letter this morning, telling her they are going with some friends to Cheltenham and perhaps into Wales, I am glad of it poor girls, as they are far from happy. it will amuse them and do them good. As *to* poor little Geo²⁹³ I think you may never see her again, of course will never hear her <u>Shagg</u>. a letter is come to Edward from Mr H[erbert], a very good and kind one, feeling for their uncomfortable situation. and pitying them, at the same time saying he <u>must</u> have His daughters with him – <the> *his* West Indies affairs [fb] are in such a state not to be left, neither can he allow them any thing if they marry, he and his daughters can manage to live tolerably there, he cannot come over, and at present he hears of no prospect of Edwards supporting a wife. why will he not suffer his girls to go to him, for a year or two – it is cruel he says, to keep them from him – this is chiefly the purport of his letter. your Father read it, and says it is a sensible affectionate letter, and much to the purpose and

referred to in both his capacity as a shoemaker and as a carrier. This letter indicates that he had been defended from a legal charge by William.

290 Not identified, but also mentioned in Letter 177.

291 Sterrys & Tweed were attorneys based in Hornchurch Lane, Romford. (Pigot's *Directory* (1823), p. 63.)

292 Members of the family of Mary Ellis Herbert, the future wife of Edward.

293 Probably a sister of Mary Ellis Herbert named Georgiana (or Georgina); Mary and Edward's first daughter was named Georgiana.

advised Edward to part with them. but he said how that cannot be, so how it will end God only knows. all your Fathers dread is that if our poor boy was to get only 200 a year he wou'd marry directly, poor Geo will certainly go this Summer.

Your Father told me about this letter, I woud not have you or Aunt Adey notice it when you write, neither do not mention it to John if he shoud come into Norfolk this Summer which he talks of doing, it is better he shoud not know that Mr H wrote such a letter. We were in Town on Saturday. the girls walk'd out and met Mr H[enry] Anson[294] and General Walpole[295] who did not know dee [Elizabeth] she was so much grown – I hope Aunt Adey have receivd her plants from Barr[296] as your Father wrote to him some time agon [fb] John have got is right Coat but we cannot find *any* for you, but I hope you have all your own at Aylsham that you shoud have. When he went to Town last week and got into the Coach who shoud be there but Mr <Kant> Kent, he coud not stop with us, as he was in a hurry on business, he told John (I did not see him) that Mrs Taswell[297] and her 2 daughters were at Fullham staying with Mrs K[ent]. He praised them as being very clever young Women and that Caroline was a beautiful girl. I think sure they must be past being girls, they now live at Margate – we dine to morrow at Mr Newman's[298] to meet Mr and Mrs Gay and daughter, our

294 Revd Henry Anson (1773–1854); brother of Charles; fifth son of George Anson. In 1804 he was instituted to living of Oxnead with Buxton. (NRO, AYL 932/3.) He was also (amongst others) rector of Swanton Abbot, 1807–26; Skeyton, 1807–54; Lyng-cum-Whitwell, 1827–54. (CCEd Person ID: 4443.)

295 Probably General George Walpole (1758–1835), second surviving son of Horatio Walpole, first earl of Orford and Lady Rachel Cavendish. He had passed through the ranks of the Dragoons, rising to brevet colonel in 1796. In 1797, on his retirement from the army, he became M.P. for Derby (2 Jan. 1797 – 1806) and then Dungarvan (1806–1820). In 1803–4 he was major commandant of the Aylsham Infantry Volunteers. In 1806–7 he was briefly under-secretary of state for Foreign Affairs under Charles James Fox. (Hist. Parl.)

296 Thomas Barr was a prominent London nurseryman. In 1791 he founded his nursery at Balls Pond in Islington, on the west side of Newington Green Road; it gradually increased in size and by 1806 covered about 11 acres. In 1809 he was contracted by Repton to carry out his plans, including planting, at Haileybury, Great Amwell (Herts). (Repton in Herts, pp. 60–70.)

297 Perhaps the widow of the former Aylsham vicar Revd William Taswell (d. 9 June 1800), who had been appointed in 1777. He was buried in Oxnead church. (J. Sapwell, A History of Aylsham (Norwich, 1960) p. 95.) In 1788 Mr Taswell and his family were visited by Parson Woodforde. (Sapwell, History, p. 84.) Repton mentions Taswell in his memoirs. (Memoirs, p. 103.)

298 A resident of Hare Street or Romford. In his memoirs, Repton mentions 'my faithful servant Robin Newman'. (Memoirs, p. 68.)

old neighbours and friends in St Giles.[299] Miss G says she knows you, and have often wishd to be introduced to you. tell aunt Adey if you shoud meet any where to introduce you to her – she is not very young, she enquired for her friend John[300] whom she rememberd, I leave you to guess her age. She is good temperd and merry notwithstanding –

I have not left room to say God bless you, and to send my love to dear Uncle and Aunt who have my best love and wishes and prayers for a Continuance of health of your affectionate Mother M Repton.

I hope to hear soon that all is as well as when I heard last.

We are going to stay with Mrs Martineau[301] the week after next. tell dear Aunt Adey I will write to her before I go. I dout you will not be able to read this written in a great hurry. Your dear Father is quite well. turn it

Address: Wm Repton Esqr, Aylsham, Norfolk
B st: RUMFORD 125; Cross Post; *charge*: 8
Endorsed: 26 May 1808   Mrs Repton
HM 40934

46. Humphry Repton to William Repton; note by Mary (Clarke) Repton

Harestreet near Romford, July. 13. 1808

Dear William

I am sorry to find that your acc[oun]t with Sir Roger K[errison] is so much more than I expected – because from Martineau's[302] statement – (who has just left us) I fear there will be great deficiency – he says 6 hun[dre]d thou[san]d Pounds Debt to be paid by sale of 13 Thou[san]d *p[er] Ann[um]* in Land.[303] Suppose it to sell at 35 y[ea]rs purchase

---

299 i.e. St Giles in Norwich, where the Reptons lived when first married and John Adey Repton was baptised.

300 The following sentences have been written in any available space; hence the instruction at the end 'turn it'.

301 The wife of Philip Martineau esquire. (See following note.)

302 Philip Martineau (1752–1829), a distinguished surgeon, son of David Martineau (1726–1768), Norwich surgeon. His seat was at Dulwich Hill (Surrey). A drawing of Dulwich Hill by Repton was reproduced in the *Polite Repository* (1805). (Carter et al., *Repton*, p. 143; Daniels, *Repton*, p. 267.) Martineau also owned Carrow Abbey and Bracondale Lodge, Norwich; the Red Book for the latter, *c.*1792, is held at NHC. (Daniels, *Repton*, p. 263; Carter et al., *Repton*, p. 158.) See also *Repton in Norfolk*, pp. 81–92.

303 The bank of Kerrison & Sons, Norwich, 'failed in 1808 on the death of Sir Roger Kerrison, apparently with debts of £460,000. The business was then taken over by Harvey & Hudsons (est. 1792) of Norwich'. (*British Banking*, p. 302.) Repton's calculations here confirm the extent of Kerrison's debts.

$$13,000$$
$$\underline{35}$$
$$65,000$$
$$\underline{39}$$
$$\overline{455,000}$$

or suppose at 30 y[ea]rs it woud be 390,000. in short I fear there will not be more that 10% in the £. Then comes the question you ask – how is it best to state your debt – & this involves unpleasant [*fb*] suppositions & such as my poor Sister will not like to see mentiond – viz –

If you are a partner – J Adey's 500 is set off ag[ains]t Your thous[an]d & leaves balance 500 – of which you get 250 & you lose 250, & no immediate call on J Adey –

If you are not a partner – J Adey will be call'd on immediately for his 500 – & you get 500 & lose 500[304]

But if an event were to take place which I suppose my sister must be in some degree hourly prepared for – & in that case the first 500 – wou'd only be paid in part if at all – then you are better off as separate from the joint concern – & from the little I know of dear J A's affairs – I cannot tell what other consequences might arise – from declaring a partnership – or not – on that much will depend as well as on the prospect of Sr Roger's debt being paid [*fb*] & you must put it every wa[y], thus suppose –

The effects pay 5% in the pound	Your 1000	loses	750
	Your 500	loses	375
if 10%	Your 1000	loses	500
	Your 500	loses	250
if 15%	Your 1000	loses	250
	Your 500	loses	125
if 20%	Your 1000	loses	0
	& Your 500	loses	0

in all the first cases you have 500 to pay –
in the latter – only to wait for your dividend.
& therefore on the whole perhaps you had better do as you propose & make J A's 500 a Sett off –

---

304 Both of these reckonings are set out with 'you get' above '& you lose'.

So little can we foresee future events that I begin to doubt if we ever act right by taking great pains to do so – & chance, or in other words providence, acts for us while we give ourselves credit for being very Clever, & then We wonder how matters turn out – there is one consideration which *we* shou'd never lose sight of – & which I have ever felt in my own concerns – that by steady confidence in the great Disposer of events – he makes all things work [*fb*] together for good – to those who love him,[305] & every days experience proves that wealth is not always the means – or end, of good – May he direct you

Believe me ever Yours Most Fondly HR

John came home on Sunday and confirmd my fears that dear Mr Adey was not quite so well, as my sister did not write to me.[306] But tell her with my kindest love to dear Dee, that I do beg and hope she will not keep any change *from me* dear Mr Adey may have, as her silence will give me great pain and I shall imagine the worst – I am quite happy to hear Mrs Brett is with her, as I know her to be a most charming good Woman. She is I am certain a very great comfort to her and I hope she will continue with you. God bless you all.

Address: To Wm Repton Esq, Aylsham, Norfolk
B st: RUMFORD 12; Cross Post; *charge*: 8
Endorsed: 13 July 1808   My father about the Concern in Kerrison's Bankr[upt]cy
HM 40852

47. Humphry Repton to Dorothy Adey

Harleston Park, Northamptonshire,[307]   August 24 1808

My Dearest Dee

I promised Mary[308] that I wou'd write in the Course of my journey – because she says you love to see my hand writing – but after writing to her

---

305 Romans ch. 8, v. 28, 'And we know that all things work together for good to them that love God, to them who are called according to his purpose'. (Authorised Version.)
306 This note from Mary (Clarke) Repton has been written upside down at the bottom of Repton's letter.
307 Harlestone Park was the home of Robert Andrew (1770–1831). Repton and his son John visited there in 1808, 1809, 1810 and 1811. (information from Stephen Radley, University of Nottingham) This letter must have been written on their first visit. The work at Harlestone is mentioned in Fragment VII, 'On Unity of Character'. (*Fragments*, pp. 21–2, and illustration.)
308 Repton's wife.

& she, I know, decants my letters into hers – You can have nothing from me but the Lees. Yet I will drain my subject to the last drop to tell you, that I have no greater pleasure than in thinking & writing of you & Aylsham

How often did I think of old times yesterday when in my way hither from Oxford I came 5 miles out of my way to see Dayrell at Lamport[309] – [*fb*] I found him with his spud stick & shooting jacket leaning on a gate – & looking like John at Oxnead quite as fat & as farmer like – I was there 2 hours before dinner & had a most cordial welcome to a very fair family dinner – with Bro' Martin's[310] mother[311] & his sister[312] as like Martin as two shrivelld peas & two of her children – & a niece a Miss Iforget We were waited on by a Mulatto girl with woolly hair – Johanna – & I got a very good dinner with a good glass of Madeira – but I cou'd not help feeling that the times were felt here as they are every where else – there was no elegance no excess of good – but it was good – & we talk'd over old stories & lived the old days over again. Our dear John Adey wou'd have liked to have joined us [*fb*]

I suppose you know that poor Stafford Baxter has been jilted by his fat frowzy friend Miss B, who is wedded to Sir –– Graves[313] – & is now Lady Graves to the great disapointment of the ambitious Stafford who expected by this time to have <u>quadrain</u> circled the fair Charmer in his arms –

N.B. It would take four pair of arms like Staffords to have reach'd round this fair volume of flesh –

I suppose Mary has told you all about Windham. he is a most incomprehensible being – & knows not what he wants – but perhaps I may meet him this Autumn – if I have much to do – & money to spare – it is not impossible but we may all come (I mean the women &c) & <u>live with you</u> if I knew how to do it without <u>living upon you</u> – [*fb*] This will call up a tear,

---

309 John Dayrell of Lamport Manor House, near Stowe (Bucks). (Daniels, *Repton*, p. 256.) In his memoirs, when writing about the 1790s, Repton mentions Edward Dayrel, a barrister 'who had a small estate adjoining Stowe', perhaps John's predecessor. (*Memoirs*, p. 58.) Contributors to *Humphry Repton in Bucks* concluded that there was no Repton connection with Lamport, citing *Memoirs* as the only evidence. However, this letter indicates that Repton had been to Lamport in the past and was on friendly terms with the family there.

310 John Dayrell Martin (q.v.)

311 Martin's mother was Elizabeth Dayrell, who married John Martin in Barbados on 3 April 1753.

312 In his will, written on 26 August 1814, Martin made bequests to two unmarried sisters – Frances and Sarah Arabella. (TNA, PROB 11/1560/226, proved 8 Sept. 1814.) His sister Elizabeth was married to Revd John Wood of Barbados.

313 On 21 July 1808 at Bath, Vice-Admiral Sir Thomas Graves KB (1747–1814) married Susanna Blacknall of Parham (Suffolk). (*Gentleman's Magazine*, vol. 78, part 2 (1808), p. 747.)

as it brings one to my Eye but it is all my Eye[314] – & the hard times will make us feel for others what we feel for ourselves. –

I sometimes hope the prospect brightens, but it is too late for me to hope much – & too soon to fear much

Thus a little of the old Mans Morality will damp the joys of declining life & my only comfort is – that I have enjoyd Life – that I do enjoy it – & why shou'd I not continue to enjoy it so long as I can say I Love You all, including J.A. & WR – HR

Address: To Mrs Adey, Aylsham, Norfolk
B st: NORTHAMPTON [illeg] Aug 25 1808; *charge*: 8
Endorsed: 24 Aug 1808   My father from Northamptonshire   Spent a day with Dayrell at Lamport   Staff Baxter's love
HM 40834

48. Humphry Repton to Dorothy Adey; note by Elizabeth Repton

Harestreet, Monday 5. September 1808

Dearest Dee

We are all returned from London where we have been to hear Dear Edwards first *Boyles* Lecture at Bow Church[315] – the Congregation very thin – but all went off quite well

I write to night to say that Mary wishes you to engage the boy mentiond – but not to send him till You hear again from her – & to make due enquiries concerning his Character, <u>Temper</u> Sobriety, honesty, <u>activity</u> &c &c – Our Charles Neale's is not a good temper – & very Lazy – so we are not sorry he is going – Duff has written to take his place p[er] mail on Friday night & hopes to reach Aylsham on Saturday – so far he is decided [*fb*] I have fifty things to say, but shall be too late for the Post if I say more than Mary's Love & thanks for Partridges which I reach'd home in time to finish – God bless dear JA & Wm

&, believe me, ever most affectionately yours HR

314 'All my eye and Betty Martin' meant 'stuff and nonsense'. (*OED*)
315 In a codicil to his will, dated 28 July 1691, the scientist Robert Boyle, left £50 per year to be an annual salary for 'some learned Divine or preaching Minister from time to time to be elected and resident within the City of London or Circuit of the Bills of Mortality, who shall be enjoined to perform the Offices following; viz. to preach Eight Sermons in the year, for proving the Christian Religion against notorious Infidels …'. Edward Repton was so appointed in 1808. His first Boyle's lecture was published and includes a copy of the codicil mentioned above. (Further details in Edward's biography in the Introduction.)

You forgot my Parcel by Betty, if W. can spare it I should not mind the expense of haveing it sent by a coach. DR[316]

Address: To Mrs Adey, Aylsham, Norfolk
B st: Rumford 1101; Cross Post: *charge*: 8
Endorsed: 5ᵗʰ Sept 1808   My father   Has heard Edwd preach his 1ˢᵗ
Boyle's Lecture   Duff is coming
HM 40835

49. William Repton to Edward Repton (draft)

[?Aylsham, September 1808]

My dearest Edward

It is impossible to read the correspondence which has passed between My father & Mr Herbert without perceiving what you in any other situation would yourself perceive, that <you are let> the whole business <of> has latterly *borne the appearance of* <becom> a preconcerted plan to urge you & Miss Herbert to a step which <must lead to your utter ruin as to> *her father imagines will* relieve <the father> *him* from the expence of supporting his dau[ghte]r but w[hi]ch must inevitably lead to your ruin. Do my dear fellow look at the plain state of the fact & you must I am sure see that if Mr Herbert can allow his dau[ghte]r £100 a year when your wife he can allow her the same if she continues in England – without marrying *or at least he can in that situation allow her £50 per annum* & how often has Mary Herbert said that she would make that sum do, if she were to be permitted to continue here – but it is *as* obvious <that> [*fb*] to dear Mary[317] <*as well as myself*> <wh> with whom I have *had* much serious conversation upon the subject *as it is to me* that Herbert can never <more pay the £100> make the payment of the £100 secure to you. & then consider Edward, for God's sake, in what a situation you are placed, <with constant calls> *deprived* <[*illeg*] you> <*and deprived*> of all those comforts *& of that station in Society* which you as a Gentl[eman] & as a Repton have *all your life* been accustomed with<out> constant claims upon you which you <will> can have no means of satisfying – <&> what is *perhaps* worse than all – I <mus> cannot help telling you that our father has more than once <sh> said "I feel William that if Edward does this, he will become an alien to me for ever <notwithstanding> I have already lost his confidence & he

---

316 This note was added by Elizabeth.
317 i.e. their sister Mary.

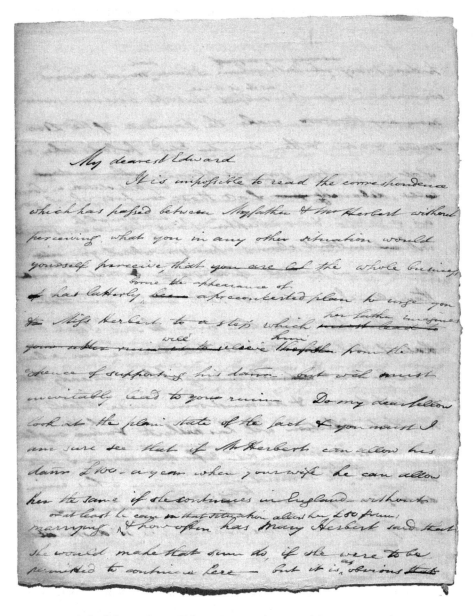

5. A draft letter from William Repton showing deletions, HM 40939

must soon cease to feel for me that affection w[hi]ch has hitherto & *which* <when> ought ever to subsist between us *and* <& for that reason> I will <[*illeg*]> never <*therefore*> be so much an accessory to his union as to give any consent *to his mar[ria]ge* while the <prospect is so gloomy> chance of his happiness is so desperate".

[*fb*] In short, my dear Edward never be so much you own enemy – so much the enemy of him for whom you feel an affection as to <consent> acquiesce in a plan which I am convinced has been formed by <her> Mr Herbert for his own purposes – <do not> exert your own good sense & do not suffer yourself to become the dupe of Miss Herbert's relations for that she is <*her* [*illeg*]> free from deception <as you are> I believe as firmly as I do that you are yourself void of reproach – & consider that <if> even if he should secure *to* you the payment of the amount he promised<s over> by the strongest personal ties in the world, could you distress your wife's father & without doing so *I am convinced* you can never get paid. I have turned the matter over in every possibl<y>e way, & have hastily written these my sentiments upon the subject, not as John Repton sometimes gives *unseasonable* advice, but activated by the strongest possible feelings of affection *towards* <for> you <& I trust my dear> *for* <and> be assured my dear fellow that in all <st > situations I must ever be

Your truly affectionate brother

[*fb*] Lest Herbert sho'd not shew you the letter which my father has written him, I send you a copy of it.[318]

Endorsed: Sept' 1808   Letter to my brother Edwd to dissuade him from marrying
HM 40939

50. Humphry Repton junior to William Repton

202 Piccadilly, 13th October 1808

My dear William

I have some doubts to whom it will be best to address this letter – but upon the whole it will be best perhaps to write to you –

I saw Edward on Tuesday & shewed him Mr Herbert's very sensible letter to my father – which I am sorry to say did not by any means produce its proper effect upon his mind – He had been spending the preceeding

---

318 Not found.

day at Hornsey & George persuaded him with some difficulty to go on Tuesday evening to a ball near Crayford, where they were received with the most marked attention by the whole neighbourhood – [*fb*] yesterday they returned to dinner at my lodgings & we passed the whole evening together which enables me to tell you exactly the state of affairs – which indeed it is absolutely necessary for you to know – Herberts daughters are at Hornsey – while he is in London – & Edward at Crayford – & Herbert desires very properly that they will not see each other to prevent his daughters acquiring the firmness necessary to enable her to leave England – Edward has unfortunately collected from her & her foolish Aunt Stone a thousand ridiculous stories about the depraved state of society in <the> Montserrat where they tell him Herberts estate is entirely peopled with his own natural children of all countries & of all colours with whom it would be death for Mary Herbert to associate – this is one of the ordinary subjects which they discuss together & she tells him that her father says she must shut both her eyes & her ears when she arrives [*fb*] at Montserrat – Another anecdote which has no small effect – is that though Herbert was even more fond of his wife than of his daughter – yet as soon as he got her to the West Indies he broke her heart by his fretful disposition & unkind treatment <u>as he will very soon do [to] his daughters</u>. these kind of stories & surmises absurd as they are joined to various other <stor> circumstances have I am sorry to find given Edward a rooted aversion to Herbert & a most contemptible opinion of all his motives & principles – which is very apparent whenever he mentions his name – on *my* pressing him to consider <u>all</u> the consequences of the step he is meditating – which you may be sure I pointed out in very strong terms & pressing him to accustom himself by degrees to meet the alternative which <u>must</u> be presented to him in a few weeks – he said that his only object was under all the circumstances of the case to prevent her from going to Montserrat from a conviction that if ever they met again (which he firmly believed it was her fathers object to prevent) he should find her degraded & debased by having lived in improper society for which the delicacy of her mind &c &c – was but ill calculated – but that if Mr Herbert was firm & there was no other means to prevent her going – he was prepared to prevent it by marrying her, even if he descended a step in society [*fb*] by adding a few pupils to the emoluments of his curacy – he says Mr Ellis who has a great regard for him, wishes him to marry[319] – & offers to give £4,000 for the Advowson of a living of £600 *per ann*[*um*] which Edward may *hold* 7 years for one of his sons – paying him £200 as Interest! – Edward had

---

319 Mr Ellis was Mary Herbert's uncle. (See Letter 111.)

promised to see Herbert[*sic*; *recte* Ellis] today but we easily convinced him
that it was dishonourable to do so <agai> unknown to her father & against
his commands – so he is gone to Crayford where George & I purpose
spending Saturday & Sunday with him to consider what more is to be done
– thus I have shewn you exactly the state of the disease that my father may
be enabled to consider the remedy – the harsh parts of his letter had not a
good effect. Lord Sidmouth has written to dissuade him from playing the
fool, perhaps if my father could get him to renew the subject it might have
a good effect as he has greater weight with Edward than any body

I have hardly room for the kind remembrances I must ever feel for all
the dear friends at Aylsham – amongst whom I beg my friend Anna[320] may
not be forgotten for <she> both she & all of you are ever remembered by
your   H Repton

N.B. George says Lord Sidmouth objected to Edward having published
his sermon[321] against which he stated many arguments. I mention this that
my father may not commit himself –

Address: William Repton Esqr, Aylsham
B st: C OC 14 808
Endorsed: 13 Octo'r 1808   Hy Repton Esq. Junr   As to Edward's
attach[men]t to Miss Herbert
HM 40925/1

51. Edward Repton to Humphry Repton

Roberson's Hotel, October 27 1808

My dear Father

I have just left Humphry and George, with whom I have been dining
in Piccadilly, and their conversation has added torture to the distress I
already feel. You do not do justice to your Edward's affection and mind,
my dear Father, if you do not believe that his conduct is attended with the
most unfeigned anguish to himself – but placed as I am, how am I to act
– and how to reconcile my own feelings and my Ideas of honour, and my
apprehensions of greater misery [*fb*] with my duty to my Father, and my
Love for my family – Mr Herbert <u>positively</u> tells me, he will <u>never</u> leave his
Daughter in England, under any other protection, than that of a Husband
– and that if he takes her away it will <u>be for ever</u> – This is his final resolve

---

320 Not identified. Duff also mentions this Anna who lived at Aylsham in Letter 55.
321 See Letter 48.

– to argue therefore upon any compromise is useless – what ever therefore his <u>motives</u> may be, it is of little use to consider – The consequences affect not <u>him</u> – but his Daughter – her Happiness, he says, is <u>his</u> first object – and her <u>comparative</u> happiness (for under the present circumstances it can only be so) is <u>my</u> first object – you cannot be surprized therefore at my preferring <*illeg*> the future prospect of misery which may never happen – to the present certainty of it, by following your wishes – A long and uninterrupted attach[fb]ment of six years is not to be given up at a minute's warning – and to be suddenly done away from Prudential motives which it is possible to obviate – and while I have health and abilities, they shall be exerted to support the Woman I love, and to prevent her from falling a sacrifice to misjudged pride – Do not my dear Father imagine that I am led away with false notions of happiness, believe me, I feel most severely the distress I am reduced to, which is most seriously increased by your forbidding Letters – I look but for little happiness – and with your displeasure, or the thoughts of giving you pain – my own apprehensions are greatly aggravated – and altho' I am too well assured of your paternal Love to believe that you could long be at enmity with any of your Sons; yet to me it would be the most distressing sight, to witness the effects of my conduct upon your mind, such as Humphry and George have des[fb]cribed to me – George tells me that William has added his fears, and his brotherly advice upon this most awful and I may fairly say most important event of my life, but I have not yet seen his letter[322] – I accept however his sentiments as a most affectionate mark of his Love – because I am persuaded – that neither he or any of my friends can have any other interest than my happiness: – but I understand he considers Mr Herbert's conduct in the most unfavourable light – and which I who have seen more of him than he can have done <I> am fully persuaded, there are no just grounds for – It is true his Pride has been roused by your Letters, and with reason, and he is determined on <u>no account whatever</u>, to depart from his resolution – he says, "had I consulted my head, rather than my heart [fb] I might have been led to follow up my first sentiments, and to agree with your Father, but foreseeing the fatal consequences to Mary's Happiness, I have preferred her Welfare, to any personal considerations" – and altho' I am fully aware that the case is widely different between a Father who is to seek protection for a Daughter, and a Father who looks to the encreasing difficulties of a Son – yet I should be ashamed of myself, were I to leave that Daughter in such circumstances, from want of exertion on my part – With my Ideas and with the habits in which I have been educated,

322 See Letter 49.

you cannot but suppose that I look upon the plan of making my time subservient to others, as most irksome, and most unwished for – but with the circumstances I have mentioned how <would> am I to act – and what [fb] advice can you, as a fond Father, consulting the happiness of your son, give? – Am I to give up the hopes I have been cherishing for 6 years – and destroy the peace of mind of a Woman who has sacrificed every thing to me, and to whom my heart is bound by the strongest ties – or am I, and ought I to sacrifice a portion of my own ease, and perhaps, respectability – by adopting that plan which can alone prevent our separation, tho' perhaps it may be attended with mutual inconvenience and dislike? – Place yourself, my dear Father, in my situation, and you will find that I am pursuing a conduct, by no means enviable – Could I have expected from you that assistance, which (altho' you write to the contrary) I [fb] am persuaded you would most readily have given – we could have lived for a year or two, (with economy) in comfort; and after a few years I have reason to expect that advancement, which my own exertions and your influence give me every encouragement to hope for – and which my Mary's friends are inclined to forward by Purchase, should our endeavours prove unsuccessful. but knowing, as I do your difficulties this I cannot expect – but for God's sake, don't withdraw from us your affection and your influence – but by your kindness, relieve the distresses we must inevitably feel, at the thought of acting contrary to your will – and add not the grievous reflection of having augmented your sufferings to the already too much afflicted [fb] Brow of your ever affectionate Son Edward Repton –

Mr H. sails the 10th of November – you may imagine therefore my anxiety to see you – and to solicit your sanction to my conduct which must very shortly be decided.

I shall be at Blake Hall Wanstead[323] on Monday, where I shall hope to learn the day of your return – – Give my affectionate Love to my dear Mother [and] sisters.

Address: H. Repton Esqr, at J Adey's Esqr, Aylsham, Norfolk
B st: [*illeg*] OC 28 808
Endorsed: 27 Octo'r 1808   The Revd Ed. Repton to my father   As to his Attachme[n]t to Miss Herbert
HM 40907

---

323   Bleak (later Blake) Hall, a large house at the west end of South Lane, Wanstead, was built *c*.1690, and evidently much extended later; it was demolished in 1909. ('Wanstead', *VCH Essex*, vol. 6, p. 319.)

52. Humphry Repton junior to William Repton

Adelphi, 29ᵗʰ October 1808

My dear William

I return with many thanks £10 – N° 6,590 which I will thank you to say you <ha> receive safe –

Edward has been at Laytonstone during the last week & will not therefore receive your letter till to day when I am to meet him at Crayford – I fear all our representations are of no avail as he has determined to marry without even my fathers consent or that of Mr Herbert – so what is to be done God only knows –

[*fb*] Mr Claude Scott has just written me a very handsome letter offering to renew my admission to Drury Lane Theatre³²⁴ – I will be very much obliged to you to take some trouble in <who> procuring him all the particulars of Sr R Kerrison's estates – perhaps they are to be had in London – if so tell me how that I may send them to him – & if not put them into a cover directed to Me – which enclose in another directed to <u>Francis Percival Eliot Esqr</u> – & that in a third addressed to the Commissioners of Audit Somerset Place – sealing each of them. This is you will say somewhat in the Lukin style – ³²⁵

[*fb*] I have this moment received my fathers letter which alters my plans & makes it necessary for me to see George immediately so if I have no time to say more I shall conclude here with every good wish to all my dear friends around you

Ever yours H Repton

Address: William Repton Esq, Aylsham
Endorsed: 29 Octo'r 1808   My Brother Hump'y   Edward will marry³²⁶
Claude Scott's civility
HM 40925/2

---

324 See Letter 9 for the beginning of this gift from Claude Scott.
325 Lionel Lukin (1742–1834) was a lifeboat designer and was related to the Robert Lukin, first husband of William Windham's mother Sarah née Hicks. Among Lukin's many inventions was an 'unsubmergible' boat. (*ODNB*) Presumably Duff means that the papers would be sent safely and securely.
326 He did indeed marry, less than a month later, on 22 November. The marriage of the Revd Edward Repton to Mary Ellis Herbert at Leyton (Essex) was reported in the *Gentleman's Magazine*, November 1808, p. 1039.

53. Humphry Repton junior to William Repton

Harestreet, 27ᵗʰ November 1808

My dear William

Instead of enlivening the Aylsham fireside with a long prosing letter, I intend to give you the trouble of reading a little poetry – which is however most unfortunately unpoetical inasmuch as it is founded upon fact – & not upon fiction. first comes the <u>Motto</u> –
"*Quid dignum tanto feret hic promissor hiatu?*"
"*Turpiter obticuit sublato jure nocendi.*"
"*Quanto rectius hic qui nil molitur inepte*"![327]

Miss Walter[328] will translate this for you – & when she does, & will give me her permission it shall be published with her translation in vellum & gold & prefaced by a long dedication setting forth <u>at length</u> her numerous amiabilities & transmitting her talents to the latest posterity – I wait with the utmost impatience for her answer! – "He may wait long enough"! – Now William I appeal to you whether this is not very unpoetical "Certainly"! On the contrary is [*fb*] is not this very poetical? –

Seven˟ doughty Knights to Stafford town
   The Shrieve by requisition led,
Insisting that to keep his word
   Our King should be petitioned.[329]

˟ "doughty in Staffordshire" "not Doughty in Norfolk"

---

327 The Latin translates thus: 'What could he bring forth great enough to match such an opening promise?'; 'He was shamefully silent when he lost the power to injure'; 'How much better this man is, who doesn't exert himself inappropriately?'. The first and third lines are from Horace, *Ars poetica*, lines 138, 140. http://www.thelatinlibrary.com/horace/arspoet.shtml.

328 Perhaps 'Anna' referred to in Letter 49.

329 This poem relates to a political incident in Stafford in early November 1808, as William noted in the endorsement, it was known as the 'Staffordshire County Meeting'. The meeting is mentioned in various issues of *The Staffordshire Advertiser*; one of the correspondents in the newspaper was Thomas Anson. He had been M.P. for Lichfield from 1789 until 17 February 1806, when he was elevated to the peerage as Viscount Anson. (*Hist. Parl.*) He was well-known to the Reptons. His property Oxnead Hall was depicted in the *Polite Repository* (1807). (Carter et al., *Repton*, p. 144.) It seems likely that Duff acquired the poem through connections in London: it was not printed in the *Advertiser* until 3 December 1808, nearly a week after this letter was written. There are some very slight differences in the two versions of the text. (See Duff's biography in the Introduction.)

S[t] Vincent[330] (of Shelburnian school[331]
    & principles political
With axioms Machiavelian, and
    Orations jesuitical)

Uprose, & said "a crowd shall follow
    "Me who lately dreaded one"
"& in <u>smooth accents</u> force our King
    "To do – what he's already done.

"Our laws, our rights, our liberties
    "By Ministers confounded are,
"Oppress'd at home, despis'd abroad,
    "Our grievances unbounded are!

"That Yeoman, Burgess, Knight & Squire
    "Are driven from society
"By taxes upon taxes heap'd
    "Has too great notoriety!

"This I maintain'd in Essex, to
    "The rich well fed freeholders there,
"Adding that these Ministers
    "Would flagellate their shoulders bare"

"My speech design'd for Essex calves
    "Arous'd John Bull with heel & horn
"To drive me, with my harangue in halves
    "Far from the land of veal & corn!

"Come on then! Men of Staffordshire!
    "Men of approved ability!
"Join hand & heart, & storm the Throne
    "With <u>insolent humility</u>!

He said! but while of heart & hand
    His Lordship was palavering,
His valiant friends withdrew their hands
    Because their hearts were wavering!

---

330 John Jervis, earl of St Vincent (1735–1823), naval officer. (*ODNB*) He was one of the
signatories to the original notice printed in the *Staffordshire Advertiser* on 29 October 1808.
331 William Petty, second earl of Shelburne (1737–1805), Prime Minister 1782–83; a
reformer and supporter of Pitt.

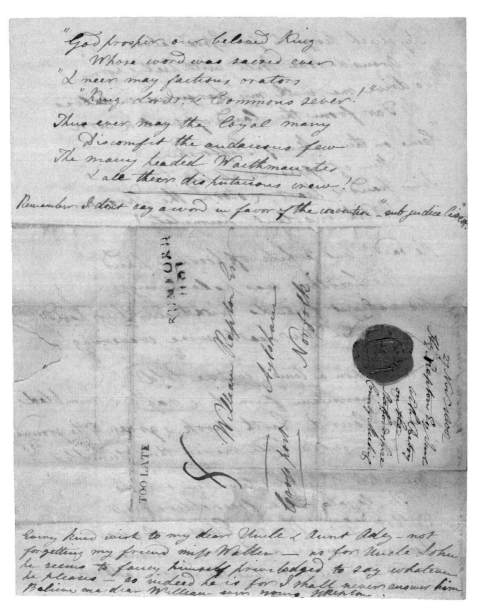

"God prosper our beloved King
"Whose word was sacred ever
"& neer may factious orators
"King, Lords, & Commons sever! ¹
Thus ever may the loyal many
Discomfit the audacious few
The many headed Watchmaurites
& all their disputacious crew!

Remember I don't say a word in favor of the convention — sub judice lis est.

RUMBOROH
1795

TOO LATE

J. William Repton Esq.
Aylesham
Cropston
Norfolk

Every kind wish to my dear Uncle & Aunt Adey — not
forgetting my friend miss Walker — as for Uncle John
he seems to fancy himself privileledged to say whatever
he pleases — as indeed he is for I shall never answer him
Believe me dear William ever yours HReptson

6. Final page of a letter from Humphry Repton junior, HM 40925/3

\# So, once upon a time, we're told
  A mountain fum'd & rag'd & rumbled,
Heav'n lour'd, Earth shook, & groan'd the ground
  Till – out a little mouse there tumbled

\# *Parturiunt montes, nascitum riduculus mus*[332]

Meanwhile to Stafford town in crowds
  The loyal, brave freeholders press
Talbot,[333] Grey,[334] Bagot,[335] Eliot,[336] Gower,[337]
  Vernon,[338] & many a thousand more,
Who, faithful, thus the Throne address

[*fb*] "God prosper our beloved King
  "Whose word was sacred ever
"& ne'er may factious orators
  "King, Lords, & Commons sever!"

Thus ever may the loyal many
  Discomfit the audacious few
The many headed <u>Waithman</u> ites[339]
  & all their disputatious crew!

---

332 'The mountains are in labour, a ridiculous mouse will be born.' Said of works that promise much at the outset but yield little in the end. (Horace, *Ars poetica*, line 139.)

333 Probably Charles Talbot, 15th earl of Shrewsbury, (1753–1827); one of his properties was Alton Castle (Staffs).

334 George Harry Grey, Lord Grey (1765–1845), of Enville Hall (Staffs). (*Hist. Parl.*)

335 Hon. Charles Bagot (1781–1843), of Hanover Square (Middx). He was a captain in the Uttoxeter yeomanry 1803–7. (*Hist. Parl.*)

336 Not identified.

337 George Granville Leveson Gower (1758–1833), of Trentham; known as the marquess of Stafford from 1803 to 1833; M.P. for Newcastle-under-Lyme 1779–1784 and for Staffordshire 1787–1799, then elevated to the peerage. (*Hist. Parl.*)

338 George Granville Venables Vernon (1785–1861), M.P. for Lichfield 1806–1831. (*Hist. Parl.*)

339 Supporters, or people who approved of the views and actions of Robert Waithman (*c.*1764–1833), who did not become an M.P. until 1818, but was a London livery man and well-known radical. In March 1808 'he led the common council campaign against sinecures and for government economy, and in October he presented a City petition to the King for an inquiry into the Convention of Cintra'. (*Hist. Parl.*)

Remember I dont say a word in favor of the convention[340] – "*sub judice lis est*"[341]

Every kind word to my dear Uncle & Aunt Adey – not forgetting my friend Miss Walter – as for Uncle John he seems to fancy himself priviledged to say whatever he pleases – so indeed he is for I shall never answer him.

Believe me dear William ever yours H Repton

You sent me Sr W [*recte* S] Romillys opinion[342] – but no letter – what ought I to do in the business – or shou'd I call on him – Bannister is paid for[343]

Address: William Repton Esqr, Aylsham, Norfolk
B st: RUMFORD 12; *stamped* TOO LATE; Cross Post; *charge*: 8
Endorsed: 27 Nov 1808   Hy Repton Esq. Jun'r   With Poetry on the Staffordshire County Meeting
HM 40925/3

54. Humphry Repton to William Repton

Kidbrook,[344] 5 December 1808

Dear William

Before I go to bed – I will tell you that the Speaker[345] desires me to look out for a purchase for Lord Nelson.[346] it must be in a Maritime County & ought to have a house on it fit for a Nobleman to be call'd Trafalgar

---

340 The meeting had been called to express opposition to 'the late Convention, concluded by the Officers commanding his Majesty's Forces in Portugal'. (*Staffs Advertiser*, 5 November 1808.) This was the Convention of Cintra, allowing the defeated French forces to leave Portugal.

341 'The case is before the court.'

342 This postscript has been written at the top of the first page. Humphry is probably referring to the ongoing court case concerning the Wallingers. (See Letter 5.)

343 The postscript is followed by a small drawing of a pair of breeches: Bannister was a London tailor patronised by the family. (See Letter 22.)

344 Kidbrooke Park, East Grinstead (Sussex); the home of Charles Abbott, first baron Colchester. Repton's first consultation there was in about 1803. (Daniels, *Repton*, p. 268.) Marcus Batty has provided a detailed discussion of Reptons's visits and proposals. Abbott's accounts record that £10 18s 6d was paid to Repton on 12 December 1808 'in summary of annual expenditure for 1808'. (*Repton in Sussex*, pp. 66–76, p. 67.)

345 Charles Abbott.

346 Following the Battle of Trafalgar, Parliament voted an annual pension of £5,000 for the new Nelson peerage settled on Horatio Nelson's brother and £90,000 for the purchase of a country seat. (Daniels, 'Cankerous blossom', p. 150.) Repton later suggested Sheringham.

– but if no such house exists *& an addition might make it such* – he thinks Parl[iamen]t wou'd grant a sum to be Laid out *by me* in adding or building – if it appear'd in other Respects desireable – Now I wish [fb] You to furnish me with such particulars of Kerrison's[347] or any other Norfolk Estate as you think wou'd come within the Compass to which the Commiss[ione]rs are limited, viz £90,000, & I have bespoke that you shall be the agent or steward. Therefore send me such statement as soon as you can – I have no time to say more now as I am very sleepy – but woud not trust to having time tomorrow morning.

My Love to D & JA & God bless you, HR

[fb] The Speaker says they wou'd prefer some elevated spot – where a Tower or flag might be seen from a distance & the[sic; that] if within View of the Sea the better – so look out sharp & write to me soon –

John is here & we go home today

Endorsed: 5 Dec 1808   My father from the Speaker's   Wishes to find an Est[at]e for Lord Nelson
HM 40853

55. Humphry Repton junior to William Repton

Adelphi, 15th December 1808

Dear William

My friend Mr Arthur Anstey[348] has desired me to write to you on the following subject –

A Gentleman (a perfect stranger to him) <M> Francis Noble Esqr of Cringleford has applied to hire his brothers house near Cambridge with 300 acres of land[349] – & Mr Anstey naturally wishes to be informed of "his substance & capacity to pay the rent" – of which he thinks you may be [fb] able to procure him some intelligence – If you can – pray write to me immediately as Mr Noble is actually in treaty for the place – He lived some time ago at or near Newmarket –

---

347 Kerrison's estate was west of Sustead. (Daniels, *Repton*, p. 91.)

348 Arthur Anstey, conveyancer, of 22 Lincoln's Inn and 78 Guildford Street, London (1805).

349 In 1805 Christopher Anstey (*c*.1757–1827) inherited from his father, also Christopher, Anstey Hall, Trumpington, just outside Cambridge. The Ansteys did not live at Anstey Hall after the 1770s but regularly let it with 85 acres. Known tenants are Nathaniel Wedd 1790s–*c*.1805 and John Hemington 1814–36; it was probably vacant in 1808. (*VCH Cambridgeshire*, vol. 8, p. 255.) See also *Alumni Cantab*.

I have written to James Marsh on this subject – & have also spoken to the Bishop of Cringleford[350] – but as the latter does not reside in his diocese he knows no such man – tho' he thinks it very probable that he may have lately taken a Mrs Somebody's house [*fb*] there – A letter would reach Mr Anstey at the Post Office Cambridge next Sunday – & if you have time it would be gratifying to him to hear from you as Mr Noble is to meet him there – If not write to me –

My best wishes always attend my dear Uncle & Aunt Adey & my friend Anna – if she will accept them

Ever yours, in haste, H. Repton

Address: William Repton Esqr, Aylsham
B st: C DE 15 808
Endorsed: 15 Dec'r 1808   My Brother Humphry   As to a Mr Noble of Cringleford who has applied for an Est[at]e of Mr Ansty's at Cambridge
HM 40925/4

56. Edward Repton to William Repton

Crayford, December 20th 1808[351]

My dear William

A most handsome reproof for my neglect – Your letter was the precursor of two fine Birds – which have found their way here – without the necessary directions that John R[352] requires for the Turkey's flight – which he promises to send provided I will inform him <u>how</u> it is to be sent but I suppose the Coach-men and Porters are better informed on that head that[*sic*] I am – so to them I shall leave it – besides there is a sort of delicacy in having <u>turkeys</u> from Oxnead – for fear of the consequent charge of undervaluing such Donations [*fb*] but however I don't wish to entertain you with Oxnead occurrences – how it could have entered my good Uncle's head, however, (or 2^d whether it ever did really do so) that I should run down fast to Oxnead to spend the Wedding night[353] – I am at a loss to understand. I cannot think he did in truth expect us – but

---

350 Perhaps a sarcastic reference to Joseph Brett, curate of Cringleford from 15/01/1805 to 13/04/1835. (CCEd Person ID: 111641.) According to Letter 57 he had been accused of neglect of his duties.
351 Date altered from 19th to 20th 1808.
352 i.e. Uncle John.
353 22 November.

certainly I never had such an intention, or such a thought – I must speak more tenderly – and indeed much more feelingly with regard to your kind invitation, my dear William, – and believe me, nothing would afford me greater pleasure, than to carry my Mary, where I know she would be so kindly and so affectionately received – I mean at Aylsham; – but alas! I cannot wander far, for many reasons, all solid and substantial: – unless indeed this extraordinary Living should call me to take possession – by the bye, pray make every enquiry about it – as it seems [fb] a most promising purchase – *prima facie*, but I should fear there are objections lurking behind, which we are not aware of – I go to Harestreet on Monday with Mary – and my Sister Mary who is now with us, for a fortnight – and from thence to Leyton and Wanstead – but I must make my appearance here on Sundays – and shall contrive not to be out of reach of Home – in case of a sudden call – Pray thank Mrs Adey for her letter – and express to her my regret that no Cake was sent to Aylsham – but it was indeed the fault of them at Harestreet, we had three Cakes to distribute – one was left at Leyton for Mary's Aunt Ellis to distribute, one at Harestreet – to be cut up for the benefit of all the Repton family – and one we disposed of oursel<f>ves to Mary's and my acquaintance[s] – but I did not learn till ours was gone – that Mrs Adey had been unprovided for – or I would have robbed half my list, rather than have suffered her for a moment to have supposed that I was unmindful of her – give my affectionate Love to her – and beg to accept [fb] my regret as an excuse – We have had our Cottage full of Visitors, every morning since my Wife made her debut at Church – and every one expresses the warmest interest in our welfare – My dear girl is courted and beloved by all – and I have little doubt that our happiness will increase – We dined out to day – and to morrow we dine with Lady Farmanaugh[354] – who will never suffer Mary to walk home – You shall hear more of our schemes when I write again which I will do from Harestreet – to which place I will thank you to direct your letter – with particulars of the Living you mention –

My Wife and Sister join in kindest Love to Mrs Adey

and believe me, my dear William, your affectionate Brother Edward

Mary is just come down stairs to read this – and says "as she is married, she may send her Love, and a Kiss" – so accept it, if worth – and give my best Love to dear Mrs Adey

---

354 Mary Verney, baroness of Fermanagh, lived at May Place, Crayford. She was the posthumous daughter (b. 21 Oct. 1737), of Hon. John Verney and his wife Mary Nicholson. She died unmarried on 15 November 1810 at May Place. (*Complete Peerage*, vol. V, p. 296.)

Address: William Repton Esqr, Aylsham, Norfolk
B st: [*illeg*] Unpaid; *b st*: B [*illeg*] 21 808; *orange st*: 3 o'Clock DE 21
KENT; *charge*: [*illeg*]
Endorsed: 20 Dec'r 1808   My brother Edward after his Marriage
HM 40910/2

57. Humphry Repton to William Repton; postscripts from Edward Repton, John Adey Repton and Mary (Clarke) Repton

Harestreet near Romford, December 29 1808

Dear William

Your Mother rec[eive]d your Turkey & was delighted to have one at last – after being on the Sharp look out for many days previous to Xmss day – & being obliged to make shift with a haunch of Ld Darnleys Venison[355] instead of an Oxnead Bird – & now lo! a bird is come from Oxnead without a single word. I cannot shew my resentment by sending a Barrel of Oysters without a letter – but I shall certainly not fail to settle that acc't by sending the barrel next Monday *to Oxnead* – & also one to Aylsham by the same Coach – if the <u>frost</u> do not return

[*fb*] Duff thanks you for his Letter – Ed'd will write – & I want to know what Estate of 11. or 12,00 [i.e. £1,100 or £1,200] *p*[*er*] *ann*[*um*] – without a house can be worth 42,000 – near 40 Y[ea]rs purchase. Why shou'd not Kerrison's Estate do[356] – Let us hear all about it – –

& then Stannard's *50£* Estimate for the bow is a stiffener – pray send to him immediately to repair the Sashes that let in the Cold – & to turn the door, that poor John Adey may not perish with Cold – for I suppose we shall have more pinching weather soon.[357]

---

355 Both Daniels (*Repton*, p. 261) and Carter et al. (*Repton*, p. 155) say that in 1790 Repton produced the Red Book for Cobham for the fifth baron/Lord Darnley, but this incorrect. Edward Bligh, Lord Clifton, later fifth earl Darnley, of Cobham Hall, nr. Gravesend (Kent), was born on 25 February 1795. (*Hist. Parl.*) The Red Book was therefore made for his father, John, fourth earl Darnley (b.1767, d.1831). Indeed *Repton in Kent* (p. 38) states clearly that the Red Book was for the fourth earl. This haunch of venison must have come from the fourth earl, as his son would have been 13 at the time of this letter. There is a long description of the 'Earl of Darnley' as a young man in Repton's memoirs. A footnote states that this is 'the 5th Lord Darnley', but as the description is of the earl when Repton first met him, this too must have been the fourth earl. (*Memoirs*, pp. 102–3.)

356 Referring to the proposal for the estate for Nelson's brother. (See Letter 54.)

357 Indicating that Stannard had drawn up plans for some replacement windows (and repairs to a door) at the house in Market Square.

Except Yourself & George – we are all together here & more than all – & we are all very happy together so I will say no more, but that our best love to John Adey & Dee comes with my Blessing & good Wishes, HR

[*fb*] Dear William – My P. S. will be but short, as I am very busy in preparing my Lecture for Monday[358] and am obliged to return to Crayford on Saturday and be separated from my Spouse for 3 days – I must thank you however for your communication concerning the living – and shall be glad to learn further particulars – I fear however that it appears too good a thing – to be had upon such terms – Poor Mrs Bretts letter seems to regard her Son Joseph[359] – whose neglect of his Duty – will be attended with serious consequences – if he does not amend – Give my love to Dear Mrs Adey and Mr Adey – and accept the same my dear William

From your affectionate Brother Edward R

Dear William

This Postscript is much shorter <but> I don't know what to say – but my Love to Uncle & Aunt Adey & hope they are well – & also to all the pretty girls at Aylsham –

Your affectionate Brother JAR

[*fb*] Thank you dearest William for the Turkey. My love to Dear Aunt Adey and tell her that the Basket is just arrived, and I am quite *glad* to hear you are all so well and happy. I wish you all a Merry Christmas and happy new year. and I sincerely *wish* we were all together but as that cannot be we must be contented. I will write to Aunt Adey with the Basket on Sunday.

Yours affectionately   M M[360]

Address: William Repton Esq, Aylsham, Norfolk
B st: RUMFORD 10; Cross Post; *charge*: 8
Endorsed: 29th Dec 1808   My Father, John & Edward from Harestreet
HM 40854

---

358 Another in the series of lectures under Boyle's bequest, to be given on Monday 2 January 1809. (See Letter 48 for the first lecture.)
359 Revd Joseph Brett (q.v.).
360 Mother Mary.

58. George Repton to John Adey Repton; note to Dorothy Adey added by Humphry Repton

East Cowes Castle,[361] Isle of Wight, January [1809]

My dear John –

I think no one can possibly dispute that the spot markd on the Plan
<u>Plot East</u> is by far that most desirable situation for the new Exchequer,[362]
and I think you are quite right to give a design for that purpose – but as
you are not to give in your Plans with the idea of so applying that spot of
Ground, I will tell you what strikes me as being the most advisable way
of disposing the general Plan – I think the South end of the <u>Plot West</u> is
a good situation for the Albany or distinct apartments for <u>single men</u>[363]
– The residue of <u>that</u> Plot I suppose to be Houses very good, but small
for the same description of people as those who inhabit what we call the
Albany, but who we must suppose to be <u>married</u> men and with families
– I should think the sort of people who inhabited this Plot would be
those whose employment belonged to the two Houses of Parliament [fb]
and to the Courts of Law in Westminster Hall, and I think by making
the rooms in the Albany and the Houses not upon too large a scale there
would be no sort of difficulty in disposing of them very expeditiously –
I also think as another reason for placing the Albany in the situation I
propose, that it appears to be <u>worse</u> with respect to neighbourhood than
any other part of the ground to be built *upon* being near all the most
objectionable streets – therefore I think would be a greater nuisance to
<u>families</u> were they to live there than it would be if divided in Chambers
for single men like one of *the* Inns of Court – and I think the side
for Entering should be where I have placed it on the South, otherwise it
would destroy the regularity of the front which from what you sent me
you appear to wish to preserve towards the Abbey – you will observe that

361 Owned by John Nash, George's employer. On his second marriage in 1798 Nash
bought a 30-acre estate overlooking the Solent at East Cowes on the Isle of Wight, where
he built the 'Gothic East Cowes Castle'. (*ODNB*)
362 By the provisions of an act of 1806 (Geo. III., *c.* 89), the southern portion of King
Street, as well as all Thieving Lane, and Broad and Little Sanctuaries were demolished
and new government buildings were to be erected. This detailed letter discusses plans to
be submitted by George and John Adey Repton for the competition to design new public
buildings in Parliament Square. They gained first prize, although their plans were never
executed. (Carter et al., *Repton*, p. 133.)
363 The Albany, Piccadilly, built in 1771–76 by William Chambers; converted into 69
bachelor apartments by Henry Holland in 1802–3. Possibly to be relocated.

I have sent two sketches for the *Plan of* this part of the Building, one supposing the whole to be as one House, the other supposing it to be divided into 4 distinct Houses – though they are very much alike yet I think the latter (that upon the thin paper) would perhaps make the best Plan – I have supposed each ten<n>ant to have one sitting [fb] room and one bed room, with a Closet w*h*ere it could be conveniently obtained – the rooms as you will perceive are not large, or ought they to be, for the description of people who will most probably inhabit *them*, if you can get them 12 or 14 ft by 16ft or 15ft sqr or rather more *or less* I think it would be quite enough – the Bed rooms of course need not be large – and as the passages will in a certain degree be very public, I think it will be more comfortable not to have an external door from the different Bed rooms – I think the Privys might be obtained in that angle which you call <in> Thieving lane. you will see I have made little <provision f>or no provision for an Hotel because I consider *it* to be a Coffee house which should have a good Coffee room with a good Kitchen under it, there[sic] business should be more for cooking dinners &c than for lodging people – perhaps over the coffee room you might make one or two (at most) private rooms for dinners, should they be desird. you can arrange what Basement rooms you may want, which I should think would not be much – as the description of people who lived in these rooms would not keep many, if any servants – you will see I have marked <in> one house as I think the rest of the Plot West might be disposed of, for such a description of people, as I before mentioned, who have families – they would make very comfortable small Houses and on the first floor [fb] would make a front drawing room 24 ft long – on the Plot East I think might be put <a> better sort of Houses of which I have sketched the Ground & first floor of one of them – these would also make very habitable houses for most respectable people and should it ever be determined to put the new Exchequer upon this spot, perhaps these good houses could better be dispensed with, than the other inferior ones – at the back of these good houses might be built small houses (as I have drawn) making a back street from George Street – and as from the name I am to suppose "Thieving lane" not to be a desirable situation to live in – that might be the best possible situation for the Stables necessary to the Houses in Plot East – it seems to me almost absolutely necessary that the corner of George Street adjoining Plot East should be purchased, and the good houses continued on to the Back Street before mentioned –

The Speaker seems to mention a great deal in his letters about the seeing the new Buildings from Whitehall which you do not seem to have thought of.[364] I therefore suppose *you* have given up all thoughts of doing *so* as requiring the purchase of too much land, or for some other good reason –

[*fb*] = thus to recapitulate what I have attempted to explain to you is thus – I think <u>Plot East</u> should have good houses built upon it, with small houses forming a back street built in such a way (as you will see I have marked so) that they can be no annoyance to the front houses, (that is supposing the new Exchequer not to be built upon this scite, if it is, then do away these Gentlemens houses altogether) – and I think this <u>Plot East</u> will in a great degree be free from the objections mentioned in the Speakers letters, of the dirty streets and being too near the school[365] – then <u>Plot West</u> I recommend to have Houses of rather an inferior size &c, (which its situation requires) with the South end of it divided as an Inn of Court for such as cannot, or do not, like to have the expence of a house – I think "<u>Albany</u>" will not be a good name to call it but "Parliament Inn Court" or some such – With respect to the <u>Elevations</u>, you will perceive that what little I have done to the Plans still leave <u>them</u> untouched, as I think they would both do extreamly well – but the <u>Grecian</u> sketch (as sent me) I think appears to want a little enrichment, particularly if that building is appropriated *to* a better [*fb*] description of Houses as I have recommended – for after all I think by the Speakers letters that the <u>Grecian</u> character is what they seem inclined to adopt – for after the specimen of <u>Gothic</u> which they have had from a Man who they have <all> been taught to believe so superior to all others, they will I fear, hardly venture to try it again – unless <u>your</u> Drawing should tempt them – I am sorry that the time would not allow me to do more – to assist you – and I am aware there is very much that you can <u>alter</u>, and <u>improve</u> upon when you come to draw it out – but I hope you will put <u>all</u> the Houses in – which is not much trouble when you have perfectly considerd and determined upon one of them. the number of people through whose hands they will pass will not well comprehend it, if there are great mas[s]es of one color left instead of putting in the Plan as in the Burlington House Plan – and let them be very <u>neatly</u> done which goes a great way with many thickheaded fellows –

Did the Speaker recommend an <u>Elevation</u> only of the proposed new Exchequer to be sent in <u>without</u> a <u>Plan</u> for that building? [*fb*] If the <u>center</u>

---

364 Humphry Repton had designed the Speaker's Garden at Westminster for Charles Abbott. A drawing of 'Lambeth Palace from the Garden of the Rt. Hon. The Speaker of the House of Commons' is in the *Polite Repository* (1808). (Carter et al., *Repton*, p. 144.) Abbott's papers at TNA include correspondence and journal entries about this work. (S. Daniels, 'View from Westminster', *Garden Museum Journal*, 36 (Winter 2018/19), pp. 26–30, p. 27.)

365 i.e. Westminster School.

House in <u>Plot East</u> must be a so much larger house than the others and must have its door in the middle in order to conform to your Elevation, I have marked in ink upon your Plan how it may be divided in a different way to what you had proposed – divide the whole length into as many houses and windows as I have marked, or as you think will do best, not minding if it should not correspond exactly to a foot with the Elevations – which might be rectified <when> *should* they really be carried into execution – when it will be time enough to think of many little details and difficulties – the only thing is to take care not to propose any thing <u>obviously</u> impracticable –

You may make something simple and pretty I think of the two Porches entering into the Quadrangle. I have given <u>an idea</u> only of something of the sort that might be proposed –

With respect to the value and cost of these buildings as nearly as I can from an opinion it would, I think, be thus –

The larger houses in <u>Plot East</u> would I think cost about £200 or upwards a sqr. to build and the Stables about £60 per square – making both together say from 4000 to £4500 *each house & stables* – cost to finish. I think they ought to let for 250£ a year, perhaps the Ground Rent would be £20 <or £25 in> in addition to what is already paid to the Dean & Chapter – the second sort of Houses in <u>Plot West</u> would I think cost about £180 a sqr. making about 1600£ – and would I think let for from 100 [fb] to £120 a year – the rooms in the Albany would I think cost from £160 to £180 per square to build; and would let for from 40 to 50£ a year. The Coffee room would let well – and the center house & end houses in <u>Plot East</u> being larger should have a rather greater rent – the small houses at the back of <u>Plot East</u> would I think cost 6 or £700 to build and would let for about £40 a year – they should be let <for> to people belonging to the Parliament &c or may from their size become nuisances to the <u>neighbourhood</u> altogether –

I think the<at> calculations *you send in with the Plans* will be of Consequence and will in a great degree influence the Committee &c – if <My> Our Father thought there would be no harm in it It would be a good thing to shew the Plans to Rowles[366] or some other one and get them to give you an idea which they from a constant habit of that sort of thing could do pretty accurately, without much trouble. I should <u>not</u> like your calculation <u>to be far</u> from the mark – but what you give in with the Plans [fb] must

---

366 Henry Rowles (bap. 1777, d.1840) trained in the office of his uncle, the architect Henry Holland, and then entered business as a builder. In about 1807 Rowles entered into a partnership with another uncle, Alexander Copland, one of the most successful of the early building contractors. (*ODNB*)

not be "say" or "suppose" but decided as your opinion therefore the more necessary not to be much out of the way – the ground rents I dare say will bear a great advance – adieu my dear John. I shall be most happy to hear of you success which will always give the greatest pleasure to your affectionate Brother   G R

Give my love to all at Harestreet. I do not write to Mary – having written so lately and having nothing particular to say to her – I send my Father Lubbocks letter – I think Gentlemen in <u>the law</u> will be glad to have a <u>house</u> in <u>Plot East</u> with their Chambers in <u>Plot West</u> –

If you think the small houses at the back of <u>Plot East</u> are likely to become nuisances – you might put the offices there for Lawyers who inhabit the Good Houses in <u>Plot East</u> with sleeping rooms over for Clerks &c.

[*fb*] Dear Dee – too much for one Cover so I have sent you this to see what a clever boy George is – God bless you – & bid William shew you his letter[367]

Address: John Adey Repton Esqr, F. A. S.[368]
Endorsed: Jan'y 1809   George's Letter to John   Explaining his ideas about the new buildings at Westminster
HM 40916

59. John Repton to Dorothy Adey

[Norwich, 9 or 10 January 1809]

My Dear Dee

I hope to shew myself at Aylsham on Wednesday from Norwich – Mr Martineau gives me great Spirits and his assurances that very little Physick is required.[369] I have certainly had to much. He has himself walkd me in the Castles Upper close and back to my Inn, which I performed better then I expected. I am glad I came to Norwich and shall be glad to see you at

---

367 This note has been added by Repton senior under the address and indicates that George's letter was subsequently forwarded by his father to Dorothy, explaining why it has survived in the archive accumulated by William at Aylsham.

368 Fellow of the Society of Antiquaries

369 Philip Martineau of Bracondale Lodge, Norwich. (For his properties see note to Letter 46.) He was the fourth generation of a family of surgeons, eventually becoming a principal surgeon, specialising in lithotomy (the removal of bladder and kidney stones). (*Repton in Norfolk*, pp. 81–2.) In other letters he is mentioned as offering advice and conferring with Taylor, the Aylsham surgeon.

Aylsham on Wedensday if Mr M consents, as I wish to *be* out of the way of the bustle of the Sessions.

Yours affectionately J Repton

[*fb*] The other side was wrote before I rec[eive]d your kind letter. I am in paper. Mr M will consent to my coming to you this Evening and so I shall be with you as soon as my letter, in short out of the way of the bustle I will get if I ever return to Norwich again – I wish I had well considered at first the consequence of having put myself under the advice of Mr Martineau – Thank you for goodness to Eliza. I suppose she stopd at Lubbocks on Sund'y night – all well with my Bro' at Woburn. Your orders for the real Steers[370] will lead me to Copy part of HR letter – here its –

[*fb*][371] Honourable mention was made of your Name [i.e. John's] by a fine fat Farmer visiting the Duke [of Bedford], he's from Holkham a John B[*illeg*] a Tenant of Mr Coke,[372] he talk's of nothing else but fat Cattle and Water-Meadows an is so fond of Watering that he recommended a Mr Cedicon[*sic*; ?Medication] to cure the chapd hands he complained of by making Waters upon them upon them[*sic*] and washing them frequently in his own Urine.

So are you to make some steers or must we bring some. God bless you William & dear John Adey and any young ones you may have with you. Mrs Brett and Mr B call and kindly stop with us at alesham

Address: Mrs Adey, Aylsham
Endorsed: 9 or 10 Jan'y 1809   My Uncle John Repton to Mrs Adey from Norwich
HM 40929/2

60. Humphry Repton to William Repton; Charles Abbott to Humphry Repton; Humphry Repton to William Repton

[Cirencester], 21 January 1809

Dear William

I sent your letter about Sherringham[373] to the Speaker – & you see by his

---

370 From what follows, it appears that 'real Steers' was a remedy for chapped hands.
371 The following paragraph has been copied from a letter from Humphry Repton to his brother.
372 Thomas Coke, first earl of Leicester.
373 At that time the Sheringham estate was owned by Cook Flower (q.v.). William had been overseeing the enclosure bill for Sheringham, so was familiar with the property; for

short answer[374] he wants further particulars – so send me all you can – with the present & supposed improved rents – & even a sketch of the 'Situation' if you can get it map'd for him without expense or trouble – I write from Cirencester 100 miles from home where I am just arrived this Saturday night 21 January 1809 – & not being able to get a place in Oxford Coach – I came all the way in hack Chaises alone – the Coldest & worst journey I ever performed – 3 horses out of the <u>pair I</u> drive have been down in the same day – & I almost capsized by one shock, but here I am alive to tell the Story & if I send this from Lord Ducie's[375] to morrow, you will know that I am safe 15 miles farther – I wish I had [fb] you as my Companion – but I hate wishing – so tell dear John Adey & D. that I am well & remember them – My Love is with you. How solitary is an evening at an Inn in Cold weather after having had nobody but one's self to speak to for the last 24 hours without any thing to say – & only filling up the time by saying it to you

I saw Duff well yesterday in Town & heard from George who is a delightful fellow – his letters are full of information if I can get a spare frank I will send you the last I had from him as a sample –

Apropos – Shall I have any rent from Norfolk to pay Claude Scott[376] this year, or must I get it elsewhere?

[fb][377] Only one Moment to say – 1ˢᵗ That next Monday the 23ᵈ is the day fixed. 2ᵈˡʸ I should wish to hear more of Sherrington[sic] 3ᵈˡʸ Mrs Abbott will thank you much for Your <u>Drawing</u> of the Cascade when it can be spared.[378]

T[illeg]

---

details see Daniels, *Repton*, pp. 90–1. Repton is referring to another possible estate for Lord Nelson. (See Letter 54.)

374 See below, dated 17 January; Repton's letter was written on the back of the Speaker's note.

375 Thomas Reynolds Moreton, fourth baron Ducie of Tortworth and first earl of Ducie (1775–1840). (*ODNB* entry for his son Henry, second earl of Ducie.)

376 Scott's bank had made a loan to Repton, on which interest of £35 was due every year; in 1810 £3 10s was deducted from this for tax. (See Letter 134.) John Repton, Humphry's father, had purchased a number of properties in Aylsham and had taken the lease on Oxnead Hall, where John's younger son, also John, farmed. When John senior died his three children, Dorothy, Humphry and John, drew up an agreement sharing the family property. Humphry wished to use his share of the rents and of the produce of Oxnead to pay Claude Scott. (*Aylsham*, pp. 170, 174, 177.) The agreement between the siblings is in NRO, AYL 1019.

377 The following note is in the hand of Charles Abbott.

378 Repton's work at Abbott's property at Kidbrooke Park included a cascade. It is depicted in the *Polite Repository* (1810). (Temple, 'Repton, illustrator', p. 172.) *Repton in Sussex* (p. 71) mentions the cascade, citing this letter, as quoted by Nigel Temple.

17. January

How like a Man of business is this Note from one of the first Characters of the present age, The Rt. Hon. Charles Abbott, Speaker of the House of Commons[379]

WoodChester Park, Sunday [22 January 1809]

Safe arrived at last – 4 horses skaiting up & down hill worse than Bath or Matlock – with a precipice on the side & a river ready to break ones fall – or one's neck – I wrote the inclosed last night from the Coldest dirtyest Inn in Glocestersh' & fear'd I might be imprison'd there so – I thought this was a better prison – & moved for a writ of habeas Corpus – which was answer'd by 4 horses & a writ of double payment & G – d – um

But here I am – & well – Lord Ducie just come in from his Cold ride & walk

Adieu HR

Endorsed by William: 23rd Jan'y 1809   My Father   From Lord Ducie's[380]
A Note from the Speaker
Endorsed by Repton: Post Script
HM 40857 & HM 40858[381]

61. Humphry Repton to William Repton

[undated, probably early 1809][382]

Dear William – Remember me dear John Adey –

If Beasy cou'd make me a pair of Strong shoes[383] – to fit me as well as my last boots – they wou'd be a treasure to me but they must like the boots be cheap as well as good – or I may as well get them in London –

---

379 Note added by Repton.
380 This letter is cited as the only written evidence for Repton's work at Woodchester (Glos). (Daniels, *Repton*, p. 260; Carter et al., *Repton*, p. 153.) John Adey Repton made alterations to the library and dining room *c.*1820. (Carter et al., *Repton*, p. 153.) The frontispiece of *Polite Repository* (1810) is 'The Entrance to Woodchester Park, Lord Ducie'. (Temple, 'Repton, illustrator', p. 172.)
381 The two letters were posted one inside the other, hence there is one endorsement. They have been separated in the archive: HM 40857 is Repton's letter from Cirencester, written on blank pages of Abbott's letter; HM 40858 was written at Woodchester Park.
382 Regarding the date surmised here, see Letters 54 and 57, which mention Kerrison's estate as a possible estate for Nelson's brother.
383 Robert Beasy, cordwainer of Aylsham.

I dont think Sheringham wou'd do – what advance of rent is expected to be made or what advantages for so dear a bargain –

You don't say any thing about why Kerrison's Estate might not do – is there not a lofty spot on it? –

You dont say if W[illiam] W[indham] has consented to the solicitorship &c –

Shall I send you my Claim of 26:5:0 to give to Mr Budd?[384]

Seal with wax as wafers always come open

Address: Wm Repton Esq, Aylsham
HM 40861

62. Dorothy Adey to William Repton

Aylsham, Thursday night [26 January 1809]

My dear William

When you talk'd of sending Barnes home on Monday, and returning yourself on Tuesday you was not *I suppose* aware of being detained so long, tho Mr Barnes says, he heard Mr Bircham[385] say the business was to last till saturday night. supposing this to be fact, I think you will be very glad to have your letters, and even if you are to return tomorrow Barnes may be of use in bringing home your Cloak bag, in short the cheif reason for my sending him, is, that two letters from your dear Father came two nights agon by the same post a thing so unusual, that I am afraid it may be necessary for you to see them, and I assure you I feel quite fidgetty to know all is well. I do think from so near a relation there cou'd have been no harm in my opening them, but I had rather incur the expence of Barnes to Holt, than do any thing that you think not right.

The Young Men had several people on Tuesday but Murrell chose to see me yesterday and if I cou'd [*fb*] have told him positively if you wou'd be at home *on Saturday* or at Holt, he wou'd have been at either place that day to have seen you, I told him I dare say you wou'd be at the Audit tomorrow if possible, however he has left his message with me. note upon note from Oxnead. the dear Ansons did intend to have been part of the week with us but John has made engag[emen]ts every day and will not part with them. I'll shew you the Court party note when you come home, and you are quite

---

384 William Windham's lawyer (q.v.).

385 Several (later) members of the Bircham family, mostly wherrymen, are mentioned in *Sail and Storm*.

in favor, and I will shew you too a letter from him that has been receiv'd at Harestreet in your dear Father's absense worse than any thing he says to me –

I have no very good account to give of dear Mr Adey so I will say nothing, but that I have never been absent from him half an hour since you left us. I am quite determind whether you come home and go with me or not, to go to James Holleys to morrow night, so let Barnes if you dont come, be home <u>before seven</u> that I may have your Fathers letters.

God bless you. Yours affectionately   D Adey

Address: Wm Repton Esqr
Endorsed by William: 26th Jan'y 1809   Mrs Adey to me when at Holt Incl[osure] Meeting
Endorsed by Dorothy Adey: Seven letters beside this
HM 40887/1

63. Thomas Blake[386] to William Repton

Norwich, 2^d February 1809

Sir

The Livings lately advertised by me to be sold consist of The Advowsons of the Consolidated Rectories of Barningham & Coney Weston in Suffolk. There is a Church in each Parish and Service once on every Sunday at each Church. There are a Barn Stable and about 32 Acres of Glebe in Barningham, but the Parsonage House (then a mere Cottage) was burnt down some years ago and has not since been rebuilt. There is a Parsonage House at Weston (altho' a very indifferent one) with about 13 Acres of Glebe. There are about 1600 Acres of Land in Barningham, about three fourths of which are Arable. There are about 1300 Acres of Land in Weston, of which the greatest Part is arable. The Rest of the Land is Meadow or Pasture Ground. I believe there is a Modus for antient Pasture Lands, but what it is I have not been informed, but it certainly does not affect Grass Lands when mowed. The annual Value is upwards of £800 *p*[er] *annum*. The Rectories are discharged of First Fruits and [*fb*] Tenths. The Land Tax is redeemed. The present Incumbent is 87 Years of Age.[387] The Price of the

---

386 Probably Thomas Blake of Norwich, barrister at law. His will, dated 27 July 1812, was proved on 10 March 1814. (Probate copy is NRO, NRS 10375, 25A5.)
387 John Barnes (1721–1818), rector of Coney Weston and Barningham, 1745–1818; son of Andrew, grocer of Lakenheath. (CCEd Person ID: 122482.)

Advowsons is £9000. The present Incumbent's Effects will be liable to the dilapidations of the Rectory of Weston, But the Purchaser of the Advowsons must take upon himself the Dilapidations of the Rectory of Barningham.

I remain Sir

Your most obedient Servant

Tho. Blake

[*fb*] [notes by William]

Barningham

1600 acres of wch three fourths are arable

Suppose 1200 acres to be worth 5/6 an acre	330–
And 400/1600 acs of Pasture at 3/–	60–
Weston	
Suppose 800 acres of arable at 5/6	120–
And 500 of Pasture at 3/–	75–
45 acres of Glebe may be worth *p*[er] *an*[num] at 25/–	56 – 5
	641 – 5

Mr Blake says it is well ascertained however that the Livings now produce above £800 *p*[er] *ann*[um]. If so, they must sure be at the utmost

The Vendor is Mr Henry Patteson[388] who has a Lease of the Great tithes of one parish during the present incumbent's life.

If he would consent to give up that to the Purchaser it might make a considerable difference in the eligibility of the Purchase.

Address: Mr Repton, Attorney at Law, Aylsham

Endorsed: 2ᵈ Feb'y 1809   T. Blake Esqr   With particulars of two Livings to be sold Communicated to Edward

HM 40953/9

---

388 According to *Alumni Cantab.*, after his ordination in 1781, Revd Henry Patteson was curate of Coney Weston, where his son John was born in 1790. Patteson was rector of Burgate, 1782–1805; Drinkstone, 1805–24; and of Wortham Eastgate, and Wortham Everard, 1782–1824 (all Suffolk parishes).

64. George Walpole[389] to William Repton

[Weybourne], February 27th 1809

If you propose being at Holt on the 2d March you will find a Bed ready at Waybourn & dinner too. remember I do not dine later than – half past five – tea at any Hour. you have heard I suppose of my poor father's death.[390]
   Ever your GW

Endorsed: 27 Feb'y 1809   The Hon'ble G. Walpole   About visiting him at Waborne after Lord Orford's death
HM 40947

65. George Walpole to Dorothy Adey

Waybourn, Monday 20th March [1809][391]

Dear Mrs Adey

   I should have been with you this Day but for the threatened appearance of the Weather – so I must put it off till next week as on Wednesday I expect Mr Dowsing from Barsham.[392]
   Ever your G Walpole

Endorsed: The Hon. G. Walpole to Mrs Adey
HM 40942/1

66. Humphry Repton to William Repton (fragment)

[April 1809]

[*torn*] You had better call again at [*drawing of a swan with two necks*] Lad lane[393] & learn the Inns *where* & the time when the Mail Changes horses – because a Chaise from Woburn after dinner by Moonlight will take you either

---

389 General George Walpole.
390 The earl had died on 24 February 1809.
391 20 March was a Monday in 1809. On the back of this note is a draft letter from William Repton to William Windham, dated 21 May 1809; printed below as Letter 95.
392 Horatio Dowsing (1757–1843), vicar of Hindringham (1783–1843); rector of Barsham (1788–90); rector of Barsham with Alby (1790–1843). (CCEd Person ID: 1044.)
393 The Swan with Two Necks in Lad Lane (off Gresham Street) was one of the London's leading coaching inns and centres for mail distribution. (D. Campbell-Smith, *Masters of the Post: the authorized history of the Royal Mail* (London, 2011), p. 95.)

back to Dunstable – <or to>   33 miles from London – or
across to Hockliffe   38 miles d° ⎤ both only 4 miles
or forward to ⎰Brickhill   43 miles d° ⎦ from Woburn
    ⎱Fenny Stratford 46 miles d°

& tis material that you should stop where the Mail Changes horses in the night

Endorsed: April 1809   My father to me in London about going with him to the Duke of Bedford
HM 40859

7. A fragment including a drawing of a two-necked swan by Humphry Repton, HM 40859

67. Humphry Repton to Mary (Clarke) Repton

[London], Tuesday morning 8 oClock [4 April 1809]

Dear Mary

I have sent to Golden Cross[394] & the Coach is full so I must proceed to

---

394 There is a crucifix here. Probably the Golden Cross Inn, Charing Cross, which Repton mentions in Letter 149. It is shown clearly in *Regency London*, plate 23, square Ba.

Woburn[395] _solus_. I did all your jobs yesterday – & Mrs Marsh[396] will bring your things down tomorrow – the little girl had a stiff neck – but that is to be well. Edward has written to Mary[397] so you know they are to be at Ellis's[398] – for a fortnight – or as long as agreable – but defer Harestreet till I am at home & warmer weather – She is a poor Cold thing[399] – I found her at Norris's[400] – with her hands in *thick* worsted gloves sitting over the fire – as if she had the itch or Childblains – & a great Shawl on. [_fb_] Young women should do – & look like other folk. Mrs Martineau went with me to call on her & I was vexed to see her so muffled up – but Edward is as much wrapt up in her, poor fellow – as she is in her shawls – so they must do as they like – I dont think she looks upon herself as much obliged to any of our family but Edward – & perhaps she is right – so we must bear with our loss of dear Edward – for lost he is to us – but there are enow of us to be happy – & happy we will be – till our Mary & our dee find [_fb_] out those they can love better than us.

God bless you dear old Girl – & expect to hear from me at Woburn – & whither I go farther North or not is of little consequence if I can't get more than for a Concern near home – tis not worth going 150 miles.[401]

Poor Dargue my hackney man (for whose Chaise I am now waiting) – thought he had a profitable *black* job to take a dead Lord to Ireland to be buried – but in his way home, he tumbled over a pail on board ship – broke his shin[402] – cou'd get no advice & <_illeg_> became a Corpse himself when he landed in England – so much for long jobs – [403]

---

395 Repton paid numerous return visits to Woburn Abbey.

396 Presumably the mother of James Marsh; she was Mary (Clarke) Repton's cousin, or cousin-in-law.

397 i.e. his sister Mary.

398 The Essex home of the uncle and aunt of Edward's wife.

399 'She' being Mary, Edward's wife. From what follows, it is clear that, rather than referring to her personality, Repton is referring her feeling the cold in England, compared with the climate in the West Indies.

400 Not identified.

401 A comment about the profitability, or otherwise, of his work. The next letter, dated the following day, indicates that he was intending to travel to Langold, then in Yorkshire, now in Notts.

402 This could be 'shin' or 'skin' – h and k are very similar in this letter – 'shin' seems more likely. Joseph Dargue (b.1756) was buried at St Paul's, Hammersmith, on 17 March 1809. (LMA, DL/T/031/012.)

403 Daniels says that this paragraph is part of a letter from Repton to William, reference HM 40859 (the fragment published here as Letter 66); but it is clearly contained within this letter to his wife, reference HM 40840. (Daniels, _Repton_, p. 38, note 70.)

Address: To Mrs Repton, Harestreet near Romford Essex
B st: A AP 4 809
Endorsed: 4ᵗʰ April 1809   My father to my mother about Sister Edward
HM 40840

68. Humphry Repton to Mary Repton

Woburn Abbey, Wednesday 5 April 1809

Dearest Mary –

Tell Mamma – I wrote yesterday – by which she will see that I go to Mr. Gally Knights[404] next week in addition to which I can now tell her that I leave this place on Saturday – & then stop a day or two with the Marquis of Tavistock[405] – at Oakley[406] near Bedford, where she may write to me on Friday – under Covers to him – but after that time I dont know Mr. Gally Knights post Town – I think she may say at Gally Knights Esqr Langold near Blythe by Retford. I wonder Mr. Simpson[407] has not

---

404 Henry Gally Knight (1786–1846), architectural writer and antiquary; the family home was Langold Hall. (*ODNB*) It has been said that sometime before February 1807, his father, also Henry (d.1808), barrister, commissioned Repton to prepare a design for Langold, a drawing of which was reproduced in the *Polite Repository* (1807). (Carter et al., *Repton*, p. 144; Daniels, *Repton*, p. 269.) However, new research into Langold suggests that Henry Gally Knight *junior* was closely involved with the Repton project from the start. It cites this letter and says 'In April 1809 Henry junior called Repton back to discuss ongoing works, before he left Langold in the care of his mother and agents and set off on a tour of Europe in July. Repton's advice on this occasion must have been comprehensive as he was paid £105 in May'. (*Repton in Yorkshire*, pp. 91–3; the payment is in C. Hoare & Co Archives 3/438.)
405 Francis Russell, marquess of Tavistock (1788–1861), the eldest son of the sixth duke of Bedford, who later became seventh duke. (*ODNB* for sixth duke.)
406 The parish of Oakley is four miles north-west of Bedford. The manor of Oakley Reynes was purchased by the duke of Bedford in 1757. (*VCH Bedfordshire*, vol. 3, p. 150.) The house at Oakley had been one of the homes of the sixth duke when he was known as Lord John Russell, i.e. before becoming duke. At Woburn Abbey's 2018 exhibition 'Humphry Repton: Art & Nature for the Duke of Bedford', it was stated that Repton began work at Oakley in 1799. A photcopy of a note from Repton about plantings at Oakley was on display at Woburn; this is the only known writing of his about Oakley; the original has been lost. The visit mentioned in this letter was obviously a return visit.
407 The Hon. John Bridgman Simpson of Babworth (Notts), M.P.; his property was not that far from that of Gally Knight. Repton prepared a Red Book for Babworth in 1790 (Daniels, *Repton*, p. 264); a drawing of Babworth was reproduced in the *Polite Repository* (1792) (Carter et al., *Repton*, p. 141); for details of the Red Book, see Carter et al., p. 160.

answerd my letter – perhaps You will send me one from him – for [fb] [I] dont like to go so near without calling – & I dont like to write to him again – so I don't know how to act – it is bitter cold weather here – but I potter about after the different workmen & come in to drop at 6. & dine at 7 – or later[408] – I miss my boy Edward here & wish poor George could have come – The Duke ask'd me why I had not brought an Aid de Camp – I said John was gone to Norfolk *& Ed[war]d married* – & he said 'where is Master Humphry' – so you see he was a little expected but I am sure he judged right not to neglect his board day – & so tell him when you see him

Kent[409] said he should call at Harestreet next Monday on his way down the road with some Gent[lema]n but cou'd not stop dinner – We are very Comfortable [fb] here – the Young Marchioness[410] a charming woman & makes the house cheerful & Comfortable – she seems to look as wives "should do when they Love their Husbands" as Shakespeare Says – & the Duke will soon be a grand papa[411] – sooner than I shall – but we have no Worsted Gloves & Shawls[412] & fancies here – God bless you all – I hope I shall get a frank for this – HR

Address: April five 1809, Miss Repton, Harestreet Romford Essex, Tavistock[413]
B st: WOBOURN 42; *r st with crest*: FREE 6 AP 6 1809
Endorsed: 5 April 1809   My father from the D. of Bedford's to Mary
HM 40842

---

408 At this time Repton used his visits to Woburn to advance his botanical reputation: in the winter of 1808–9 he gathered information on ivy, presenting a paper on it to the Linnean Society in April 1810. (Daniels, *Repton*, p. 178.) The entry for June 1810 in the *Polite Repository* is a drawing of 'The Thornery, at Woburn Abbey. Seat of His Grace the Duke of Bedford'.

409 Nathaniel Kent.

410 Anna Maria Stanhope, daughter of Charles Stanhope, third earl of Harrington. She married of Francis Russell, marquess of Tavistock, on 8 August 1808. (*Alumni Cantab.* for Francis Russell, marquess of Tavistock.)

411 The Shakespeare quotation has not been identified. The Tavistocks' only son, William, was born on 1 July 1809; he became the eighth duke (d.1872).

412 A reference to his daughter-in-law Mary's methods of keeping warm that he mentioned in Letter 67.

413 Free post via the marquess of Tavistock: he was M.P. for Peterborough from 14 March 1809 to 1812; then 1812–1832 for Bedfordshire. (*Hist. Parl.*)

69. Dorothy Adey to Mary (Clarke) Repton

Aylsham, [Wednesday] April 12 [1809]

My dear Mary

I have this morning parted with my dear William and tho he has left me in the good Company of both my dear Johns (for poor John[414] came to us last night and is staying here <u>comfortably</u> to day) yet my poor William is so much of a sheet Anchor to me that I feel I look in vain for him all day long, as to writing and telling you when he wou'd see you I cou'd not for all the post was in yesterday he cou'd not himself absolutely determine, and now how he goes from Norwich I am sure he did not know when he left Aylsham as no place was taken and now that all Lawyers [fb] are making the best of their way to Town I think it is very like he may find a difficulty in getting a place. My directions are to send his letters every Saturday in a parcel by Basey, if the Basket does not go, so that he may have them every <u>Sunday morning</u> at Harestreet, and if he is not there of a Sunday He says he shall tell you to have the goodness to forward them to him, so that next Sunday my dear Mary I hope and trust you will have the comfort of seeing him, yet if he finds it necessary to run down into Staffordshire, I suppose you will not, but of course you will hear of him as soon as he gets to Town. Barns goes up with him, and Mileham[415] I fancy will follow next week, but I am to hear from him today when he is to go, and now as to dear John I am right happy to have him once again and he appears happy and comfortable himself and two things I hope I have accomplish'd <it> at least <u>whilst they are here</u>[416] the one to persuade [fb] his Wife not to continually talk of his being ill and the other not to stop him from talking, that He was the best judge what hurt him and woud not talk if it did. John and all said I was right, and she has been better in both respects and in that He is certainly the better for being <u>here</u>. I am afraid he will go home tomorrow but now that he has once been I hope he will come again –

Your letters are arriv'd. I was sure I might open yours to William and I will return that and Pierses with the [?]saucege basket if any to be had, or

---

414 Her brother, John Repton of Oxnead, whose health is discussed later in the letter; the other John is her husband.

415 Another employee of Adey & Repton; he was a clerk; perhaps the Harry Mileham who was left a bequest in one of the codicils to William's will. (NRO, AYL 1157, papers relating to will of William Repton.)

416 i.e. her brother John and his wife.

in any parcel to William. I find by the postillion that drove him he was too late for the Mails and went by the Expedition. I am quite glad Dufs under Lodgings are disengaged, it cannot [?]signify to dear William what it is he pays for the time he may want them. I am sorry for my poor Girls both of them and shall be heartily Glad to hear you say they are both better. write to me when you have seen or heard of my Boy.

Yours affectionately D Adey

Address: Mrs Repton, Harestreet near Romford, Essex
B st: AYLSHAM 132; Cross Post; *charge*: 8
Endorsed: 12 April 1809   Mrs Adey to my Mother
HM 40885

70. Dorothy Adey to William Repton

[Aylsham], Friday Afternoon [14 April 1809][417]

My dear William

I am writing dear Mama so long a letter that I have nought to say to you save God bless you and to day all of us drinking your health. Your uncle Adey who is <u>uncommonly</u> himself to day said plain and loud (now really and truly I dont tell a story) 'success to what he is about'. Copeman has call'd and said it was no matter he wou'd take some other opportunity of telling Mr Ives[418] what he wanted. Mrs Tillet[419] call'd and seem'd to say she was excessively surprisd that she had not seen you before you left Aylsham. Mileham set off [*fb*] yesterday for Lynn and George says he does not expect him home till Sunday but I suppose that will be before your summons comes for his going to Town. John is gone to dine at Johnson Gays.[420] He and young Fisher call'd here yesterday. now I bid you adieu and am going to scribble to Mama again.

Yours ever Affectionately DA

---

417 The originals of Letters 70 to 75 are dated very loosely and some of William's endorsements say only 'April 1809'. They were written hurriedly by Dorothy during her husband's final illness. The order in which they have been published here seems to be the logical sequence.

418 Robert Copeman was an Aylsham lawyer, so it might seem unlikely that he would call George Ives, William's clerk, 'Mr Ives', but there are no other alternatives for 'Mr Ives' in Aylsham at this time.

419 Possibly Mrs Anne Tillett (b.c.1781), a widow, who in 1823 married Frederic Roe, many years her junior. (*Aylsham*, p. 277.)

420 At Saxthorpe, near Aylsham.

I have this moment your kind letter. A thousand thanks to you for it. I do hope all will go smoothly and I hope you will have a Trip into Staffordshire[421] but most of all I hope you will secure the Lodgings in Duffs house never mind paying a <u>little</u> Extra for a great <u>Comfort</u> let me beg of you to get them yet again and again.[422]

Thank you DA

Address: Mr Wm Repton
Endorsed: April 1809   Mrs Adey
HM 40887/2

71. Dorothy Adey to William Repton

[Aylsham], Friday Afternoon [21 April 1809]

Your yesterdays letter my dearest William I have this instant receiv'd, and truly and sincerely congratulate you on your success on the Sher[ing]ham Bill,[423] and trust and hope the Swanton will go on as smoothly,[424] but I dont like that Mr Wright[425] and wou'd give a small trifle to know the contents of the note the man brought from him on Tuesday and which I enclose you, and the one from Doughty. no other letters or parcels have arriv'd this week by the post. I wrote to you on Wednesday so did George & Mileham, but by directing to Piccadilly I doubt (as you say you go to Harestreet to day) you will not have had them, so enquire at 202 before you set out for Staffordshire. as to my Letters to Mrs Anson[426] and Lady Katherine[427] if it is not pleasant to you to give them yourself <put them> some time <u>before</u> your return into Norfolk, either put them into the penny

---

421 On business for a member of the Anson family.

422 This letter has been dated Friday 14 April because of the reference to William trying to secure lodgings in Duff's house, also mentioned in the previous letter, dated Wednesday 12 April.

423 PA, HL/PO/CO/1/55, Proceedings at Committees on Private Bills & other matters 19 Jan 1809 – 19 Jun 1809, 1 volume of Unpublished Select Committee papers (volume 55), Sheringham Inclosure Bill, fo. 112; Local and Personal Act, 49 George III, c.19; NRO, C/Sca 2/252.

424 NRO, C/Sca 2/284, Swanton Abbott, Lammas and Buxton enclosure award 1824; 3 maps. The relevant enclosure act was passed in 1809.

425 Not identified.

426 Mary Anson, née Venables-Vernon was widow of George (d.1789). One of their estates was at Shugborough (Staffs); they lived at Orgreave (Staffs). https://landedfamilies.blogspot.com/search?q=anson%2Cthomas.

427 Lady Katherine Walpole (q.v.).

post office or get a Frank at Shugborough[428] because [*fb*] if they do not get them at all it will be necessary for me to write and explain, which having written once I do not wish to do, but if I understood you right you have been with Mrs Anson. she of course wou'd enquire for me, and you of course I shou'd suppose wou'd say you had a letter for her.

You dont say if your dear Father is <u>perfectly</u> recoverd but I hope with all my heart He is, poor John is (he writes me word) again at Oxnead, and comes to us tomorrow but I send chapter and verse to your dear Mother and will not teise you. dear Mr Adey is again this afternoon very much inclind to break his back with bending forward, and when an hour agon I talk'd on the subject and endeavour'd to straiten Him, he made use of an expression that cut me to the heart, that He wish'd he was in heaven and then he shou'd be easy. I cou'd say no more. John[429] left us this morning, and said He shou'd go by tomorrows Mail, but I dare not trust to him, so shall [be] sending packet by Beasy, with Gingerbread to your dear Father.

I am sure all at Harestreet will be heartily glad to have you with them tonight else I [*fb*] cannot help wishing you had accompany'd Duff to his Ball. you are too good a dancer not to be an acquisition at <u>any Ball</u> and your Brother John told us last night, the different Qualifications of <u>all</u> his Brothers. He did not know enough of his Brother William he say'd to speak about him as he did of D, E, and G, but that all his Brothers were <u>real Gentlemen</u> but Brother William more a Gentleman than any – I am sure you will have a delightful visit in Staffordshire and I hope you will have no letter to prevent you going thither, give me a line dear William when you get there

I intended in my last to have ask'd if you had seen Mr Windham for I fancied you must have had his answer to your Sherringham Bill. you will hear by John that Stannard has seen the windows, and is to give Him an Estimate. he says that when he talk'd of three pounds a window he supposes he must mean to have put these present Glasses into broad mouldings <but that> but that he had intirely forgotten all about what passd. he now I understand purposes to have twelve panes instead of eighteen, but by all means over rule John's idea of the six open windows being done and the three [*fb*] stop'd up ones remaining <u>as they are</u>.[430] Nancy Holly desires her love to all, so does my little Eliza, neither poor John <and> *or* his Wife tho they knew I wrote continually ever said 'give my love' but I hope it might be accident not design.

---

428 Shugborough Hall, Great Hayward (Staffs); home of the Anson family. For a history see: http://www.shugborough.org.uk/theshugboroughestate/EstateHistory.aspx.
429 William's brother.
430 Letter 57 refers to the sash windows of John Adey's property requiring attention.

Yours ever affectionately   D Adey

Peter Durrant[431] has brought the printed Tables for you, your uncle, and Mr Henry Anson, to be filed[432] and said he must have them again as soon as he coud. I told him you might not be home of[sic] three weeks. he said before three weeks he wou'd deliver them, but he wou'd call again. John brought me a Bill of 4 pounds of Beasys to pay and said he wou'd send me the money by you, but I told him he had better give the account and the money to you, and I offerd him three Guineas to put in his pocket, but he said without paying that Bill he had quite sufficient to take him home

Address: William Repton Esqr, Harestreet
Endorsed: 21st April 1809   Mrs Adey to me at Harestreet
HM 40887/3

72. Dorothy Adey to William Repton

Aylsham Saturday [22 April 1809][433]

My dear William

I depart from my directions, but these two enclos'd letters arriving by todays post, surely it will be better for you to have them at Shugborough than wait for seeing them till to morrow sent. Beasy came home to day with an account of most prodigious good news, having arriv'd at Norwich the the[sic] Mail Coach men were coverd with Blue Ribbands, and printed papers, and we hop'd and thought you wou'd have sent us a newspaper, but I suppose you were at Harestreet when the news arrivd in Town.[434] all at home as usual *Brother* John did not come to day as he promised but when he sent for Eliza said it was too cold to venture in the Cart, but that he was tolerably well. I shall like to hear you say I have not done wrong in forwarding these letters to you, and with <u>Love</u> to Mr Charles and Mr Henry

I am yours ever Affectionately D Adey

Address: William Repton Esqr, Shugborough
Endorsed: April 1809, Mrs Adey to me at Shugborough
HM 40887/4

---

431 Peter Durrant (1773–1824) of Aylsham; son of James and Elizabeth; married Ann Branton in 1797; licensee of the Bull Inn.
432 'filed' meaning 'filled, completed'.
433 Written for William's arrival at Shugborough; dating his visit there to 23–26 April.
434 Probably news of the Battle of the Basque Roads, 11–13 April; a British victory over the French fleet at the mouth of the Charente.

73. Dorothy Adey to William Repton

[Aylsham], Friday night [28 April 1809]

My dear William

I have been looking at the papers Mr Durrant[435] left and I see the 21 days notice expires on the 8th of March.[436] surely you had best fill them up and send them to me before that time in a Parcel, else it appears to me there is a penalty of 50£. Durrant was here on Saturday and said he wou'd call again. I meant to have defer'd writing till tomorrow morning but George says (for Mileham I suppose is taking leave as he is not in *the* Office this afternoon) he understood he intends to be off at 7 tomorrow morning as he has a good deal to do at Norwich so I shall prepare for him tonight

There is so little alteration in dear Mr Adey for these last three days that it is of no use worrying you or myself on the subject. He has not taken so much nourishment of Broth today as yesterday and he has had [fb] Bork[sic; ?Pork] and Port wine rather more, for I am sorry to say the little place you have heard me complain of his having for some weeks is now a great deal worse, and Mr Taylor very kindly dresses it every day, after this sort of prospect before us my dear William, tho it distresses me to say so, yet if you have not already call'd on Ravenscroft[437] it may be as well not to do so, we can write to him at any time –

By this time to day I think you are arriv'd in Town without danger from floods, I hope. After I had had your letter I saw in the London Paper very terrible [fb] Accounts of accidents from floods. I can easily conceive your Dear Fathers alarm. I have this moment had the most kind letter from him, and I shall write to night and thank him for his goodness. He hopes and so do I, that no real distressing change may take place till you are at home again. I am afraid next Wednesday fortnight the 17th is the earliest day I must look for you, as I recollect the Tivetshall meeting[438] is on the 15th and I think you will be glad to take that in your way home. a fortnight is a long time to look forward to, but I hope I may look forward to it, and if I shou'd be mistaken I hope the moment you hear from me your [fb] good Brother

---

435 See Letter 71.

436 It seems likely that Dorothy has written 8 March by mistake; 8 May would fit. Later in the letter she mentions 'Wednesday fortnight the 17th': 17 May 1809 was a Wednesday; 17 March 1809 was a Friday.

437 Perhaps the London wig-maker in Serle Street, Lincoln's Inn. In 1792 the business was owned by Thomas Ravenscroft. (*Universal Directory* (1792), p. 264.)

438 Probably relating to the Tivetshall enclosure. NRO, AYL 440, comprises Tivetshall enclosure act (1808) statement of claims, commissioners' minute book, 1808–1809.

Duff will have the goodness to come to me by the first Mail. I am afraid I cant bear to be quite by myself. God bless you.

Yours affectionately D Adey

Address: W R—
Endorsed: 28th April 1809   Mrs Adey   a bad account of poor Mr Adey
HM 40887/5

74. Dorothy Adey to William Repton

[Aylsham], Friday night [28 April 1809][439]

My dearest William

At your return *to London or Harestreet* I am sure you will give me a line. I am also sure you will hear of the alarm I <u>have</u> been in from your dear Mother and therefore I do not enter into it with you, farther than to say, I hope nothing at present will happen as most certainly wou'd have been the case had we grown at all worse but I thank God a <u>little</u> alteration for the better is perceptable and I hope we shall not lose the ground we have got but supposing it shou'd be the Almightys will it shou'd be so, rest assured I will make myself as content as I can rather than you shou'd by absence lose the obtaining your Bill, or in any way whatever be injur'd by returning before <u>all</u> your business is got through to your wishes.

The Young Men have had several people with them but I told Mileham to write to you if necessary. I thought when I went into the Study to put up my Tea it felt cold and rather damp, and I ordered a Fire to be made on Wednesday. that day and every day since they have been up to the ears in dirt and dust, it was so uncomfortable to me [*fb*] [to] *see* Books and papers strew'd all over the room, that I complain'd of the appearance. George says it is quite necessary, and that he had your orders to do what he is about, and I do see today (for I had no heart to look in yesterday) two or three of the Lockers are cleard and in good order, but I still think a little method might have made it an easier job. I am afraid you have had but bad weather for your Staffordshire Excursion. I have you may be sure, thought and talk'd of you every day and am truly happy that by <this> the time you get this I hope to have you a hundred miles nearer to old Aylsham

God bless you, Yours affectionately D Adey

---

439 Assigned to 28 April as this was a Friday. The second of two letters written that night. The accounts of Mr Adey's health differ, but otherwise this dating fits with the other letters in this sequence.

Flowers[440] man brought a letter which I send and told me his master sent his Comp[limen]ts to me, and if Mr Repton was from home, beg'd I woud give the servant leave to put his Horse into the stable till his return as his letter required an answer. I sent my Comp[limen]ts and you was not returnd from Town nor did I know when to expect you. I had a mind to have written and said the Sherringham Bill was nearly ended, but on [fb] second thoughts I did not. yet surely my dear William you shou'd give him a letter yourself of its safety. dear Nancy had been a great comfort to me. she is to go to Ardens[441] on Monday for a week but will if I wish it give up her engagement. I do not wish it. I shall do vastly well so that I have not Mrs John. o dear William you have not an idea what it is to have that weak woman in the House day after day when poor creature she is in trouble.

Address: Wm Repton Esq
Endorsed: April 1809   Mrs Adey to me at Harestreet
HM 40887/6

75. Dorothy Adey to William Repton

[Aylsham], Saturday Night [29 April 1809][442]

My dear William

A Thousand thanks to you for your letter from Shugborough, which I have this instant receivd. to hear you are well and happy in your Excursion, and to know that you will enjoy your visit is the pleasantest of all pleasant things to me my best of Boys, and tho I am sorry you cannot allow yourself to make it longer, yet if call'd upon to speak honestly I am monstrous glad to hear you are coming again a hundred miles nearer home.

in all probability you will get this letter before you have the one I have sent to Harestreet by the Basket, or hear from your good Mother the alarm I have been in (according to custom *in your absence*) on your dear Uncles

---

440 Cook Flower (1766–1842); married Ann Hindry in 1798. Flower owned the house at Sheringham that Repton suggested be purchased as a country seat for Horatio Nelson's brother. In his contribution to Armstrong's *History of Norfolk* (1781) Repton described Sheringham in glowing terms. (Daniels, *Repton*, p. 91.) In 1811 Flower sold Sheringham Park to Abbot Upcher and Repton subsequently worked there. See note to Letter 158.
441 Francis Edward Arden (1777–1855) and his wife Rachel neé Pinckard, who married at Blickling in 1803; they lived at Gresham, (*Aylsham*, p. 255.) See also Letter 75.
442 In his endorsement William has 'qu[ery] 22d April 1809', but this was written in response to a letter from Shugborough, so 29 April, which was also a Saturday, is more likely.

account. I will not bore you to death with farther accounts, let it suffice, that I do not now foresee <u>immediate</u> danger, yet for fear of leaving off our attention too soon, I will not give up the having one or other of the Maids sit with him all night.

John Repton goes on ill and well, his note tonight when [*fb*] the Child was sent for, was rather good than not. I have told Mileham your wishes and I have said to George, that as you find there is a possibility of getting an allowance for two Clerks you are under the necessity of saying He this year must not think of a Journey to town, and the poor Lad said, 'I am very much oblig'd to Mr Repton Madam for thinking and mentioning me'. perhaps you will bring him some little remembrance from Town, somthing for a Waistcoat, or a Silver Pencil, or somthing of a Bettermost sort of a portable inkstand, not a watch chain, cause why? He has no Watch to put it to.

pray dont forget to give my letter to Mrs Anson.[443] I am sure you will call and say how you left all in Staffordshire, and as to Lady Katherines letter must be given her as I have told <Mrs> Lady Mary[444] that I have written to her by you. I wish if you go near George *St* you wou'd enquire at Ld Carleton's if H. B.[445] is in London. I wish Belmont[446] had fortunately been within a morning ride, but twenty miles is rather too far to Bump, and meet no pleasure at the end of the fatigue.

Dear Nancy was to have gone to Gresham yesterday, in order to prepare [*fb*] for the Christening on Monday, and Arden came over to fetch her, but all I cou'd say she wou'd not go till Monday, with the Holleys. If Mr Adey continues mending or even as he is, she does not come home before Saturday, and don't you fancy that <u>I mind</u> being alone, upon my word and honor I do not. <u>I am perfectly well</u>, and so that I do but escape the worry of Mrs Johns Tongue I am content. Taylor[447] was at Norwich last Saturday and in conversing with Martineau about J[ohn]: R[epton]: Martineau said, 'there is certainly a vast deal of hurry and nervousness about him, but surely Mr Taylor that Wife of his must hurry and fatigue him, how incessantly she talks'. You will see Mrs Doughtys[448] letter to me, and my Answer.

---

443 See Letter 71.
444 Lady Mary Walpole, daughter of the first earl of Orford, Lady Katherine's sister.
445 Harry Botham. In Letter 15 he wrote about sending a package via Lord Carleton.
446 The home of Mr and Mrs Sneyd, who lived near Lichfield (Staffs).
447 Samuel Taylor, the Aylsham surgeon.
448 Ann Doughty, wife of Robert Lee Doughty (q.v.). They had married in 1776; she was the daughter of Thomas Powys esquire, later first baron Lilford (Northants). (*Repton in Norfolk*, p. 45.)

Mr Churchill came last night to enquire how your uncle did. it is impossible to say how very kind the whole Parmeter family, Tounsend,[449] Mr Holley, in short every one who understood how very bad Mr Adey was, have been in their attention.

I fancy poor Taylor gave the alarm. he was here at two oclock *on Thursday* and went from hence to Ld Orfords Audit at the black Boys and I find since, he told Izzy where to send supposing I can't go on. so never mind, thank God he has been mistaken and all I meant to say was, that Mr Churchill says the Doughtys set out for London on Monday. I have given Mr Doughty your direction to 202, but I suppose you will leave your address there. I am sorry your own Lodgings are gone, but I hope you will be in the [fb] Neighbourhood and not have a long walk of a night. Mileham desires I will say he sent a parcel <for> to you, which he thinks wou'd be at 202 on Wednesday and if you have not receiv'd it desires you will say so. George told me with great Glee tonight, that He shou'd intirely finish his job on Monday night. I said I was glad of it, but that I saw a novel of Mrs Dyes[450] laying on the Desk and I was afraid that might take up his time: 'That's Mr Mileham. He dont help me at all. Mr Repton desired me to do it.' 'O very well' I said 'you [are] a good Lad I dare say'. so ends this medly.

Yours ever Affectionately D Adey

Nancys love

My kind love to dear Duff. tell him I shall hope for the pleasure of hearing from him in August, bid him enquire for my this years number. I dont know if your Mother will tell it to him, 82 or 81 or some such foolish thing.[451]

Address: William Repton Esqr, Piccadilly No: 202
B st: AYLSHAM 132; *r st*: B May 1 1809;[452] *charge*: 9
Endorsed: qu[ery] 22ᵈ April 1809   Mrs Adey – Mr Adey better
HM 40887/7

---

449 Not identified.

450 From 1790 until his death in 1797 Robert Dye owned The Dog in Norwich Road; after his death his widow Elizabeth took it over, until her death in 1810. (M. Vaughan-Lewis, ed., *A New History of Aylsham Public Houses* (Aylsham, 2018), pp. 71–3) This was probably a book belonging to Elizabeth Dye: there was no readily identifiable novelist called Mrs Dye in this period. (W. D. Adams, *Dictionary of English Literature* (London, 1880); M. A. Bald, *Women-writers of the nineteenth century* (Cambridge, 1923).)

451 This probably refers to a lottery ticket. See also Letter 194.

452 i.e. the letter was not posted until 1 May.

76. Dorothy Adey to William Repton

[Aylsham], Tuesday Morning 6 [a.m.] [2 May 1809]

Dearest William

A very good discharge from the Bowels last night, a quiet night free from Cough and is now asleep very comfortably
  Yours ever DA

Address: W Repton Esqr, 202 Piccadilly
Endorsed: qu[ery] 2ⁿᵈ May 1809   Mrs Adey's note of Mr Adeys health
HM 40887/8

77. Dorothy Adey to William Repton

[Aylsham], Wednesday 6 oclock [3 May 1809]

My dearest William

I dont ask you to pity your dear old Aunt. I know you do, but I shall soon I trust be surrounded by those you love *for* Taylor assuring me a change must inevidently[sic] shortly take place, I have accepted your dear Fathers Kind offer and have summon'd them to me. in short I have sufferd so dreadfully the whole of this day intirely by myself, from hearing his most distressing Groans that I find I am not equal to it any longer. Mrs Parmeter and Charlotte <he> were here last night, the latter wou'd not leave me and Mrs Parmeter has made Mr Taylor promise to send for her when he sees it right to do so, and then she will not leave me till your dear Mother arrives, and this kindness of hers, has led me to refuse poor Mrs Bretts offer of leaving the bedside of poor Hardy (who is dangerously ill) but I am sure I feel her kindness.[453] it is unfortunate dear Nancy haveing engag'd herself to the Ardens, but as she desir'd me to send if I wou'd have her come home I shou'd have done so, if Mrs Parmeter had not so kindly offerd me her attention, and of the two she is certainly best.

I have two letters for you, I think you will not now go down to Harestreet on Saturday, I will therefore send [fb] them with this and make a parcel of the whole. you will as one of the letters have been here some days be glad I shou'd think to have them. We have flatterd ourselves my dear William that

---

453 Susanna Brett's husband was named Hardy; his being ill is also mentioned in Letter 99.

so gradually as our dearest Mr Adey has all along gone, He wou'd at last have left this world without pain. Taylor says he is not clear he <u>feels</u> pain now. what then can occasion the dreadful and distressing groans he incessantly makes. if he shriekd to be heard across the Market and I cou'd afford him <u>one moments</u> aleviation from pain, you know me too well to believe I wou'd shrink from it, but I cannot do so, and therefore I go occasionally but I do not stay by him, nor am I this afternoon able to bear the <u>sitting room</u> but am come down into the parlour. what will become of me to night I dare not think but perhaps as I had no sleep last night I may be tired out and drop to night. it is a real comfort to me to think (when I think as I ought to do) that you unhappy as I am sure you must be, be where you will, have not nor are in the way to hear him as I do –

write to me my dear William that you are safe in Town, and as to seeing you, I am sure I shall when your business will permit, but remember my good William it is <u>you</u> now that is all in all to me and that if you encounter any unnecessary fatigue to expedite you getting back and lay yourself up, you will add to the distress you mean to lessen. George (who dines here poor boy ever since Mileham left Aylsham) tells me somthing about the Court at Matlaske[454] in the course of next week that will bring you home. I am [fb] almost sure, from what little I know of the business you are upon, if you are not in Town <u>till Friday</u> it never can be concluded for you to get down to a Court, and I think in the multiplicity of business you have had on your mind you may possibly have forgotten this same Court. If I should be right in my conjecture write and tell George what to do.

Mr Taylor has just been in and insisted I do not sleep tonight in the little bed. I believe he is right, for I think I cou'd *not* hear him and retain my reason, so I shall take Eliza and sleep in the patchwork room. Barnes has slept in the House ever since Thursday night. The poor maids sit up by turns. Izzy looks worn to death, but sits in the room with patience and Kindness. Mr Taylor thinks no change will take place just at present, if it does I will send Barnes with a letter to put in the post before it goes from Norwich, so I will make up my parcel for Beasy to night because to write to dear Duff this morning I was up at 5, and so was poor Taylor.

so God in Heaven protect you my dearest William. I will do all I am able, depend <illeg> upon it to bear my trying affliction. I want to ask many questions, and say many things, but I have not the heart. Duff will be with me and direct me right and on toward I hope [fb] your Dear Father & Mother. poor dear JR very very bad again. he sent tonight to know if I

---

454 i.e. the manorial court.

woud have a load of straw to lay in the street but no noise or any thing in the world affects him again

    God bless you DA

Address: Wm Repton Esqr
Endorsed: Wednesday 3ᵈ May 1809   Mrs Adey's letter to me in London preparing me to hear of Mr Adeys death
HM 40887/9

78. Dorothy Adey to William Repton

                [Aylsham], <Wednesday> Thursday [4 May 1809]

My dearest William[455]

    I am better writing to you than not at ½ past eight I saw your dear Uncle at nine he was releas'd God love you & write to me let me see who I will do you write

    to your truly afflicted but affectionate D Adey

Address: [*torn*] Wm Repton Esq, No 202 Picc[adilly] Lo[ndon]
R st: B May 6 1809; *charge*: [*missing*]
Endorsed: Thursday 4 May 1809   Mrs Adey's letter to me in London that Mr Adey died on this day at 9 in the morning
HM 40887/10

79. Dorothy Adey to William Repton

                  [Aylsham], Thursday afternoon [4 May 1809]

    The joy and Comfort your letter has given me my dearest William is not to be told. to have you in London a whole day earlier than I thought is most comfortable and you I am sure will be made comfortable by hearing of the kindness of all my friends. Mrs Parmeter came to me this morning and will not leave me till your dear Mother arrives. I have had the kindest offers of attention from Mr & Mrs Collyer and from Mr & Mrs Holly and dear Mrs Brett has repeatedly written, but what is best of all, and what I am sure you have comfort in being told, your dear Uncle John and my sister come before dinner. they go home to night and will come to me again to morrow. I dreaded more than any thing our meeting for fear of hurting him but thank

---

455 A single sheet, torn in half; absence of punctuation as in the original.

God I had resolution to behave well and I have the <comfort> happiness to say I find him much better than from report I had expected. He hopes in your hurry you will not forget an application [*fb*] to the Fishmongers.[456] most heartily glad shall I be to have the meeting between you and me over, but I shall have all my good friends about me and will wait with patience till all your business is done and ended. so do not my dear good Boy distress yourself for

Your truly affectionate D A

Address: Wm Repton Esq, No 202 Piccadilly, London
B st: AYLSHAM 132; *r st*: B May 6 1809; *charge*: 9
Endorsed: Thursday 4 May 1809   Mrs Adey to me in London after Mr Adey's death
HM 40887/11

80. George Repton to William Repton

[London], Thursday afternoon 5 o Clock [4 May 1809]

Dear William

Duff is going to Harest[reet] this Evening supposing he shall find you there as you have not calld <u>here</u> since the morning – but should you still be in Town, and happen to call here this Evening, I wish you to extend your walk to Dover Street where I shall be all this Evening

Your affectionate Brother George

the enclosed is Duffs key – as he proposes leaving Harestreet tomorrow morning for Norfolk – his bed you will occupy of course

Endorsed: 4th May 1809   My Brother George's   Note to me in Piccadilly on Mr Adey's Illness
HM 40918/1

---

456 The Worshipful Company of Fishmongers of the City of London were (and still are) the trustees of Gresham's School, Holt. Adey & Repton did business with the Fishmongers' Company, but how this might relate to John Repton is unclear. NRO, AYL 250 is a bundle of correspondence the between Fishmongers' Company and Adey & Repton re. Gresham's School, Holt, including copies of statutes; NRO, AYL 420 is a bundle of papers, mainly correspondence with Fishmongers' Company regarding the Holt enclosure.

81. Humphry Repton to John Wodehouse, first baron Wodehouse (draft);
Humphry Repton to William Windham (draft)

Harestreet near Romford, May 6 1809

My Lord

When I was last in Norfolk I had the honor to call at Kimberley[457] &
introduced my son Mr William Repton who has <for many> *of late* years
acted for his Uncle Mr John Adey as <Your Lordships> Steward <for> *to
your Lordships* Courts held by him – I have just learned the death of Mr
Adey & take the liberty – to beg *the favor that your Lordship will continue
<the>*< Your Lordships continuance of> the same Courts to My Son –
<with such further Confidence as Your Lordship may be pleased to grant
him> – & I have the honor to be, My Lord
    Your Lordships Most obedient humble servant H Repton

Harestreet <by> near Romford, May <7>6 1809

<My Lord>

<When I was last in Norfolk I had the honor to call & introduce to your
Lordship my Son *Mr* William Repton who has of late>
    Dear Sir
    I have just received an account of the death of your sincere friend John
Adey who for many years enjoyed your Confidence. I now take the liberty
to request that you will have the goodness to consider my Son Wm Repton
as his Representative & that you will bestow on him those Courts formerly
held by his Uncle, for whom you know he acted during the last years of his
lingering decay. I have the honor to be, Sir
    Your most obedient humble servant HR

Endorsed by Repton: Copy of letters for Courts for Wm   6 May 1809   To
Lord Wodehouse[458] & to Rt Hon W Windham
Endorsed by William: 6 May 1809   My Father's L[ett]res to Mr Windham
& Lord Wodehouse applying for Courts
HM 40883

---

457 Kimberley Hall (Wymondham). Prior to his elevation to the peerage on 26 October
1797, as baron Wodehouse, John Wodehouse was M.P. for Norfolk. (*Hist. Parl.*; http://
www.thepeerage.com/p3635.htm#i36344.) He married Charlotte Norris on 17 November
1796. Through her father she had inherited Witton Hall; in 1801 Repton had prepared a
Red Book for Witton Hall. (*Repton in Norfolk*, pp. 98–104.)
458 Altered from Woodhouse.

82. John Wodehouse, first baron Wodehouse, to Humphry Repton

London, May 8th 1809

My Dear Sir

I should have great pleasure in complying with your wishes, Did I consider that I should act kindly towards a young Man to whom I am much obliged, were I to do so. I am aware that There is no Professional Gentleman in the county whose Character stands higher than that of your Son, and it is impossible that anything can be more pleasing than his manners. But Mr Gilman[459] is a young Man that holds my other Courts and I am so much Indebted to him for the very great attention he pays to my Concerns on all occasions, that I feel that I can do no [fb] less than add the Manors of Crownthorp & Wicklewood to those he already holds for me.

I am Dear Sir
Your very faithful Humble Servant Wodehouse

Address: London May eight 1809, Humphry Repton Esq, Harestreet near Romford,
Wodehouse[460]
R st with crown: FREE 8 My 8 1809
Endorsed: 8 May 1809   A very civil Letter from Lord Wodehouse to my father about the Wicklewood Courts
HM 40951

83. George Repton to William Repton

29 Dover Street, Monday – May 8th [1809]

My dear William

I have just sent off the Servant with your Portmanteau and deal box – with directions to take them to the White Horse Fetter Lane and desire they may go by this afternoons Expedition Coach – I therefore hope you will receive them safely – the black pantaloons I put into the Portmanteau – and in the pocket of the pantaloons is a letter which has come for you since your departure – the Seals had <u>not</u> been sent,[461] and I feard the time

---

459 Perhaps Samuel Heyhoe Le Neve Gilman (1773–1860), lawyer, of Hingham.
460 Indicating Wodehouse's privilege of free post.
461 Seals from Halfhide. George first mentioned obtaining seals for William in July 1807 (Letter 12). The seals mentioned here were eventually sent on 15 May 1809 (Letter 90).

for sending them by this day's *coach* would have elapsed had I made enquiries for them – but <in> if I can forward them to you in any other way you may point out I will do so – upon Duff's Chimney I found two letters one to Charles Kent[462] the other to myself. the former I have put into the twopenny post – the request in the latter I will attend to the first time I go out *you may therefore consider it done* – give my affectionate [fb] [love] to all at Aylsham and believe me, Dear William

your affectionate Brother GSR

Your two packages are directed to you at Aylsham Norfolk. tell Duff I see a Card from Claude Scott on his Chimney, to invite him to dinner on some distant day. I do not exactly recollect for what day – but think it was for next Saturday –

I open this to put in my father's letter[463] and to join with him in hoping that My dear Aunt will return to Harest[reet] with you –

Endorsed: 8 May 1809   My brother George   Has sent my portmanteau
HM 40918/2

84. Humphry Repton to Mr Charles Repington of Tamworth[464]

Harestreet near Romford, 8 May 1809

Sir

I desired one of my Sons who has lately been in Staffordshire to make some enquiries concerning my name, when he confirmed what I had understood from my father thirty years ago, that his father was Rector of the Parish of Stoke upon Trent in 1692, but I can trace the name no farther back in that Register.[465]

The name of Repton has evidently been changed from Repington, like the Town & Hundred of the same names in Derbyshire, & as I can

---

462 The son of Nathaniel Kent (q.v.). (See Letter 145.) In 1822 Charles had a house in Cromer Road, Blickling. (*Aylsham Directories*, p. 6.)

463 There is no letter in the collection to William from his father, dated 8 May 1809; presumably the letter that George had enclosed was the copy of Repton's 'extraordinary Letter to Mr Repington of Tamworth'. (See Letter 84.) They have been separated in the archive.

464 Charles Edward Repington (26 October 1755 – 27 June 1837), of Amington Hall, near Tamworth (but now in Warwickshire). (http://www.rippington.me.uk/indiI3793.html accessed 17/9/19.)

465 A John Repton resigned as rector of Stoke on Trent on 20 November 1697. (CCEd Person ID: 58169.) A Humfrey Repton had served in a chapelry of Stoke on Trent until 1676. (CCEd Person ID: 58167.)

discover no person of either names except yourself I have taken the liberty to address you on a subject which to a Stranger might appear impertinent as it is merely to gratify that sort of Vanity which naturally belongs to an ancient name – but perhaps you may have heard at what time or on what occasion the abbreviation took place – although such abbreviations often occur, as in the very ancient name of Wyndham from their original Estate at Wymondham in Norfolk & many others –

I will therefore hope you will pardon my addressing you in consideration that however distant the consanguinity I may possibly have [*fb*] the honor to be a relative and as such beg leave to subscribe myself, Sir

Your most obedient humble Servant H Repton

Endorsed by Repton: Copy to – Repington Esq ab[ou]t name &c
Endorsed by William: 8 May 1809   My father's extraordinary Letter to Mr Repington of Tamworth
HM 40838

85. Lady Katherine Walpole to William Repton

Bruton Street, May 11ᵗʰ 1809

Dear Sir

The great esteem I have for Mrs Adey will no longer allow me to be silent upon the Late Melancholy Event. However encreasing infirmities might have prepared her for her loss, yet I am fully sensible when the stroke comes it is a heavy one & such as time alone can relieve. There is, however, both to herself & to you much subject of Consolation. His Situation has been gradually that of sinking both in body & mind for a Length of time & his release from this world to a better has placed him in a happier state than the happiest here could have afforded him during his long indisposition. The unremitting attention & care with which he has been attended [*fb*] by Mrs Adey & you must be a source of the highest Comfort. I beg of you to say everything from me & from us all to her. I was going to answer her Letter when the sad news arriv'd & when you are at leisure may I beg you will believe My Anxiety about her & I am, Dear Sir,

Your oblig'd &c K. Walpole

Address: W Repton Esqr, Aylsham
Endorsed: 11 May 1809   Lady Kath Walpole   On Mr Adey's death
HM 40949

86. Hon. Mrs Mary Anson[466] to William Repton

Queen Ann Street,[467] May 13th 1809

My dear S'r,

I did not hear of the Event of your poor Uncles death till yesterday, & need not say how truly I feel for your dear Aunt on this greatest of trials. for tho' she must have really been long prepared for it, in her own mind, yet when the blow does come it must ever be severely felt, especially where there had been so much happiness for so long. Your good Uncle was a worthy valuable Man, beloved by all that knew him, & I had indeed a very [fb] sincere regard for him. To himself it is a happy release & I hope he did not suffer much at last.

I had not heard any of him since I saw you here. I hope you was returned home before the Event happened, as I know your Aunt would receive every comfort & attention possible from you, & will feel it a great relief to have so kind a Nephew with her, & I beg you will be so good to let me know how she really is & trust her health will not suffer materially from all the fatigue & anxiety she has gone through. Pray give my kindest Love to her & assure how sincerely I share in her present affliction, but doubt not her being properly supported under it by [fb] that good Providence who never fails them that submit with due Resignation to his Will.

We have also had a melancholy Scene in the death of poor Ld Harcourt[468] which is a great concern to all the family. L[ad]y Harcourt is very indifferent & my friend L[ad]y Elizabeth Lee[469] has been greatly affected.

I hope you will excuse this hasty scrawl but I was unwilling to omit a post enquiring after your dear Aunt & expressing my concern for you all, & beg you will believe me, Dear S'r

Yours Sincerely M Anson

Pray how is Mr John Repton.

We have not yet heard from my Son George.[470] L[ad]y Anson[471] came to

---

466　See Letter 71; Letter 92 is William's draft reply.

467　The London residence of the Anson family.

468　George Simon, second earl Harcourt, died on 20 April 1809, without issue. (*ODNB* for his brother William, third earl Harcourt (1743–1830).) Lord Harcourt's wife was Elizabeth Venables Vernon; she was the half-sister of Mary Anson.

469　Lady Elizabeth Lee was Lord Harcourt's sister; she had married Sir William Lee on 20 June 1763. (http://www.thepeerage.com/p46162.htm#i461614.)

470　Mary and George Anson's second son, George: Gen. Sir George Anson (1769–1849) GCB.

471　Lady Anne Anson (1779–1843), wife of Thomas, first viscount Anson (1767–1818). (See

Town on Wednesday & my Son was to go to Leamington last Tuesday. I am sorry Charles & Harry[472] are not <u>now</u> in Norfolk

[*fb*] The Stuarts & Samb[rook]e[473] desire me to say every thing kind from them

Address: Mr William Repton, Aylsham, Norfolk
B st: A MA 13 809
Endorsed: 13th May 1809   The Hon'ble Mrs Anson   On Mr Adey's death
HM 40894

87. William Repton to Lady Katherine Walpole (draft)

Aylsham, 14th May 1809

Madam

Both Mrs Adey & myself are very much obliged by your Ladyship's kind and friendly letter on the subject of our recent Loss, for such as a matter of feeling, we must *undoubtedly* consider poor Mr Adey's departure, & though reason & reflection ought to satisfy us <that from> under existing circumstances that he whom we lament is but released – yet the remembrance of former scenes <of pleas> in which he participated *with us* cannot but excite those feelings of regret & anguish which <time alone can> *are to be* subdued by time alone. Mrs Adey I am happy to say exerts her natural good sense as much as <it can> [*fb*] <be expected in> any one so situated <to be> can be expected to do – *& my fat[her] & mother being here with us* I have hopes that she may be induced <when my mother> *to accompany them* into Essex <when> on their return, more particularly as I <must return to> *must be again in* London soon after the Whitsun Holidays in order to complete my business in Parli[ament] which has been for a while delayed by this distressing event – Again I thank your Ladyship for having so kindly remembered us. And have the honor to be
    Your Ladyships Most obliged & very humble &c WR

Endorsed: 14th May 1809   L[ett]re to The Right Hon. Lady Kath' Walpole On Mr Adey's death
HM 40941

---

note to Letter 53.) They had married on 15 September 1794 at Holkham, she being Lady Anne Margaret Coke, second daughter of Thomas William Coke, first earl of Leicester.

472 Charles and Henry Anson. Letter 91 is Charles' letter of condolence.

473 Mary and George Anson's third daughter, Catherine, had married Henry Stuart in 1807. Lt-Col. Sambrooke Anson (1778–1846), was their seventh son.

88. Mrs Ann Doughty to Dorothy Adey

Hanworth, Thursday [May 1809]

Dear Mrs Adey,

I cannot help troubling you with a line to offer our condolence on your late melancholy loss, the severity of the shock I trust will be in some degree softend, by your having been prepared to expect it, & I hope in time you will recur to the consolitory[sic] reflection [fb] that by your unreserved & affectionate attention to your good Husband you afforded him every possible comfort.

We are going tomorrow to Town for a short time, when we return I intend taking an early opportunity of calling upon you, in the mean time, Mr D. unites with me in all good wishes, & I remain

Much yours A Doughty

Address: Mrs Adey
Endorsed: May 1809   Mrs Doughty to Mrs Adey on the Mr As death
HM 40901

89. John Repton, with notes by Humphry Repton

Oxnead, May 15th 1809[474]

This Will having been made at the time of a little disagreement with my own family – I hereby confirm every part thereof with this exception only <of> that instead of the name of James Marsh Esquire – I have inserted the name of my Nephew William Repton of Aylsham Attorney at Law & hereby constitute & appoint him to be <my> *a joint* Executor <with> and Guardian with my friend William Lubbok – & Elizabeth my Wife, as witness my hand in the presence of

My beloved brother Humphry }
& my Nephew & Niece[475]   }

[fb] [*notes by Humphry Repton*]
Power to Collect & receive – Moneys due from any person – or &c any

---

474 The Huntington Library dates this as [1809] [14 Jan<] i.e. after 14 January 1809, but the note by John Repton is dated clearly 15 May 1809.

475 The nephew and niece are not named, but from Letter 93 it is likely that the nephew was Duff. The niece would have been Mary as she was 23 in May 1809, whereas Elizabeth was only 18 and therefore under age.

acc[oun]t whatsoever whether arises <from> under the Will of my late father John R Eq deceased or otherwise –

to Eliz[abeth] Ex[ecuto]rs not to be acc[ounta]ble for more money than comes into their hands – each – nor by any Loss – – neither one answerable for the other – &c &c but each for himself – and also – Ex[ecuto]rs may reimburse themselves all such loss Costs & reasonable exp[ense]s as they or either of them may incur in the execution of this will.

Money to be vested in funds & accumulate till Eliza is of age.

If she dies before – all goes to his wife *if single* – with power of disposing by will but not giving it out of the family of his Bro[ther] & Sister or if both die – then the prop[ert]y to be divided among them & their representatives

Endorsed: May 1809   My father's memos about John Repton's Will
HM 40856

90. George Repton to William Repton

Harestreet, Monday May 15ᵗʰ [1809]

Dear William –

enclosed I send your two seals which Mr Halfhide denies having promised to send to Duffs, on the contrary he says that they have been ready for you some time past. I offerd to pay him for them, but he said it could remain untill you came to Town – I have not yet paid Jewells Guinea,[476] but have been once to the place in Holborn – and found nothing could be done after 2 oClock. I will therefore take an early opportunity of going there again before that hour – adieu

Your affectionate   GSR

Endorsed: 15 May 1809   My brother *George* abt my Seals from London
HM 40918/3

---

476 Not identified; presumably Jewell had a business in Holborn.

91. Revd Charles Anson to William Repton[477]

Sudbury [near Lichfield], May 16th 1809

My dear William

From a Letter recieved from Henry[478] he with much concern informed me that the Norwich Newspaper contained the melancholy intelligence of the Death of our worthy & most justly esteemed Friend at Aylsham[479] – The situation he has been in for so long a time allows I doubt but little room to hope that the information may not be correct, & I can easily conceive what real concern the loss of such a valuable member of your society must have been to you all. I feel most deeply for poor dear Mrs Adey, & am sure her affliction will be severe, but trust her natural strength of mind will enable her to bear up with fortitude [fb] & resignation against certainly one of the severest trials that human nature has to encounter – viz – a separation from all that one has held most dear in this world. To offer or to intrude with officious consolation on such a subject may be truly deemed impertinent – Time, when aided by a patient submission & humble acquiescence to the divine will, can only mellow that sorrow which it cannot heal. It cannot indeed obliterate the remembrance of what has been, but it may render that remembrance more pleasing & less painful. – I am in hopes that severe as the blow must be, that poor Mrs Adey was in some degree prepared for it. She must have perceived that gradual decay of Nature <that must have> *which* precluded any hopes of amendment. She has the satisfaction of knowing that his latter days have been rendered comfortable to him by her constant & unremitting attentions, indeed <her> *unusual* exertions of fortitude have been frequently called for throughout his illness. [fb] I do not know the time of poor Mr Adeys decease, as I have only heard of it by report, but I <question> *fear* whether the fatal event might <hap> have happened during your absence from home – which would be <doubly> *greatly* distressing to your Aunt, & I am sure would be equally so to yourself, as it would have been a great comfort to her to have had you with her.

Pray have the goodness to write me a line to inform me how poor Mrs Adey does, & how she supports herself under her affliction:- Assure her that I feel for her most sensibly, I could not bring myself to write to her

---

477 Letter 96 is William's reply.
478 His brother.
479 A brief report of John Adey's death is in *The Norfolk Chronicle*, Saturday, 6 May 1809, issue 2041, p. 3.

on this melancholy occasion – though had I not had an opportunity of gaining intelligence of her through you I certainly should have done so – Frederick[480] *begs* I would say every thing proper for him, & feels anxious as well as myself for an account of you all, [fb] which I hope you will have the goodness to send us as soon as convenient – He laments also not having had the pleasure of seeing you when you were in this Neighbourhood.

With kindest regards, & every good wish to poor dear Mrs Adey believe me ever, my dear William,

your affectionate Friend Chas Anson

Direct to me, Rectory, Sudbury, Lichfield

Address: William Repton Esqr, Aylsham, Norfolk
Orange st: LITCHFIELD 119 MAY 17 1809; *charge*: [illeg]
Endorsed: 16th May 1809   The Revd C Anson   On Mr Adey's death
HM 40895

92. William Repton to Mrs Mary Anson (draft)

Stratton,[481] 16 May 1809

Dear Madam

I beg to return you many thanks for your very kind & friendly letter on the subject of the loss we have recently sustained in poor Mr Adey's death. it is indeed a loss for which we have been <long> *gradually* prepared by his increasing age & infirmities, yet as you observe with much justice <when the a separation> it is a blow which must be severely felt by <Mrs Adey> my aunt *especially* when we consider that the union which is thus dissolved has been of 40 years contin[uan]ce.

My brother[482] & myself <attended> performed the last office<s> of attention & respect by following my uncle's *remains* to the Grave <at Mrs Adey's request> having found that such was Mrs Adey's wish tho' she hesitated to ask it lest it sho'd be imposing *on me* too hard a task. She poor soul exerts *herself as much <her>* her natural good sense as much as

---

480 Revd Frederick Anson (1779–1867), eighth and youngest son of George and Mary Anson; at this time rector of Sudbury (Derbys.), 1803–10; later dean of Chester Cathedral, 1839–67. (CCEd Person ID: 4442.)

481 William was staying at the White Swan in Long Stratton: see the next letter, addressed to him there.

482 Probably Duff, as on 3 May (Letter 77) Dorothy Adey had asked him to come to Aylsham.

it wo'd lead us to expect & can be expected – of any person <so situated> *in her situation* [fb] to do – <and> It is a great comfort to her to have my dear mother & sisters with us – & I sho'd hope when they leave Aylsham Mrs Adey will be tempted to accompany them home for a short time, more especially as I must return to Town for about 10 days to complete my business in Parli[ament] w'ch has been interrupted for a while by this melancholy event.

On my return from Shugborough (<after passing a most delightful week there>) *after passing a most delightful week there* I of course intended to have had the honor of calling in Queen Anne St't in order to give you an account of those with whom I had spent <a most delightful week> my time so pleasantly & of whose welfare you wo'd be desirous to hear but <finding> I found at my lodgings a letter *from Mrs Adey* which determined me to leave London without delay –

I am sorry to say it is not in my power to give a good account of my Uncle John Repton. The medical Gent[leme]n who attend him seem to be confident that his complaint is Water in the Chest – if such is really the case we may indeed have reason to dread the Result. [fb] He appears to be much rallied by the <sight of> *society of* my father & <much> was very desirous that we sho'd all be with him at Oxnead on Sunday

I beg my best remember[an]ces to Col: Sambroke & all who so kindly remember me. And have the honor to be, D[ear] Madam

Your *obliged &* very faithful humble servant WR

Endorsed: 16 May 1809   L[ett]re to the Hon'ble Mrs Anson on Mr Adey's death
HM 40937

93. Dorothy Adey to William Repton

Aylsham, Wednesday [17 May 1809]

My dear William

d: [Elizabeth], Eliza and myself came home to breakfast this morning in order to meet dear Nancy from Gresham, who I am sorry to say is gone home extremely ill. Mr Murrell came about eleven with your letter, and as he says, and as you also say *you* think you can be spar'd. I have no hesitation whatever in saying your being at Oxnead <u>as soon as you can</u> (not taking any notice of my saying so, but as a thing of course which your poor uncle expects in your road to Aylsham) seems absolutely necessary, for he was very Anxious on Sunday after we all came away to consult with your dear Father on his disposal of his affairs, and on [*fb*] Monday Morning your Mother with great pleasure told me every thing was settled intirely to his and also to Mrs John's satisfaction and that your Father had written a Codicil⁴⁸³ which was signd before and witness'd by Duff, not one word of which Codicil I am very sure is of the smallest consequence and this from the little knowledge of Law that I possess I have convinc'd all except the dear one most concern'd *is the case* <of> to him not one word is said, and whether it pleases God to allow him Life or not till your return, I am satisfied his wishes are, to not withdraw himself from his own Relations, but He is not to be told one word on any account untill you are on the spot, so that of course if you can get to Oxnead in any tolerable time tomorrow *Thursday* you will, but we are all wish'd to be in Bed at ten, that he may not be prevented sleeping. so if you dont get this letter in time for that, do not come till Friday Morn, and then, as your Uncle says, he knows you will <come> to Oxnead in [*fb*] your road to Aylsham.

Mr Martineau din'd with us yesterday *when* your Father said he wou'd try and see the event of a few days, he shak'd his head and said a few months might not determine, and there was no saying a few hours might not, he is quite sure the disorder is not water in the Chest but one equally fatal. I dont know the name but an enlargement of the Heart – Mr Martineau told us of your being on the outside a Mail Coach and I with pain learn the Horse you took from Aylsham made this necessary, very dear William, I shall never be comfortable till you can find you are able to have a Horse of your own.

d: says the intelligence of Mr Marsh's⁴⁸⁴ death can not be true. I think they must have talk'd of your uncle and confounded Mr Marsh with Him. I remain, God love you

Yours ever affectionately D Adey

Address: Wm Repton Esqr, White Swan, Long Stratton, Norfolk
B st: AYLSHAM 132; Short post; *charge*: 5
Endorsed: 17 May 1809   Mrs Adey giving an account of John Repton having settled his affairs while my fat[he]r was with him
HM 40887/12

---

483 See Letter 89.
484 The father of James Marsh.

94. William Windham to Humphry Repton; Humphry Repton's draft reply

Pall Mall, May 18th 1809

Dear Sir

The death of our late friend, in the circumstances in which it has happened, cannot be considered an affliction, and is only affecting as it recalls times past; with the affectionate remembrances connected with them; and *as it* reminds us of the general decay of life. It deprives us of no joys to be looked to in future – the last time that I was in Aylsham, upon my asking Izzy, whether my approaching Mr Adey & speaking to him, would be any gratification to him, she discouraged the intention, & seemed to think, that he would either be wholly insensible of it, or that it would give him more annoyance than pleasure. In such a state of living-death as he had been for some time past, his final release cannot be in itself a subject of regret, however it must for [fb] the time be felt as an awful change by those, whose happiness and interests had been united with him during so large a portion of their existence.

Though <my> regard for Mr Adey & the fear of wounding him in the latter period of his life, would have prevented me, had such an intention existed, from withdrawing from their *house* the business, which he had been accustomed to do for me, yet there has in fact *been* no such intention, & his death will therefore make no difference in the connexion before subsisting, & which I certainly could not break off without much pain, as well with respect to the living, as with respect to those who are no more. I should think myself peculiarly unfortunate in any necessity of taking from your son & from Mrs Adey at this moment, what would now probably be of some value, than at any future period. – Should any new instrument be necessary to transfer the appointment formerly given to Mr Adey, <he> your son will be so good as to have it made out.[485]

I do not like to mix with my regrets for a person, whom I valued so much as I did Mr Adey, concerns so foreign as those of alterations at Felbrigg, on which I have a word [fb] or two to say, but not such as are pressing, or may not be reserved to any future opportunity.[486]

With best respects to Mrs Repton, believe me to be Dear Sir,
Your very faithful Humble servant W Windham

---

485 Windham's positive response to the original of the letter drafted by Repton in Letter 81.
486 See Letter 24.

[Aylsham?] [Whit Sunday, 21 May 1809][487]

Dear Sir

The satisfaction you must have felt in writing your kind & benevolent leter of 18th Inst' will be increased by knowing <that> *how* it was received at Aylsham in the Circle *of friends* which you meant it should cheer & console – <*under an event*> <& while what for more than 30 years has never put on the ?terrible apendage to that awful event which> *the late Event* you beautifuly observe although it has deprived us of no joys to be looked to in the future – must be felt at a nearer time perforce the [?] affliction never known concealed with them & as it reminds us of the general decay of life.

<Mrs Repton & my daughter came to> It is a most singular circumstance that our family circle has never known the loss of a relative or put on black *clothes* for more than 30 years – this tends to increase in us the effect of that change which however long expected is always awful – & can only be alleviated by the kind notice of those who can share in the pity excited – Your letter convinced us all of a long continued & unabated participation in the interests of our family & I trust you will find my son's attention to your interests as far as that goes – will supply the place of his late Uncle – but that is a small part if the feelings which your letter has excited. It seems like a renewal of former times when mutual confidence & esteem first made those bonds of connection <which> *that* began at Felbrigg & Sustead were drawn together by [?]debate & political [?]animation which would be *so much more* seem likely to loosen than to rivet the Chains of friendship – It is only in the hour of Mourning that the finest feelings of man can be excited – We are this day <(Sunday)> *Whit Sunday* assembled to perform the most solemn rite [fb] of Christians in the Church where our poor friend Adey has quietly been deposited, & where a very few years must bring us all to the same quiet termination of *all* our hopes & fears <in> *relating to* this world – but where we are taught to look beyond that termination that knowing <to> what we are to expect – Gratitude <for *the sad that is* part> must however be our most acceptable sacrifice & while we thank Heaven for all the good we have enjoyed – we will not be unmindful of <those> benefits <which we> derived from the friendship <& of dear> of those around us – & among these for your renewed Confidence.

I have the honour to be &c

---

487 Repton's draft answer, in faint pencil, begins on the back of Windham's letter and continues on the back of the wrapper.

Address: London. May eighteen 1809. H Repton Esqr, <Harestreet
Rumford> at John Adeys Esqr, Aylsham, W Windham[488]
R st: FREE 18 MY 18 1809
Endorsed by Humphry Repton: W Windham May 18: 1809   an excellent
Letter of Condolence & appoint[men]t of William
Endorsed by William: and my father's excellent Answer
HM 40950

95. William Repton to William Windham (draft)[489]

Aylsham, 21ˢᵗ May 1809

Sir

  I beg you will accept my unfeigned thanks for having conferred on me
that <of which I have> the Stewardship of your Norfolk Courts *which I
have been accustomed to consider* so much the object of my ambition. If
any thing can add to the obligation it <will> is the handsome <manner>
terms in which you have been pleased to <grant> *convey to* me this
proof of your confidence – I <do not> conceive no written authority will
be necessary from you in order to enable *me* to fill the office so long held
by <poor Mr Adey> *my poor Uncle* as <I> *it* do*es* not *appear* <find
on> from <investigating> his writings that he had ever [*had*] a written
appoint[men]t from you. I have the honor to be, Sir
  Your most obliged & Very faithful humble servant   Wm R
The Rt Hon Wm Windham
Pall Mall

Endorsed: 21 May 1809   L[ett]re to Mr Windham   thanking him for his
Courts
HM 40942/2

---

488 i.e. dated and signed by Windham for privileged free post.
489 This draft was written on the back of a note from G. Walpole, dated 20 March 1809
(Letter 65).

96. William Repton to Charles Anson (draft)[490]

Aylsham, 23rd May 1809

My dear Sir

I beg you will accept my best thanks for your very kind letter of consolation & condolence on the subject of our recent loss, for such as a matter of feeling we must undoubtedly consider poor Mr Adey's departure, & though reason & reflexion must & ought to satisfy us that he whom we lament is but released from a world of cares, it is time alone which can subdue our regret, by placing at a greater distance those scenes <of care or pleasure> in which we have been accustomed to enjoy his participation during so long a period [fb] The Severity of the Shock was certainly much lessened by poor Mr Adey's gradual decay & my aunt I am happy to say bears the event as well as under all the circumstances can be expected. She certainly has the comfort of recollecting that my Uncle had not a wish ungratified which it was in her powers to <gra> accomplish, & that there never was a union of greater harmony & affection.

I am sure from my knowledge of the kind & friendly interest which you take in *any thing which tends to* our advantage you will be pleased to hear that Mr Windham has given me his Courts <which, of all the Courts in which my uncle formerly held are inferior only to those which I enjoy from your Brother's[491] kindness & favor announcing> *announcing* the intelligence by a letter to my father which by <kindness its kindness & feeling> *the style of feeling it contains* adds much to the obligation – These Courts, of all the concerns which poor Mr Adey formerly had are [fb] inferior only to those which I enjoy from your brother's favor & kindness. You will thefore see it is a great point gained.

I shall be in Town on Monday to resume *my* <the> proceedings in Parl[iamen]t which have been for a while so painfully delayed & Mrs Adey intends to remain at Harestreet during my absence w[hi]ch cannot *I trust* be more than 10 days or a fortnight.

We beg you wo'd <make> *give our* best regards & Compl[iment]s to Mr Frederic & again thank you for having so kindly remembrd us – I remain my D[ear] Sir

Yours very sincerly WR

Endorsed: 23d May 1809   Letter to The Revd C. Anson at Sudbury

---

490 William's reply to Letter 91.
491 Probably Henry Anson, since he lived at Lyng.

Rectory, Staffordsh[ire]   In answer to a kind letter of condolence on Mr
Adey's death
HM 40936

97. Charles Cooke[492] to Humphry Repton

Semer, 24 May 1809

My Dear Sir

Your letter gave us the first intelligence of the late melancholy change at
Aylsham, which, notwithstanding the long hopeless state of our late worthy
Friend must have deeply afflicted Mrs Adey; however, every one to whom
Mr Adey was known cannot but derive the greatest consolation from the
reflection that his truly exemplary conduct through life must have ensured
him the happiest change – Your account of Mr John Repton's state of health
gives us great concern but, we hope we may flatter ourselves that your
anxiety for him may have magnified his danger – We have had a very sick
Family, our eldest Daughter[493] was brought home from School at Easter,
who suffered greatly under a long continued nervous Fever.

We have since had three more of our Children affected in a similar way &
we judge from the same cause, the late inclemency of the season. Mrs Cooke
herself is only now recovering [*fb*] from a very severe illness, the foundation
of which I attribute to her fatigue in nursing & anxiety for our little ones.
By Dr MacLean's[494] recommendation we move next week to Aldborough
where we purpose staying a Month for the benefit of the Sea Air to assist
in bracing[495] – Mrs Adey may expect to receive a letter from Mrs Cooke as
soon as she feels herself equal to the task –

My opportunity of encreasing an acquaintance with our Friends at Hare
Street, be assured, would give us the greatest pleasure; the attendance on
a family of six young ones necessarily keeps us very much at home. Mrs
Cooke has not passed through Hare Street since she called upon Mrs
Repton in her way from London last Christmas twelvemonth with our

---

492 Charles Cooke (1762–1838); rector of Semer (Suffolk) 1793–1838; and of Bromeswell
1790–1838; Suffolk J.P.. (CCEd Person ID: 112320.)

493 Probably Mary Cooke, baptised at Semer on 19 August 1798.

494 The Reptons and the Cookes shared the services of Dr MacLean (q.v.), who was
Mrs Cooke's brother-in-law. (See Letter 182.) MacLean married Mary Young (aged 21)
at Norwich, on 26 April 1794; Charles Cooke married Elizabeth Young, at Clare, on
22 August 1797.

495 Aldeburgh (Suffolk) rather than Aldborough (Norfolk).

eldest Son,[496] who was at that time so much an Invalid that he could not leave the Carriage. My Journeys to & from London have been by the Stages, which like the Tides will stop for no man – I expect to see Dr Maclean [fb] this week, when I will communicate the melancholy subject of your letter – Mrs Cooke unites with me in every good wish to all our Friends at Aylsham & Oxnead under their present Affliction – Believe me

My Dear Sir Yours very truly Chas Cooke

Address: H Repton Esqr, Mrs Adey's, Aylsham, Norfolk
B st: HADLEIGH [*illeg*]; *charge*: 7
Endorsed: 24 May 1809   The Revd Chas Cooke to my father on Mr Adey's death
HM 40899

98. John Dugmore[497] to William Repton

Swaffham, 2 June 1809

Dear Sir

I understand that your Sheringham Bill has passed. I beg therefore to Inform you that it will be very convenient to Me (if it suits Mr Dehague[498] & yourself) to have the first Meeting fixed for the 13 July to qualify & receive Claims, & to perambulate the Bounds of the Parish the following Morning. I presume that the Meetings must be at Holt.[499]

I am Dear Sir, Yours faithfully J Dugmore

Allow me to offer my Condolences on the late Event which has happened in your Family. But, Poor Man, He is happily released. He can have had but little Enjoyment of this World for a long time.

Address: Wm Repton Esq, Aylesham
B st: SWAFFHAM 95; *charge*: 8

---

496 Probably Charles Cooke, baptised 10 August 1799; d. 1820.
497 John Dugmore (1757–1844) of Swaffham, land surveyor. See for example, NRO, MC 3/589, 516X9, letters from J. Dugmore to Lord Suffield concerning estate and manor court business on the Gunton estate and Stockton enclosure and renewal of lease of the manor of Stockton from the Crown.
498 Probably Elisha De Hague junior (1755–1826), lawyer, town clerk of Norwich 1792–1826.
499 Indicating that the Sheringham enclosure commissioners were Dugmore, De Hague and William. See NRO, AYL 940, Sheringham enclosure commissioners' minutes, 1809–1810.

Endorsed: 2ᵈ June 1809   Mr Dugmore   Sherringham Inclosure first
Meeting   Mr Adey's death
HM 40902

99. John Repton to Dorothy Adey; Susanna Brett to Dorothy Adey

Oxnead, June 7ᵗʰ 1809

My Dear Dee

There never was such good people for writing. you make me ashamed and I cannot plead Illness as an excuse, no excuse but that I have nothing to say – some what you wish about myself which in one word is that you will find me better – The Bell tolling for poor Threadwell[500] my Wife dreaded wo'd hurt me and therefore very considerately sent Jonathan over without my knowing it for Mrs Brett and Miss Bulwer[501] and they you know all kindness came into the place at once and are now with me. therefore to save my shaking hand perhaps Mrs Brett will make my letter worth postage –

my Brother letter was rec[eive]d and he shall hear from me a second addition of a family bundle the Moment I have time and power and subject to write it – Elizas thanks for your letter which she read very well. You never wrote so well since you left Old Massingham in your life[502] – Eliza is improved in looks very much but she brings a bad Acco[un]t of poor Anna[503] at Aylsham with her [?]knees, all which George I suppose has wrote about

My dear Mrs Adey

It was my intention to have written to you last Saturday or Sunday by way of taking about half the time I thought you would stay at Harestreet, but you find by your dear Brother [*fb*] John's letter, that I am at Oxnead – where I have been with Miss Bulwer since Sunday morning. It is with

---

500 John Threadwell was a paper-maker at Oxnead mill. He died in 1809, aged 55, and was buried at Oxnead on 6 June 1809. (http://www.norfolkmills.co.uk/Watermills/oxnead. html (accessed 5 Feb 2019); NRO, Archdeaconry of Norwich Probate Records, ANW, will register, 1809–1811, (1809) fol. 89, no. 58, Threadwell, John, of Oxnead.)

501 Probably not Elizabeth Bulwer, born in Aylsham in 1796. (*Aylsham*, p. 209.) Related to Augustine Bulwer, rector of Heydon (see next letter).

502 Perhaps a reference to a person involved with Dorothy's education: there is no place called Old Massingham and no discernible connection with Great Massingham.

503 Perhaps the Anna mentioned in Letters 50 and 55.

a degree of comfort I little expected that I have passed my time with this long valued and truly beloved Friend. I found him so much better than I had any hopes of doing that it gave me inexpressible pleasure to *have* obey'd the summons, that carried us to him – and I encourage the hope that with care and attention he will again be restored to his family & friends. I know it will be a great gratification to you to hear me say he has been cheerful, animated and pleasant as usual. We walked about the farm by the side of his Donkey Cart both forenoon & Afternoon and at the end of each ride he always said he felt the better for it. Pray Heaven he may continue to amend & as the Summer creeps on I hope he *will* gain strength to combat his complaint. We return to Norwich this forenoon and before I go I am happy to catch the opportunity of adding a little to your Brother's letter to assure you how glad I was to hear you are at Harestreet with your good friends, from whence I find you will return with dear William and I hope the better for a little change of Air & change of scene.

I have not yet heard from Mrs Holley, but I find She is got very finely – She has been very ill and has had a deal of fever. I left poor Hardy again in bed with the Gout, from having taken cold, but I trust I shall find him better on my return to day (Wed). [fb] Poor Threadwell was buried yesterday, therefore that little hurry will be over before we leave Oxnead. Miss Bulwer must return today as she is going to Heydon on Friday to pass a week or ten days there with her Aunt[504] & Major Fuller.[505] Eliza was highly delighted with your letter & the *History of the Baby house*,[506] as were all the great Children. I need not I hope *add* I was glad to come in for a share of a letter from you, and to hear you say you were well. If you stay longer than this week I shall look for a letter from you, and I know you will not disappoint me. Remember me kindly to all and every part of your dear family and believe me

as ever Affectionately Yours Susanna Brett

Miss Bulwer sends kind love

Mrs Repton will thank you to bring her six Yards of crape trimming like Mary's best gown – it was done at Rumford at 4d a yard.

Address: 7 June 1809, Mrs Adey at H Reptons Esqr, Harestreet, Romford, Essex

---

504 Perhaps Mary Bulwer (1759–1821), sister of Augustine (q.v.), rector of Heydon.
505 See Letter 176 for the auction of Major Fuller's household goods; he cannot be identified further.
506 Not identified.

B st: [illeg]; *charge*: 8
Endorsed: 7 June 1809   My Uncle John Repton's Last letter to Mrs Adey
Mrs Brett's letter with an account of his health   Died on 14th June
HM 40929/4

100. William Repton to Revd. Henry Anson (draft)

<Aylsham> *Oxnead Hall*, Thursday 15th June 1809

My dear Sir

I cannot without much pain communicate to you that we have received another stroke of affliction in the loss of one for whom you have I am sure been accustomed to feel sentiments of friendship & regard – my poor Uncle John Repton is no more – He had on Friday a violent return of Spasm & other alarming symptoms of his disorder which <occasioned> *in consequ[en]ce of a Letter from* Mr Taylor <to send for Mrs Adey & myself> *occasioned Mrs Adey & myself accompanied by my mother [?]imm[ediatel]y to set off for Oxnead*. We found him extremely faint & weak & <notwithstanding> *he continued with little* [fb] <the assistance of Dr Reeve⁵⁰⁷ & Mr Martineau, he gradually became more so> *or no variation, & without pain <till*> until 5 o'Clock yesterday when all was over. Mr Martineau had <left Oxnead> returned to Norwich half an hour before with a conviction that nothing co'd be done – Mr Martineau *indeed* appears to have been all along of opinion that the disorder was an incurable one, but from my Uncle's natural good spirits, & the flattering appearance which his disease at times assumed, <wh> we had I believe all of us, but <partic> my father in particular entertained hopes that this case might have been a singular exception to the many others which have preceded it – but all our hopes are thus at an End –

[fb] My Uncle latterly expressed a wish to be buried in the Oxnead church near the<ir own> pew in which he was accustomed to sit – & finding there wo'd be no time to hear from you previous to the day when *it* will be necessary that the funeral *sho'd* <to> take place, I have this morning, as one of the Ex[ecut]ors *ventured* to give directions for <opening &> preparing the place in question – & <so this> I trust you will approve what I have done –

It is not in my power at present to enter much upon any other subject – but I will trouble you to say with my respectful Comp[limen]ts to

---

507 Not identified.

<Ld Anson> your brother[508] that Spinks' Es[ta]te at Heigham[509] <will> *is to* be sold by Auction – <in order> that <his Lordship> *your brother* may not lose <have an> *the* opportunity of purchasing. I again beg to thank his L[or]dship for the kind hospitalities which I experienced at Shugboro'.

Believe My dear Sir Very faithfully & sincerely Yours Wm Repton

Endorsed: 15 June 1809   Letter to the Revd Henry Anson on John Repton's death
HM 40938

101. Humphry Repton to William Repton (fragment)

[Hare Street, just after 14 June 1809][510]

To the Memory of John Repton Esqr who died 14 June 1809 aged 56

of whose virtues there is no room to say much, because His foolish Widow desires to have room left for hers, but as she can neither write nor read I will do it for her

>   Our poor Brother John
>   For ever is gone
>   Bequeathing his foolish wife Bess
>   She long buckled his Shoes
>   Then slipd on the Noose
> And he Married – "He coon't du no less".

What a Melancholy reflection that we cannot look back on any part of poor John's conduct that was not influencd & embitterd by his dotage for this low woman – even *in* his last moments she counteracted his intentions by adding a stranger to the trust for his daughter [*fb*] and thus has laid the foundation for future disputes & squabbles in the management of that dear Girls Education but I will not dwell on such subjects[511]

Why do we not see you at Harestreet? I must go to London on Monday – & we have many things in which we should like your advice & assistance

---

508   Thomas Anson (1767–1818), first viscount Anson.
509   This might be in Heigham, a suburb of Norwich, or in Potter Heigham. By 1828 Oxnead Hall had been sublet to a John Spinks. (*Aylsham*, p. 177.)
510   Dated by the HL catalogue as: [1809] [14 Jan<] i.e. after 14 January 1809, but it should be after 14 June 1809, as that was the date of John Repton's death.
511   This letter shows the low regard Repton had for his sister-in-law, Elizabeth, and provides the reason for the notes that he made on his brother's will in Letter 89.

– can you come Saturday – or if I take the girls on Monday to the rehearsal will you see them home safe that night & I will bestow a Chaise upon them – but I shall not then be at home with you on Tuesday. in short you are in great request here &[512]

HM 40855

102. Mary (Clarke) Repton to Dorothy Adey

[Hare Street], Sunday noon [June 1809][513]

My dearest Dee

I shoud have written to you last night but was too tired, and we did not get home till a late dinner. Thank God I had the happiness to find my dear Humphry, Boys and girls, quite well, and very very glad to see me again, the former looking charmingly well, but you will not wonder at his being low at first seeing me – tell my poor Sister John, that he did <u>wish</u> and hope that she woud have changed her mind, and <have> come[514] with dear Eliza and me to Harestreet, but he with the rest of our family sends kind love to her, and she will *they * [hope] soon consent to accompany you my dear dee and come to us. We *will* do all in our power to make you both as happy as you can ever be without our dear deceas'd friends whom we can never have again in this world, – therefore it matters not, where we are, we shall always feel a want of those we have lost and we must look up to the dear ones that are left us – to Comfort and support each other in all *our* troubles and afflictions, and the more we can be together, the happier I trust we shall all be.

My heart was too full when we parted to say much on this subject, but my thoughts of you both agitated me a great deal, which brought on [*fb*] a sort of uncomfortable Feeling in my Bowels which rather alarmd me. I did not let dear William know this: he will have told you that we found James and his wife at home.[515] she asked if we went by Cambridge, she said Nancy and her Brother Samuel were at home and woud be delighted to see me.[516]

---

512 The page ends here; it has been torn along the fold.

513 After the deaths of both John Adey and John Repton.

514 Changed to 'came'.

515 Probably James Marsh and his wife Frances, neé Black; they were married at St Mary in the Marsh, Norwich, on 2 May 1797. (NRO, PD 499/6, p. 129.)

516 Members of the Marsh family: witnesses to the marriage of James and Frances included S. C. (Samuel Clarke) Marsh and Anne N. Marsh (Nancy was a diminutive of Ann). (NRO, PD 499/6, p. 129.)

I was quite rejoiced at the Idea and consented to go that way knowing how much more comfortable it woud be to me to be there if I was ill in the night than being at Ipswich, and it woud be a change of Road. We got there about 9 oclock (after stopping at Newmarket to see Capt[ai]n Barclay walk).[517] Nancy, Samuel and Marian Marsh (as it is Commencment week)[518] were gone to the Concert to hear Mrs Billington[519] and Bartleman.[520] Her excellent Servant <u>Anne</u> Bustled about, got a good fire laid the Cloth got supper ready and our Beds, and said her Misstress woud be home at 10 oclock. I laid on the sopha and was quite refreshd, and did not think the time long. Poore Nancy delighted to see me, after a eating good Supper we sat chatting till almost one oclock. I slept well and lost my complaint, now I am sure you will agree with me, that the plan was a good one – I think you will want to hear somthing more of Capt[ai]n B.

When we got to the last Turn pike to Newmarket we asked what time he woud walk [fb] the *woman* said a Quarter before 7 was the time he woud start – when we drove up to the Bear Inn it was but 6 oclock. What shoud we do till that time. dear John said he woud certainly see him.[521] "God bless my soul, many people would give 10 Guinea to see him and we are so near and not see him wou'd be a shame". so I found I must consent (and as we did not go by Bungay I did it with a good grace). I orderd some *Tea* which we had, with good cream and Toast, and was *much* refreshd; I orderd the Chaise to be quite ready, and the man was to drive not a hundred yards from the house where the Walker was to start, and we shoud see him come out and cross the Road. it raind very hard just as we set off. We waited about a Quarter of an hour, rather <u>impatient</u> and we said he woud not come perhaps as it raind. 'Oh yes' the post Boy said, 'he must come let the weather be ever so bad'. "There Mam there he is now coming out at the door["]. He walkd close by us, and crossd the Road <to the> and got into his path on the turf where a row of Lamps are put the length of

---

517 Robert Barclay Allardice (1779–1854), known as Captain Barclay, was a famous 'pedestrian'. His most noted feat was walking 1 mile in each of 1,000 successive hours. 'This feat was performed at Newmarket from 1 June to 12 July 1809. His average time of walking the mile varied from 14 min. 54 sec. in the first week to 21 min. 4 sec. in the last, and his weight was reduced from 13 stone 4 lb to 11 stone.' (*ODNB*)

518 Commencement: 'the great ceremony when the full degree of Master or Doctor are conferred, at the end of the academical year.' (*OED*)

519 Elizabeth Billington [née Weichsel] (1765–1818), originally an opera singer but from 1806 a concert singer. (*ODNB*)

520 James Bartleman (1769–1821), singer, 'a bass-baritone, with a range of over two octaves …'. (*ODNB*)

521 i.e. John Adey Repton.

a mile, the Boy drove a little way on the Turf and we saw him walk about ten minutes, which was enough for us to see, a man came out of the house with him, and presently 2 more followd him which I suppose where to watch him, that he did right. – Capt[ai]n B walkd very Lame indeed. some said his feet where sore, but Duff says, 'no it is his *knees* are stiff'. there are many bets he says, that he will not go through with it. dear Humphry says we shoud have staid and seen him walk [fb] his mile and back again but we saw quite enough of it, and where much surprizd there where not 6 people to look at him, either the rain prevented them, or that the novelty of the thing is over – I shall think no more of it, but at the time it amused us, and at the *same* time diverted my thoughts from thinking of my friends I had left behind me, and I hope the reading this account of this wonderfull man will divert your attention for a time, how ever short – from dwelling too much on your present sorrows and affliction. You have both my dear sisters, all our kind wishes for health, and Restoration of <u>that</u> happiness and peace of mind, so recently lost. And my prayers for many years of health and happiness. Kiss my dear Eliza as often as you like for us all. I do not forget my dearest William neither[522] his kind attention to me nor how much I am in his debt in Cash.

Yours affectionately M Repton

Address: Mrs Adey, Aylsham, Norfolk
B st: RUMFORD 12; *b st*: TOO LATE; Cross Post; *charge*: 8
Endorsed: June 1809   My Mother after having left us
HM 40933/3

103. George Repton to William Repton (sketch enclosed)

29 Dover Street, Thursday [20 July 1809]

My dear Brother

Enclosed I send you a Sketch for the Monument of our poor Uncle – which I have endeavourd to keep as plain as possible, at the same [time] giving it so much ornament as will make it rather above the common description of such kind of Tablets.

With respect to its being done <u>here</u> or in Norfolk, that will, of course, rest entirely with you. I will make the Drawing to its full size – which (by the scale) you [fb] will perceive is about 2 ft 9 in long by 1 ft 3 in high. I

---

522 From here to the end of the letter is written upside down at the top of the first page.

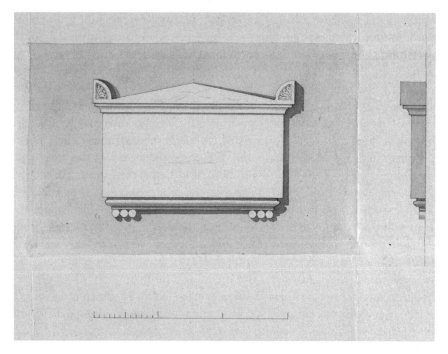

8. Sketch of monument for John Repton by George Repton, HM 40918/4

think it cannot well be much less – and I have shewn it to a Mason here who tells me the expence of doing it with the inscription, will not exceed 15 Guineas.[523] if therefore you can agree with the Man you employ to do it for less, I will send you the large Drawing for it – but he must engage to do it with pure statuary Marble, which is now <u>exorbitantly</u> dear from the Impossibility of importing it from Italy – but if the difference is but a trifling sum – I should recommend you to have it done in London.

A Letter from my Father this morning says Mrs Burroughes has written to him for his terms[524] – he may <u>perhaps</u> therefore (should She agree to them) have to go down to her, and he has written *to me* to know if I can accompany him, but I am so uncertain what are my plans that I can scarcely answer him – for I am daily expecting a summons from Nash to go to the Isle of Wight – at any [fb] *rate* I shall be happy to go with my Father if I

---

523 Samuel Adson of Fitzroy Square Statuary. (See Letters 135 and 147.)
524 Christobelle Burroughes lived at Hoveton Hall. The proposed work was to build a new house there: plans by Humphry and John Adey Repton survive from 1809, indicating that the terms Humphry provided were acceptable. (*Repton in Norfolk*, p. 139.)

can do so – as it will give me the opportunity of knocking up your Quarters at Aylsham – though perhaps <though> for no longer time than my last short visit to you ––

give my best and affectionate love to Aunt Adey. I acknowledged the rec[eip]t of her letter in a postscript to my Mothers on Sunday last – and also give my love to Mrs John – and believe me always my Dear William

your very affectionate Brother G S Repton

Endorsed: 20 July 1809   My brother George   With Sketch of a Monument for John Repton – Mrs Burroughes
Enclosed: drawing
HM 40918/4

104. George Repton to Dorothy Adey

29 Dover Street, August 1ˢᵗ 1809

My dear Aunt

I expect to be obliged to go to the Isle of Wight in ten days or a Fortnight from this time – and as I shall probably remain there till Christmas, I shall not have the opportunity of accepting your kind invitation to accompany Duff into Norfolk in September – I have therefore determined to pass a few days with you and William at Aylsham before I go to the Island – and shall be with you one day the end of this week – but which – I cannot decidedly say – as I am uncertain about passing a day at Chelmsford. however my dear Aunt do not expect me till I arrive – and this letter will prevent your supposing when I do arrive, that I am come down express with bad news – [fb] as you imagined when last I saw you – adieu my dear Aunt with best love to William –

believe me your very affectionate G Repton

if Williams business should carry him to Norwich about Friday or Saturday – tell him to leave word at your Inn (I think the Maids head)[525] and I will ask there, if they know any thing of his being in the Town –

Address: Mrs Adey, Aylsham, Norfolk
B st: A AU 1 809

---

525 The Maid's Head, Tombland, Norwich, still survives. The oldest parts above ground date from the fifteenth century. The bar and snug were added in the late sixteenth century. It was a busy coaching inn during the eighteenth century. (https://www.maidsheadhotel. co.uk/about/our-history/ accessed 20/02/19.)

Endorsed: 1 Augt 1809   My brother George   to Mrs Adey – that he is coming
HM 40915/1

105. George Repton to Dorothy Adey

Hare Street, Monday August 28ᵗʰ 1809

My dear Aunt

My Mother tells me I ought to write to you upon my return from Norfolk – which I am sure you will agree with me to be almost unnecessary, if it is only to say, how sensible I feel at yours and my dear Brothers kindness to me during my stay at Aylsham – which I regret I could not prolong – and though it may *be* long before I again have the power of being so completely an <u>idle man</u> for the same length of time, yet, my dear Aunt you may be assured I will always avail myself of every opportunity which may occur, of passing a few days with you – which I hope you will enable me [*fb*] <ne> to do next Spring at <u>Harestreet</u> –

As I found my dear Mother did not care about having either of the Rings, and considerd it would be the same thing <to her> if her Girls had them, I distributed *them* in the way Mrs Sᵗ John⁵²⁶ directed – and Mary is now writing a proper letter of thanks for the same – Whilst my Mother, with <u>Fudge</u> & <u>Venus</u>,⁵²⁷ is putting her Nose into one of the many <u>Rat</u> holes we have got, and lamenting over one of her <u>bottle stands</u>, which they have mutilated in the most barbarous manner possible – for you Must know a <u>whole</u> <u>Colony</u> of those destructive animals have lately arrived in this [*fb*] neighbourhood, and distributed themselves partly with us, and partly with Mr Page⁵²⁸ – but directions are given for various traps, and Duff is reading accounts of how they are to be caught – <we> therefore *with <u>his</u> <u>Theory</u> & <u>Thomas</u>⁵²⁹ <u>practice</u> we* live in hopes of being able to supply all our friends – and if you should wish for any to p[*damaged*] up for the Winter – Duff will take as many with him as you may require – *by the mail on Monday 4ᵗʰ Sept as he hopes to have the pleasure of joining you at Aylsham on Tuesday 5ᵗʰ*

Tell William that though Mrs John gave me directions to order the Monument, yet we were to determine upon the spot what would be the

---

526 'Mrs sister John': George had just returned from Aylsham.
527 Presumably Fudge and Venus are two of the family's cats.
528 Repton's immediate neighbour at Hare Street.
529 Another cat, or possibly a manservant.

best size for it, therefore he had better slightly mark upon the wall the size I described in the letter I wrote to him (which bye the bye I now forget) and tell him to let me know if he thinks it should *be* a little larger or [*fb*] smaller – and also I should like him to obtain Mrs John's consent to have the monument to our poor Uncle <u>only</u> and not any space left for <any> other persons name*s*.[530]

A letter from my father on Saturday morning. he is quite well and wrote in good spirits – highly pleased with a letter he had recieved from the Duke of Bedford asking his advice about the the Buildings and Grounds at Tavistock Abbey[531] –

I do not exactly know the time I shall sett off for the Island but expect about the end of this week but Whether <in> I am in London the Isle of Wight or any other part of the Country, a letter from you will always give me the sincerest pleasure <when> *which* I hope you will bear in your recollection – With best love to William, Mrs John &c

believe me always my dear Aunt your affectionate Nephew George Stanley

My Mother says that as I have told you all is well at Hare Street she will not <now> write untill the end of the week – but sends her affectionate love to you & William, as does all the Reptons here –

Your letter[532] did not come to day untill very late – I am glad you put the plain question to Harbord[533] – an <u>open</u> opponent is better than a <u>concealed</u> one – and William now knows to whom he has to trust – I suppose Harbord wanted him to be Copemans "*locum tenens*" – and did not wish decidedly to shew what he intended to do, untill Copeman returned into the County.[534] My Mother says dinner is ready, therefore once more adieu –

Address: For Mrs Adey, Aylsham, Norfolk
B st: RUMFORD [*illeg*]; Cross Post; *charge*: 8
Endorsed: 28 August 1809   My Brother George to Mrs Adey
HM 40915/2

---

530 Cf. Letter 109 indicating that space would be left.

531 The commissioning letter from the sixth duke of Bedford was dated 12 August 1809. (Carter et al., *Repton*, p. 151.)

532 This final paragraph is written upside down at the top of the first page.

533 William Assheton Harbord (1766–1821), of Blickling and Gunton Hall, who had married Caroline Hobart of Blickling. He became second baron Suffield in 1810. (*Hist. Parl.*)

534 Robert Copeman (q.v.), Harbord's manorial steward. See, for example, NRO, MC 3/61(a), 466X3, an account between the Hon. Colonel Harbord and Robert Copeman for estate expenses, 1802–1808.

106. William Repton to Col. William Harbord (draft)

Aylsham, Saturday Morning [9 September 1809]

Sir

<I beg leave> *I think it right* to apologise to you for hav[in]g yesterday in shooting with my brother <tres> inadvertently trespassed upon two <part> of your Aylsham fields. On learning from your Serv[an]t that we were upon a part of your property, we of course imm[ediatel]y left the place; & I shall in future be careful that you may <never> *not* again experience any annoyance from me, or my friends.

<I feel anxious to explain that because I have the honor of being known to you I do not, on that account presume to be troublesome> *I feel anxious to explain this circumstance because* <& that> I sho'd <at the same time> be very sorry to rank in your <good opinion> *estimation* [fb] with those, <from whom whose conduct has been for some time obnoxious to you> *from whom you have* for some time past experienced many incivilities

I have the honour to be Sir, Your very faithful <se't> & obedient humble servant WR

Address: The Hon[oura]ble C[o]l: Harbord, &c &c &c, Blickling
Endorsed: 9 Sept 1809   Letter to Col: Harbord   Apologising for hav'g trespassed upon him in shooting
HM 40954/2

107. William Harbord to William Repton

Blickling, Monday [11 September 1809]

Sir

I have received your note and beg to assure you I am perfectly satisfied with the explanation it contains.

I am, Your obedient humble servant Wm A Harboard

Endorsed: 11 Sep'r 1809   The Hon. Col: Harbord   As to my apology for shooting upon him[*sic*]
HM 40953/10

108. John Johnson Gay[535] to William Repton

Saxthorpe, Tuesday December 12th 1809

Dear Repton

If you are disengaged on Monday next (the 18th) I shall be extremely happy of your company to take a family dinner with me, and if agreeable to accompany Mrs J. Gay & myself to the Holt Assembly that evening – We shall dine at half past four oclock, but shall be glad to see you as much earlier as may be convenient, & you may rely upon having a well aired bed upon your return. I hope you have no engagement on the following Friday December 22nd as I expect a party of friends to dine with me on that day and it will give me great pleasure to join your name to those whom I hope to see – Have the goodness to send me word if I may expect the pleasure of your company – Mrs J Gay joins me in best Comp[li]m[en]ts to Mrs Adey

I am D[ea]r Repton, Yours truly J J Gay

Endorsed: 12 Dec 1809   Mr Johnson Gay's   Friendly invitation to dine with him & go to the Holt Assembly
HM 40903

109. George Repton to William Repton

East Cowes Castle, Isle of Wight, December 18th 1809

My dear William

Your letter was forwarded to me here – and in consequence of it I lost no time in making out a Working Drawing to the full size for the Monument – but in doing so I made some trifling alterations from the sketch I sent you, and also added a little more ornament to it, which I thought it required – but knowing that these alterations would of course increase the expence – I have sent the Drawing to Town to know what the additional expence will be – and I have but now received the Statuarys answer – that it will cost £26 – I have therefore not given him any farther directions untill I hear from you – but I should add that the little ornament I have made (in addition to [*fb*] the design I sent you) is I think a great improvement, and I am very much inclined to think the increases of price is not <u>wholly</u> owing to the enrichments, I have added, but also to the daily increace in the price of Marble, for as the means of importing it is entirely shut up, it of course

---

535 See note to Letter 32.

increases in cost as it every day becomes more scarce – the expence of the inscription will be extra but that will be but trifling – for indeed the size of the Tablet will not allow much to be said, and still less for our poor Uncle, if Mrs John insists upon having room left upon it for herself, but I agree with you that it ought to be so, if she desires it, though the Monument will certainly look better if it is not too much crouded with letters – thus it rests at present and nothing farther will be done, untill I hear from you – if you say that I may go to the expence I have mentioned, for the Monument itself I will then give directions to the Statuary in town to go [fb] on with it, and I shall by that time be there myself and will see that it is well done –

I have not heard very lately from Hare Street but propose being there myself the first week in January. I shall leave this place on Friday next *on my way to* Lord Ducies[536] in Glocestershire and from thence to Hare Street – you say nothing about coming to Town this Spring, which I very much hope you will have occasion to do. I cannot <probably> receive[sic] your answer here before I leave it, but a letter will find me at Lord Ducies any time between the 26ᵗʰ & 30ᵗʰ ins[tan]t – directed at the Rt H'ble Lord Ducie's, Woodchester Park, Minchinhampton Glocestershire –

pray give my affectionate love to Aunt Adey, tell her the postscript to your letter I will not accept in lieu of a much longer one whenever she has nothing better to do – also remember me kindly to Mrs John & Eliza – and believe me always, My dear William,

your very affectionate George Stanley

Endorsed: 18 Dec'r 1809   My brother George   from the Isle of Wight about the Monument for Uncle John
HM 40918/5

110. Edward Repton to William Repton

Leyton, Essex,[537] December 27 1809

My dear William

Through you, I must return thanks to Mrs John for a very nice Turkey – which I had the satisfaction of enjoying with my Friends here, yesterday, and it was perfectly sweet – tho' it was so long since she had said "Gobble" – pray say every thing that is right for us –

---

536 Indicating that George would be working in conjunction with his father at Woodchester Park: Repton senior had been there in January 1809. (See Letter 60.)
537 His wife's uncle and aunt lived in Leyton.

My Wife left home on Wednesday and stayed till Saturday in London – when I sent her down to her Uncle Ellis, and went to Crayford by myself – but got away time enough on [Chris]tmas day – to cross the Water and reach the circle here in the Evening – You learnt from my [*fb*] Mother before I left Yorkshire that I had no vote at Oxford[538] – and that if I had – I should have disposed of it, as you requested – I did not therefore think it necessary to write to you purposely on that subject. Indeed we shall soon be looking out for you again – I understood that you were likely to be up before [Chris]tmas – but I hope some good thing will bring you to Town in the Spring – For now you know I have a new sight for you – my great <ugly>ˣˣ Boy[539] – Tell Aunt Adey he will be glad [*fb*] to be introduced to her – but I fear that is not likely to happen unless I get much richer than I am – and can move about with more satisfaction. –

Our Dear Father's prospects are brightening very much – and I think John and George have got their feet firmly fixed – and will do well – The Yorkshire Journey was a profitable one[540] – and will lead to something more –

We return on Saturday – to Crayford – and shall remain there I think for some time – for the inconve-[*fb*]nience of travelling with a Maid and a Child is very great –

Mary unites in kindest Love to yourself and Aunt Adey – and Mrs J[ohn] &c

Believe me ever Yours affectionately ER

ˣˣNo such thing – a <u>Cherub</u> – M E R.[541]

Address: Wm Repton Esqr, Aylsham, Norfolk

B st: DE 28 809; *orange st*: 7 o'Clock Dec 28 [*illeg*] NT; *charge*: [*illeg*]

Endorsed: 27ᵗʰ Dec'r 1809   My brother Edward   Seems well & happy Oxford Election

HM 40911

---

538 The election for the chancellor of the University; William Wyndham Grenville (prime minister 1806–7) was elected in December 1809.

539 Edward Eardley Harris Repton, b. 18 Sept 1809, baptised at St Paulinus, Crayford (Kent), 22 Oct. 1809.

540 Repton's first visits to Oulton Hall, owned by John Blayds, and to Armley, owned by Benjamin Gott, both near Leeds, were in 1809. (Carter et al., *Repton*, p. 164.) In the Red Book for Oulton Hall, Repton states that he was 'On the Spot Nov'r 1809'. (*Repton in Yorkshire*, pp. 95–114 (Oulton), pp. 115–136 (Armley).) Edward's earlier mention of being in Yorkshire suggests that he was there with his father.

541 A note added by Edward's wife (Mary Ellis Repton); she had crossed out 'ugly'.

111. Edward Repton to William Repton

Crayford, January 12 1810

Dearest William

My Mother and the Girls are all here – they came for a dance at Belvedere Lord Eardleys[542] of which you will I dare say hear the particulars through the usual and regular channel – but d. [Elizabeth] says such accounts must not be blended in a letter of business to William, so for the purport of this. – Mr Ellis my Wife's Uncle is desirous of purchasing a large Estate – his Object is partly speculative, and partly for his own convenience – he wishes for a residence for himself – and not [fb] I imagine over large – but he thinks that there are so few purchasers of very considerable Estates – that he might reserve (from a purchase of perhaps £80,000 or 100,000) such portion as he required for himself, and dispose of the rest in smaller lots – with a profit perhaps, or at least without any loss – This I know has been done in many cases – His object too, is to have an Advowson attached to the purchase, as a provision for a Son now a child – with the hope of its being a benefit to me till his Son can take it – Should such a purchase present itself in your Neighbourhood or County – it might also be a means of extending your connections. [fb] There have been two or three Advertizements lately in the Papers, of Estates near Norwich[543] – one in particular seems to hang heavily on hand – I believe the Estate to which Dr Columbines Living is attached[544] – and one in *the times* of yesterday with the Rectories of Saxlingham and Frostenden between Norwich and Yarmouth[545] – particulars are to be had at the Angel Inns at Norwich and Yarmouth – – What was the estate you enquired about for Lord Nelson? In short if you meet with any thing that appears a desirable and improveable purchase, let me know of it. – The Saxlingham &c is to be sold by Auction on the 18th.[546] Could you learn [fb] particulars before that time? –

---

542 Sampson Eardley (formerly Gideon), first baron Eardley (1745–1824), of Belvedere (Kent) and Spalding (Lincs). (*Hist. Parl.*)

543 The sale by auction of the presentation to the 'valuable Rectory of Little Plumstead with Witton and Brundall' was to take place on 17 January. (*The Norfolk Chronicle and Norwich Gazette*, Saturday, 6 January 1810, issue 2076, p. 1.)

544 Dr Paul Colombine (1756–1821/22), rector of Little Plumstead with Witton and Brundall. (CCEd Person ID:109558.)

545 These two rectories were advertised in *The Times* on 4, 6 and 8 January 1810. Frostenden is a small Suffolk villlage about 12 miles south-west of Wrentham.

546 According to *The Times*, they were to be auctioned by M. Burrell, Bartholmew Lane (London), on Thursday 18 January 1810.

Altho I must not enter into chit chat – yet I shall not conclude without sending kindest Love to Aunt Adey – in which they all join –

Your affectionate Brother Edward

Address: William Repton Esqr, Aylsham, Norfolk
B st: DARTFORD 15; *r st*: E 13 JA 13 1810; *charge*: [*illeg*]
Endorsed: 12 Jan'y 1810   My brother Edward   Mr Ellis wo'd like a p[ur]chase of £100,000 in Norfolk – Livings
HM 40912/1

112. Humphry Repton to William Repton

Harestreet near Romford, February 9 1810

My dear William

Our dear John is coming to make a final Settlem[en]t with Mott[547] & Stannard at Barningham – I wish I could have been with him – because from his not hearing distinctly all that is said – he is often apt to mistake & make answers which may commit him. For tho he means always right – he sometimes says what is better not said – for this reason I know it would be a satisfaction to him as well as to me if you could be present with him & witness what passes – & how the accounts are Closed[548]

[*fb*] You are aware that it is our duty as Architects to see justice done between Mr Mott & his Contractor & there may be points arising out of the words of the Contract that require Your advise as our Lawyer but do not either let John enter into useless Cavils about triffles – or Stannard take unfair advantage of any material departure from the Contract. Whatever excess is fair – is to be allowed – & of Course we have a right to 5 P[er] Cent on the same – but John talk'd (a little idly) of taking P[er]Centage on no more than the Amount of the <u>Contract</u> – this would be foolish – & instead of looking well would seem as if he had derived advantage from the Contractors instead of Mr Mott –

[*fb*] Let us hear how you go on – & fix the days for Mr Mott that may suit you to go with him, as I am afraid in so important a matter that the plausibility of Stannard may be an overmatch for dear Johns straightforward honesty & Simplicity.

---

547 i.e. John Thurston Mott (q.v.).
548 Surviving architectural drawings (now in private hands) for work at Barningham are mostly dated 1807, but some may be later. (Reproduced in *Repton in Norfolk*, pp. 195–7.)

We are all well & I am off for Lord Ducie's.[549]

So God bless you all – Ever Yours HR

I have been looking into my Acc[oun]ts & cannot find when we had any settlement about the Estates &c at Aylsham – have you any means of making them out that I may know which way the balance stands between us or whether the Rent will pay Claude Scott this year

Address: To Wm Repton Esq, Aylsham
Endorsed: 9 Febr'y 1810   My father's Letter about John's examining Stannards Work at Barningham
HM 40863

113. John Adey Repton[550] to William Repton

[Maid's Head, Norwich, 17 February 1810]

My dear William

Upon examining the Books – I find that a place has already been taken for me & <u>Paid for</u>. It will not do to throw away 2£ 8s – for the sake of a few days staying in Norfolk – I am sorry I shall not have the pleasure of returning to Aylsham – But give my love to Aunt Adey – & hope she will excuse it –

Pray will you have the goodness to send my Portmanteau to Harestreet & any thing remaining may go by the Basket –

Pray give my Compliment to our good [*fb*] friends Mr Charles & Mr Henry Anson & also to Mr Lubbock & his Lovely Daughter when you meet them at Lammas[551] on Monday –

I remain Dear W Your affectionate Brother   J A Repton

Pray excuse this Wafer

Address: Wm Repton Esqr, at the Maid's Head – to be forwarded to Aylsham by the Post

549 Woodchester Park, near Minchinhampton
550 The HL had catalogued all five letters under this reference as being from John Adey Repton; in fact the other four were written by John Repton of Oxnead and have been reproduced in Appendix 1 as they are impossible to date. He died in June 1809.
551 William Lubbock (q.v.) lived at Lamas. His daughter may be Anne Elizabeth (1779–1855) who married Hugh Brown (before 1806). (R. Birkbeck, *Notes on the history and genealogy of the family of Lubbock* (London, 1891).)

Endorsed: 17ᵗʰ Feb'y 1810   My brother John   At Norwich on leaving
Norfolk
HM 40931/5

114. James Marsh to William Repton; William's draft reply

London, March 1st 1810

Dear Sir

As by the Death of Mr. Foster[552] I am likely to have my old Client Mr.
Shalders[553] for whom the former had some time since made Application
to you relative to yourself and Brothers conveying the St George Es[ta]te
formerly Capt[ai]n Clarke's to him, for which purpose your father entered
into a Bond on Sale and having been already applied to by Mr. Shalders
as well as Mr. Hart for that purpose I will during my Stay in London ask
my Conveyancer as to the necessity of a fine and prepare the necessary
Conveyance. I <was> have no doubt but I can persuade these Parties to
bear a proportion of the Expence which is more than in strictness we
could expect but which from the difference in the Stamp Duty is but fair.

Shalders is now so fast advancing *in age* that it is desirable his Affairs
sho'd be settled and in the Event of the females marrying more Expence [*fb*]
and Difficulty might arise. I think I lent you the Drafts of Conveyance to
Shalders and Hart but as I have the Deeds themselves it is not very material
that you should now return them.[554]

As Lady Day is approaching I should like to peruse the Draft of Security
from Mr. Doughty to Mr Repton's Ex[ecut]ors previous to its Engrossment.
I shall be in London I fear several days that a Letter directed to <the> me,
Bull Inn Yard Bishopsgate will duly arrive. I am waiting the Event of a
Tryal against my Brother at the Baptist Coffee House,[555] Keeping my Door

---

552 Mr William Foster, aged 74, 'for many years an eminent attorney in this city', died
on Thursday 22 February 1810 (*The Norfolk Chronicle and Norwich Gazette*, Saturday,
24 February 1810, issue 2083, p. 3.)

553 Jacob Shalders, grocer in St George's Colegate; d. 14 Jan. 1816; buried at the Old
Meeting House (Independent).

554 The matter of the conveyance of land to Mr Jacob Shalders continues through
several letters; it was finally settled in 1814. See NRO, AYL 835, Copy conveyance
Marsh and Repton to Shalders of property in parish of St George Colegate, Norwich
1814 (undated). The final signatories were Mr Samuel Clarke Marsh and Miss Elizabeth
D. Repton.

555 Perhaps his brother Samuel; Baptist Coffee House was in Chancery Lane.

barred to avoid a *Subpoe[n]a* by my Opponents but am rather fearful we shall not [?]come on to day and I hate Confinement.

I am D[ear] Sir, Yours very obediently James Marsh

I breakfasted with Mr Kent[556] on Monday wishing to speak to him relative to Palgrave's Lease[557] from Lord Anson. He said he had their *papers* in London but that you had the Draft which I [*fb*] could at any time see. He will probably mention this Circumstance to you as I may leave London previous to his Return

Deaths
Died Thursday last, at Gunton Hall
Harbord Lord Suffield, that is all,[558]
Heralds can nothing more record,
Than that he was, & died a Lord.
Ask of the Rich, if they can shew
What more he was, they nothing know
Ask what he was of all The Poor,
They'll say a Lord and nothing more

From such Lords, Good Lord deliver us.

The above Placard I copied from one in the Angel Coffee Room at Norwich.

Aylsham, 2d March 1810

Dear Sir

I have rece[ive]d the favor of your letter on the subject of Messrs Shalders & Harts Purchase & can have no objection to your consulting some Convey[an]cer as to the mode to be pursued for perfecting the title, but it appears to me that any steps which may be thought necessary to be taken on behalf of these purchasers must be at their expence as my father will no doubt think it quite sufficient if he is called upon to pay Lawyer Repton without anything further. indeed I do not think it improbable that the Repton Fraternity may say they ought to be at no expence whatever & that the purchasers may be very well satisfied <if> to get their title substantiated –

---

556 Nathaniel Kent (q.v.).
557 NRO, Y/D 51/1401–1402, includes a 60-year lease, dated 1770, from Thomas Anson to William Palgrave for property in Great Yarmouth.
558 Harbord Harbord, baron Suffield, died on 4 February 1810. (*Hist. Parl., 1754–1790.*)

Mr Doughty's Deed you shall of course see before it is ingrossed
Believe me Dear Sir Yours very faithfully WR

Address: Wm Repton Esqr, Solicitor, Aylsham, Norfolk
B st: 1 MA 1810
Endorsed: 1ˢᵗ March 1810   Mr Jas. Marsh   Ex[pe]dite Shalders   Doughty
to Repton's Ex[ecutor]s   Palgrave's Lease from Lord Anson   My Answer
HM 40953/11

115. George Phipps[559] to William Repton

Bank Street, Norwich, March 3ʳᵈ March [1810]

Sir

Mr. Marsh being now in London has written to me to send him the
Deed, Humphrey[*sic*] Repton Esqr. to Mr. Jacob Shalders, which I believe
is in your <D*illeg*> Possession; If therefore you will send me it by Return of
Mail as Mr. Shalders requests you will, you will much oblige
Sir Your obedient servant Geo Phipps
PS. Pray direct to be deliv[ere]d immed[iate]ly <as>

Endorsed: 3ᵈ March 1810, James Marsh's Cl[er]k   To send Draft of
Shalder's Deeds
HM 40953/12

116. George Repton to William Repton

Dover Street, March 7ᵗʰ 1810

My dear William

I some time since wrote to you from the Isle of Wight upon the subject
of Uncle Johns Monument.[560] I have to day had a letter from John to say
he has hitherto forgot to mention it to me, but that Mrs John has desird
him to tell me to order it to be made – now I of course shall not think any
more about it unless I am requested to do so by you – whom I consider
the authorized person to give directions upon the subject – but it is not
necessary to tell her so –

---

559 James Marsh's clerk.
560 The most recent letter on the subject in this collection is Letter 109, 18 December
1809.

You no doubt rejoiced at the famous division in the House last Monday night.[561] I think our [fb] present stupid fellows must e'er long turn out – but I am afraid not before they have uselessly sacrificed more Men & Money in their foolish expeditions – did you see Cobbetts paper a fortnight Ago about your friend W Windham.[562] It was in consequence of the latters speech upon the Newspaper Reporters[563] – and Cobbett proves that Windham is the last Man who should abuse them for that he has had his speeches sent down to Felbrigg before they were inserted in the work he *(Cobbett)* edits of Parliamentary Reports – for Windhams corrections – And that the Work has been delayed & an additional expence incurrd in consequence – however all the papers appear to have been offended [fb] by it – Windham the other night (I understand from a Member) made a most brilliant speech. The Newspapers one & all merely said "Mr Windham spoke against the question" or "a Member opposed the question" – this must annoy your friend not a little, who Mr Cobbett attests used to go into the Gallery to ask what effect his speeches had & if he modulated his voice well, – if you have not seen that Weeks paper & wish to do so I will endeavour to procure one & send you.

I heard from Hare Street this morning all well – Mary comes to town tomorrow to stay with Mrs Scott[564] until Monday – I fear there is but little chance of your coming to us this year – with affectionate love to Aunt Adey, not forgetting Mrs John. believe me My dear William

Your very affectionate G S Repton

561 The debate on Whitbread's resolutions on 5 March, relating to failure of Walcheren Expedition (Sept.–Dec. 1809). *The Times* (6 March) reported that William Windham 'spoke at great length and concluded by saying he would support the motion'.

562 William Cobbett (1763–1835), political writer and farmer; his *Political Register* was published, almost without exception, every week between January 1802 and his death in 1835. (*ODNB*) George is referring to *Cobbett's Weekly Political Register*, dated London, Saturday, February 24, 1810: Vol. XVII, No. 8, which includes a letter, columns 297–301, from 'A friend to the Truth', dated 15 February 1810. In col. 300 the writer says '[Mr Wright's] publication is not a newspaper; it is a Collection of Speeches complied and printed sometime after they have been delivered, with a view to the information of posterity, and corrected, in many instances, by the speakers themselves. Mr Windham appears to be one of the speakers who render this assistance, and it would have been strange indeed if he had thought it necessary to censure a publication to which he himself contributed'.

563 Windham's speech was recorded in *Cobbett's Weekly Political Register*, dated London, Saturday, February 17, 1810: Vol. XVII, no. 7, report of Windham's speech 'Summary of Politics' 'Shutting up the Gallery' (i.e. the Press gallery).

564 Claude Scott's wife; see the next letter regarding Mary's stay.

Endorsed: 7ᵗʰ March 1810   My brother George   Oxnead Monument
Windhams Speech in Cobbett on Newspaper Reporters
HM 40919/1

117. Humphry Repton to William Repton; Mary (Clarke) Repton to Dorothy Adey

Harest[reet], 7 February [*recte* March] 1810[565]

Dear William

I dont know how our Acc[oun]ts stand – but all I expect from my hopeful property in Norfolk is to pay Cl[aude] Scotts Interest. 35£ p[er] a[nnu]m which is due about this time & if you can spare a draft for that Am[oun]t & direct it to me under Cover to Claude Scott Esq. Bruton Street so as to be <u>there next Monday morning</u> – I shall receive it that day & not let the payment appear in my Bankers Acc[oun]t –

With respect to Shalder's business – am I to make good his Title so long after I have done with the Estate? & must all the Children be of age – because D wants 2 Years of it? – at all events I will sign nothing of James Marsh's production & refer 'em to you. The Girls will want all the room in this Sheet – so God bless you all –

[*fb*] My Dearest

I was indeed very uncomfortable on Sunday not to have a letter from you, at the same time supposeing the post Basket was lost, as I knew if there was no provision, you wou'd write by the post. In future when that is the case, be so good as to write on the Saturday, which I shall get a day sooner. My fidgets are over, and we are happy to hear all is well, and when the Basket comes next send your long letter you have written, for they are my dear Dee always a great treat to us –

My dear H has been at home this last fortnight very hard at work drawing and making Books[566] and we are kept in constant employ of reading to him: he with the 2 girls went last Monday *to* the rehearsal of Ancient Music:[567]

---

565 The date is written in Repton's hand but in a different pen from the rest of letter. The endorsement by William says it is 7 *March* 1810. Repton refers to 'Shalder's business' which was raised by James Marsh's letter of 1 March 1810 (Letter 114) and Mary mentions their daughter Mary going to stay with Mrs Scott the next day, which George had mentioned on 7 March.

566 Perhaps books for the Yorkshire properties mentioned in Letter 110.

567 James Bartleman (q.v.) often performed at the Ancient Music concerts.

Ld Darnly[568] admited them all to go in his name, and he had given Mary his Gold Ticket to go to morrow night, and she is going to morrow morning to stay with Mr and Mrs Scott and go with them, and stays till Monday, when we are to go by Ld Darnleys admission to the Rehearsal, dine [*fb*] at Mr Scotts, and bring Mary back.[569] This is a great favour from Ld D – who is always very attentive and notices Mary. When you hear from us again you shall know all about it. I have have[*sic*] often lookd out for poor Mrs Windham.[570] What is she going to Town for. Poor thing I shoud have been glad to have accommodated her in any way, if she woud have calld, but perhaps she woud not have liked to have stopt. did she know she shoud go past our house.

I hope the old woman who makes sausages is not affronted at our finding fault and will not make more, as I shall hope to have some on Sunday.

God bless you all and, best love Your affectionate M R

Address: To Mrs Adey, Aylsham, Norfolk
B st: RUMFORD [*illeg*]; Cross Post; *charge*: 8
Endorsed: 7 <Feb> *March it is* 1810   My father   Cl[aude] Scott's Int[eres]t   Shalders' business   My Mother to Mrs Adey
HM 40862

118. Humphry Repton to William Repton

12th March 1810

Dear William

I acknowledge re[ceip]t of your draft   31.10 –
No time for more
H Repton

Address: To Wm Repton Eqr., Aylsham, Norfolk, *written on the back of a wrapper addressed thus:* Claude Scott Esqr. M.P., Bruton Street, London
R st, with crown: FREE 12 MA12 1810; *b st*: AYLSHAM 132
Endorsed: 12 March 1810   My father acknowl[edge]s Rec[eip]t of £31 10
HM 40864

---

568 John, fourth earl Darnley (1767–1831).

569 In his memoirs, Repton recalls attending some of the rehearsals for the 'Ancient Concerts' and also his daughter Mary and himself being given tickets by Lord Darnley and Lord Uxbridge for one of the concerts in the Hanover Square rooms. (*Memoirs*, p. 129.)

570 Cecilia Windham, b.1750; m.10 July 1798, at Binfield (Berks); d.5 May 1824; third daughter of Commodore Arthur Forrest. Probably 'poor Mrs Windham' because William Windham was seriously ill. (See note to Letter 135.)

119. Humphry Repton to William Repton

Harestreet near Romford, March 16 1810

Dear William

I can only account for your having again received the draft you sent me for £31:10 by Mr Scotts having accidentally put it in the Cover with my letter to you & *he* has probably supposed it to be lost or Mislaid – You will therefore be so good to return it to him in Bruton Street – & write over my Name on the Indorsment

pay to Cl[aude] Scott Esqr – or order

We are all well – & I returned last night from Sudbury where I went to meet Mr Greenwood[571] & felt my self half way [fb] to those I love too well not to think of with a wish to be nearer

God bless you HR

[fb] Mr Repton begs the favor of Mr Scott to read the inclosed & afterwards to direct it to Wm Repton Aylsham

Mrs R & the Girls unite in best regards & thanks to Mrs Scott & Yourself –[572]

HM 40865

120. Claude Scott to William Repton

Bruton Street, 20 March 1810

Dear Sir

It is very true I did by mistake include the Draft in the Letter from your Father I address'd to you and imagined I had mislaid it – be so good at your leisure to return it to

Dear Sir Yours truly C. Scott

---

571 In Letter 5 Mary (Clarke) Repton told Dorothy Adey that at that time (December 1806) Repton had decided against a visit to Sudbury, because it was winter. The *Polite Repository* (1811) includes a drawing of Auberies (Suffolk), the property of Mr Charles Greenwood (1748–1832). (Daniels, *Repton*, p. 266; Temple, 'Repton, illustrator', p. 173.) Greenwood had purchased the property in 1806. (SRO (Bury), 613/747, Printed sale particulars of 'Auberies', Bulmer, Essex …, 25 Sept. 1806.) Auberies was previously owned by Mr Andrews, whose portrait was painted by Gainsborough in the well-known painting of him with a gun and hunting dog, with Mrs Andrews sitting on a bench under a tree. (http://www.bulmerhistory.co.uk/page49.html.)

572 No address or endorsement, but see Letter 120; the two have been separated in the archive.

Address: London March twenty 1810, Wm Repton Esqr, Aylsham, Norfolk, C Scott
R st with crown: FREE 20 MA 20 1810; *b st*: A 20 MR 810
Endorsed: 16 & 20 March 1810   My Father & Mr Claude Scott about Draft for £31.10 returned to me by mistake[573]
HM 40953/13

121. Claude Scott to William Repton

Bruton Street, March 24th 1810

Dear Sir

I am favor'd with your Letter of the 23[d] returning the Draft for £31.10.s which I had sent you by mistake. I beg leave to thank you for your attention, and to assure you I am with much respect
Dear Sir
Your faithful and obedient humble Servant Claude Scott
Wm Repton Esqr., Aylsham, Norfolk

Endorsed: 24[th] March 1810, Claude Scott Esq., Acknowledges Rec[eip]t of £31.10 by my Draft
HM 40953/14

122. George Repton to William Repton

29 Dover Street, March 22 1810

My dear William

I have applied to my Father for the inscription upon Uncle Johns Monument – he has sent me the enclosed this morning[574] – which you will perhaps think rather too concise – but if you make any addition to it, you must bear in recollection that there is not room for a great deal [*fb*] particularly if a space is to be left for Mrs Johns name hereafter – Would not "Sacred to the Memory" be better than "to the Memory" as my father has written? and has he put the right day & age? – You had better I think by no means let any but Aunt Adey see the enclosed letter – but you can tear

---

573   i.e. Letters 119 and 120 were originally filed together by William.
574   The enclosed letter that George refers to as being from his father is not in this archive, but see Letter 128 which has a later version of the inscription to be put on John Repton's monument.

the top inscription off, if it is necessary to shew it to your colleagues – the Mason will want the inscription as soon as you can let me [*fb*] have it – with best love to Aunt Adey believe me always my dear William

Your affectionate Brother George

Endorsed: 22ᵈ March 1810   My father to George & George's note to me about the inscription on Uncle John's monum't
HM 40919/2

123. Humphry Repton to Dorothy Adey

Harestreet, March 27 1810

Dearest Dee

As we have no basket to send & you will think it hard not to have a letter – & mine come more rarely – you may as well pay postage for one from me as from any body else & you may answer it gratis next week under Cover to H. G. the D. of B[575] *Woburn* & so now I have ask'd old Mary what she has to say. – Nothing on Earth – a pretty business – so I will turn over a New Leaf

[*fb*] A New Leaf,

We are to have some <u>fringe</u> as Mrs John calls her friends – to dine on Sunday & wish we had Turkeys &c &c &c to be paid for – Mind that – & when in the time for Crabs – & Potted Lobsters which you may do & not be paid for – Mind that –

Old Mary has got pain in her back

Lumbago

Young Mary pain in her head

Megrims.

[*fb*] & poor Dee [Elizabeth] *has* neither Aches nor Pains but takes a great deal every day

in Learning Italian.

John is quite well. Ditto I. & so no more as the man is come for the Letters & is to drink till I have finished this – & if I don't finish quickly he will finish my Tub of Drink

& Mrs Madam & Mr William have you seen the Trimming Windham has had from The [?]dragon[576]

---

575   i.e. His Grace the Duke of Bedford, Woburn, indicating that Repton was planning a visit to Woburn in early April. Letter 127 indicates that he did go.

576   Perhaps a reference to a newspaper article on William Windham. The press was

In haste Ever HR

Address: Mrs Adey, Aylsham, Norfolk
B st: Rumford [*illeg*]; Cross Post; *charge*: 8
Endorsed: 27th March 1810   My father to Mrs Adey
HM 40836

124. Cook Flower to William Repton

Sherringham, March 31st 1810

Dear Sir

As I am not Certain whether there is a seperate acc[oun]t from Mine Kept at Messrs Gurneys,577 by reason of the Money advanced by them on account of the Sherringham Inclosure, I shall be Obliged to you to wait 'till the Latter end of Next week, at which time will ride Over to aylsham, and settle respecting it –

I am Dear Sir Yours Truly Cook Flower

Address: Wm Repton Esqr, Aylsham
Endorsed: 31 March 1810   C Flower Esqr   Sherringham Inclosure money at Gurneys
HM 40953/15

125. Humphry Repton to Mr Stevenson578

Harestreet near Romford, April 1st 1810

Sir

I have received repeated letters about News papers which I desired my son Mr William Repton of Aylsham to answer by telling you that I always

---

no longer reporting his speeches, but *The Times*, Saturday, 24 March 1810, issue 7936, p. 3, reported on the previous day's debate in Parliament, including an exchange between Windham and Richard Sheridan which included innuendoes about Windham's motions.

577 Gurneys' bank became the most important in East Anglia, its influence extending throughout the region either by the establishment of local private banks in which the Gurney family was an important participant or through marriage to other local banking families. (*British Banking*, pp. 246–8, entry for Gurneys, Birkbecks, Barclay & Buxton, Norwich.)

578 Although meaning of the reference to stained glass is unclear, mention of newspapers suggests that 'Mr Stevenson' was the stationer Stephenson of Matchett and Stephenson, printers and stationers, 47 Market Place, Norwich. (*Norwich Directory* (1802), p. 34.)

considered the balance the other way & that in Consequence of your own Proposal to me respecting Stained Glass – you were my debtor – either 10£ or 20£, I forget which – so I thought it might work itself out in News papers till your very persevering hints obliged me to stop the papers – & therefore if you please now the matter is explained – you may balance the Acc[oun]t by continuing to send the papers free – but, to avoid [*fb*] the unnecessary postage I must trouble you to shew this letter to Mr William when he calls at your house & not answer it to me, because I have of late felt that I had not reason to be well pleased or I could have been <of> much more use*ful* to you in the Sale of the Stained Glass –

I am notwithstanding Yours very faithfully H Repton

Address: To – Stevenson Esq, Surry Street, Norwich
Cross Post[579]
Endorsed: 1[st] April 1810   My Fathers L[ett]re to Mr Stevenson of Norw[ic]h about P[er]Centage on Stained Glass
HM 40882

126. George Repton to William Repton;[580] Humphry Repton junior to William Repton

[London], April 2d 1810

Private
Dear William

Your letter does not precisely describe, the nature of the Bond which you mention <my> *our* Father to have given – whether simply a Bond for the amount of the Purchase Money – or a Bond of forfeiture – should his Children not confirm his part of the Contract[581] –

With the anxious wish that we all of us feel that the remainder of our dear Fathers days should be as uninterrupted and happy as it is in our power to make them, and feeling equally anxious, that his character should continue such, as it has ever hitherto been, for the strict fulfilment of all his engagements – we think there cannot be a doubt, but that we are bound (for these reasons) to confirm his act, as submitted in your letter for our opinions – and also, from what you describe, of our Father having

---

579 This letter was not actually posted, but sent as an enclosure to William to send on. (See Letter 127.)
580 Unsigned but clearly written in George's hand.
581 Referring to the conveyance to Shalders. (See Letter 114.)

covenanted to defray all expences necessary for the regularly obtaining our consents – we [*fb*] do not see how, we can in honor, require of the other parties to pay the *whole (if any) of* those expences – but we decidedly object to executing any deed now – if our Sister D is to be subject to the same expence hereafter – We therefore decline doing so, untill our Sister becomes of age, and is capable of acting with us – unless it is particularly understood that she is not to be put to any expence whatever, whenever she may sign the deed – but in either case, we shall of course require, that our Father is released from all Bonds, and Engagements, he may at any time have entrd into –

Such Dear William is the light in which we view the subject, and in so determining we have put a great reliance upon your opinion, who doubtless have carefully examined all the documents upon the subject – though we cannot but feel some surprize, at James Marsh's so urgently pressing for our signatures –

[*fb*] [London], April 4th 1810

Dear William

George has exactly expressed what I meant to say, & what indeed was the subject of our previous conversation. Indeed there can be but one opinion on the subject – we are bound in honor under all circumstances of the case to confirm whatever my father has thought it right to do, unless there are some circumstances in the Agreement with which I am unacquainted – of the best means of carrying my fathers stipulation into effect you are the best judge, having all the documents before you – The bond I understand to be a penalty of double the purchase money in case of failure to complete the bargain – We have [*fb*] seen nothing of Marsh & shall of course neither sign nor discuss any thing without your sanction –

Edward agrees with us exactly. John I understand demurs, – but as his acquiescence is, fortunately unnecessary it is not worth while entering into the subject with him – have you read Cobbetts attack on Mr Windham? a decided blackguard has no delicacy in stating home truths, his last number attacking the House of Commons under the cloak of an Essay on Bonapartes Government[582] is worse than any of his former performances –

I wish you were coming to Town this Spring – but what avails wishing – ever yours H Repton

---

582 Referring to *Cobbett's Weekly Political Register*, dated London, Saturday, March 31, 1810. Vol. XVII. No. 13, Columns 481–493, 'Summary of Politics': 'What is Despotism'.

Address: London April five 1810,   Wm Repton Esq., Aylsham, Norfolk,
L Worsley Holmes[583]
R st: FREE 5 AP 5 1810
Endorsed: 2ᵈ & 3ʳᵈ[*sic*] April 1810   My brothers George & Humphry
About Shalders' business To execute Deeds   Windham & Cobbett
HM 40926/1

127. Humphry Repton to William Repton

[Woburn], 4 April 1810

Dear William

That puppy Stevenson is always dunning me for News Papers so I wrote the inclosed[584] – but perhaps you had better shew it him & not send it till you go to Norwich

Apropos – about Income Tax. You say right – 31.10 – is to pay 35 so I save – £3: 10s:0 – but how is Gov[ernmen]t the better for my getting it & Claude Scott not getting it? – Am I to pay it in to any body & reveal my secret pray expound – Master expound.

[*fb*] I am quite well – & have been on foot from 11 – till 6 – & am tired & hungry but as dinner is not ready – I tell you so
   & Bless you HR

Endorsed: 4ᵗʰ April 1810   My father from the Duke of Bedford's
Property Tax   Stevenson's Glass
HM 40866

128. George Repton to William Repton, with a draft inscription

29 Dover Street, April 5ᵗʰ 1810

In the Vault near this spot are deposited the remains
of John Repton Esqʳᵉ
who died at Oxnead Hall June 14ᵗʰ 1809 aged 55[585] years

---

583 Leonard Thomas Worsley Holmes, (1787–1825), of Pidford House, I.o.W., was M.P. for Newport (I.o.W). (*Hist. Parl.*) George, through his acquaintance with the Isle, was making use of this M.P.'s free postage.
584 Letter 125.
585 14ᵗʰ and 55 added in different ink, by William.

Multis ille bonis flebilis occidit[586] –

(put in age & day of death)
(Born on 25 Aug't 1753)[587]

My dear William

The above I have written for the Monument, to which Duff has added the quotation from Horace, to which I think there can be no objection – if you approve of it altogether let me know as the man has asked me for it – I think it expresses every thing necessary, in as little compass as possible but alter it in any way you like – only [*fb*] let me know about it that I may put it into the Workmans hands –

Sacred to the Memory[588]
of
John Repton Esq[re]
late of Oxnead Hall
Who died the 14th day of June 1809 aged 55[589]
and whose Remains are here interred

Multis ille bonis flebilis occidit

I heartily join with Duff my dear William in wishing you had a <u>profitable</u> call to London, which I fear is now too late in the year to be probable – my friend Ferris much wishes me to take a cruize with him in his Frigate[590] – if only as far as Yarmouth [*fb*] but my various other employments at this time will not I fear permit me to do so –

We have all cause to lament the general agreement which appears to have taken place amongst the <u>Editors</u> of Newspapers for the exclusion of Windhams speeches[591] – I understand from one of the most able men in

---

586 'That man has died mourned by his many good friends'. (Horace's Ode 1.24, To Vergil on the Death of Quintilius.)
587 This phrase added by William.
588 The following version is not in George's hand; possibly Duff's. It is not the inscription by their father 'enclosed' with Letter 122, because here it says 'Sacred to the Memory' whereas George specifically stated that their father had simply written 'to the Memory'.
589 Again 14th and 55 added in different ink, by William.
590 Not identified: there are several men named Captain Ferris mentioned in Admiralty papers held at TNA for the years 1800–1820.
591 Owing to Windham's earlier complaints about newspaper reporting, from 23 March whenever he subsequently rose to speak, 'all the reporters struck work. Detailed reporting

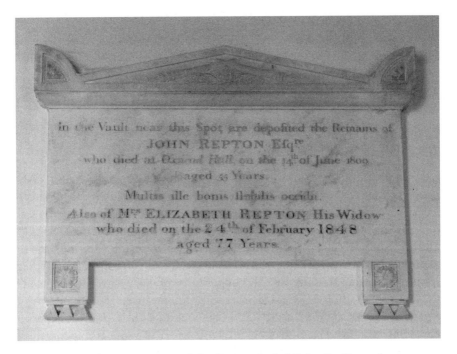

In the Vault near this Spot are deposited the Remains of
JOHN REPTON Esqr
who died at Oxnead Hall on the 14th of June 1809
aged 55 Years.

Multis ille bonis flebilis occidit.

Also of Mrs ELIZABETH REPTON His Widow
who died on the 24th of February 1848
aged 77 Years.

9. The monument to John Repton in St Michael's, Oxnead
(photograph by author)

the House of Commons – that for the number of years he has been in the House <of Commons> – he never yet heard such a speech as that Windham made on Friday night, upon the great division on the Scheldt Inquiry[592] – he says there was not a line or scarcely a word in the whole speech that it appeard possible to correct and [*fb*] that he was particularly happy in all his quotations & allusions – I will not attempt to tell you any news of Harestreet. it is most probable you know more of them than I do, for I am sorry to say it is more than 2 months since I have had an opportunity of going there but I hope to do so this week if possible – My father left town yesterday morning for Woburn – with best love to Aunt Adey – believe me my dear William

ever your affectionate Brother George

---

of his speeches was not resumed until 10 April'. (*Hist. Parl.*, Windham.) In line with the press ban on Windham, *Hansard* 1st ser. Vol. 16 c. 409 (30 Mar. 1810) simply records that he 'spoke at length' in favour of original resolutions.

592 The division ended in a victory for the government, after a debate lasting until 7.30am on Saturday.

Address: Wm Repton Esqr, Aylsham
B st: [*mostly illeg*] NORWICH   117; *charge*: 7
Endorsed: 5 April 1810   My brother George   Inscription for Uncle John's
monument   Likely to sail to Yarmouth with Capt. Ferris   Windham's
good Speech – not in the Newspapers
HM 40919/3

129. William Repton to Nathaniel Kent[593] (draft)

<Aylsham 9> *Holt 11[th]* April 1810

Dear Sir

I have in pursuance of the Comm[issioner]s directions written Chas[594] a kind of official letter *about* the Swanton &c Inclosure Meeting[595] – In addition to what I have there said which you will of course *see* I beg leave to call your attention to the <importance of> subject of Lord Anson's Claim – In the first place as to its *great* importance. The Commons of Swanton contain by the Survey 229 <*ave*> acres – the Land in the parish belonging to Lord Anson may be fairly estimated in value at one fourth of the whole parish – <the question therefore you will perceive involves his Ldship's property to the amount of at least 50 acres of the Common> *His Lordship's* probable share of the Commons if his Claim can be substantiated, will be at least 50 *average* acres – If the[re]fore <of> we have any probable chance of success, <I wo'd> the object is such that I sho'd <contend it the> be very unwilling to relinquish the Claim & the delay in the Inclosure is *I think* between ourselves of little consequence compared with Lord Anson's inte't[596] but at the same time if <the business> we are unable to produce any <testimonies> evidence in support of our Claim, proprietors will say why <delay> *sho'd we* cause a delay unnecessarily – I have hinted that your testimony in point of information may be material & that you or Lord Anson himself may be in possession of ancient Records or other Documents <essential to the Case> *relating to the question* & that at all events we must beg the business may not be pressed in such a manner

---

593   Kent managed the Norfolk estate of Thomas, Lord Anson, hence this letter about the enclosure of Swanton.
594   Charles Kent, Nathaniel's son who was a surveyor. (See Letter 145.)
595   NRO, AYL 495, papers relating to the enclosure of Swanton Abbott, Buxton and Lamas: a bundle containing commissioners' minutes, 1809–1823; two copies of 1809 Act, four copies of statement of the claims, four notices under the award and one draft notice.
596   Probably, 'interest'.

as to deprive us of the means of having <all the> *such* aid *as* our case
may <require> admit of

Mr Nash is desirous[597] of having his Lease of the Lands *which have
been* purchased of him, <the> it having been[598] one of the Conditions of
the sale that he sho'd have a Lease. <Pl I ha> I have not heard from you
relative to the admissi[on] in the Manor of Horsford[599] under < the> Sir
P. Stephens will[600]

Endorsed: 11 April 1810   L[ett]re to Mr Kent   As to the Swanton
Inclosure question   Hayneford Lease to Nash   Lord Ranelagh's[601]
admis[sio]n
HM 40954/3

130. James Marsh to William Repton

House of Lords, Wednesday Noon [11 April 1810]

Dear Sir

I have called several Times upon both your Brothers who seemed disposed
to confirm the Conveyance made by your father, and I wrote to Edward
requesting his Attendance in London tomorrow. It not being convenient for
him to do so I again called on Humphry for him to appoint his own Time
when all might meet for the first time. he expressed his <u>Ignorance</u> of the
Business that he <u>had written</u> to you but has not <u>heard in Return</u>. In short
he seemed disposed <u>not to confirm</u> his father's Act and intimated I was at
liberty to take any Steps I might deem necessary ag[ain]st that[*sic*] Father.
This has put me in a most awkward and distressing Situation. I lament that I
<have> *am* so placed yet I feel I have a paramount Duty to [*fb*] my Clients
to perform this I cannot fly from and I shall to morrow tender the Deeds for

---

597 In faint pencil above this: Lord Ranelegh.
598 In faint pencil above this: Hayneford. Hayneford, now Hainford, is between Aylsham
and Norwich.
599 Horsford is about 3 miles south-west of Hainford. There are numerous documents
relating to the manor of Horsford in NRO, AYL.
600 NRO, AYL 125/7 comprises 'Abstracts of property in Horsford purchased by Lord
Suffield from Preston family, incl. Preston and Harbord family settlements, title to other
Suffield property, abstracts of title to property purchased by Sir Philip Stephens, etc. (18th
century–early 19th century). The will of Sir Philip Stephens of Saint Faiths, Norfolk, was
granted probate on 5 January 1810. (TNA, PROB 11/1507/69.)
601 Thomas [Jones], sixth viscount Ranelagh, born 3 February 1763, died 4 July 1820.
(http://www.cracroftspeerage.co.uk/online/content/ranelagh1628.htm)

Humphry's [Duff's] signature, *if he refuses* shall then endeavour to see my Uncle[602] when sho'd his Influence over his Children be of no Avail Things must take their Regular Course.

I had hoped to have been Home to morrow as I expect getting thro the Lords to day but am disappointed by this unpleasant *Business* which now <un>necessarily, will *yet unnecessarily* keep me in Town perhaps several Days. Sewell and Blake are both here that I suppose my Absence does not prevent Mr Doughty's[603] Business being concluded. Should this however be the Case I beg you will not consider my looking at the Papers as necessary as I shall rest satisfied with your Correctness.

All Parties *in the House* seem to have given up Sir F Burdett[604] for his intemperate Conduct but not so a very large Party out that House.

Yours truly James Marsh

[fb] Perhaps it would be as well for you to write to Hare St[reet] or Humphrey[sic]

Address: Wm Repton Esq, Aylsham, Norfolk
B st: A 11 A 810
Endorsed: 11th April 1810   James Marsh's acco[un]t of his visit to Duff to sign the Deed of Convey[an]ce to Shalders &c
HM 40904

131. Humphry Repton junior to William Repton; note from George Repton

Adelphi, 11th April 1810

Dear William

I neither understand Mr Marsh's object nor his behaviour – he has just been here in a violent hurry & agitation – "I'm going to the house of Lords & cant stop a moment" – "read this letter from Edward" – a letter in answer to one from him desiring him to attend at his lodgings tomorrow to sign a

---

602 Referring to Humphry Repton senior; the family connection was between Marsh's mother and Mary (Clarke) Repton, who were cousins.
603 Presumably Robert Doughty (q.v.).
604 Sir Francis Burdett, fifth baronet (1770–1844), radical politician. On 5 April 1810 he had been found guilty of breach of privilege by the House of Commons. On 6 April the Commons had voted to commit him to the Tower of London, whereupon he challenged the speaker's warrant and barricaded himself in his London house. Clashes followed between troops and the crowd. He was seized on the morning of 9 April and was confined to the Tower until the end of the parliamentary session on 21 June. (*ODNB*; see also *Hist.Parl.*)

conveyance & inviting him to dinner – Edward says if he is sure of meeting us he is perfectly willing to attend & do what we think right – if not it will be <very> inconvenient for him to come to town <& therefore>

I said I had written to you on the subject & when I saw the papers in question, or heard from you what was to be done I was perfectly ready to do it – till then I could of course not form an opinion on a subject on which I was <ignorant> *not fully informed* [*fb*] he flew into a violent rage & said – "I cant be kept here day after day in this manner – it has now arrived at that pass that you must either say you will or will not sign this paper" – "Till I hear from William I can only repeat what I have already said" – He jumped up, laid hold of the handle of the door – & said "William has had the papers in his possession three years – your father engaged to pay the whole expense & you may depend upon it I shall take other means to compel him – I shall not tell you that William has behaved unhandsomely in this business" –

By this time he was half way downstairs & it is lucky he was, or the affair would have taken a turn that I am on reflection glad to have avoided – Now, my dear William, what is to be done – I conceive it to be highly improper in a lawyer to proceed in this manner to transact business with a gentleman who tells him that he has [*fb*] written to his brother "learned in the law" on the subject under consideration –

I am ready to do immediately of course whatever you tell me to do – but am always unwilling to do this or any other act of business in a violent hurry as if it was a matter of life & death – & I shall take care to have only the necessary communication with Mr Marsh on the subject –

You will of course not suffer your judgement to be influenced by our common feelings on his threats to my father – for we will take care that he shall never see any letter <from> upon the subject –

The moment we know your decision on the course to be pursued we shall do what is necessary but dont let a single iota of that course depend on Mr Marsh's discretion. –

We live in strange times – while I was singing glees at Mr Eliots[605] on Saturday night, a clerk of Heatons[606] was shot at my door in Piccadilly – I called on Charles[607] & sat by the man's bed side – a ball passed thro' his knee without injuring the bone[608] so I hope he is doing well – The House of

605 Duff's superior in the Audit Office.

606 Not identifed further. Later letters refer to Mr and Mrs Heaton, who were probably inhabitants of Hare Street, but it is impossible to tell whether there was a connection.

607 Not identified; unlikely to be Charles Kent as he lived at Craig's Court.

608 *The Times* reported at length on the riots in London in support of Sir Francis Burdett on Saturday 7 April. Troops were on hand, not only Horse Guards but also two brigades

Commons have decided that Sir F[rancis] B[urdett]'s letter shall not appear on the Journals "– <but> "that it is a <u>high</u> & <u>flagrant</u> breach of privilege – but as he is in the Tower it is not necessary for the House to proceed further on the subject" – so much for strong measures & a weak administration –[609]

The town is now perfectly quiet & has been for the last two days[610] – love to all,

ever yours HR

[*fb*] Dear William

The *Morning Chronicle* of yesterday gave the proceedings relative to Sir Francis Burdett so fully,[611] that I procured <a> *that* paper to send you, not knowing that Duff had done the same – you are therefore now I suppose quite learned upon the subject – let me know about the inscription for the Monument –

yours affectionately GSR

Address: William Repton Esqr, Aylsham, Norfolk   single sheet
B st: C AP 11 810
Endorsed: 11 April 1810   Duff's account of James Marsh's visit to him at the Auditor's Office with Deed of Conveyance to Shalders &c
HM 40926/2

132. George Repton to William Repton

Dover Street, April 13 1810

Dear William

Duff and myself have to day signed the deeds which James Marsh brought to us for that purpose – Duff tells me Marsh left what you had written with him yesterday, and to day brought him that same sort of thing engrossed – he therefore signed it – Marsh and another man came to me afterwards – and told me, Humphrey[*sic*] had signed the deeds, and that

---

of artillery and 150 men from the 15th Light Dragoons. The focus of the disturbance was in Piccadilly. 'Some shots were fired in the course of the night; some by the populace and some by the military. Several persons [unnamed] among the crowd were wounded.' Duff's letter provides an eyewitness account, and some identification, of one of the rioters who was shot. (*The Times*, Monday, 9 April 1810, issue 7949, p. 3.)

609 See *Report from the Select Committee on Proceedings Relative to Sir Francis Burdett* (printed 11 May 1810).

610 After the demonstrations in favour of Burdett.

611 *The Morning Chronicle*, Tuesday, 10 April 1810, issue 12766, p. 1.

he had read them through before doing so – this upon <u>seeing them</u> I did not feel inclined to do, but put my signature on the same <u>three</u> papers that Duff had previously signed – they had some sort of commission to wait upon us – it is granted – (I understand from Duff) on the ground[s] four being incompetent from bodily infirmities, otherwise to execute the deeds – they are going to Crayford, and from thence cross the water to Harestreet for Marys signature – as Marsh seems to say he stays in London only to complete this business –

When you tell me about the inscription for the Monument tell me also by what Waggon you will like to have it sent, & to whom directed –

With love to Aunt Adey, believe me Dear William

Your affectionate Brother in haste G S Repton

Address: William Repton Esqr, Aylsham, Norfolk
B st: A A 13 810
Note in pencil by William: wrote to George: 14 April
Endorsed: 13th April 1810   George   That he & Duff have signed the Convey[an]ce to Shalders &c
HM 40919/4

133. Edward Repton to William Repton

Crayford, April 25 1810

Dear William

I have just received an Answer from Mr Ellis to whom I forwarded the contents of your letter – he has been in Wales (which prevented my hearing sooner) where he had made a considerable purchase – the Estate as he says, contains more than 2,000 Acres – and there are two Advowsons upon it – the next presentation to one of them, is however withheld – and he hopes the other will fall in while he holds the Estate for if he can get a good profit he intends to sell again – so I suppose it is an entire Job – with him – but if the living becomes vacant – and he presents me – we will not quarrel [*fb*] with his intentions – He did not consider Monk Soham [Suffolk] very reasonable – as he says he could purchase an Annuity for a trifle more – which would be a Sinecure – of course, therefore he gives it up. –

James M[arsh] has been here – he came with a <u>blear</u>-eyed, ill-looking fellow on the outside of the Coach – <which> with an old green velvet bag – which I told him looked as if it had *been* made out of an old Pulpit Hanging – he produced a popularity of Papers – to all of which, where I saw your signature, I put mine, which is a proof, observe, that in such matters I give you credit for knowing more than I do – and also, a tacit acknowledgement that I consider you an honest fellow – but to return to our amiable [*fb*] Cousin – When we were getting something for them to eat – the shabby fellows confessed they had ordered a beef steak at the <u>Inn</u> – So to the Inn they went – and I followed shortly after – lest my Parishioners should imagine that two such ill-looking fellows – (who professed to come to see me, and could not get any thing to eat at <u>my</u> house) were sent to arrest me – After they had crammed down Beef steak and Porter – at ½ past Eleven – they started for Harestreet – the result of their walk[*sic*] you will have heard <at> from H: Street –

My Father and Duff cross from Tunbridge[612] to Crayford tomorrow – and we dine at Lord Eardly at Belvedere[613] – so I shall keep this open till I see him. – Tell Aunt Adey – that my poor Mary had made up her beautiful Gown to go to a Dance last night – and the Lady who was to have taken her could not go – so the gown is reserved for another occasion. – Give our kindest Love to her – and a kiss from her fat faced Nephew – the little – –

Yours Ever ER

[*fb*] [*in pencil*] Thursday night [*26 April*] – We have just left my Father at Lord Eardleys – with Duff who are both well – and as jolly as a skin full of Champagne and Claret can make them – Love to Aylsham ER

Address: Wm Repton Esqr, Aylsham, Norfolk
B st: [*partial*] A 2 81
Endorsed: 25th April 1810, My brother Edward   Ellis purchased Livings in Wales   Jas Marsh's visit to them at Crayford   Sister Edwds gown
HM 40912/2

---

612 Perhaps Repton and Duff had visited Summerhill, near Tonbridge, the home of William Woodgate. Joseph Farington recorded that Repton has been there prior to Farington's own visit in July 1810. (Daniels, *Repton*, p. 37.) (See details in the section on Summerhill in the Introduction.) Indeed, in letters below written by Repton after the failure of the Tonbridge Bank, of which Woodgate was one of the owners, there are hints that he and his sons had a commission from Woodgate that was never paid for. Alternatively on this occasion Repton and Duff may have been visiting Vicesimus Knox, who lived in Tonbridge. (See Letter 169 for both Woodgate and Knox.)

613 Belvedere was not far from Crayford. Belvedere was pictured in the *Polite Repository* (1810), suggesting that Repton had visited before 1810. (Daniels, *Repton*, p. 261; Temple, 'Repton, illustrator', p. 172.) Certainly his wife and daughters visited in January 1810. (See Letter 111.) There is a connection with another of Repton's commissions. Lord Eardley's daughter Charlotte (d. 15 September 1826) was married to Sir Culling Smith, second baronet (1768–1829). (*ODNB* for Sir Culling Eardley [formerly Smith], (1805–1863), third baronet, their son.) Sir Culling Smith, first baronet, Charlotte's father-in-law, owned Bedwell Park (Herts), where he had commissioned Repton to suggest improvements in 1809. (Letter 26.)

134. Humphry Repton to William Repton

Harestreet, May 1st 1810[614]

Dear William

You have not answered my Qu[estion]:
A Lends B on bond 1000 – at 5 P[er] C[en]t In[teres]t
B pays only 45 instead of 50 £ deducting Income Tax.
Qu[estion]: how is Government to get the Five pounds
I suppose by A giving in his income £50 & paying <45> £5 but don't you see in this Case that B is benefitted & actually borrows at 4½ P[er] C[en]t instead of 5 P[er] C[en]t –

I can understand this in Cases of Mortgage – but Mortgage & bonds often go together – as in my Case with Cl[aude] Scott – & I don't see how the Income tax gets into the hands of Governm[en]t – I know I save it in the interest I pay – by deducting it – but the lender [fb] suffers, While the borrower gains – & Govern[men]t knows nothing of the transaction between them –

I know I pay £31.10. instead of £35 – P[er] ann[u]m
I know C.S. gets 31.10 instead of 35 – his due
& the difference never can find its way to Govern[men]t unless I go & say here is £3.10s for you, which I certainly never shall do unless call'd upon.

Now Mr Legisperitus[615] – expound – expound. When shall we see one another – I have a nest egg near Mistley[616] for the Summer, perhaps I may extend my flight a little farther – but all this is uncertain – as Buonaparte may be hatching eggs for us of a different kind & preparing the Yokes for the fools who with Burdett are hatching mischief & playing his game –[617]

[fb] We are now so wise, that we can only be kept in order by the bayonet – & if people are to be shot & trampled under Horses feet in the Streets of London – it matters very little whether by French or English Soldiers – while we look at Lord Camden &c &c &c receiving thousands & thousands from our Taxes –[618]

---

614 Daniels, 'Cankerous Blossom', p. 150, dates this letter to May 1814, but both Humphry and William have written May 1810 clearly; also, this letter mentions Sir Francis Burdett. (See Letter 130.)

615 lawyer; learned in the law.

616 Apparently a commission near Mistley (Essex), but it is impossible to identify.

617 Burdett had been critical of the way in which the war was being conducted. He was still in the Tower at this time.

618 John Jeffreys Pratt, second earl Camden (1759–1840); amongst other offices he was Teller of Exchequer 1780–1834. Just before he left the government in 1812, there was a

There is something Rotten in the State[619] & like Rotten Cheese, we shall either be ruind by the rats. – or by the little Mites who are undermining all that is sound & good but what signifies saving the Cheese if they rob us of our bread. – thank heaven mine of late has been well butter'd – except at Breakfast this morning when we were driven to honey from bad butter.

Address: To Wm Repton Eqr, Aylsham, Norfolk
Endorsed: 1ˢᵗ May 1810   My Father   Property Tax on Int[eres]t   Sir Fras Burdett
HM 40867

135. George Repton to William Repton

29 Dover Street, May 31 1810

My dear William

The Mason tells me this morning that the Monument is ready for me to see. I must therefore request you will inform me, by what conveyance, and from what place you wish it to be sent.[620]

I fear your friend Windham will not recover, the Bulletin at his House <u>yesterday</u> was "that he had passed a quiet night, & was not worse". I have not heard of him to day – but had there been time before the post went out, I would have sent to his House, that I might give you the latest intelligence but the time will not permit me to do so – with best love to Aunt Adey – believe me my

dear William your ever affectionate GSR

[*in pencil*] Thursday[621] 5 o Ck at Ws door in Pall Mall – Bulletin "Mr Windham has passed a restless night but is not worse this morning"

1 O Clock "Mr W is become worse since the morning" –

---

scandal over his income as Teller. His income from the office had increased tenfold since he was awarded it, to £24,000. (*Hist. Parl.*) See also Daniels, *Repton*, p. 21, where there this section of the letter is quoted. In 1800 Repton had produced a Red Book for Lord Camden's property of Bayham Abbey (Kent). (See *Repton in Kent*, 'Bayham Abbey'.)

619 An allusion to the famous speech by Marcellus at the end of act I, scene IV, in *Hamlet*.
620 In a letter to William, dated 8 January 1812, Samuel Adson, statuary, of New Road, Fitzroy Square, complained that the 'the account of the Marble Monument for the Memory of John Repton Esq.', dated 13 June 1810, for a total of £26 1s 10d, was still unpaid. (NRO, AYL 438, bundle of papers labelled 'John Repton's Extors'.)
621 31 May 1810 was a Thursday.

Endorsed: 30[*sic*] May 1810   My brother George   As to the Monument for Mr J Repton ready   Mr Windham's illness[622]
HM 40919/5

136. John Steward, Mayor of Norwich,[623] to William Repton; William's summary of his reply

Norwich, June 12 1810

Dear Sir

In order to arrange the precedency at the Country Table[624] on the 19th, I have to request the favor of your information as to a Gentleman of the Walpole family. The hon: Mr Walpole of Wabourne has done me the honor to accept my invitation & I shall be much obliged to you to inform me whether he is the Son or Brother of the Earl of Orford & what rank he is intitled to. Pray let me [*fb*] have your answer by return of post, & excuse the liberty I have taken

Yours very truly J Steward

[*fb*] 12 June 1810   Answered the Mayor = That The Hon. Gen[era]l Walpole is a younger Son of the last Earl of Orford[625] & that in precedence he follows the Eldest Son of a Viscount & that I know not of any person likely to be at the Guild & entitled to take place of him except The Lord Lieut[enan]t[626] The High Sheriff[627] Lord Walpole Lord Primrose[628] Lord

---

622 Windham died at his house in Pall Mall, London, on 4 June 1810, from complications following an operation on his hip (*ODNB*). According *Hist. Parl.*, 'he had injured his hip on 8 July 1809 while helping to rescue Frederick North's valuable library from a fire; he ignored the injury, but a tumour developed, and the operation on 17 May (1810), though apparently successful, was too much for a constitution already greatly impaired'.

623 Mayors of Norwich were elected on 1 May and sworn in on Guild Day, the Tuesday before midsummer, with dinner in St Andrew's Hall.

624 The 'Country table' is referred to in the newspaper report of the event mentioned in note 631.

625 The 'last Earl of Orford' died in 1809. His second son William had died on 21 December 1764, aged 8. (N. Walpole, *The Walpoles of Wolterton* (Lewes, 1986), p. 96.) The 'Hon. Gen. Walpole' was George Walpole (1758–1835), third born but second surviving son. His elder brother Horatio (1752–1822) was the current earl of Orford. (See *Hist. Parl.* biographies of the father and both sons.)

626 William Assheton Harbord, second baron Suffield.

627 Nathaniel Micklethwait, esquire, of Beeston.

628 Probably Archibald John Primrose, viscount Primrose (1783–1868), eldest son of Neil, third earl of Rosebery; the third earl's third son, Hon. Francis Ward Primrose (1785–1860), was of Bixley Hall.

Bayning[629] or Mr Herbert who is the Earl of Carnarvon's Son,[630] but it will be seen by the List of invitations & table of Precedence whether I am right in that supposition – & if I can be of any use, he may command me

That Gen[era]l Walpole & the Mr Ansons will <come> be with me at Aylsham on the preceding night & we shall go *to* the Guild together[631] – WR

Address: Wm Repton Esqr, Sol[icito]r, Aylsham, Norf[olk]
B st: NORWICH 117   Ju 12 1810; *charge*: 4
Endorsed: 12 June 1810   The Mayor of Norwich   Desiring to know what Rank & Place of Precedence Gen[era]l Walpole is entitled to at the Guild
HM 40953/16

137. William Repton to Thomas William Coke[632] (draft)

Aylsham, 4ᵗʰ July 1810

Sir

I have the honor to inform you that I have just learned the death of Mr Corbould[633] a Gent[leman] who held the <preferment> *<two small> livings* of Bawdeswell & Eccles <two small livings> in the Patronage of Sir John Lombe.[634] Will you allow me to request your kind intercession with Sir John in favor of my brother Edward Repton who is a young man in full orders, of exemplary conduct with a wife & family <&> *but* without any <Church Preferment> *Living* to whom *therefore* the preferment *in question though small* must <be therefore> be an object – *I think if I am not mistaken Edward has the honor to be one of the D[uke] of Bedford's Chaplains –*

I trust to your usual <gr> kindness to excuse <the> my presumption in

---

629 Charles Townshend, first baron Bayning (1728–1810).

630 Revd Hon. George Herbert (1789–1825), at this time vicar of Tibenham. (CCEd Person ID: 76907.)

631 *The Norfolk Chronicle and Norwich Gazette*, Saturday, 23 June 1810, Issue 2100, pp. 2–3, reported at length on the events of the Guild Day and dinner. The Hon. Gen. Walpole gave a toast 'from the Country Table'.

632 Thomas William Coke (1754–1842), of Holkham; created earl of Leciester in 1837. (*Hist. Parl.*)

633 John Corbould (1768–1810), son of John Corbould of Norwich; curate of Felthorpe, 1792; rector of Bawdeswell 1807–10; rector of Eccles 1808–10. (CCEd Person ID: 112340.)

634 Sir John Lombe, of Great Melton (d.1817); he acquired the Bylaugh estate in 1796.

making such a<n application> *request* to you *but I well know the high opinion which Sir J Lombe entertains of your Recommendations*

And I have the honor to be Sir Your most obliged & Very faithful humble &c

Endorsed: 4 July 1810   Dra[ft] Letter to Mr Coke asking for the Livings of Bawdeswell &c for Edward
HM 40954/4

138. Thomas William Coke to William Repton[635]

Holkham, July 7th 1810

Sir

It would be encroaching to much upon the Liberality of my Friend Sir John Lombe to request the living of Bawdswell, after having obtained two livings from him – which I am sure neither you, or others who have applied to me upon this occasion could have been informed of. I will trouble you to present my best Compl[iments] to Mrs Adey, & I remain – Sir
    Your Obedient Humble Servant Tho Wilm Coke

Endorsed: 7[th] July 1810   T. W. Coke Esqr   Declines applying to Sir Jo[h]n Lombe for the Living of Bawdeswell for Edward[636]
HM 40953/17

139. Augusta Disney[637] to William Repton

Elmers, July 17[th] [1810]

Sir

Mrs Windham requests me to express her sense of <Gla> Kind condolences on her present heavy afflictions – she bids me say that she is much aware of the friendship that has so long subsisted between parts of your family and Mr Windham and of course cannot have any wish or intention of altering any arrangement of his in regard to you – she is concerned your letter has remained so long unacknowledged but her reluctance to writing was the

---

635 Reply to the original of the draft, Letter 137.
636 Corbould was succeded as rector of Bawdeswell on 6 September 1810 by Philip Duval Aufrere; and as rector of Hempstead with Eccles on Sea on 24 September 1810 by William Heath Marsh. (Aufrere is CCEd Person ID: 99558; Marsh is CCEd Person ID: 114036.)
637 Augusta Georgina Disney (*c*.1764–1847) of The Elmers, Kingston-upon-Thames, apparently a friend whom Mrs Windham visited after death of William Windham.

cause and she has at last commissioned me to write for her – she begs [*fb*] her kind remembrances to Mrs Adey and compliments to you – I request you will offer mine to Mrs Adey – I remain sir

    your obedient Humble servant Augusta G. Disney

Address: William Repton Esqr, Aylsham, Norfolk
B st: A   JY 18 810
Endorsed: 17ᵗʰ July 1810   Mrs Windham by Mrs Disney   Continues me in the office of Steward of the Norfolk Courts
HM 40900

140. Horatio Walpole, second earl of Orford[638] to William Repton

[London], July 18 [1810]

Dear Sir

    I have heard a report that Lord Suffield is dangerously ill[639] & as I wish to know whether it has any foundation I trouble you with this, requesting you will give me any information you may have, not mentioning however to any one that I have made this inquiry. I am

    Sir Your obedient servant   Orford

Address: London July Eighteenth 1810 Orford,[640] William Repton Esqr, Aylsham, Norfolk
R st with crown: FREE 18 JY 18 810
Endorsed: 18 July 1810   The Earl of Orford   As to Lord Suffield's illness
HM 40948

141. Dorothy Adey to William Repton

[Lyng], Thursday morning [2 August 1810]

My dearest William

    I have very great hope we shall see you here on Saturday or Sunday yet for fear it shou'd not be so I shall send this by the <u>Lyng Butcher</u> to tell you

---

638 Horatio Walpole, second earl of Orford (1752–1822), of Wolterton. (*Hist. Parl.*)
639 The letter was definitely written on 18 July 1810, so refers to William Assheton Harbord, second baron Suffield; the first baron had died on 4 February 1810. (See Letter 114.)
640 The earl of Orford's privilege of a free frank.

that when your old Aunt begins gadding there is no knowing when the fit is to end. never any thing was more kind than Mrs Branthawaits attention to me yesterday in the most friendly manner she invited me to make one of the party from hence during the whole of their stay at Taverham.[641] it was in vain to refuse and when I said I really expected friends from Cromer on Thursday there was no getting an excuse for going to her till that time. the objection to my not haveing the [fb] means of getting my Carriage from hence to Taverham she obviated at once by insisting on sending a pair of Horses. I am therefore going thither on Tuesday and I have (for fear you may not be at home to receive this) written to John Secker[642] to send me horses to Mrs Branthawaits on Wednesday afternoon.

I think my dear William you will not object to the visit I am about to make for believe me it is and ever will be my wish to have your approbation in all I say or do as much as ever it has been hitherto to have that of our dear departed. He was ever pleas'd to find me respected by respectable people and you I know are equally so, but indeed except I cou'd have positively told of any engagem't before the Thursday without great incivillity I cou'd not have been excus'd. Yesterday we paid a morning visit to Mrs Custance.[643] to Morrow we are to have the Browns[644] to dinner but I very much hope I shall eer you get this letter tell you all this myself but my mornings from early rising [fb] are so much longer than the mornings of other people that I have plenty of time for writing. yesterday I wrote a long letter to Harestreet and now before I go down I shall write to dear Duff. God bless you

yours affectionately   D Adey

Address: Wm Repton Esqr, Aylsham
Endorsed: 2ᵈ Augt 1810   Mrs Adey from Lyng about visiting Mrs Branthwayte at Taverham
HM 40888

---

641 Mary Branthwaite, widow of Miles Sotherton Branthwaite (d.1807) of Taverham. Nathaniel Kent had commented on Branthwaite's agriculture at Taverham: 'River weeds and sedge have lately been used to very great effect, for turnips, by Mr. Coke [of Holkham], and Mr. Branthwaite, of Taverham, who assure me that no manure whatever answers better'. (Kent, *General view of the agriculture ... of Norfolk* (1796), p. 42.)
642 There were several John Seckers in Aylsham, one living in Schoolhouse Lane, Aylsham in 1822 and another the tenant of the Black Boys Inn after 1825. (*Aylsham Directories*, p. 6; *Aylsham*, p. 292.)
643 Mrs Frances Custance, neé Beauchamp-Proctor, married in 1778 John Custance (1749–1822) of Weston Longville.
644 Perhaps Ann Brown née Lubbock and her husband. (See note to Letter 113.)

142. John Thurston Mott to William Repton

Barningham, Thursday [2 August 1810]

Dear Sir

I am really quite shocked at my stupidity in not recollecting that Mrs Adey told me she was going this week to Mr Ansons,[645] and also that you were to remain at Aylsham – The Note sent this morning was to request the pleasure of Mrs Adeys and your company to a dance tomorrow Evening – we are very sorry to find Mrs Adey is not at home, but if you will give us the pleasure of your company, we shall be happy to see you and shall have a bed much at your Service. I am afraid it would be presumption to suppose she would do it, or unfair to ask Mrs Adey to leave Mr Ansons, but if they will do us the honor to accompany her, we shall feel much flatter'd, and be very happy to see them – perhaps you will have the goodness [fb] to get some Man (on my account) to go down with a Note from you, containing my request

In Mrs Adeys Note sent this morning, there is one for Miss Churchill, which Mrs Mott will thank you to burn, as she has sent her another – No answers are necessary; if you or any of the party can come, we shall be happy to see you at ½ past seven.

Believe me Yours very truly J Mott

Address: W. Repton Esq, Aylsham, to be deliverd <u>immediately</u>
B st: AYLSHAM 132; *charge*: 2
Endorsed: 2ᵈ Augt 1810   John T: Mott Esqr   A Friendly invitation to a Ball at Barningham
HM 40905

143. Humphry Repton junior to Dorothy Adey[646]

[London, 10 August 1810]

My dear Aunt Adey

As I must send this cover to George before I go out – I have only a moment to acknowledge the receipt of your very kind letter – & that I always read your letters with the greatest pleasure whether addressed to me

---

645 From previous letter, written on the same day, it is clear that Dorothy Adey was staying with Charles Anson at Lyng.
646 Probably a reply to the letter that, in Letter 141, Dorothy said she was about to write.

or to the circle at Harestreet where I see them every week – I look forward
with great pleasure to joining you at Aylsham but do not yet know the day
I can leave London <u>with George</u> – Give my love to William & tell him I
will thank him to write & tell me if such people as Messrs Scott (manufacturers I beleive) are to be found in Norwich & where![647] They appear to
have furnished clothing for the Bredalbane Reg[imen]t of [*fb*] fencibles nos
94 – 95 & 96[648] – I ask this for a friend who has had a letter directed to
Messrs Scott Norwich returned from the Post Office – & who is anxious to
find the people –

ever affectionately yours   H Repton

Address: London Tenth of August 1810, Mrs Adey, Aylsham, Norfolk, M
Wood[649]
B st: STAFF; *r st*: FREE 10 Au 10 1810
Endorsed: 10th Augt 1810   My brother Humphry to Mrs Adey about
coming to see us
HM 40922/1

144. Humphry Repton junior to Dorothy Adey

London, 11th September 1810

My dear Aunt Adey

You will I fear think me a most harem scarem chap to have been so
long without telling you when I expected to have the pleasure of joining
you – but I know you will excuse me when I tell you that business as much
as pleasure has kept me within ear shot of Mr Eliot – You must have seen
part of a Report of Bankes's Committee on the Audit Office[650] [*fb*] this is

---

647 Perhaps either Scott and Spaw, Manufacturers, Colegate Street, or Barnard and Scott,
Manufacturers, Muspole Street. (*Norwich Directory for 1811.*)
648 The Breadalbane Fencibles were volunteer troops raised by the Campbell earl of
Breadalbane. The original fencibles were in existence from 1792 to 1799; then there were the
Breadalbane volunteers, 1799–1811. (Archives: GD112/52. Military papers, in the papers of
the Campbell family, earls of Breadalbane (Breadalbane Muniments), listed in the catalogue
of the National Records of Scotland.)
649 The signature is not clear but must be that of the M.P. who franked this letter for
Duff. Perhaps Mark Wood, I (1750–1829), of Gatton Park, Surrey, who was M.P. for
Gatton 1802–1818.
650 Henry Bankes, M.P. (1757–1834) leading Evangelical economic reformer; he 'made
public economy his chief goal during a parliamentary career that spanned five decades'.
(*Hist. Parl.*; *ODNB*) For the background to the issue of control of goverment expenditure

likely of course to affect us & made it desirable for me to consider with Mr Eliot their proposed arrangements – & therefore, whilst I was happy to avail myself of his invitation to make cricket matches at Richmond & Hampton Court, this though the ostensible was not the only or the principal motive of our meetings –

We are to meet again tomorrow at Hampton Court & the moment [*fb*] we part – I shall put myself into the mail & be with you in a trice – but whether that will happen tomorrow or Thursday or Friday I cannot exactly tell till I see him but I am unwilling to leave you in suspense & therefore write this letter –

The delay that has taken place in my Norfolk journey has only increased my desire to begin it – Love to William &c &c –

ever most affectionately yours H Repton

Address: Mrs Adey, Aylsham
B st: B SE 11 810
Endorsed: 11 Sept 1810   My Brother Duff to Mrs Adey   About coming to see us
HM 40922/2

145. Humphry Repton junior to Dorothy Adey

Adelphi, 15th Oct 1810

My dear Aunt Adey

Who would have thought that within two miles of Aylsham I should hear news yesterday so distressing as poor Kents melancholly end[651] – & the manner in which the intelligence was communicated was by no means calculated to lessen the effect of the news itself – for Tom Rackham[652] stopped the gig & said in the same breath "How do you do! Mr Kent is

and elimination of corruption see P. Harling, *The Waning of 'Old Corruption'* (Oxford, 1996) p. 116. One of a series of reports into various branches of expenditure, this report criticised the excessive number of commissioners and higher officials in the Audit Office and its deficiency of subordinate clerks. It concluded 'Economy, at all times necessary to the welfare of the State, cannot in the present circumstances of the Country, be too highly estimated, but must be considered to increase in its consequences in proportion to the growing exigencies and expenses of the nation'. See *Select Committee on Regulations to control Branches of the Public Expenditure in Great Britain & Ireland, Fifth report, Part II (Audit of Public Accounts)* PP 1810 II (371), presented to the House 20 June 1810.

651 Nathaniel Kent.

652 Perhaps related to the Rackhams living in Aylsham. In 1804 Thomas Rackham of

dead"! – you may suppose what I felt – & as I knew you were gone to
church I begged of him to call on William & to tell him what had happened
that you might not hear it too abruptly – [*fb*] the same reason prevented my
mentioning it before Eliza – but is alas too true –

I called at Craigs Court[653] the moment I reached London & the clerk
with tears in his eyes gave the following account. He reached Baldock in his
way from Lincolnshire to Town with Sam[654] last Wednesday night – eat[*sic*]
a good supper – went to bed – rose in the morning perfectly well & in high
spirits – & came by the stage to London – walked from the Inn along Fleet
Street & opposite the Temple took a Hackney coach – the coachman says
he appeared very well tho' rather fatigued with walking & he must have
been perfectly collected by his desiring the man to drive him to No 5 Craigs
Court – when the coach [*fb*] reached the Office <door> poor Charles[655] &
Mr Pearse[656] opened the door to welcome him – & Charles found him in the
coach dead – can any thing be more shocking[657] – No man could be better
prepared to die however suddenly – but unfortunately few men could be so ill
spared – he may truly be said to have been the constant friend of those who
had <bee> few other friends <of> those who most wanted them –[658]

This melancholly subject has so entirely occupied my mind that I can
scarcely find spirits to begin <th> to thank you for the very pleasant visit I
have made you. & I therefore fear that you must be satisfied with my good
intentions – tho' if I wished to say ever so much after saying I thank you I
dont know [*fb*] what I could say more – give my love to all around you – my

---

Rippon Hall, Hevingham, was appointed one of the executors to the will of Anne Jewell; he
was later of The Grange, Cromer Road, Aylsham. (*Aylsham*, p. 200.)

653 By 1793 Nathaniel Kent had a land agency in London at Craig's Court, Charing
Cross, in partnership with John Claridge and William Pearce. (*ODNB*; *Dictionary of land
surveyors*, 2nd edn., vol 2, p. 293, entry K88.)

654 Not identified: perhaps an employee.

655 Charles Kent, Nathaniel's eldest son; from 1804–1810 he was in partnership with his
father and William Pearce as Kent, Pearce and Kent. (*Dictionary of land surveyors*, 2nd edn.,
vol. 2, p. 293, entry K88 for Nathaniel Kent.)

656 William Pearce, Kent's nephew. (*Dictionary of land surveyors*, 2nd edn., vol. 2, p. 400,
entry P147.)

657 Concerning the death of Nathaniel Kent, his *ODNB* entry simply says that 'He died
of apoplexy at Fulham, Middlesex, on 10 October 1810'. This is account given by Duff is
very detailed and obviously from a direct source.

658 Repton's poem 'The Save all' is dedicated 'To the Memory of the Late Nath'l Kent
Esq're and many other departed friends'. Its ending reveals detailed knowledge of the
circumstances of Kent's death. Repton noted that 'Mr Kent always express'd a wish to die
suddenly & he was taken dead from a Carriage at his own door – having sunk on his knees'.
(Avery Library, MS 3233; microfilm MICROFOR F a4379.)

Aunt Repton (poor Uncle John is spared the pain of losing Kent – & has perhaps at this moment the pleasure of being with him)[659] Kiss dear Eliza for me & do <u>not</u> <u>forget</u> Mrs Brett –

I hope William will give my <u>best respects</u> to all friends at Hadisco – for a <u>grimmer</u> set I never encountered.[660] I shall send a paper containing glorious news[661] – I hope the result will be as usefull as the action is glorious – but I have doubts on that subject.

ever most affectionately yours H Repton

Address: Mrs Adey, Aylsham
B st: C OC 15 810
Endorsed: 15 Octo'r 1810   Duff to Mrs Adey   On Mr Kent's death
HM 40922/3

146. George Repton to William Repton

East Cowes Castle Isle of Wight, Thursday night December 14 1810[662]

My dear William

I have seen in our Paper of this day (for the first time) an advertisement from the Magistrates of your County, for Designs for a proposed new <u>Lunatic Asylum</u>, to be built near Norwich[663] – it so happens that I have lately turned my attention to *the purposes of* that particular Building, and might perhaps be able (with less trouble than it would otherwise give me) *to* send in a plan – if you think there would be any probability of success – of this you will perhaps have the goodness to inform me

---

659 Kent had recommended John Repton's farming methods at Oxnead. (Kent, *General view of the agriculture of … Norfolk* (1796), p. 56; Daniels, *Repton*, p. 69.)

660 Haddiscoe, north-east of Beccles. The manor of Hadiscoe was held by George Grimmer (1777–1845) at this time. See, for example, NRO, NRS 23537, 82X2, Abstract of Title of George Grimmer to the manor of Haddiscoe and an estate in Haddiscoe. Duff is punning the name of the family; perhaps William was steward of the manorial court.

661 The defeat by Wellington of the French in the Battle of Busacco (Portugal) on 27 September.

662 14 December 1810 was a Friday, so perhaps George was up on Thursday night writing this. William endorsed it 14 December; the postmark is 15 December.

663 For the new asylum, see S. Cherry, *Mental Health Care in Modern England: the Norfolk Lunatic Asylum/St Andrews Hospital, c.1810–1988* (Woodbridge, 2003). Eventually the competition was won by William Browne (Ipswich), 70 guineas prize, with Good & Lockaby (of ?) 30 guineas; but the commission was given to the County Surveyor Francis Stone who incorporated best features of the two successful entries. (Cherry, *Mental Health Care*, p. 30.)

– the advertisement you may probably have seen in the provincial paper[664] – directing that the Drawings should be sent "on or before the 4th of January – to Mr Simpson the County Treasurer"[665] – whom you may perhaps know – if so, you can learn from him (or some one else, who may *have* to do with the concern) – the sort of situation [fb] upon which the new Building is to be placed – whether a confined spot which must regulate the Plan – or whether such a space as to admit of any form of building to any extent? also if it is near the Road? to which it should present a Front? and if so, what aspect? if the nature of the Soil will admit of digging to any depth? all these are principal, and very important points not to be totally ignorant of – otherwise a very good Plan of an Asylum may be sent, which would be quite inapplicable to the spot fixed upon – and the advertisement gives little or no information whatever, to guide any professional Man residing at a distance, and wholly unacquainted with Norwich and its neighbourhood – indeed the manner in which the whole of it is worded, appears to have been done by some one, quite unused to the subject – they generally refer you to some person for farther instructions of what is required and also who will shew you a Map of the Ground – none of which seems to be held out in the article in this days paper.

You will also be able to judge from the Persons who are <principally> the most active in the direction of *the* new Building – if it is likely to be [fb] a fair competition, or whether the local Carpenter or Builder are sure to be the successful Candidates, from their personal acquaintance & interest – the Advertisement says nothing about any paticular number of Drawings required, and to a particular scale – as desired by the Governors of Bethlem Hospital In their late public notice for Designs[666] – or does it say that they

---

664 *The Norfolk Chronicle and Norwich Gazette*, Saturday, 8 December 1810, issue 2124, p. 4, had an advert requesting 8 to 10 acres of land to purchase near Norwich where the asylum could be built. The advert for the competition was not in that edition; it first appeared in the next issue on 15 December 1810, issue 2125, p. 3, together with another request for suitable land. Eventually the Norfolk lunatic asylum was situated in Yarmouth Road, Thorpe St Andrew near Norwich.

665 Probably William Simpson, who was also clerk to the Norwich Corporation, 1791–1826; he was also treasurer and clerk to committee of Visiting Justices concerning lunatics. NRO, MC185/1, is a presentation copy of a resolution, dated 1826, passed by the Governor, Deputy Governor, Assistants, and Guardians of the Poor of the City of Norwich that the thanks of the Corporation 'are pre-eminently due to William Simpson Esquire' for his 35 years of service as clerk.

666 Founded in 1247, the Bethlehem Hospital had moved to Moorfields in 1676, but in 1793 the governors decided to build on a new site. They acquired St George's Fields in Southwark in 1810 and held a competition to design the new hospital.

are to be sent in <u>anonymously</u> And with Mottos – this you will be able to tell me, and I think at any rate it would be better, <u>not</u> to mention for whom you are applying – when the Candidate does not succeed, it is generally as well not to have it known that he made the experiment – for after all, those kind of things are like a ticket in a Lottery – which do sometimes succeed, as at Westminster –⁶⁶⁷ The premium is of course a secondary object, to the good it does every young Man to be known in his profession – and I think no opportunity should be lost in trying – for after all, if I do not *succeed* I am but where I was – none the worse for it – except having worked a few hours later at night, than I otherwise should have done – with the advantage of having turned my attention to a particular description of Building which I otherwise should not have done – John & I have now some Designs before the Governors of Bethlem Hospital, which he very unwillingly consented to join in, though at a time he was not doing any thing else.⁶⁶⁸ x

[fb]⁶⁶⁹ x having once sent them in, we think no more about it, and surely you will allow that I was right in proposing to him a little trouble for <u>a chance</u> of obtaining the reputation of Building of such Magnitude – thus you will understand what I wish to know from you, if your Business should happen to Carry you to Norwich soon – for as I cannot do any thing <in the Business> untill I hear from you – you will suppose I shall not have much time (if sufficient) to do <t>what <which> must be at Norwich <u>on the 4ᵗʰ of January</u> – let me know if that is really the <u>latest time</u> they must be sent to Mr Simpson – and any other information you may think serviceable – if they expect large highly finished Drawings it will be out of the question, my time now being fully occupied I can only make slight Drawings and upon a small scale – yet I am unwilling to lose the opportunity of doing something in Norfolk if you think it really an opportunity. I suppose the same advertisement must have been in other papers long since – otherwise they could hardly expect to have many designs sent to them upon so short a notice – without wishing to have any unfair advantage of other Candidates it is a great thing to understand something of the wishes of those who principally have the direction of the Building – in all concerns of that sort there are always two or three active men who do everything –⁶⁷⁰

---

667 Referring to the success that he and John Adey Repton had had in 1809 in securing first prize in the competition for public buildings for Parliament Square, Westminster.
668 In fact they achieved second prize for their New Bethlehem Hospital design. (Carter et al., *Repton*, p. 133.)
669 The following paragraph has been written in various spaces on the address page.
670 The next letter indicates that George did indeed submit a set of plans for the new Norfolk Asylum.

I will not my dear William make any excuse for thus troubling you with so long a letter, well knowing your readiness to afford all the assistance in your power when required by

    your ever affectionate Brother George Stanley –

The Man who made the Monument[671] has not spoken to me since about it – but should he do so, may I tell him to send his Bill - <&> *But* to whom [*illeg; covered by seal*]

I do not know when I shall leave the Island,[672] but I think not this Month – it in some degree depends upon whether I go to Glocestershire, where my noble client appears to be again <u>nibbling</u>,[673] after <a> some months without my hearing from him – from thence I should go into Herefordshire, to a small concern of Nashs,[674] which is to be a joint one between us – I heard a few days ago from my Father, he & John where then going into Devonshire,[675] when they will return I know *not* – from Harest[reet] I have not heard very lately, I am anxious about my poor Mother, who I fear is not so well as she should be – but that I cannot learn for certain, as all my sisters letters are seen by her – Give my affec[tiona]te love to Aunt Adey. tell her months ago when I was at Harest[reet] one of her letters said "tell George I am going to write to him in a day or two" but I fear she meant <u>year</u> or two – or her letter has miscarried

Address: William Repton Esqre, Aylsham, Norfolk
R st: D 15 DE 15 1810; *charge*; [*illeg*]
Endorsed: 14th Dec 1810   George from the Isle of Wight
HM 40919/6

---

671 For their uncle John Repton.
672 This paragraph is written upside down on the front page.
673 Perhaps the 'noble client' was William FitzHardinge Berkeley, first earl Fitzhardinge: he owned the manor of North Nibley in Gloucestershire, and George's comment about 'nibbling' would fit with the family's liking for puns.
674 Perhaps Belmont, Clehonger (Herefs), the property of John Matthews. Humphry Repton had advised there before 1794 and Matthews later employed Nash and George to design several cottages. (Carter et al., *Repton*, p. 153.) See also Letter 153.
675 Most likely to Tavistock Abbey, one of the Duke of Bedford's properties in that county.

147. George Repton to William Repton

East Cowes Castle, I.W., January 1ˢᵗ 1811

My dear William

I have delayed thanking you for all the trouble you have had on my account untill I could say that I should certainly take my chance for the New Building – I have this day sent my Drawings to Dover St – to be forwarded on to Mr Simpson at Norwich. therefore unless any unnecessary or unforeseen circumstances should delay them upon the road, they will certainly be with him by the time specified – I have not (as you will readily believe) had time to do so much as I could have desired and if I had had more time should probably have drawn the Plans to a larger scale – as it is, they are sufficient [fb] to shew the general arrangement – I am sorry to understand in your first letter that the <u>detail of the Plan</u> would not be much attended to – unfortunately it is <u>that</u> in which must <principally> consist the principal merit, as the nature of the building will not allow a shewy architectural Elevation – St Lukes Hospital (a Building universally admired by every body who have seen it)[676] is <u>quite plain</u> without any enrichments whatever – when your second letter *came* My drawings were very *far* advanced. I have made the Building higher than you seem to think they will like – from the assurance of the very intelligent Master of St Lukes that no inconvenience whatever was felt from it – care being taken in the formation of the Stairs – a high Building afford better subdivisions for the different classes of Patients – and also saves [fb] the expence of a<n> *more* extended roof. I should certainly have very much like to have seen Dr Foxs book[677] which I have never met with – so much for this subject which I fear you will be tired of – and I again thank you for the trouble you have had –

I had a letter from my Father a few days ago written in good spirits – safe returned from his Journey –[678] At dinner at my friend Lord Henry

---

676 St Luke's Hospital for Lunatics, Old Street, London; designed by George Dance the younger, it opened in 1786. (Drawings held in the Sir John Soane Museum.)

677 Dr Edward Long Fox who established an asylum in Brislington House near Bristol in 1806. The 'book' referred to here may be 'An account of the establishment of an asylum for lunatics, lately erected near Bristol', by Ed. Long Fox, M.D., in R. Reid, *Observations on the Structure of Hospitals for the Treatment of Lunatics* (Edinburgh, 1809), pp. 71–7. Fox's asylum catered mainly for the wealthier members of society. Its unique design, with seven distinct houses, enabled classification of patients according to social class as well as behavioural presentation. See L. Smith, 'A gentleman's mad-doctor in Georgian England: Edward Long Fox and Brislington House', *History of Psychiatry*, 19 (2008), pp. 163–84.

678 To Devon, with his son John.

Seymours[679] the other day I met a Captain Sneyd[680] who was going out to Lisbon to join the Myrtle sloop of war[681] to which he is just appointed – he says he was at Aylsham at his Brother in laws John Hollys[682] some years ago. he gives a melancholy account of the health of our poor Uncles sister[683] who he says is living at Litchfield but he has not seen her for some years – he saild yesterday after waiting here for an East Wind a most tedious time –

[fb] best love to Aunt Adey – tell her I do not accept her short two lines in lieu of her promised long letter whenever she has nothing better to do –

I did not know you had Adsons Bill[684] – let me see <the> a Copy of it before it is paid, that I may ascertain if it conforms to a written agreement I have from him for the price of it before it was begun – believe me always, My dear William

your very affectionate Brother George

I have just rec[eive]d a letter from my Father[685] I think not written in such good spirits as I could have wished – much of it being upon the prospect of our poor Brother Edwards difficulties which we have all of us so long feard & foretold –

Address: William Repton Esqre, Aylsham, Norfolk
B st: B 3 J[*missing*] 811
Endorsed: 1 Jan'y 1811   My brother George   About Plans for Norfolk Lunatic Asylum   Capt. Sneyd   Bill for Oxnead Monum't
HM 40920

---

679 Lord Henry Seymour (1746–1830) lived at Norris Castle on the Isle of Wight. The building was designed by James Wyatt. It is pictured in the *Polite Repository* (1805), suggesting that Humphry Repton had advised there. (Daniels, *Repton*, p. 261; Carter et al., *Repton*, p. 155.)

680 In 1817 Clement Sneyd held the rank of Post Captain, having been appointed on 3 April 1811. (TNA, ADM 9/3/575.)

681 A 'sloop-of-war' was a relatively small ship-of-war, carrying a maximum of 18 guns on the upper deck only (*OED*). For the movements of HMS Myrtle in 1812, under Captain Sneyd, see TNA, MP 1/105/69, pp. 342–342a.

682 In February 1796 John Holley of Holme and Aylsham had married, as his second wife, Mary Ann Sneyd. She died in December 1799. (*Aylsham*, p. 251.)

683 John Adey's half-sister, Mary Sneyd.

684 For John Repton's monument; the bill was not paid until at least January 1812. See note to Letter 135.

685 This paragraph is written upside down at the top of first page.

148. Humphry Repton junior to William Repton

Harestreet, Wednesday [2 January 1811][686]

Dear William

I have only time to say that Mr Percival[687] was outvoted yesterday on his <u>fifth</u> resolution – Lord Gower[688] moved an amendment to leave out certain words after "the Queen's most excellent Majesty" & to add "together with the sole direction of such persons & establishment as are suitable in the present circumstances to the care of the Kings person & Royal dignity"[689] – this amendment was [fb] opposed by Hiley Addington[690] – Stephen [–][691] Wilberforce[692] – Ld Dysart[693] – Fuller[694] (who <caused> *raised* a laugh by saying he stood there as a <u>legislator</u>) & Percival – & was supported by Johnstone[695] –

---

686 William has endorsed the letter '5 Jan'y 1811', probably the day it was received; it refers to events in Parliament on 1 Janaury.

687 Hon. Spencer Perceval (1762–1812), M.P. for Northampton, 9 May 1796 – 11 May 1812; prime minister from October 1809 until he was assassinated on 11 May 1812. (*Hist. Parl.*)

688 George Granville Leveson Gower, II, Earl Gower (1786–1861), of Trentham (Staffs); M.P. for St. Mawes 1808–12; Newcastle under Lyne 1812–15; Staffordshire 1815–20. (*Hist. Parl.*) See also Letter 53.

689 The debate reported here was reported in the press, e.g. *The Times*, Wednesday 2 January. It concerned the nature of the Regency and how far a separate household for the Queen would lead to greater expense and party influence; the King had last been seen in public on 25 October and the Regency was declared on 7 February, following passing of Regency Bill. Care of the King was entrusted to the Queen advised by a Council of seven members of Privy Council, headed by the Archbishop of Canterbury: a move designed to limit the Queen's influence.

690 John Hiley Addington, (1759–1818), of Langford Court, Somerset, brother of Henry Addington, Lord Sidmouth. Hiley voted 'against Gower's amendment to the fifth resolution of the Regency bill, 1 January 1811'. (*Hist. Parl.*)

691 James Stephen (1758–1832), M.P. for Tralee, 1808–12; East Grinstead, 1812–15. (*Hist. Parl.*)

692 William Wilberforce (1759–1833), leading abolitionist, M.P. for Kingston-upon-Hull, 1780–84; Yorkshire, 1784–1812; Bramber, 1812 – Feb. 1825. (*Hist. Parl.*)

693 Hon. Wilbraham Tollemache (1739–1821), of Calveley Hall (Cheshire); succeded as sixth earl Dysart on 22 February 1799; he was an M.P. from 1771–84. (*Hist. Parl., 1754–1790.*)

694 John Fuller (*c.*1756–1834), M.P. for Southampton, 29 Jan. 1780 – 1784; Sussex, 16 July 1801 – 1812. 'He rallied to ministers … on the Regency proposals, putting in a word for the "old King".' (*Hist. Parl.*)

695 Sir John Lowther Johnstone, sixth baronet (1783–1811), M.P. for Weymouth and Melcombe Regis, 29 June 1810 – 24 Dec. 1811. 'No speech by him is known, but he voted with the opposition majority of 1 January 1811 on Lord Gower's amendment to the Regency proposals.' (*Hist. Parl.*)

Martin[696] – L[or]d Milton[697] – Romilly[698] – Adam[699] – Canning[700]
– L[or]d Castlereagh[701] – & Whitbread[702] –

    for the amendment   226

    against it   <u>213</u>

                 13

This is all I have time to say except love to my dear Aunt Adey &etc &c ever yours H Repton

[fb] We are just going to sit down to a Haunch of Venison from Stoneleigh Abbey[703] – in excellent order – & last night arrived half a doe from Sir H Featherstone[704] of which the Haunch will find its way to Aylsham p[er] to morrow's Coach – I wish it had been killd sooner that you might have enjoyd it while your friends are with you but it is dated killd 31ˢᵗ Dec.

---

696 Henry Martin (1763–1839), M.P. for Kinsale, 1806–18. (*Hist. Parl.*)

697 Charles William Wentworth Fitzwilliam, viscount Milton (1786–1857), M.P. for various places, including Yorkshire, 1807–30. 'He spoke and voted against the Regency proposals, particularly on the concessions to the Queen in the Household, 1 January 1811.' (*Hist. Parl.*)

698 Sir Samuel Romilly (1757–1818), M.P. for various places, including Wareham from 20 April 1808 – 1812. 'In opposing Perceval's Regency resolutions, 1 January 1811, he attacked Pitt, whose name had been used to justify ministerial proceedings.' (*Hist. Parl.*)

699 William Adam (1756–1839), M.P. for Kincardineshire, 1806–18. (*Hist. Parl.*)

700 George Canning I (1770–1827), M.P. for various places, including Hastings, 1807–12. 'He favoured an unhampered regency and backed Lord Gower's successful amendment trimming the Queen's power on 1 Jan. 1811, though privately he believed that two-thirds of the nation would prefer the King, "blind, deaf and mad", to the Prince.' (*Hist. Parl.*)

701 Hon. Robert Stewart, viscount Castlereagh (1769–1822), M.P. for various places, including Plympton Erle, 1806–12. On 1 January 'he was critical of the dual royal household and of all unnecessary limitations of the Regent's powers, so he supported the successful opposition amendment'. (*Hist. Parl.*)

702 Samuel Whitbread II (1764–1815), M.P. for Bedford 1790 – 6 July 1815. 'Whitbread's behaviour during the Regency crisis of November 1810 to February 1811 revealed that his ambitions for office, albeit on his own terms, were still very much alive.' (*Hist. Parl.*)

703 Stoneleigh Abbey (Warks) was owned by the Leigh family. Repton produced a Red Book in 1809; the proprietor at the time was the Revd Thomas Leigh. (Rogger, *Landscapes*, p. 209.) A drawing of 'The Gate House at Stoneleigh Abbey. The Revd Thos. Leigh' was published in the *Polite Repository* (1810). (Temple, 'Repton, illustrator', p. 172.)

704 Sir Harry Fetherstonhaugh of Uppark, South Harting (Sussex). Repton's statement of account, produced in March 1814, summarises his involvement at Uppark. He first visited in August 1810, for which his charge was £52 10s, i.e. 50 guineas; in that same month he charged £42 for his 'Report on plans for ground'; he made further visits in 1811, 1812 and 1813. (M. Meade-Fetherstonhaugh and O. Warner, *Uppark and its people* (National Trust, new edn., 1995) p. 77.)

The dear little Reptonini & Reptonina[705] are both well & by their squalling enliven our little Circle – but we are all snow & cold & I must go to London on Thursday to meet the Duke of Bedford – but my voice is come & my Cough is gone – All join in Love to all

Ever & ever Your own Brother Humphry

Address: To Wm Repton Esqr, Aylsham, Norfolk
B st: RUMFORD [*illeg*]; Cross Post; *charge*: 8
Endorsed: 5 Jan'y 1811   Duff – Division in the House of Commons on the Regency   My Fathers Venison &c
HM 40927

149. Humphry Repton to William Repton

Harestreet near Romford, January 21 1811

Dear William

It is not often that we honor each other with Letters in owr own hand writing – but having lately seen one from Mrs Adey – interlarded by yours (in duplicate) to Edward – I think I will send you one entirely of my own – concerning my own business – & first – in Looking into last years Acc[oun]ts I find £26:5s:0d against the Name of Rt. Hon. W. Windham – which I shall not send to you – but to the executors if you will tell me who they are – & how to direct to them – I never got a shilling by W: W: & dont see why I should loose £26:5 – which was a bargain between him & me & for which he said he was obliged to me –

[*fb*] 2^{ndo}: – A Basket containing 2 br[ace] of Phea[san]ts & 1 br[ace] of Hares was sent me from Sr Harry Featherstone 21st December 1810 & mark'd off as delivered to the porter by the bookkeeper at Golden + Charing Cross[706] – who says he took them to Romford Coach – but no such entry appears & there was 7/6 Car[ria]ge to pay – *ergo* – the fellow stole them & I have written to Mr Bolton[707] to replace the same or I shall enforce it – <u>by Law</u> – Now as you have got 10/6 out of this fellow before – pray how can you act by your Agents Baxters[708] so as to get me my game

---

705 The syntax of Duff's Italian suggests that Edward and Mary now had at least two sons and one daughter, but he then refers to 'both': in January 1811 Edward and Mary had one boy and one girl. Georgiana Repton was born on 12 Nov. 1810 and baptised at St Paulinus, Crayford, on 13 Dec.
706 The Golden Cross Inn, Charing Cross.
707 At the Golden Cross.
708 Either Stafford Baxter (see Letter 14) or Baxter & Bowler (see Letter 199).

– & pay yourself for the game you have to play – & what is to be done more than threatning this Cross Man[709] – propound – propound

So now the paper is open to the P: S: of all the family[710]

Address: To Wm Repton Esqr, Attorney General to the Repton family, Perpetual Church Warden of Aylsham &c &c &c &c &c &c &c
Endorsed: 21 Jan'y 1811   My Father   Debt due to him from Mr Windham's ex[ecu]tors   Bolton of Golden Cross has lost his Hares and Pheasants
HM 40868

150. Edward Repton to William Repton

[January 1811]

Dear William

You will see that I lost no time in making the proper application – I could not go in person – as I think it would have surprized the old Lady[711] too much – and should she have already made up her mind about the disposal of the Livings – I should not have like a point blank refusal – after a long journey into Sussex –– I <u>might</u> [*fb*] have received an answer this morning – but it is not come – She is a very precise, steady Lady – and if this Young Man have done any thing to make her consider him – as an improper Person to be an Example to others – depend upon it, she will not present <u>him</u> to the Livings – but she has little else to do in Sussex – <but> *than* to sit and talk with Miss Merry upon the chances of old Howmans [*fb*] Life[712] – and to settle what course she is to pursue in all cases – I greatly fear therefore that she has long ago determined in what manner to dispose of them – and your poor brother I doubt has but little chance – Accept my sincere thanks however for your thoughtful attention – You shall have her answer soon after I receive it – What do they ask for the Presentation to Thorpe Living *near Norwich?* I see it advertised.[713] Love to Mrs Adey and believe me

Dear William yours ever ER

---

709 i.e. Bolton at the Golden Cross.

710 No postscripts were added.

711 Mrs Merry, who lived near Ardingly (see Letter 10).

712 Revd Edward Howman, rector of Gissing and Flordon, both in the diocese of Norwich, who died in March 1811. (CCEd Person ID: 109739.)

713 The sale by auction of the presentation to the 'very valuable rectory of Thorpe next Norwich' would take place on 2 February. (*The Norfolk Chronicle and Norwich Gazette*, Saturday, 12 January 1811, issue 2129, p. 1.)

[*fb*] I inclose your Nephew with the many names for your Perusal – it is very like him – The Master you will readily know – send him back in safety – ungreased – unturkeyfied – [714]

Endorsed: Jan'y 1811   My brother Edward   Mrs Merry's Livings   Little boys Picture
HM 40913

151. Revd Charles Anson to William Repton

Lyng, January 21st 1811

My dear William

I just write a line to ask what length of stay you make at Dereham – & whether it will not be possible for you to pass a day or two at Lyng as I shall be at home – I hope your Springall Clients[715] will be exact to their time. I have delivered your message to them. – What are your plans [*fb*] & engagements for next week & are you likely to be at home – I write this by our Female Post – you may return an answer by the same conveyance
Believe me ever yours truly Chas. Anson

Address: William Repton Esq, George Inn, Dereham
Endorsed: 21 Jan'y 1811   The Revd Chas Anson   Desiring to see me at Lyng when at Dereham
HM 40896

152. Dorothy Adey to William Repton; postscripts from D (Elizabeth) and George

[Hare Street], Tuesday February 19th [1811]

My dearest William

According to custom I have been up this age, have made up my bundle for Izzy to send to Mrs Bell[716] but they need not be returnd hither

---

714 No picture of Edward's son has survived in the archive so perhaps William did return it.

715 Not identified. There were Springalls at Baconsthorpe, Felthorpe and Norwich in the period.

716 In 1821 there were two families named Bell living in Aylsham: one Bell and four female family members in Hungate Street and John Bell and three female family members in Newel's Yard. (*Aylsham in 1821*, pp. 8, 17.)

untill I send send[*sic*] my next parcel or she hears from me again, and now before any one is down I am inclind for a little Chat with you but I wish I had a better Pen and cleaner Ink tho on reccollection if it was the best in the world you wou'd say your old Aunt wrote so as not to be read[717]

well that being so, this does as well as any other to tell you your dear Father <u>allow'd</u> <u>himself</u> to be better yesterday than he had been yet tho towards night he found out a new complaint, soreness in his back from the embrocation but as for an hour and a half before we retir'd we heard no more of [it] I conclude it was not very bad. he amus'd himself a long time yesterday in contriving something made of cane by way of cradle for his arm to prevent the bed cloathes touching it but we all laugh at the idea of his sleeping sound all night on either Arms and thinking of such a thing He is this moment come down, says he has had a charming night and is going on bonnily, –[718]

Mary is down and has given me one of her sunday pens and now I shall write till I tire you,[719] and the first thing I do must be a memorandum of what I forgot <u>the paste Buckles</u>. I think you will find them in one of the square boxes in the top drawer of my dressing table and you I believe have the case belonging to them in your possession. here comes d. [Elizabeth] come d. you must [*fb*] write to Brother William, 'O yes I dare say I shall, He will say 'silly Child what does she write to me for', <u>crumple</u> the letter up put it in his pocket and think no more of it.' Mary says 'I'll coppy your next letter Aunt Adey for you have said all I have to say' – they are two trumpery Girls and I will put my letter away and they shall see no more of it

[*Elizabeth's hand*] D desires her love and a kiss notwithstanding; Aunt Adey will not tell you about Mrs Boyd[720] because she says she does not like her, but we have had another letter, in which she hardly tells us how Mr B. goes on but after <u>Three Pages</u> of flummery about <u>kindness</u> <u>gratitude</u> &c &c she says "but if I go on in this way you will think I am as crazy as my dear husband"! so much for a good feeling observation; and, for fear you should think I have copied her style, I will eat my breakfast and wish you goodbye. N.B. I would recommend you to put on <u>gloves</u> when you

---

717 The ink Dorothy was using gave a patchy appearance to her writing.
718 This letter was written three weeks after Repton's carriage accident on 29 January 1811. (*Memoirs*, p. 23.)
719 The ink is better from the beginning of this paragraph onwards.
720 According to Letter 172 Eliza Boyd was Elizabeth's godmother.

read this as Aunt Adey has complained of an odd sensation in her hand which Mr Andrews[721] thinks rather <u>suspicious</u>.

[*Dorothy Adey again*] I have this moment read your letter in the drawing room and George is doing so to the family party in the Study. I am most sadly sorry my dearest William for the trouble brought upon you. I think I remember your carrying papers up into your own room before you left [*fb*] Aylsham and I dare say if there was Cash or Bills in the Desk drawer you took them also, else I shou'd be afraid you might have contributed more than half a Guinea, they are all come in, and I can not get them to be serious, however in this <u>all</u> agree that you have done exactly what is right, – all the way.

Your Father is a sad rogue. John says 'poor Mileham. I pity Mileham, woman seduc'd him I know, they always do, I wish William had not turn'd him away', but George tells him, that a Man who wou'd take his friends Wife, will not hesitate *to take* his Masters money,[722] but he also says, he takes it for granted if Collyer[723] reads you a lecture you will give him the choice of the door, or the window, your dear Mother and myself are very very sorry for the troubles and worry you met with on your first getting home. I am quite glad the poor fellow met with kindness from Izzy, more than meets the Eye about his very great offence at Smiths, must have hapned to have caus'd him to be held in such <u>utter</u> <u>detestation</u> in the Town of Aylsham, because if all the men in the Town were refus'd a Bed in a <u>private</u> or <u>publick</u> house because they had sin'd in this way, we shou'd have a pretty parcel of them in the Market, and we are all anxious to hear more, & I am very very much so to hear that you have engag'd some one that in your next absence you may have confidence in and be equal to transact anything necessary to be done in your absence / it has unhing'd me for a correspondent in my usual ratling way, and therefore I will resign my pen, and I hope dear George, or <u>Par</u> or <u>Mar</u> will add to it.

if you see the Parmeters say I will write by next Basket and tell me about James Holley and if he has found his pocket Book [*fb*] I will send you H:

---

721 James Andrews was a doctor in or near Hare Street. Repton's poem 'The Swallow' was dedicated 'To my long tried friend James Andrews', who 'keeps us all alive from year to year'. (Avery Library, MS 3233; microfilm MICROFOR F a4379.)

722 William's clerk Mileham had become involved with the wife of one Smith. Although George's comment suggests that the two men had been friends, a letter from James Marsh to William, dated 26 June 1809, indicates that Mr Smith had been assaulted at The Dog, in Aylsham, and that Mileham was alleged to have been a party to the assault. (NRO, AYL 438, papers labelled 'John Repton's Extors'.)

723 John Bedingfield Collyer, curate of Aylsham. (CCEd Person ID: 112308.)

Ansons last letter which I think seems between jest and earnest not quite one I like. I have written to intirely give up all idea of of[sic] going untill I am in Town. I send you the parcel and all the letters that came in Sundays Basket. God bless you farewell and continue to write to

yours affectionately   D Adey

[*George's hand*] Mrs Adey says I must say something to you my dear William – but I have only to express the regret with which I heard yesterday upon my return from the Island[724] – that you had returned into Norfolk – but I hope nothing will prevent my seeing you when next you come & if you will let me know when that will be, I will take care so to arrange my business as not again to miss seeing you<r> – your poor Clerk seems to be too hardly punished for what he has done if no more than you describe it. I think Collyer himself could not have read him a better lecture than you appear to have <done> *given him* – however I think you have done right not to keep "a dog with a bad name". I did not know Aylsham had been so moral a place – perhaps all the sober Householders have a fellow feeling for Mr Smith –

yours ever affectionately   GSR

Address: Wm Repton Esqr, Mrs Bretts parcel to be sent by Beasy
Endorsed: 19 Feb'y 1811   Mrs Adey, d, & Geo: My father's illness
Paste Buckles   Mileham's conduct   crim. con. with Mrs Smith
HM 40889/1

153. Dorothy Adey to William Repton; Humphry Repton to William

[Hare Street], Sunday February 24th [1811]

My dear William

Mary promises to write by the Basket but I do so by the Post to day, because it is quite impossible our Ham bone can find food for us much longer, and therefore as I suppose you will have get[sic] this on Monday, have the goodness to tell Betty to put one of hers into a Brown paper (give her a proper direction) and let Beasy take it to Norwich on Wednesday, and the Bury Coach will bring it hither on Thursday, another material cause for my writing, is, to tell you George has an engagement in Herefordshire[725] and He is unwilling to fix any time for his going till He

---

724 i.e. the Isle of Wight.
725 Perhaps Belmont, Clehonger (Herefs). (See Letter 146.)

knows your plans for fear [fb] of being out of Town when you are in it, you had therefore better write to him by the post as soon as you get this and direct your letter to <u>Doverstreet</u> and he will settle his journey when he had that letter.

I dont seem to have any thing to tell you, but that Mary and d: walk'd to Mr Heaton's[726] on <Thursday> *Wednesday*. d: came home on Thursday, and brought home a Miss Thompson to make up for the loss of dear Mary who staid with Mrs Heaton, but as <she> *Miss Thompson* was not quite as desirable a companion to any of us, as our own dear Girl, we did not regret to part with her on Friday.[727] That you can make Mileham useful to you at Norwich is all well, but it seems to be the joint opinion of this fire side it wou'd be highly improper to bring him back to Aylsham, I think in your absence you will feel it highly necessary to have some person you have <u>confidence in</u> to take notes of who calls, and competent to answer common Questions, and I am not a little anxious to hear you [fb] have already or are likely *soon* to meet with one.

I have been working over old Izzy's account, and it amounted on Friday night to £4/11s/6d a just and true account, so that I doubt she will require more money if you will be so good to give her some; I see by the Norwich News an Inclosure meeting[728] is fix'd for the 4th of March, we were rather in hopes your letter this morning wou'd have told us you expected to be here by that time. I hope soon to hear you say your time for again leaving Aylsham is fix'd. I was going to say what I think of your dear Father, but it will perhaps be to the [damaged] as satisfactory to you to hear him say what he thinks of himself, so God bless you

yours affectionately D Adey

[*Repton's hand*] I think I am mending every day – but tis Slowly & I am right glad our old bone of Ham is going to be thrown away for I never see them scraping & digging at the joint but I always feel a Sympathetic jar in my Elbow – which makes me say to my self – yanng! yanng! yanng! – and then they say I pull faces & accuse me of fancies but I begin to think I shall do again but hang time & patience I never had either

---

726 See Letter 26.

727 Miss Thompson was probably a local resident. In 1823 Thomas Thompson of the High Street, Romford, was a perfumer and haircutter. (Pigot's, *Directory* (1823), p. 64.)

728 The Swanton Abbott, Lamas and Buxton enclosure meeting would be held at the New Inn, Aylsham, on 4 March. Notice given by William Repton dated 25[*sic*] February 1811. (*The Norfolk Chronicle and Norwich Gazette*, Saturday, 23 February 1811, issue 2135, p. 3.)

Address: Wm Repton Esqr, Aylsham, Norfolk
B st: TOO LATE; RUMFORD [*damaged*]; Cross Post; *charge*: 8
Endorsed: 24 Feb'y 1811   Mrs Adey & my Father
HM 40869

154. Mary Repton to William Repton; notes by Elizabeth and Humphry senior

[Hare Street, early March 1811]

My dearest William

Our Aunt Adey is the torment of my life, as I have heard of nothing but writing to you every day since you left us, what pleasure or information she expects my letter to contain I am at a loss to guess but she says write I must, so here goes.

First when do you mean to return to us, George writes to enquire and we can give him no information, but conclude he will hear from you. Edward likewise enquires when you are to be here as he will visit Hare street when we are [*fb*] all together. Aunt Adey says you will be off to Town as soon as you arrive here, but our Ball is on the 11ᵗʰ and I am sure you wont be so shabby as to desert us before then, because you give that amiable man Mr Mileham plenty of work, during your absence, not only that it may keep him out of mischief but that you may not be hurrying home as Aunt Adey means to have a great deal of fun in London and Old Mrs Anson[729] will be in dispair if I cannot give her at least a week of my company. You were told of our wonderful gaiety in being from home two [*fb*] nights, but you did not hear the whole history. Mrs Heaton was so anxious for me to stay another day that D and Miss Thomson were sent home, but there was much debating of how they were to get here. The common was entirely mud, to walk by Romford was too far and it was too late to send for horses before dinner, but at last a carriage was ordered to the door in the shape of a Tilted Cart with a horse from the Plow. The two young Ladies mounted and jog'd on most comfortably, but their pride could not bear the riding thro Romford so they were to be set down in the dirty Lane to walk home, but as ill luck would have it while in the act of decending from their Vehicle with proper grace, the Miss Dilions[730] appeard in great haste to render their assistance to what they supposed was a market cart [*fb*] upset in the ditch,

---

729 Perhaps Mrs Mary Anson (q.v.).
730 Two sisters living in the Hare Street area; not identified.

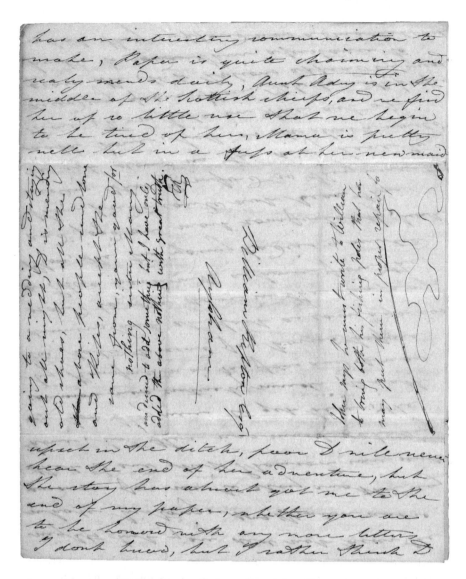

10. Final page of a letter from Mary Repton,
with sketch of fishing rod by her father, HM 40932/1

poor D will never hear the end of her adventure, but the story has almost
got me to the end of my paper,

whether you are to be honoured with any more letters I dont know, but
I rather think D has an interesting communication to make, Papa is quite
<u>charming</u> and realy mends daily, Aunt Adey is in the middle of *The Scottish*

chiefs,[731] and we find her of so little use that we begin to be tired of her, Mama is pretty well but in a fuss at her new maid going to a wedding and staying out all night, D is mending old shoes, but all the <*illeg*> above people send love and Kisses, accept the same from,

your good for nothing[732] sister Mary

[*Elizabeth's hand*] I am desired to add something but I have only added the above nothing with great truth.   ER

[*Repton's hand*] John says he must write to William to bring both his fishing poles that he may put them in proper repair so [*sketch of fishing rod with a fish*]

Address: William Repton Esqr., Aylsham
Endorsed on front page: March 1811   Sister Mary
HM 40932/1

155. Dorothy Adey to William Repton

Harestreet, Sunday 10ᵗʰ [March 1811]
I hope you have a Plum pudding[733]

My dearest William

I thank you a thousand times for so kindly giving me the proof of your affection as I receive from your Dear long letters, which we all enjoy and scramble who first shall read. every day that keeps you from us after the 17ᵗʰ the day a former letter gave *us* the hope of seeing you, we *shall* look upon three times as long as any that preceed the 17ᵗʰ, because we had quite made up our minds to the impossibility of your being with us before. as to that 8ᵗʰ of April business at Dereham is worse than all the rest, I dont know if at that meeting you are Com[mission]ner or Solicitor but be which you will, you have so much ear of all, and every one, that we can not forbear to hope you will defer that meeting till after Easter.[734] I have all along known that on Easter Monday you cou'd not be absent from home.

I am very unwilling to give up the [*fb*] visit at Semer, and the cheif reason of my writing to day, is, to beg of you to give me a line as soon as you get

---

731 *The Scottish Chiefs*, by Jane Porter, in 5 volumes, first published in London in 1810.
732 'for nothing' added in Elizabeth's hand.
733 This phrase has been written as part of the dating; it was not added as a postscript.
734 The East Dereham enclosure act was not passed until 1812, perhaps this was a preliminary meeting. (NRO, AYL 1025.)

this, to tell me if I may write to Mrs Cook[735] and tell her we will be with her on Wednesday the 3ᵈ of April. I shall enquire where we turn off the Colchester road nearest to Semer, and I have not a doubt but they will send their Horses there for us, and also take us to Stowmarket on the Saturday. We all still hope you will bring Eliza with you from Schole,[736] but even if not, she can meet us there on our return, and Mrs Johns[737] Horses be ready at Stratton to convey us home, and thus I think I have plan'd our return as cheaply and well as it can be, for dear Mary has quite given up all idea of accompanying us, she says if Mrs John comes up <for> at Mids[umme]r she will come back with her, and stay till Duff leaves Norfolk in the Autumn, that if she returnd with us she is sure she shou'd make a very very short visit, so that I do think on the whole she has decided right.

Another thing I have to enquire about is, if you dont think the week we shall next [fb] probably be in London will be on Monday the 25ᵗʰ to Monday the first because if so, Duff or George will endeavour to get us places at Covent Garden for Bluebeard on the 28ᵗʰ for George writes word he cou'd not secure places for Mrs Nash[738] of three weeks, and Col: Brown[739] who has just calld says he took great pains, but the Boxes were engag'd for a Month to come.[740] I think you will laugh at this <u>weighty matter</u> but I assure you having nothing at present to look forward to more Gay than the <u>Romford Ball</u> tomorrow, the play is really a principal business

your dear Father does often make the best of his complaints I do firmly believe, and at others He sighs and thinks worse of himself than I cou'd wish, but I am sure you will be glad to hear He thinks of going to consult Home or Heaviside.[741] Edward writes word He shall be here tomorrow, and

735 See Letter 97.

736 Scole on the Norfolk/Suffolk border.

737 Dorothy's sister-in-law, John Repton's widow.

738 The second wife of John Nash, Mary Anne (d. 1851), younger daughter of John or Robert Bradley. (*ODNB*)

739 Not identified, but see Letter 168 for General Brown, a companion of Humphry senior.

740 On 18 February 1811 the actor John Kemble revived the pantomime of Bluebeard, which had first been produced at Covent Garden in December 1791. Crowds flocked to see it. Despite its critics, the play was a great success, and was acted 44 times in the season. (H. S. Wyndham, *The Annals of Covent Garden Theatre from 1732 to 1897*, 2 vols. (London, 1906), vol. 1, pp. 351–2.)

741 In 1790 these two men were recorded as London surgeons: Everard Home practised at Green Street, Leicester Fields and John Heaviside at George Street, Hanover Square. (*Universal Directory* (1790), p. 448.)

one day this week your dear Father will go with him. Andrews advises it, and I have strongly recommended it ever since I have been here.

I dare say I shall write by the Basket tho I am afraid you will be off for Tivetshall[742] and therefore it is I write by the post that I may hear as to the Semer business and I have been at the post office today for the girls and I walked [fb] to Romford Church, to enquire about the letter being said to be too late, but like all post masters or rather I ought to say post mistresses for they all tell me the man is remarkably civil, she was quite crumpy,[743] so I shall give a little girl 2d to go down on purpose with this before we dine and I will scribble again by the basket, which you will get when you come home from Bungay or Harleston.

give your Mothers love to Mrs John and thanks for her Hares. God bless you now and when are we to have a day to be all together here. Poor dear Dash, how very very glad I shall be to see him again.[744] I hope no more ill will betide him before I get home

yours ever affectionately D Adey

Address: William Repton Esqr, Aylsham, Norfolk. sent to the Romford post office before 6 oclock March 10th
B st: RUMFORD [*illeg*]; Cross Post; *charge*: 8
Endorsed: 10 March 1811   Mrs Adey from Harestreet
HM 40889/2

156. Dorothy Adey to William Repton; Mary Repton to William

[Hare Street], Monday Morning [8 April 1811]

My dearest William

We all thank you for your letter from Norwich, it has been a source of satisfaction to know you were so near home safe and well and I hope and trust I shall find you so on Saturday, Marys cold is better, mine not so well, and all beside are well, whether I shou'd be able to say this to morrow is another matter, for d:, Eliza, and Mrs John, after shopping, riding, walking, and visiting in London bid fair for Colds, for the weather with us is more like Winter than it has been since I left Aylsham.

---

742 See Letter 73. The eventual Enclosure Award and Map for Tivetshall (1813) is NRO ACC 2017/21.
743 The Romford Post Office was in the Market Place; in 1823 the post master was William Warwick. (Pigot's *Directory* (1823).)
744 Perhaps 'Dash' was a family pet at Aylsham.

Yesterday I took leave of dear George, this morning I have bid a long Adieu to your <u>dearest Father</u>,[745] to morrow John bids farewell, Duff thinks He shall be here [*fb*] on Thursday, with all this and the goodbyes I look forward to a few days hence, and the long Journey (which nothing but my dear little Eliza cou'd make in the smallest degree comfortable), I am ill calculated for a correspondent, and so I shall turn you over to Mary as the greatest kindness I can do you, and say no more but that I am at this moment, and for ever

yours ever most affectionately D Adey

Dear William,

Aunt Adey has cram'd this sheet of paper down my throat ever since breakfast and says it must be fill'd, but when there is nothing pleasant, interesting wonderful or necessary to be said what is the use of writing. The only event of importance which has happened since they left us this morning [*fb*] is a visit from Miss Hamilton and her all delightful brother,[746] the former the picture of misery and wretchedness on going to <stake> take possession of her new Lodging at Hornchurch, the Brother looking like a wild heart from the ?Peners[747] and I have no doubt of almost as ferocious a nature for he appears to have very little of the milk of human kindness about him, he is to set her down in a Gig and then return to the old Lady, and may they eat their dinner without any unpleasant feelings on her account. we had a beau here yesterday in the shape of John Wallinger from Yorkshire, not the little Boy we knew [*fb*] but a very smart young man,[748] who has at the tip of his tongue, various pretty speaches, and delicately <turn"d> turned compliments, for the amusement of <u>girls</u>, <u>not quite so old as I am</u> but I was amused to see so great a change in one short year, I declare I have fill'd my sheet, "wonderful". poor Mama and I went without our Kiss the other night, my next will be in Norfolk so keep yourself in readiness and believe me

ever your affectionate <u>Mary</u>

Address: Wm Repton Esqr, Aylsham, Norfolk
B st: RUMFORD [*illeg*]; Cross Post; *charge*: 8
Endorsed: 8 April 1811   Mrs Adey & Mary from Harestreet
HM 40889/3

---

745 No indication where Repton was going.
746 Not identified, other than as Hare Street residents about to move to Hornchurch.
747 Or, 'Teners': from the context meaning forest, or similar.
748 The 'little John' Wallinger mentioned in Letter 5, now 4½ years older.

157. Mary Repton to William Repton

[Hare Street, ?Spring ?1811][749]

My dearest William

Dont fancy from what Aunt Adey says that I have given up the Idea of spending some time with you both at Aylsham, as that is certainly not the case, but were I to return with her, at the end of a <u>month</u> one of my Brothers would be sent to fetch me back. Aunt Adey has and[sic] Idea of my passing the Summer with her and perhaps the Autumn, but these people here would fancy me, realy dead and gone, and mourn for me accordingly, so that perhaps as I have so many chances at getting to you, I dont at all [fb] consider it as given up, but Aunt Adey will not leave us these two months and we may all change our minds before then.

I am very busy at the little picture, and if you are very good you shall have a sight of it when you come, with best love and a Kiss

ever your affectionate Sister Mary

Address: Wm Repton Esqr.
Endorsed: Dear Mary's Letter about coming to see us
HM 40932/2

158. Humphry Repton to Mary Repton[750]

On Deafness – written at the New Inn Ventnor Isle of Wight September 28 1811[751]

The Wind was fair – the tide oppos'd our sail
And rolling billows bellowd to the gale
Pleas'd to behold a scene to me so new
With wondring Eye – each swelling wave I view

---

749 The HL cataloguer suggested 1811, there is nothing in the letter that fixes a date but it fits in this sequence.

750 The endorsement on Letter 159 indicates that this poem was sent to his daughter Mary about a month later. The two have been separated in the archive.

751 In September 1811 Repton took a holiday on the Isle of Wight with his son John. The visit was made after securing the commission from Abbot Upcher (1784–1819) for Sheringham, but before making a site visit. The Upchers were on the Isle at the same time. (Daniels, *Repton*, pp. 93–4.) Upcher had purchased Sheringham through William Repton's agency in July 1811. (Daniels, *Repton*, p. 91.) This poem suggests that Repton was going deaf; the endorsement by William on Letter 159 describes it as 'My father's letter to Mary with very good Poetry on his deafness &c'.

Watch the long foaming track, that marks our way
Nor fear the dashing froth or <frequ> hissing spray
Because forsooth, by sailors I am told
"Salt water never gives nobody cold"
This I could just distinguish in the roar
Of jarring Elements – then heard no more –
Yet oft at times – as buzzing in my ear
The War of jarring Elements I hear
While other sounds have almost lost their force
And people <u>bawl</u> to me, till they are hoarse –
I see lips move – but feel with some vexation
To me is lost, all share in Conversation
Th' Eolian harp should with the wind resound
I feel the puffing wind – but hear no sound
Shall I not mourn, the pleasures thus bereft.
No! rather let me think on what are left
I <u>smell</u> the balmy air – I <u>feel</u> its pow'r
I <u>taste</u> its produce in the woodbine bowr
I <u>see</u> all <u>Nature</u> smiling to my view
I mark each scene as beautiful, as new,
And with my pencils <u>Art</u> I make it mine
For loss of <u>hearing</u>, shall I then repine?
Hearing which only tells what others see
With sordid views, that seldom trouble me
[*fb*] Thus when I look upon the Verdant Ley
One tells me – "it produced but little hay"
And when th' Umbrageous Copse I first beheld
Another bawl'd – "tis time this Copse were felld"
But when from steep hills height, Ocean appears
I gaze in silent Adoration – till my ears
Are rouz'd by stories of French Privateers"
Then <u>hearing</u> – why regret thy loss or why repeine?
Since <u>feeling</u> – <u>smelling</u> – <u>Taste</u> & Sight, are mine
Perhaps I loose some Compliment, some speech,
Directed to the ear, it cannot reach
But e'en such flattring proofs tis surely better
To see – than hear – as Witness Upchers Letter[752]
"Where Nature smiles to see, by Reptons Aid

---

752 Reflecting on a complimentary letter from Upcher.

"A sweeter Landscape than herself had made"
Grant me such praise to deserve – and I
Will give you both my ears to save my eye.
Then why regret a Casual want of hearing?
Or deem it Misery beyond all bearing
Rather with Hunca munca[753] say "for sartain
<u>Hearing</u> – is all my Eye – and Betty Martin".

[*fb*] Thus my dear Mary did I amuse myself with making the best of my own infirmity – & next morning while sitting at breakfast in a room with glass doors onto the Lawn looking towards the Lea[754] –

Enter a duck to eat the Crumbs under the Table –
My little quakking quaking friend draw near
Quacks thou for joy – or dost thou quake with fear?
E'er long alas! it will your Master please
To introduce you with a dish of pease
Then quack away, as long as you are able
Since you must soon, be <u>dish'd</u> upon this table.

There Enter a Terrier – presuming from Scripture that he had most right to the crumbs under the Table,[755]
and Exit Duck in a fright
So ends the story of the dog & Duck

HM 40841

159. Humphry Repton to Mary Repton

[Rochester,[756] 23 October 1811]

You will be pleased, my dear Girl, to hear that Lord Darnley Your favorite has behaved uncommonly handsome – My Acc[oun]t sent in at Christmas was 45 – including one visit to Cobham[757] not charged – & my trip from

753 Princess Huncamunca, a character in Henry Fielding's play *Tom Thumb* (1730).
754 'Lea' rather than 'Sea'
755 A reference to Matthew, ch. 15, v. 27. '… even the dogs eat the crumbs that fall from their masters' table'.
756 Repton had been visiting Cobham Hall; Rochester is about 4 miles east of the village of Cobham.
757 A return visit to Cobham Hall: Repton produced Cobham's Red Book in 1790. (Carter et al., *Repton*, p. 155.) Repton was involved at Cobham Hall between 1790 and 1816. ('Cobham Hall: "this venerable pile"', *Repton in Kent*, pp. 34–57.)

Ramsgate only the expenses. he sent a draft for £100 – & said he beg'd my acceptance of it on my own Acc[oun]t only as a Compliment for all my past services – & hoped I would make him another visit with John if at leisure – & also hoped to see George when he could spare time from other engagements – but that he consider'd he had an acc[oun]t to settle with my sons for the business done at Cobham & Sandgate.[758]

So here we are – & in high favour

It is pleasant to be well with people whom I like & only regret that I cou'd not afford to give what I feard He could not afford to pay for –

A letter from Lord Sheffield[759] wonders I have not brought my daughter to Sheffield Place[760] – but you & I have had some fish to fry

I am delighted that Dear D [Elizabeth] likes her glass &c &c

I think I have an engagement early next month for Gosfield near Hedingham[761] & Clare &c – can't I contrive to fetch you – or meet you at Bury or Sudbury – write & say –

Address: Rochester Oct twenty third 1811, Miss Repton, Aylsham, Norfolk, Clifton[762]
B st: Rochester 29;   *r st*: FREE [*illeg*] 1811
Endorsed: 23 Oct 1811   My father's letter to Mary with very good Poetry on his deafness &c
HM 40843

---

758 Indicating that some time before 23 October 1811 both George and John had done some work for Lord Darnley at both Cobham and Sandgate (Kent). They became Lord Darnley's chief architects following the death of Wyatt in 1813. (*Repton in Kent*, p. 50.) Between 1817 and 1820 George designed the library, dairy shed and entrance-lodge at Cobham Hall. (Carter et al., *Repton*, p. 134.) Lord Darnley also owned the Enbrook parkland estate at Sandgate. The only known work there by a Repton is the 'Sandgate Episcopal Chapel', designed by George Repton, for Lord Darnley, consecrated on 28 May 1822. (Carter et al., *Repton*, p. 134; Historic England website: https://historicengland.org.uk/listing/the-list/list-entry/1061187.)

759 John Baker Holroyd, first baron Sheffield (1735–1821).

760 Repton had advised on Sheffield Place (Sussex) in 1789. He later commented that this was 'almost the only place of consequence on which I did not deliver my opinion in a Red Book' (quoted in Carter at al., *Repton*, p. 163). See also 'Sheffield Place: the seat of elegance and the resort of hospitality', *Repton in Sussex*, pp. 1–8.

761 Gosfield Place, near Sible Hedingham (Essex), owned by J. G. Sparrow, a banker; mentioned in *Excursions into Essex* (1819). (Daniels, *Repton*, p. 258.)

762 Baron Clifton was another of Lord Darnley's titles; Repton had obtained a frank for this letter from him.

160. Humphry Repton to William Repton

H[are] S[treet], 21 April 1812

My Dear William

I must write on purpose – for I always forget it – Be so good to remit a draft to Claude Scott – Bruton St: as before – & place it to my Acc[oun]t –

The times look portentuous[763] – & the Prince at the Levee look'd Careworn[764] – all the Country seems in Arms. how do your weavers go on – have they begun to throw the Meat about the Market instead of throwing their Shuttles[765] –

We never Correspond but then we have rare deputies in the Women & our Letters blend with theirs so I know you are well & what is better good – for Dee [Dorothy] when she talks of her boy William always puts on the Trumpet [*small sketch of a trumpet*] & now I talk of a trumpet I will tell you that we have got a New Organ which is to be opend next Sunday sennight May the 3ᵈ[766] – & Edward is to come [*fb*] & trumpet forth the praise of organs in Churches – I wish you & dee could hear him – for I have written his Sermon[767] & My birth day is on the 2ᵈ & my Wedding day on the Fifth of May. – very proper that I shou'd be born first & married afterwards – so we shall have all our organs employed in eating plum puddings the 2ᵈ 3ᵈ & 5ᵗʰ –

---

763 The Prince Regent had just taken over from George III.

764 Repton had attended the levée of the Prince Regent; later in the letter he implies that the Prince had commented on his waistcoat. Repton is not mentioned in the extensive list of attendees at the levée. (*The Morning Chronicle*, Friday, 17 April 1812, issue 13399, p. 2.)

765 A reference to riots that were occurring in various parts of the country at that time. Some involved the destruction of industrial and agricultural machines, others were complaining against food prices. On 17 April, page 3 of *The Morning Chronicle* included reports of riots in Stockport, where weavers had attacked 'power looms'; in Sheffield, where foodstuffs in the market had been destroyed and the milita's store of weapons broken into; and in Macclesfield, where a 'manufactory' had been destroyed.

766 The church of the Virgin Mary and St Edward the Confessor, Romford, was technically a chapel rather than a parish church. Writing in 1814, Elizabeth Ogborne stated that at the west end of the chapel was a gallery, with an organ that had been erected by voluntary contributions. It must be this organ in the gallery to which Repton was referring. (E. Ogborne, *History of Essex* (1814), p. 123.) The medieval church was demolished and replaced in 1840.

767 The sermon that Repton wrote for Edward in 1812 has not survived, but a sermon that he wrote in 1814 has: *The Work of Twenty Years Brought to a Crisis in Twenty Days! Addressed to the Fashionable World, at the West End of the Town* (London, 1814). The only known surviving copy is in the NHC.

Mary Seniora[768] wanted room for a P.S. but she had nothing to say but that she had rec[eive]d the parcel & admires !!!!!!! so do I – & shall soon send Aunt Adey a patt[er]n for a Court waistcoat – her old Chenille being quite jaundiced & turn'd yellow & the Prince wonder'd to see it again –

the Girls are at William Daniels[769] in London & I go to fetch them home tomorrow – The Taswells[770] are here *& desire me to squeeze not them – but their Comp[limen]ts to Mrs Adey & Love to you of Course* & are very agreable & put us in mind of old times. I sent Lord Sidmouth 4 lines for which at the Levee he said – 'I will thank you in plain prose for your verse' – & he prais'd its Conciseness – yet wishd it had been longer – I said there was more – 'Then pray send it all' –

[fb]To the Lord Viscount Sidmouth

Like Various Metals, we assay Mankind:
Some pure as Silver, some as Gold refin'd,
Too ductile to be useful; some like Steel
Hard & untractable, make others feel;
Some dull as Lead; – others all sound & Noise
Like empty Brass; – yet each man has a Voice
Boasting his Worth, his Parts, his Eloquence:
Forgetting Virtue, Wit. & Common Sense.

———

From Metals various to compose one Mass
Of Gold & Silver, Steel & Lead & Brass
Strength add to Splendor; Use, to Decoration;
Tis You must prove the Amalgam of the Nation.

Tell D [Elizabeth] – that to blend any two Metals together they always use some third which is call'd the Amalgam – & thus in mixing Oil & Vinegar – the Egg is the Amalgam
    and I am Your humble Servant & Daddy   HR

Address: To William Repton Esq. &c &c &c Aylsham, Norfolk
B st: RUMFORD 12; Cross Post; *charge*: 8
HM 40870

---

768 i.e. Repton's wife.
769 William Daniell, the artist (1769–1837); he married Mary Westall in 1801; they had a house in Camden Town. (*ODNB*)
770 See Letter 45.

161. Dorothy Adey to William Repton

Harestreet, June 29 [1812]

My dearest William

We arriv'd safe and well yesterday, sufficiently early to have convey'd the intelligence to you by yesterdays post, and I began to prepare my writing materials, but being Sunday my letter wou'd have been "too late" for Romford post and you wou'd have seen it withoutside the letter to morrow

the beginning of our journey and the continuance of it as far as Thetford was any thing but comfortable, for unfortunately your dear Father espy'd on the table in the Oxnead Hall the Cushions belonging to Mrs Johns <Cart> Gig and with his usual impetuosity call'd out, 'O! these are the very things I have been wishing for, in with 'em, in with em, Jonathan', it was in vain we urg'd their not filling our Carriage, the thickness &c, have <them> them he wou'd, and in we all bundled [*fb*] with a wooden Box, a large bag bursting full with Mrs Johns well air'd sheets, three Cloaks, and a pelisse, a handkercheif and two paper parcels, and also Elizas Map given her by her Uncle, our own Carriage cushions were by your Fathers directions to be put behind his Back, O! dear there is no describing the fatigue I went thro till I go[t] to Thetford, and then when he went into the House, we put our Cushions under the others, and made the surface even by rolling his great Coat up between the Oxnead ones which before were so far from meeting, that a part of me had a resting place and a part had none, by this managem[en]t we travell'd on the rest of our journey as well as 4 in a Carriage with bundles cou'd be suppos'd to do and at my journeys end I had the heartfelt satisfaction of finding your dearest mother to the full as well as I expected to see her, but she certainly is in more pain and weaker by far than when she was with us last year. she will not at present hear of getting into a Carriage, but I hope some day this week to prevail on her to go with me to call on Mrs Heaton. Your Father talks of the Fair on Friday,[771] but I am convinc'd He wou'd as soon get her to attempt a Voyage to [*fb*] the East Indies.

---

771 A reference to Fairlop Fair. The frontispiece of the *Polite Repository* (1808) was 'the Ruins of Fairlop Oak, in Essex, taken during the fair held annually the first Friday in July'. (Carter et al., *Repton*, p. 144.) It 'was founded early in the 18th century by Daniel Day (1683–1767) a block- and pump-maker of Wapping, who owned a small estate near Hainault Forest. When he went to receive his rents there, on the first Friday in July, he used to take a party of friends to eat bacon and beans in the shade of the Fairlop Oak. By about 1725 this private picnic had developed into a regular fair.' (*VCH Essex*, vol. 5, p. 218.)

the Lady <u>Wyats</u>[772] it seems were here in the morning to ask the two Girls to be of their party in a Waggon, and to take a picnic cold dinner. They are to have Wallengers, and Newmans,[773] and Captains, &c &c, and had only <u>two</u> places for <u>Ladies</u> and as many Brothers as chose to be of the party, and last night old Wyatt was here, to repeat all this, but your father was tired and sleepy and promis'd he wou'd be of the party, but not in the Waggon as his old Mary shou'd go, which his old Mary certainly will not, so how it is to be setled will be the history of a future Letter.

Duff was here last night and is gone to Town this morning. John is well but older in Looks a great deal than his Father. the Girls set me upon him to have his Hair cut, and this morning I have obtain'd his leave to send to Romford for a Hairdresser.

at Attleburgh we met with Miss Coke,[774] going post to Taverham, you wou'd have been pleas'd to have seen with what unaffected pleasure she greeted your old Aunt. we chatted for five minutes and when I said 'I will not detain you longer', she call'd out to the postilion, 'stop, stop, I must shake hands with you again. good bye, good bye.' We pass'd dear Mr Henry[775] about a Quarter of a [fb] mile from the Norwich Gates. He was laughing and look'd happy and well and sitting Backward at the farther corner from our Carriage, but I think as I put my head out and nodded I saw him look as if he knew me

have the goodness my dear William to speak as you go thro Norwich about the necessary painting and varnishing to G. Brograve[776] and if the steps can be manag'd so as to allow of my getting in better I am sure you will <alter> *order* it to be done. I want you here dear old Boy, but write to me when ever you can spare the time, and I will continue to do so to you. Your dear Mother says she wishes her Boy William was here. I dare say she does and I am sure so does

your old affectionate D Adey

Eliza is writing to Miss Threadwell[777] for good things. the letter will be

---

772 From this letter and others below it is clear that there was a family local to Harestreet named Wyatt, the daughters of which were friendly with Mary and Elizabeth Repton. The title 'Lady' is affectionate, or sarcastic, rather than actual.

773 The Newmans were another local family mentioned in various letters.

774 One of the three daughters of Thomas Coke of Holkham Hall; perhaps Elizabeth Wilhelmina (b.1795). By this time her elder sisters, Jane Elizabeth (b.1777) and Anne Margaret (b.1779) were married.

775 Perhaps Henry Anson; otherwise someone whose surname is Henry. (See Letter 175.)

776 A coachmaker, or someone employed by a coachmaker; see next letter.

777 Probably a daughter of John Threadwell of Oxnead, who had died in 1809. (See Letter 99.) This paragraph has been written at the top of the first page.

directed to Aylsham. let the sixpenny woman carry it to Oxnead directly. Elizas love Mrs Johns Ds love Marys love

Address: Wm Repton Esqr, Aylsham, Norfolk
B st: RUMFORD [*illeg*]; Cross Post; *charge*: 8
Endorsed: 29 June 1812   Mrs Adey from Harestreet
HM 40890/1

162. Dorothy Adey to William Repton; Elizabeth to William

Harestreet, 6ᵗʰ July [1812][778]

I did not so soon intend you another letter my my[*sic*] dearest William, but Mr Weston[779] came in yesterday nearly as dinner was going on the Table and was prevail'd on not to leave us till the evening, tho he talk'd of having three and thirty miles to go home,[780] he is a most pleasant Gentlemenly Man, a somthing that I cannot define made me look upon him more like to my poor dear Mr Windham than I ever before met with. I believe it was a sort of throwing back of the shoulders as he stood talking with anyone, and the being[*sic*] the height and size, your Father and George employ'd him in franking for them, and tho I fancy'd I shou'd like one to you I did not like to trouble him further, but George said 'Mrs A: has left a good Brother of mine at home, she writes to every day, pray let her next history go free', so free it will come and a day or two earlier than I intended, for I think you will not be at Aylsham when it arrives, and under that idea I could write to day to Miss Threadwell for we were all terribly disappointed yesterday at receiving no basket from Oxnead, your dear Mother had laid out chickens for yesterday and a Goose for today, and promis'd Sillabubs [*fb*] Creams Custards &c. according to Custom poor old Aylsham bears the blame. Mrs John is sure the Basket was sent to Aylsham but that <u>my</u> <u>maids</u> forgot it or <u>they</u> never let Miss Threadwell have the empty basket which contain'd her orders for its being sent. I hope it wont be found to be so. O the naughty pigs but I had rather lose a Chicken or two and see them *the Pigs* about the Yard so the misfortune will answer one good end at least.

What a stupid<e> you must be my dear William not to comprehend me about the chaise. I meant that it cou'd not too soon be sent to A & B[781] for

778 Opposite the date, written in a different hand: not so <u>oh</u>.
779 Charles Callis, Lord Western (1767–1844), of Felix Hall, Kelvedon, Essex, at this time M.P. for Maldon (*Hist. Parl.*); mentioned in *Memoirs*, p. 93.
780 Kelvedon *is* about 33.5 miles from Hare Street.
781 Adams and Bacon, coachmakers, St. Stephens without side the walls (*Norwich Directory for 1811*); probably where Brograve (mentioned in the previous letter) worked.

the necessary alteration, but that, supposing it to be done when we pass'd thro Norwich whether it wou'd not be better to let it remain there than so late at night change it as to do so, all our packages must be disturb'd, and take some other opportunity of going to Norwich and exchanging it, now I am clear old Boy.

Mrs Wyndham[782] came to us soon after eleven. Mary you know she was ever a most prodigious favorite with, and now d: too is in raptures, all the boys too enjoy'd her good spirits and good humour, and our day was particularly pleasant, but as she wou'd not fancy there was any sort of danger in travelling ever so late, we cou'd not prevail on her to order her Horses before eight, we all disliked her leaving us by herself <u>so</u> <u>late</u> and persuaded her to send the Hacks without the Carriage and take a pair from hence this morning, and Duff and George will go home with her. knowing the state of the Rooms *you* will wonder how we cou'd accommodate but with a little <more> management we did, and all like her Company and she seems pleas'd with her visit, and is to repeat it on Wednesday, and brings dear George with her.

He and his Father have talk'd over the Sherringham concern and they part friends, but George said this morning "reverse it Aunt Adey, what wou'd my Father have said if Mr Nash and I had taken a concern from him".[783] he told me he wou'd write a line to you and took my sheet away to do so, but breakfast prevented and they all went away directly afterwards, so he bid me say he shou'd write from Town.

Dear Mamma eat sour Cherries yesterday and they crip'd and she went [fb] to bed before our supper but thank God she is as usual this morning, so I shall keep her from sour Cherries in future.

Mr Wallenger is gone with Mr & Mrs Roberts to Town to day and is to return at night and the Girls are to walk and invite Matilda and Mr Birmingham[784] to dine here with the Erskines.[785] I tell them so very <u>tinderish</u> as Matilda is she will be over head and Ears in Love presently with Cousin Birmingham. Mrs Wallenger says they are going out together in the Curricle this morning and she cannot say if they will come to dinner – I know I am right, and you will find it turns out so.

---

782 The widow of William Windham.

783 See note to Letter 158. Repton made his first site visit to Sheringham in June 1812. (Daniels, *Repton*, p. 91.) The comment by George suggests that Nash and he had been offered the commission but there is nothing to corroborate this.

784 Mr and Mrs Roberts and Matilda and Mr Birmingham were local residents; not identified further.

785 Lord Erskine's wife, Frances, had died in 1805; he married his long-standing mistress, Sarah Buck in 1818 (*ODNB*). See note to Letter 9 for details of his political career.

Mrs Wyndham said yesterday if <u>she</u> possess'd the power of preventing it the Court Books shou'd never be taken from you, and repeated it to your dear Mother afterwards, therefore there can I hope my dear William be little doubt of you retaining them for I have no idea if the great Mr Budd[786] (who George says is now appointed receiver of Mr W Poles[787] Rents) is ever so desirous of them, but the Lord Chancellor[788] wou'd listen to any request of Mrs Wyndhams and I will take care she shall make the request if it becomes necessary. You continue to be a prodigious favorite with her, and this morn she told me she lik'd George prodigiously, and more so because he so much <u>reminded</u> her of you.

Mrs John fidgets and fidgets about what I am to say to <u>Oxnead</u>, and so interferes with what I feel[sic] going to say to <u>you</u> that I shall turn you over to Mary or d: and write her letter and have done with it. before I leave off I must say how concern'd I am at your pull'd to peices house, but you know I fully expected you wou'd have been absent last week and that all wou'd (with the exception of the patchwork room) have been in clean order at your return. I count very much upon seeing all the dear Edwards tomorrow

Yours ever affectionately D Adey

[*Elizabeth's hand*] Mary says she wrote in the last letter dearest William, therefore it is I who am to honor you in this. Aunt Adey has told you how much we are delighted with Mrs Wyndham, but has forgotten the best part of her visit, which is that she has invited Mary to spend a few days with her in town and she is to do so next week and tho' it is not quite so pleasant an acquaintance or so desirable a situation as our fashionable [*fb*] friends in <u>No 1 little Rider</u> street,[789] yet she is not a little pleased with the prospect of her visit, but it is a very tiresome thing that we did [not] know before of her being in town, as a few weeks would have made a great difference in point of gayety. It is not fair of me to ocupy all the frank, therefore I shall leave

---

786 See Letter 39. In 1811 Budd moved to 32 Bedford Row, London, and became a founding partner of Budd, Brodie and Hart.

787 i.e. Walpole.

788 John Scott, first earl of Eldon (1751–1838), of Bedford Square (Middx), Eldon (Co. Durham) and Encombe (Dorset); Lord Chancellor 1807–27. In 1817 George Repton eloped with his eldest daughter Lady Elizabeth (1783–1862). (See George's biography in the Introduction.)

789 Little Ryder Street was off St James's Street, near St James's Square. (*Regency London*, plate 22, square Ca.) It is likely that the 'fashionable friends' were the Anson family. In Letter 187, when discussing the Ansons, Dorothy says 'we may be asked to St James's Square'.

the rest for Papa who will be much more entertaining, tho' he cannot love you more than

your ever most affectionate sister <u>D</u>

Aunt Adey says she did not mean Papa to see this, therefore my excuse for not writing more will not do, and I may as well tell you the <u>real</u> one, which is, that in <u>romping</u> with that saucy fellow George I tore the gown which I am to appear in to day and, as Papa will in a few minutes want me to read \<and\> I shall have no time to make it wearable; we are reading the most entertaining book that ever was written *The Countess and Gertrude*.[790] I wish you would read it for it is totally unlike any <u>novel</u> and does not deserve to be calld such –

Endorsed: 6 July 1812   Mrs Adey & d from Harestreet
HM 40890/2

163. Humphry Repton to William Repton, postscript by Elizabeth[791]

Harestreet near Romford, September 27 1812

Dear William

The post is the Cheapest way of sending a small parcel as I find – having this morning paid 4s/11d for a present worth 5s/- from a Man at Birmingh[am] of a Copper Medal of Lord Wellington[792] – so I send you the inclosed papers for your advice & consideration – I don't understand it a bit – you may & if you do – send me a speedy answer to satisfy the Valiant Knight & Learned Doctor[793] – & Make the trustee worthy to be trusted.[794]

---

790 *The Countess and Gertrude; or, Modes of Discipline*, by Laetitia Matilda Hawkins, in 4 volumes (London, 1811).

791 As Elizabeth signed herself 'D', the HL catalogued this as a postscript from Dorothy Adey.

792 Arthur Wellesley (1769–1852), later first duke of Wellington, had been elevated to the peerage as Viscount Wellington in August 1809 following his victory at the Battle of Talavera (27–28 July 1809). Numerous medals were struck in Wellington's honour, with copper ones in 1809, 1810 and 1811.

793 Dr Lachlan MacLean: he was knighted in July 1812, when alderman of Sudbury; he purchased Sudbury rectory from the Upchers in 1812; he was a well-known figure in Suffolk, e.g. involved in the Suffolk Bible Society; d. 7 Nov. 1843; obituary in *Gentleman's Magazine*. (December 1843), p. 668. (See also note to Letter 2.)

794 There is nothing in the archive that would have been enclosed with this letter; Letter 165 refers to Repton's co-trustee Mr Lane.

Here is now a vast blank space to be filled up by somebody so I shall lay it by till I have dispatched other business & only tell Duff – that being Sunday we miss him – but we learn to do without our old Comforts – Mary is gone – & Dee preferd staying with old Mrs Bauvis[795] last night to walking home with me, so I walk'd home in the dark alone – & found poor John[796] who was sorry he did not know it in time to come & meet me – a spasm in the Stomach reminded me that it might have happend I should only alarm those who had been my Companions & I have lived Long enough to walk alone – poor Erskine's last born infant walk'd off with a Spasm last night,[797] just as ours have done – hiccupd – turnd yellow – & gave a kick. it has been saved many a bilious headache & heartburn – but burn it never mind – & I forget I have more leisure than you – so God bless you all

Ever Yours HR

Poor Woollands is packing up to remove on Tuesday[798] & we have removed all our papers &c &c – from the office to a room hired next door at Ward's.[799] this is only a prelude to the future removal from poor old Harestreet. William Wallinger[800] removes from Hare hall to Horn Church – by order of Removal from Mr Cope[801] as bad a brute to cope with as the Black Gent[lema]n[802] who came to look [fb] at my house & garden & see

---

795 A Hare Street or Romford resident, possibly related to the income tax commissioner mentioned in Letter 6.

796 His son John.

797 Lord Erskine's first wife had had four sons and four daughters, his eldest son, David, being born in 1776; his second wife, for many years his mistress, had had several children, the last being born in 1821. (*Hist. Parl.*)

798 This section of the letter is discussed by Daniels in 'Cankerous blossom', p. 155. William Woollands was the wheelwright in Hare Street. Repton, in his memoirs, described his character and noted that 'his landlord drove him from the Wheelwright's shop by doubling his rent'. (*Memoirs*, pp. 68–9.)

799 Perhaps a room in the premises of Alfred Ward, attorney, which were in the Market Place, Romford. (Pigot's *Directory* (1823), p. 63.)

800 William Wallinger was the second son of John Wallinger I. (Searle and Brazier, *History of Hare Hall*, p. 13.)

801 John Coape of Hanover Square, London, who had purchased Hare Hall for £15,599 10s in July 1812. He refused to allow the Wallingers to remain as tenants in the empty house. Coape was the leading member of a profit-making syndicate intent on a quick resale. (Searle and Brazier, *History of Hare Hall*, pp. 14–15.)

802 Alexander Black, Wollands's landlord. In 1802 Black had purchased Gidea Hall, one of the two big estates in Hare Street, from Richard Benyon (see note 804). Black was a government contractor for tents and bedding, as Daniels notes, 'precisely the kind of war

what he could make of it – he staid half an hour & made it stink so, that we could not live in it for some hours. Poor man his Name will stink as well as his body[803] – when I said that poor Woollands would be a loss to the neighbourhood – he call'd him a thief – & said he stole his Chesnuts – on enquiry I found that one day Woollands after a high wind pick'd up 3 Chesnuts under a tree in the Park when Black gallop'd up to him & caught him in the fact of taking the husk off one of them – & abusd him for a thief. I ask'd him if he ever liv'd in the Large rooms at Gidea Hall which poor Benyon had fitted up with such care & cost[804] – oh no! he said he only lived in one small room – thus his house like his property is useless to himself & others – he acknowledged that he did not care what others said of him – but he could not always satisfy his own mind – he said some men had more pleasure in making Money than others in spending it – & that was his turn – I advised him to persevere in it & told him that he was only a Machine in the hands of providence to amass a Sum which some other was to render useful – & he acknowledged that he did not know, who that might be – This Wretch is to have the Trees I planted!

[*Elizabeth's hand*] You see dear William from Papas letter yesterday all thoughts of my Norfolk journey are at an end. I cannot help feeling disappointed, particularly as I shall be as far from Mary as *if* I were with you. Give my best love to dear A. Adey & tell her not to blame me for leaving Papa last night for it was his own doing and while I was cloaking up he sat[*sic*] off without me and told the girls I had better stay and sleep there.
    ever yours affectionately D–

Address: To William Repton Esqr, Aylsham, Norfolk, May be opend in his absence
B st: RUMFORD 12; Cross Post; *charge*: 1/6
Endorsed: 27 Sept'r 1812   My Father   With Papers about Dr Maclean's Settlem[en]t
HM 40871

---

speculator Repton reviled'. (Daniels, 'Cankerous blossom', p. 155.) Repton was a tenant of the Gidea Hall estate.
803 Although Repton's dislike of Black is obvious from this letter, it seems that he really did smell: in Letter 176 Dorothy also comments on Black's 'stink'.
804 In 1745 Sir Francis Styles had sold the manor of Gidea Hall to Richard Benyon, governor of Fort St George in the East Indies; in 1802 his son, Richard Benyon M.P., sold it to Alexander Black. (Ogborne, *History of Essex*, p. 130.) See also Daniels, *Repton*, pp. 59–62, for a discussion of Hare Street and its inhabitants.

164. Humphry Repton to William Repton and Dorothy Adey;
Mary Repton to Dorothy Adey

[Hare Street], 16 November [1812]

Dearest William & Aunt Adey

You will rejoice to know that Mary & I are safely returnd after a journey together of 32 days in which we traveld 466 miles – & I spent £70 & earned 3 times as much – without any accident – mishap – or misfortune except rain when the Sun should have shone & that Severn Salmon was not in season – [805]

Here I found your Dear Mamma much as I left her – not better – & determind to write & state her Case to Sir L. Macleane – but before I do so I ought to know what you have done respecting the papers I sent you – therefore write & tell me & this forms all I had to say to you [fb] having a good deal to say to other people I shall let other people finish my letter – after only saying

God bless you   HR

[fb] [Mary's hand] Dearest Aunt Adey,

I have been so employd this morning that I meant to wait till tomorrow before I wrote to you, but Papa has just brought in this letter with all this blank paper that it must not go empty, tho I shall not call an account [of] me and my travels. I find Mama sadly and it is but poor consolation to tell me she has only been so since the bad weather as it gives me a specimen of what she was and will be the whole winter. I find her added to her general weakness with more decided <u>pain</u> <u>fixd</u> in <u>one</u> <u>thigh</u> and which when violent prevents her moving or standing, her spirits [fb] fail her sadly and I dread the effects of frost and severe weather, she is upstairs while I write this and you shall frequently hear from me how she goes on. it is dark and dinner time so good bye

ever your affectionate Mary

---

805 Repton had been on professional visits, with his daughter Mary, in the vicinity of the River Severn but it is impossible to say where exactly. Most of his reports and Red Books for places in Gloucestershire, Herefordshire, Shropshire and Worcestershire were produced in the 1790s and 1800s. It was not until 1814 that he produced a report for Abbots Leigh in Bristol. (Daniels, *Repton*, p. 265.) On the other hand, he had produced a Red Book for Hewell Grange, near Bromsgrove, in early 1812, having visited in December 1811; perhaps his journey in October/November 1812 included a return visit. (*Repton in the West Midlands*, pp. 90–101.)

Address: To Mrs Adey, Aylsham, Norfolk
B st: RUMFORD 12; *charge*: 9
Endorsed: 16 Nov 1812   My Father & Mary   account of my mother's
health
HM 40872

165. William Repton to Humphry Repton (draft or copy)

Aylsham, 17ᵗʰ November 1812

My dear father

<Mr Lane> your Co-trustee *Mr Lane* writes like a sensible *prudent*
man & a good man of business and I think you may concur with him in
the Sale of the Stock in question – provided Sir Lachlan will grant you a
Mortgage on his House or any other <Property of> *Estate of* which he may
be in possession of an adequate value – and also grant you some proper
indemnity against any Claims which may be hereafter made in consequence
of the transfer of the Stock. At the present period when the Funds are so low
– I am rather surprised that Dr Mc'Lean sho'd be desirous of <selling this
Stock, at the present inferior price> *adopting such a plan as that which he
has proposed* & should have thought *it* more <desirable to> advantageous
to him to have borrowed the money of a Stranger on the Security of that
Estate which is to be pledged to the Trustees rather than to sell out of
the Funds at a time like the present when it <must> *will* be done at the
probable Sacrifice of some pounds p[er] Cent.

With regard to Sir Lachlan's idea of [*fb*] placing the writings of his house in
the hands of the Trustees or their Sol[icito]rs with a Minute or Memorand[um]
on the back <saying> stating for what purpose such a Deposit is made &
giving a Bond of Indemnity – I cannot recommend that such a course sho'd
be pursued & I think *it would not be approved by Mr Lane*[806] The plan
pointed out by <Mr Lane> *him* (no doubt with the concurrence of his Son
who is in the Law <at Lyng>) is the <most prudent means> only measure to
be adopted if Sir L continues to wish *for* the Transfer of the Stock. In that
case the first step to be taken is to show us the title to that property which he
proposes to grant in M[ortga]ge to the T[rust]ees.

The other part of Mr Lane's letter sho'd also be attended to – I mean
the part which relates to the M[ortga]ges & Securities for money settled

---

806 SRO (Bury), HA516/8/1-4 and HA516/9/1-9, are collections of documents relating to
property in Clare formerly owned by the MacLean family.

on Dr M's Marriage & *some of* which <by some> *appear to* have been <paid> *released* to Mrs Young[807] without any account to the Trustees – The first object *here* is to ascertain the Extent of the mischief to learn w[hi]ch of the Securities have been disch[ar]ged & *effectually* to prevent the others from being so improperly disposed of, & it will then be *no more than* right to call on Mrs Young's Repres[entat]ive to replace the monies w[hi]ch have been rec[eiv]ed <the> since the Mar[ria]ge Settlement without the knowledge of the Trustees –

Endorsed: 17 Nov 1812   L[ett]re to my father About the Trust monies under Dr Mc'Lean's Settlem[en]t
HM 40940

166. Revd Charles Norris[808] to William Repton

Fakenham, November 23 1812

My dear Sir

I am very desirous of performing the office of a Friend – &, so minded, shall, I doubt not, have your excuse for my interference in other's concerns.

In talking over various things with my Wolterton-friend[809] the other day I had occasion to mention you. My friend spoke with some dissatisfaction. I know not exactly how he express'd it, but it seem'd to be on account of some <u>delay</u> on your part of some business (whether it was Lease-making or what I forget) which he was impatient to have done. Now this whatever it be you will I doubt not understand & with this intimation [fb] will presently be able to remove his dissatisfaction & in doing so will feel a satisfaction on your part which will induce you, I trust, to forgive this my forwardness to give <u>hints</u>, not ill intended, to those I wish well to –

I must not omit this opportunity of thanking you My good Sir, for the very pleasant day <u>in spite of the weather</u> which you afforded me lately in conjunction with my good friend Mrs Adey, to whom I beg kindest remembrance & am, dear Sir,

Very sincerely yours C Norris

No one will know from <u>me</u> any thing of this Letter.

---

807 Mrs Young was Dr MacLean's mother-in-law. (See Letter 97.)
808 Revd Charles Norris was rector of Fakenham from 22 April 1790 to 26 April 1834; he had also been rector of Wolterton from 21 January 1791 to 1 April 1801; he was vicar of Aylsham from 24 October 1800 to 13 June 1834. (CCEd Person ID: 100143.)
809 The 'Wolterton-friend' was Lord Orford of Wolterton Hall.

[fb] That paper of Bunham's,[810] left with you, appearing to be an investigation of the quantity of land occupied by <u>Pitman's</u>[811] *Tithe* <u>Tenants</u>, from which, Small Tithes are due to me, the Survey made by Messrs. Pearce & Co[812] wou'd in all parts of it be very useful to us to be compar'd with this paper – this Survey I can at any time have access to.

Address: Wm Repton Esq, Aylsham
B st: FAKENHAM [?]118; *charge*: 9
Endorsed: 23ᵈ Nov 1812   The Revd C Norris   Hints about Ld Orford's Leases   Survey of Tithes
HM 40953/18

167. William Repton to Thomas Erskine, first baron Erskine (draft)

[Aylsham, 4 December 1812]

My Lord

I have the honor to address your Lordship in consequence of an application which has been made <to> *to me on behalf of* my Client Mr Flower of Southrepps[813] in this C[ount]y for the Loan of £10,000 on an Est[at]e belong[in]g to your Lords[hi]p in Sussex.[814] Mr Flower <has now waits has is now> has determined to view the Estate & as I under<stood> *stand* <him> he intends <&> to call on your L[or]dship in his way through London – I <have> take<n> the liberty <to mention the> *of stating this* circumstance <as the means of> *in order to* facilitate<ing> any conversation <which> *betw[een]* your Lordship <may> *& Mr F which may be* thought necessary –

Mr Withers[815] – thro' whom the application on this subject was originally made to <us> *me* has offered to <shew Mr Flower the Property & when> <*point out the property &*> shew the Property – & when Mr Flower has

---

810 Not identified.

811 Revd Samuel Pitman (q.v.).

812 Probably Pearce and Kent: as noted above, after Nathaniel Kent's death his son Charles went into partnership with William Pearce.

813 Cook Flower, previously of Sheringham, now residing at Southrepps.

814 Lord Erskine had purchased an estate at Buchan Hill, near Crawley, Sussex. According to his *ODNB* entry, by 1811 '[m]uch of his fortune was wasted in American investments, and financial straits forced him to sell the bulk of his property in London. Having bought an estate near Crawley in Sussex, he dabbled in farming; the land was infertile, and he lost heavily when he tried to convert the produce into raw material for manufacturing brooms'.

815 Perhaps William Withers of Holt, receiver of rents on the Bulwer estates at Heydon.

satisfied himself on a view of it, your Lordship will be so good as to <give> direct that <the> Abst[rac]ts of the title be forwarded to me, when the business may be ended with as little *delay* as possible –

I have the honor to be My Lord

Your Lordships Very faithful humble servant

Endorsed: 4 Dec 1812   L[ett]re to Lord Erskine   Estate in Sussex in Mort[ga]ge

HM 40954/5

168. Humphry Repton to Dorothy Adey (some in the hand of Elizabeth);[816] Humphry Repton to William Repton

Harestreet, December 11 1812

[*Repton*] Dearest Dee

As you say write often – Dee shall copy my Letter to Si[r] Lackland which will tell you how we go on[817]

[*Elizabeth's hand; Repton's words*] Monday. A severe return of Bilious pain and evacuations. Tuesday, much easier and sat up and playd Cards. Wednesday A day of great pain both from the Rhumatism and from a bilious paroxysm.

Thursday rather easier but at night we had an alarming attack and great flutter and debility from Evacuations. Friday the stomach easier a quiet night but little sleep and this morning great pain in the Thigh. Her diet has been very strictly attended to, but she has no desire for food and only takes slops, as she calls them, because she is thirsty and they moisten her mouth. These are, Sago, Tapioca, Barley water with a little Madeira and, last night, plenty of ginger as I found her pulse sinking and cold extremities with symptoms of fainting and terror. The excessive discharges appear to follow at stated times or when the [*fb*] bowels have received a given quantity of nourishment, and then the powders and draughts seem to check the paroxysm for a time.

[*Repton*] Friday night severe pain in Thigh till one – notwithstand[in]g she took 3 Laudanum pills – Saturday morning still dosing but the pills produced no sleep till 8 o Clock –

---

816 The HL endorsement says 'Mostly in the hand of his daughter Elizabeth Repton. Elizabeth Repton to William Repton'. The text is her father's; it is the hand that is Elizabeth's. The first part of the letter is to Dorothy Adey.

817 viz. Repton's account of his wife Mary's illness that was sent to Dr McLean.

Mr & Mrs Cook of Seemer have call'd here in their way from London, & took my Letter to Dr. Macleane, with Andrews's desire to know if we may begin the new medicines in a day or two, should the Bile keep off.

With respect to myself – My Cold is better – I go on Monday with Gen[era]l Brown to the Levee[818] – & on Tuesday with Lord Erskine to Sussex – so you see I am not confined to the house either by Mary, or my own indisposition – & if the P[rince] Regent says any thing about my beautiful Jasmine Waistcoat[819] – you shall know it in my next letter – but I have a long Letter to write to Dear William (private) by which I don't mean you Dear Dee are not to know it – but not to speak of it –

[fb] Dear William – The Walking talking Essex Gazette – Widow Wallinger – brought from Colchester the following News.[820] Mr Upcher is gone mad – entirely owing to the Estate for which he gave 50 thous[an]d[821] – & has offerd it to sale & nobody will give more than 30 thous[an]d – Supposing part of this might be true, I calld on Dr. Heberden & stated the report & in confidence told him perhaps I might obtain a Purchaser if he thought it would assist poor Upcher – he acknowledged great depression – but not Madness[822] & this morning he writes, that he had seen his patient & has authority to request I will proceed in the business – Now I will tell you what had occur'd to me –

Some time ago before, I knew Sherringhams Capability – I had some Conversation with the Speaker ab't it for the Nelson Trust[823] – he did not think it then of sufficient value – & objected to the want of a Mansion – but afterwards said that might be got over by a house built – Now I have made

---

818 *The Morning Chronicle*, Tuesday, 15 December 1812, issue 13606, pp. 1–2, has an extensive list of attendees at the levee on 14 December, including General Brown; again Repton is not mentioned. His comments in Letter 169 suggest that he did attend.

819 See Letter 160, where Repton also mentions comments made at a levée about his waistcoat.

820 Daniels discusses this letter in detail. (Daniels, 'Cankerous blossom', p. 151.)

821 In June 1811 Upcher had signed the purchase contract for Sheringham, agreeing to pay Cook Flower £52,500, with a view to taking possession in Michaelmas 1812. (*Repton in Norfolk*, pp. 146–50.)

822 'In October 1812, shortly after taking possession of Sheringham, Upcher fell ill with a "violent nervous fever" and had to go to London for three months to convalesce.' (*Repton in Norfolk*, p. 152.) It is known that one of Upcher's doctors was a Dr Heberden, who, in 1817, was living in Kent; in that year the Upcher family moved to Brompton in Kent to be near the doctor. (*Repton in Norfolk*, p. 153.) In 1792 the practice of Dr W. Heberden, fellow of the Royal College of Physicians, was in Pall Mall. (*Universal Directory* (1792) p. 444.)

823 Charles Abbott (q.v.). For the Nelson Trust, see note to Letter 54.

2 most striking views of the Place with the House proposed & the hill with Sit[uatio]n for a Column or obelisk will render it very appropriate[824] – add to this it is on the Coast – in Norfolk – & adjoining to Land of a Relation to the Nelsons.[825] I mean to ask the Speaker for an interview & shew him these drawings – if possible next Tuesday – before I go into Sussex – Now dear William could you furnish me with an Answer to Robersons Hotel[826] to the following qu[erie]s?

Qu[er]y 1[st] – Is there any truth in the Estate having been so depreciated –

2[d] – Is there any chance if the Speaker objects to it as too small – to obtain any addition from the Walpole property by purchase or exchange? Perhaps it might suit your *noble* client to accommodate a Relation to accomplish a National purpose – It is a fair stalking Horse –

3[d] – Is there any Chance of Flowers Letting Upcher off his bargain & upon what terms – that I may have two strings to my bow, if I fail with the Speaker – my first object is to save poor Upcher, whom you know I Lov'd almost at first sight – as another myself[827]–

And on Canvassing the Subject in my own Mind I think it is possible I may yet have some benefit from building the house – & you from sale & resale &c &c &c, but I hope you will make Flower pay well for your agency – & consider on the Sale of such an estate you ought to have a p[er] Centage. Your advice added 2,500 Slap. & the odd 500 should be yours – ha! Slap.

Address: To Mrs Adey, Aylsham, Norfolk
B st: RUMFORD 12; Cross Post; *charge*: 9
HM 40837

---

824 The Sheringham Red Book (folio size) is dated July 1813, and it records site visits on 11, 12, 17 and 23 June 1813. (Rogger, *Landscapes*, p. 209.) However, from this letter it is clear that Repton had visited the site before December 1812 and had made some drawings. For a detailed account of his work at Sheringham see *Repton in Norfolk*, pp. 144–54.

825 Nelson's father, Revd Edmund Nelson (1722–1802), rector of Burnham Thorpe, had married Catherine (1725–1767), daughter of Maurice Suckling, prebendary of Westminster. Catherine was a great-niece of Sir Robert Walpole and a cousin of Horatio, second Lord Walpole, who was Nelson's godfather and after whom he was named. (*ODNB* for Horatio Nelson.)

826 Roberson's Hotel, St Martins Lane, London.

827 For the 'immediate rapport' between Repton and Upcher, see Daniels, *Repton*, p. 92.

169. Humphry Repton to William Repton

London, December 15 1812

My Dear William

Many thanks for your Letter rec'd this morning. I have been with the Speaker & he desires a full acc't of the Value present & improveable with price & full particulars – therefore you must make out such a particular as will not commit your judgement – & yet may not frighten them quoad[sic] produce for Capital & I think you may set the Woods & Game & improve[men]t from Inclosure pretty high – then add so much for Situation & beauty – & write this at once to the Right Hon. the Speaker &c &c &c Palace Yard – as by my desire & make the best of it you can – – I told the Speaker when he ask'd what was the Rental – that there was no leases – & the Newly inclosed Land greatly improveable but I said – who shall in these times dare to pronounce [fb] the value of any thing 7 years hence – when we have lived to see Gold of no Value – & Rags[828] the only Wealth this cannot last long + I have just heard that the Tunbridge Bank is[829] faild – by which I loose £200 which Major Woodgate ought to have paid long ago.[830] He is one of the Firm – but nothing is firm now. Report at Lloyds[831] – Buonaparte dead! for Certain.

Here am I kicking my heels in London – waiting to go into Sussex with Lord Erskine to morrow – I know not what for[832] – but there is nothing

---

828 A reference to paper currency in place of gold standard.

829 Tonbridge Bank (Kent) was established/first known of in 1796. It had various names/incarnations. In 1812 it was owned by (or known as) Geo. Children, William Francis Woodgate & William Scoones; in 1813 as Sir Geo. Children, Knight. (*Country Banks and Bankers*, vol. 2, p. 587.)

830 William Francis Woodgate was a major in the Tonbridge troop of the volunteer cavalry. (A. H. Neve, *The Tonbridge of Yesterday* (Tonbridge, 1934), p. 56.) Repton's comment suggests that Major Woodgate was a client, rather than that Repton had invested in the Tonbridge Bank. As already noted, he had visited Tonbridge in April 1810 (Letter 133); £200 represents nearly four times his standard charge of 50 guineas for a consultation. This letter strongly suggests a commission, which had not been paid for. See Letter 197, where the sum owing is said to be £119 5s.

831 Lloyd's insurance office. It originated in a coffee house kept by Edward Lloyd in Tower Street in the 1680s; by the time of this letter it was situated in the Royal Exchange. (*London Encyclopaedia*, pp. 464–5.)

832 Daniels (*Repton*, p. 268) tentatively suggests that this visit relates to a commission at Buchan Hill, but considering content of William's letter to Lord Erskine above (Letter 167), it seems unlikely that Erskine would consider landscaping the estate. In 'Rumours of Repton at Buchan Hill', Pippa Potts discusses whether this letter is an indication that Repton offered advice to Lord Erskine at Buchan Hill. (*Repton in Sussex*, pp. 120–2.)

doing so I am doing nothing – & Harestreet without your poor Mother or with her in Torture, is no pleasing Retreat. Alas! I counted of a Christmas at Aylsham & a job in Norfolk to pay the piper – but we must leave off dancing – & eating too, if things go on thus –

[fb] I have been walking with Old Vicessimus Knox[833] – quite to Kensington to see fools skaite on a piece of Ice surrounded by Water – & have got a famous appetite for my dinner – but I have not earnd a dinner for my Appetite – – Nash is ill – the 3 D[octo]rs say it is Cancerous in his Jaw –[834]

& while I was speaking to George[835] The Prince's Servant came to enquire after his health – he ask'd me how I did yesterday as usual but never said a word about my waistcoat. What a Shew of Gold & Silver on the Uniforms of Generals Admirals &c &c – all to be paid by us & I fancied I was the only person in the Rooms not paid for my attendance in some shape or other. Such things can't last long – any more than

Your old affectionate father –

Address: To William Repton Esq, Aylsham, Norfolk
B st: B DE 15 812
Endorsed: 15 Dec'r 1812   My Father   The Speaker wishes for a Part[icu]lar
of Est[at]e   Lord Erskine   Prince's Reception of him at the Levee
HM 40873

170. Edward Repton to William Repton

Crayford, <December> *January*[836] 4 1813

Dear William

Your beautiful Birds and thundering big Hare deserve a better and longer letter than my budget of Interest can supply – but you shall have our hearty

---

833 Vicesimus Knox II was a distinguished headmaster of Tonbridge School for 34 years from 1778. He was preceded as headmaster by his father, also called Vicesimus, and followed by his son Thomas. Between them they ran the school for 70 years. Beyond the confines of school and town, Vicesimus II was widely known as a writer. His popular anthologies and views on education were well thought of by such people as Jane Austen and Dr Johnson, and he was even awarded a doctorate by a college in America. He died in Tonbridge in 1821. (http://www.tonbridgehistory.org.uk/people/vicesimus-knox.html.)
834 Whatever his illness in December 1812, Nash did not die until 1835. (*ODNB*)
835 i.e. Prince George, the Prince Regent.
836 Edward had written December then he, or William, crossed it out in pencil and added January.

thanks – and it will be the more gratifying to you to know that they were most acceptable – for we have had our little Cottage crammed full – and mouths out of number to cramm also –

My Mother is so good a news monger – that I can say little of Harestreet which you do not learn better from her – I was there a few weeks since – and certainly thought my dear good Mother was about [*fb*] to leave this world of pain, for so indeed poor Soul! it is to her – never is she <u>one instant</u> free from pain – and gets little or no rest – I am glad Mrs Adey did not come up – at the time they wrote. – Of my Father, I suppose, they say but little – but certainly in some respects he is a <u>different</u> Man – not for the worse I think, by any means – James Marsh says, "he is a Methodist" – but James M. does not know perhaps what a Methodist is.–[837] He is employing the latter part of his busy Life, in looking back upon all he has gone through – and not without some proper views of what is to come – We who know him – know that his active mind cannot be at rest – and that on whatever subject he thinks – whether Divinity or any other – his thoughts will be original – and perhaps at times a little extravagant but I see no mischief or Methodism in his present occupations –

[*fb*] Of ourselves a little – My Wife is better than I ever remember her – and by means of Barley Water and Porter supports herself and a fine little fat Baby – who promises to be beautiful – *comme une*[838] *Ange* – with regard to myself – and future schemes I know but little – I give up the Duty here at Lady Day – and have partly engaged my time in London but whether I shall reside in London or not – will, I believe, depend upon my procuring a few Pupils in town whom I could attend in the Morning at their own Houses – or have them with me – without <u>boarding</u> with us – which is destructive to all domestic privacy and comfort. Are you likely to hear of any thing of this sort amongst Lord Orfords Friends?–

There is not a Creature at Crayford whose acquaintance is worth keeping up – and we think that by extending [*fb*] our Connections in London – we may <u>perhaps</u> get on – but Wallinger leaves me at Easter[839] – and I have no other in view – What is to become of us? Alack alack! – *Je ne sais pas* – but

---

837 In relation to religion, a 'Methodist' was one took part in or sympathized with the evangelical movement begun by John and Charles Wesley and George Whitefield in 1729. The movement had for its object the promotion of piety and morality. (*OED*, definition 4.)
838 The 'e' was added in pencil, indicating a girl: so by January 1813 Edward and Mary had at least 3 children.
839 Indicating that 'Wallinger' was a paying pupil of Edward's; probably William Wallinger, son of William, of St John's Westminster, esquire, who matriculated at University College Oxford on 17 February 1813, aged 17. (*Alumni Oxon.*, p. 1490.)

as my Father says the Sparrows feed – and find food – and so I hope shall I and <I> my little Cherubs! – Love to Dear Aunt Adey, in which Mary shall add her's – in her own hand –

Ever William Your ER

Address: Wm Repton Esq, Aylsham, Norfolk
B st: DARTFORD [?]13; *r st*: E 6 JA 6 1813; *charge*: [*illeg*]
Endorsed: 4 <Dec 1812> January 1813[840]   Edward   My father altered, Edwd's future plans
HM 40914/1

171. Claude Scott to William Repton

Bruton Street, June 14th 1813

Dear Sir

Your Favor of the 11th came here to Day and bro[ugh]t safe the Notes &c to the amount of £31.11.6 in the discharge of the year's Interest due from your good Father, leaving an excess of 1s/6d to his credit – I did expect your Father wou'd have deducted from this Interest what I owe him for what we understood to be a <profess> *sort of half-* professional Visit at Lytchet[841] last Summer, and for some Drawings, which pray remind him of. We leave Town Tomorrow for the Summer. Mrs Scott desires to join me in best respects to Mrs Adey and yourself.

I am dear Sir truly Yours C. Scott

Address: To Wm Repton Esqre, Aylsham, Norfolk
B st: B JU 14 1813
HM 40953/19

---

840 Amended in pencil.
841 Claude Scott 'had retired from business in 1810 and purchased the Lytchett Minster estate in Dorset from John Jeffery'. (*Hist. Parl.*) Following a visit in the summer of 1812 Repton had produced some drawings for Scott's house, which has recently been identified by as Sans Souci, 'a delightful villa overlooking Poole Harbour'. Scott devoted his energy and wealth to improving the estate. Following his death in 1830, sales particulars stated that the house and gardens 'had been modernised and improved at considerable expenses[*sic*]' and were 'now in the most perfect state of substantial and ornamental repair'. (From abstract for Sarah Fitzgerald, 'Sans Souci, a "new" Repton site discovered', paper given at 'Discovering the Real Repton', The Garden Museum, 5 Nov. 2018.)

172. Eliza Boyd[842] to Elizabeth Repton[843]

Ipswich, September 17th 1813

My dear D

It gave me great pleasure to hear that my *people* were attentive to you & it wou'd have given Mr Boyd & me much greater cou'd we have witnessed it. I got a peep at you all *from* our dear Humphry.[844] I hope its not too late to say how happy we shall be if you will both give us a day on your return. I shou'd have made this request sooner but expected Mr & Mrs Cox[845] from Norwich to stay a few days last week but they did not *come* but sent their daughter who only left us on Wednesday. Yesterday I was prevented writing as I intended to tell [fb] that the Bed that Humphry slept in is at liberty & there is a second in a little attic that sometimes young Friends think not very uncomfortable. I truly hope I may not be too late in telling you that you & our William may indulge with a peep on your return. I shou'd have sooner thanked you for your attentive note but waited till I coud offer a sleeping accommodation. I was unwilling to delay doing so longer the first moment that I had at liberty [fb] to tell you so but it is so very short a one that I have scarcely time to scribble even *in* this beautiful way. I hope Humphry has heard of his five pound note. do give Mr Boyds & my best love *to him* & accept the same yourself, my dear God daughter – from

your Affectionate Friend Eliza Boyd

Pray give my best comp[limen]ts to Mrs Adey & every Body at Harestreet when you write, particularly to dear Mrs Repton of whom we are delighted *to hear* such a good account. tell *her* I shall *not* now quite despair of one day seeing [her] under my Roof. I cannot tell her what pleasure it wou'd give me

Address: Miss D Repton, Mrs Adeys, Alesham[*sic*], Norfolk
B st: IPSWICH 69; *charge*: 8
HM 40897

---

842 See Letter 152.
843 The HL catalogued the recipient as 'Dorothy Repton'.
844 Comments later in the letter indicate that this was Humphry junior.
845 Not identified.

173. Mary (Herbert) Repton to William Repton; Edward Repton to William; Edward Repton to Dorothy Adey

Crawford Street,[846] <February> March 1st [1814][847]

Dear William,

I fear from Sarahs earnestness to have a second character from me that she finds some difficulty in getting one from those, with whom she has lived since she left me, which otherwise she certainly would have done but could I have spoken favorably of her conduct while with me – a lapse of 3 years, may have made a great alteration in her – it is true she was the only nursery Maid <I> We had for our 2 first Children but we trusted her with them as little as we could possibly help, from the conviction that she was too unsteady to have the charge of them. This we had too many opportunities of witnessing, & this was my reason for writing as I did to Mrs Elwes[848] – feeling that if I had Lent my real sentiments, I should have entirely <have> prevented her taking Sarah as Nurse – for which situation she certainly was *not* fit during my acquaintance with her – both Edward & I feel [fb] as Parents on the subject, & know the great responsibility a Nurse has – & think it unjustifiable in any one, to recommend a Nurse whom they know is not fit for the Charge. for this reason my Husband, (whom you must know I consult in such important matters) thinks with me that I am not justified in giving Sarah a Character as a Nurse. Thus far, Dear Brother William, in plea of my letter to Mrs Elwes – but at the same time I should be sorry to do, or say any thing to injure Sarah, and pray tell her I should willingly recommend her as House Maid or in any other capacity, & will say all I can to enable her to get any Situation – <but as the a Nurse one> except that in which she is to have the care of Children. – We were sorry we had so little of y[ou]r Company – but as George says – "The loss was yours" – With kind love from Edward & me – believe me

yours affectionately M E Repton

Dear W

Thank you for your hint of Mr H[849] – I conceived somewhat the same of him – and his concerns – thank you too for the hint of the Turkey – and

---

846 Crawford Street is in Marylebone. Several letters were written by Edward from there. In Letter 190 the address is given as 1 Crawford Street.

847 The postmark indicates that the letter was posted on 3 March 1814.

848 Or, Elmes; perhaps an Aylsham resident, as this is addressed to William.

849 'Mr H' cannot be identified; the context is too vague.

still better one of your intention. I have been ill for some days – but am getting right again –

Yours ER

[*fb*] Tuesday – 2 oclock – March 1

My dear Aunt Adey

Had it not been for this abominable illness – I should have been at Harestreet to welcome your arrival – but as it is I must rest contented with the hope of seeing you <u>here</u> – for there is little chance of my Wifes getting to H.S. even had they a bed for her – indeed I don't know what they will do with the 2 Children. Now the rest of my Letter you must not read for a day or two – and then proceed <u>thus</u> – If you are at all likely to come to Town on <u>your own</u> account, so much the better for our chance of seeing you – if not – and you will come for a day or two on <u>ours</u> – we will give you a comfortable bed (don't let the Girls puzzle their heads to know how that is to be, nor my Mother call out – "no my dear dee, we shan't let you go to London") and then you may see the rest of the fry – and my Wife into the bargain should it prove practicable to do so in the beginning or middle of next week – you might perhaps bring the young ones with you – otherwise I must run down for them – for I think they must be tired of them of H. S. and we begin to sicken to see them. – I am better to day – but my hand is unsteady – and so is my head – <And> yet I am wrapping up – to go in the Carriage to [*fb*] Hornsey – where we shall stay till Friday. –

Pray tear off the other side and send it p[er] Basket or otherwise to William – and Kiss my dear Mother for me and the Girls – and my own little ones – and tell them to kiss Aunt Adey for her affectionate Nephew ER

Address: Mrs Adey, H Reptons Esq, Harestreet, Romford
B st: A MR 3 814
HM 40935

174. Dorothy Adey to William Repton

Harestreet, Friday Morning [4 March 1814]

My dearest William

I wish the enclos'd had been sent at once to you, because, I have no means of sending it but making you pay a double letter, and that must be done as the sooner the poor girl is put out of expectation the better,[850] there was at our breakfast table this morning a great diversity of opinion, we three elder think it hard Mrs Edward shou'd object to saying Sarah had certainly the intire care of her two elder children from their birth, and I think there cannot be a great proof of her having no <u>very</u> material objection to her nursing the 1st Child, by suffering her to take charge of a second. Mary thinks Mrs Edward perfectly right in <making> *considering* the parents of a Child of more consequence than the Nurse, in short, you will see what she says and so I need have said nothing but sent the letter at once. Your Father says its spite spite, and I doubt myself if there is not more *ill* temper *to Sarah* than good will to Mrs Elwes.

we found the dear Children here and [fb] Edward is as much my favorite as he was two years ago, Georgiana is a nice little thing but Edward you know is elder by a year, and I think talks as plain and as sensibly as many Children three or four years older. I have been exhibiting the profiles[851] and I suppose he told in the Kitchen what he had seen and he has just been in to tell his aunt d: 'Sally[852] hopes Aunt d: will take a profile upon my face to shew my Papa & my Mama' –

We have had uncomfortable weather for travelling but it wou'd not have [been] better at home, so we thought not of it, but jog'd on some times fast, and sometimes slow, as our postillions and good or bad Horses were dispos'd. Webster desired his Horses might go to Schole and they went most capitally, but the Lad dare not take less than 1s 9d a Mile notwithstanding the Schole Landlord told him nobody charg'd more than 1s 6d and I was not ask'd for more all the way from Schole to Harestreet, so that I did not pay the Lad, but told him I shou'd leave you to settle with his Master. we arriv'd at Ipswich about seven and met with the "<u>comfortable</u> reception [fb] the dear good old Lady talk'd of"[853] and very uncomfortably for me I had ocasion to give her more than usual cause for attention, for the illness that came on me the day before I left home, was not better for my journey, & God bless her little bustling soul, she thought she cou'd never do enough for me, and "I must eat this, and must not eat th'other & so on", and I

---

850 From the text of this letter it is clear that the previous letter from Mary and Edward, dated 1 March 1814, (Letter 173) was enclosed with this one. They have been separated in the archive.

851 From this and the following letter, it appears that Elizabeth had taken to drawing profiles of residents of, and visitors to, the Reptons' home.

852 Sally was a servant of some kind in the Hare Street house; she may be Sally Gibbs, who, in April 1814 had been recently widowed. (See Letter 183.)

853 The 'dear good old lady' might be Eliza Boyd, who lived in Ipswich. (See Letter 172.)

consented to all she advis'd <u>except</u> writing to Harestreet for my dear sister not to expect me, and sending to her <u>best</u> apothecary that ever liv'd to give me medicine, neither of these things I cou'd comply with. at Colchester I began to feel stronger than I had done ever since I left home, was bonny all yesterday, have had a goodnight and felt this morning as if I was in a fair way of getting rid of all pain and loseing the cadaverous hue that has ting'd my Cheeks for the last day or two, and I cannot give you a better proof of my being well than by treating you with this sick history, for if I was *really* ill I am sure I shou'd not tell of it.

I am delighted with the appearance of your dearest mother. I dont care twopence about her *not* <u>being</u> as lusty as I am, her Eyes are bright, she feels inclination to make exertion, and busys and amuses herself with her <u>beautiful</u> patch work, and <u>I am as happy as a Queen</u> with her and your dear Father, who had a head ach last night, which my <u>Acton</u> nightcap has left no remains of this morning. I have begun one for your Mother tho as John has treated himself with a cropping against my arrival, I think He will probably be the first to [*fb*] take possession of it.[854]

I saw by a paper I met with at Ipswich there is a chance for parliam[en]t being proro<gu>ed[855] (I can't spell it and your mother can't help me) and if so, surely it will give you a fortnight longer to prepare your Bill,[856] and uncle John's indecision must be a desirable thing.[857] it never occur'd to either d: or me that if Mr & Mrs Kent[858] went from Bungay to town this must be their road. pray if they are not set out, tell them we all hope for the pleasure of seeing them on <*illeg*> their way home, Mrs Holley too we look for every day, of course if she means to travel this road we shall have a line from you or from her.

God bless you all at Oxnead today, I hope you will remember I have left one umbrella at home, and God bless you at Oxnead & Aylsham and in every part and corner of the world prays

    your ever affectionate D Adey

---

854 In this context, rather than a drink or medicinal remedy for a headache an 'Acton nightcap' seems to be an item of headgear. An 'acton' was a 'padded jacket or jerkin worn under armour for protection; (also) such a garment worn on its own' (*OED*), so perhaps a padded nightcap.

855 Parliament was prorogued on 1 March 1814 for three weeks.

856 The bill relating to the enclosure of the parishes of Skeyton, Burgh next Aylsham and Tuttington. The Act is Local and Personal Act, 54 George III, c. 37. (PA, HL/PO/PB/1/1814/54G3n278.)

857 Referring to the indecision of William's (deceased) uncle, John Repton; had she meant John Adey, she would more likely have referred to her 'dear husband'.

858 Charles Kent (q.v.).

Address: William Repton Esqr, Aylsham, Norfolk
B st: RUMFORD 12; Cross Post; *charge*: 1/6
HM 40892/1

175. Dorothy Adey to William Repton; note by Elizabeth

Harestreet, March 10th [1814][859]
67 years old I believe today[860]

My dearest William

A most glorious long morning I get for writing, for tho I am in bed an hour after my usual Aylsham time, yet as nobody thinks of breakfast till ten oclock, I have a prodigious long time for execution of my genius but as a stuffy cold in head and stomach (which we all and every one have more or less throughout the House) has led me to indulge in bed this morning, I shall most probably break off before my paper is fill'd, and the Flaps I shall certainly devote to family concerns ——

thank you dearest good William for your long and interesting letter, for I confess I left home with fears that your enclosure wou'd <u>never</u> go on. I dont quite agree with you as to the Tuttington gentry commoning too, depend upon it that Parish is to be without Enclosure till Colby and Banningham join, but I shou'd try hard but I wou'd have a finger in that pie whenever the event takes place.[861] I am glad you have length of time to adjust your Bill for I dreaded the hurry of getting it into the House by the 4th or 7th I believe it was, that parliament was first intended to meet. a concatenation of ideas from mentioning the presenting [*fb*] the Bill brings Sir Jacob[862] to my mind and leads me to enquire if Saville and Miss Astley are married,[863] for

---

859 This letter has been catalogued out of sequence: HM 40886/13. It refers to several elements of the previous letter (HM 40892/1), which was written on 4 March 1814, such as meeting Mr and Mrs Kent and Mrs Holley and Dee making profiles, and also other elements in the following letter (HM 40892/2).

860 This phrase was written as part of the date. Dorothy was born in 1747. (Stroud, *Repton*, p. 15.)

861 In fact, the eventual enclosure act that included Tuttington did not include Colby and Banningham. (NRO, C/Sca 2/261, Skeyton, Burgh next Aylsham and Tuttington Enclosure Award 1821; the relevant enclosure act is dated 1814.)

862 Sir Jacob Henry Astley, fifth baronet (1756–1817), of Melton Constable; M.P. for Norfolk 15 Nov. 1797 to 1806 and 4 Mar. 1807 to 28 Apr. 1817. (*Hist. Parl.*)

863 Sir Jacob Astley had 3 sons and 6 daughters but it has not been possible to identify which 'Miss Astley' was going to marry 'Saville'. No Astley-Saville marriage has been found via Ancestry.com.

I have not seen it <announced> in the Norwich paper, nor have we yet read of Martha Holley and her little disagreeable Youth becoming one.[864] we have neither seen or heard of Poor Mrs. Holley, and conclude she travell'd some other road. we hope all the Kents have done so also, as they have not given us a call.

except walking last <Friday> Saturday morning as far as the Bridge with little Edward for my beau I have not been out of the House or have the Girls or any of the family save John, (who wisely walks ½ an hour before dinner every day be the weather as it may,) stir'd from home. Your dear Father had an appointment in Town for yesterday, and shou'd have been with Lord Cambden[sic][865] to day, but as his L'dship wrote to postpone his visit till he cou'd see the Ground which at present the snow prevents, he has defer'd going to London till the weather changes, when that will be we none of us know. Old Andrews told us yesterday there was a great deal of snow yet lock'd up in Norfolk. Do give the Key a turn and the weathercock a turn, and let it all go back to Norway.

½ past 3, it has snow'd without ceasing all morning but the day has been warmer than any I have felt since I arriv'd and I hope we shall feel no more bitter cold. Your dear Mother stands it all wonderfully well, tho she draws [fb] as close over the fire as any of us. Miss Wilson, Ann and Mary Wyatt[866] call'd upon d: on Friday but we have seen nothing of any of the family since the Old Man is safely shut up some where. Mrs Wyatt has not call'd & I take it for granted does not intend it and you may be sure I like best to be forgotten –

d begins to be expert at Profiles. Col: Ferrier and a Mr James[867] came to dine here on Tuesday, and like the tooth drawer we have heard your dear knell[sic; ?Nell] talk of who introduc'd the subject and had the mans tooth out in a moment, so d: the moment the poor men came to us after dinner clap'd them down in the Corner of the room, and went to work upon their faces in an instant.   by the way the old Col[one]l who I expected to [have] a disgusting pimply Face, is no such thing, but a [?]good [damaged] tall millitary looking Man of about 50 with a Face mark'd with small pox, and a Gentlemanly pleasant man. I was agreably disappointed

---

864 Martha Elizabeth Holley married Matthew Thurlow Nelson of Holme on 24 Feb. 1814. (*Aylsham*, pp. 252–3.)
865 John Jeffreys Pratt, first marquess Camden (q.v.). In 1814 Camden invited Repton to return to Bayham to offer his opinion for possible new locations for the new house which had been suggested in the earlier Red Book but never built. (*Repton in Kent*, p. 94.)
866 Local friends. (See Letter 161.)
867 From the Romford barracks. (See note 909.)

in him: He is no great conjurer at Whist, but the subaltern plays an excellent Game.

I hope when you next are so good to write you will tell us your cold is gone, when do you go to Southwold not this cold weather I hope. Duff met Mrs W[illiam] Walenger at a dinner the other day and she told him she had had a letter from you but did not mention the subject [or] say if she agrees to one plan or the other – what is become of your *ci-devant* Client George Holley, and where are our good friends the Ansons. have you had the promised visit from Mr Henry[868] yet.

and now for my Flaps. first, giving [*fb*] to you the united love of our fireside – will you write to Dorrel and Pearce,[869] or shall I. I had rather you wou'd, but if you tell me you do not I will. have a fire in the best parlour once a week whether you go to it or not. I did tell Izzy not to let the pork Lard in the bladder be made use of whilst I am out, as it will be difficult to procure in summer and may now be bought as wanted but this I forgot to mention to the Cook, pray speak about it – I wish Betty Barns would look out for two good Legs of pork and two heads, and make the Legs into hams and at the same time pickle the Faces, and when ever the present hams and Bacon is taken out of the pickle, the Lard will be at Liberty for the others, and she must take the intire management of them as before. the Cloth I purchas'd of Clover for your sleeves was not paid for before I left home, the Bill (30 shillings) I think is on your desk. take care of your Cold and ride or drive safe Horses and now God Bless you

Yours ever affectionately   D Adey

[*Elizabeth*] Dearest William

Aunt Adey says she has left room for a few lines, but Papa is asleep and the rest are all reading so I am the only one who can spare time to send best love and to say that Aunt Adey has left nothing else to communicate. I have some most capital ornaments for your bedroom window and when there [*damaged*] [?is an] opportunity of getting them to Aylsham I expect th[*damaged*] present [?]Rolls will be turn'd out.

Ever most affectionately [*damaged*] own sister   D

Address: William Repton Esq, Aylsham, Norfolk
B st: RUMFORD [*illeg*]; Cross Post; *charge*: 9
HM 40886/13

---

868 Probably Henry Anson. (See also Letter 162.)

869 Dorothy talks about writing to these two men (variant spellings) in this and the next two letters. Pearce is probably the surveyor William Pearce; a comment in Letter 177 suggests that Dorrel is John Dayrell of Lamport, rather than John Dayrell Martin.

176. Dorothy Adey to William Repton; notes from Humphry, Elizabeth and Mary (Clarke) Repton to William

Harestreet, March 17th [1814][870]

My dearest William

I am afraid I shall have you think that the moment you are so good to write me a letter I slap bang another in return directly, but the fact is, had I had or had not a letter to day I shou'd certainly have written to you, because I feel myself that I have pleasant intelligence to convey. your dear Father calls it *so* also <so>, but I am not quite sure either the Girls or John are of the same opinion, (Mamma, you know, always thinks as Papa) and now for the weighty news.

Old Black was here yesterday long enough to make the ladies sit with the door wide open after his departure, tho being from my still most obstinate Cold depriv'd of smell taste &c I knew nothing of the stench. I think you will be surpris'd when I tell you, he ask'd your Father only 30£ a year, I have made my 3 plain, for fear you shou'd mistake it for 80. I shou'd have lik'd the business to have clos'd directly, but your Father told him you wou'd be here after Easter, and if he had no objection to the waiting till then he shou'd be glad to avoid a positive answer till he saw you. The old man very handsomly desired he wou'd take his own time and [fb] indeed appeard to speak so fairly and honestly that I have not the least doubt of his standing to his agreement. He makes a point of a fourteen years Lease being taken, to this your father rather demurr'd but He seems now to think it no objection to the bargain, as there is little doubt but whenever dispos'd to let it, he will find no difficulty in procuring a Tennant. He talk'd last night of writing a note to the old man that he wou'd agree to the proposal but I thought afterwards seem'd dispos'd to wait and hear if you wou'd have him do so, but as the old fellow gave us an account of falling on the Floor after a violent cough, and being he believ'd nearer dying than ever he had been before, it will not be amiss to give us a line as soon as you can –

You know your old Aunt too well my dear William to expect when every[sic] this is agreed and setled she will throw a single obstacle in the way. I am most perfectly and intirely content and every thing in my power to do, to make the young man comfortable,[871] and you happy, I give

---

870   Assigned to 1814 due to several connections with the preceding letter which had been written on Dorothy's 67th birthday.

871   A new young man would shortly be working in William's office. In June 1814 Arnold Wallinger was apprenticed to William. See Letter 194 and notes thereto.

you my word and honor shall with my usual <u>grace and pleasantness</u> be done. thank you for your kindness in acceding to my wish of not being depriv'd of a Bedroom, but as to all that business may be transacted at my return, and any bed in the House he can be accommodated with till we get him a proper one, perhaps with the knowledge that you expected [*fb*] to stand in need of one you were provident and bought a Feather bed at old Fullers Auction.[872] I am glad to find Shelford[873] stands a chance of being in London. I think it will be pleasant to both young men to see each other and I sincerely hope they will be as happy together, as I have no doubt but you and I shall be with both

You are my dear William so very very good to me, and give so many proofs of your kindness that you give me no opportunity of believing myself forgotten – but so decidedly as you set your face against the remembrance of a Birth day; I do think your making <u>mine</u> a red letter day was such a proof of your having me in mind as made me snivel, and so you see at home or abroad I am equally an old fool.

you have not mention'd the Ansons, I conclude you must have seen each other, or do you tell me if <u>you</u> have written to Mr Pearce or Dayrell because I think they shou'd be written to by one of us –

I had a letter yesterday from Harriet Kent with a most kind invitation to pass a week at Fulham.[874] I shall write tomorrow and decidedly refuse such a long visit, and indeed whether I am to go thither at all will remain undetermind till your arrival, and I hear what you think of that, or even my going to Town at all. To Harry Botham I have not written yet, but as I am afraid I stand no chance for you of our party there, I think I ought to get that visit over before you come up [*fb*] but in this also I shou'd like to hear what you advise.

Poor Taylor is a good creature as ever liv'd. I have not altogether as great faith in his skill as in his kindness and his humanity but he has the knack of making, d: [Elizabeth] says and I say so too, the best of all possible Emulsions and we have over and over wish'd for it, and d thinks we might

---

872 The auction of the household goods of Major Fuller of Aylsham who was going to 'leave his situation' would be conducted at Aylsham by James Roofe on 15 and 16 March. (*The Norfolk Chronicle and Norwich Gazette*, Saturday, 12 March 1814, issue 2295, p. 2.)

873 By articles of agreement, dated 17 July 1813, Leonard, son of Ellen Shelford (widow), of North Tuddenham, was apprenticed to William Repton. John Bird and Dorothy Adey were witnesses to the articles, sworn before Samuel Shaw on 30 July 1814 and subsequently entered in the records of the court of King's Bench. (TNA, KB 105, Piece 24.)

874 Probably Nathaniel Kent's widow, Arminia (q.v.): Kent had lived in Fulham. Dorothy has definitely written 'Harriet'; perhaps Armina was known to friends as Harriet.

have a pint bottle put in a Basket and sent by Beasy directed to come by the old Bury coach. I shou'd think if Taylor has no objection to your sending us a prescription in a letter that wou'd be the best way, however I do assure you it is so totally different to the Emulsion little Edward had from Mr Andrews that we shou'd all like to have it right. I meant the flaps for your Father but this little bit is all he can have

ever most Affectionately yours D Adey

[*Humphry Repton*] A pint of Emulsion, a pint of Oxnead Cream would be better by half to make a pint of sending her my thanks for a hare & perhaps if she knew of this pint of Emulsion on the point of coming she would make a pint of not letting one pint bottle come without a Companion but dont put the contents of the two pint bottles got together in one quart, *cela n'yra point*

[*Elizabeth*][875] Aunt Adey should not have said the girls are not quite content. I feel it a most comfortable thing that let what will happen we have a Lease for 14 years.

[*Mary (Clarke) Repton*] Thank you for good Faces and hams. I conclude the Girls say you was too delicate to mention hams. John is gone to his Antiquarian meeting.[876]

Address: William Repton Esqr, Aylsham, Norfolk
B st: RUMFORD 12; Cross Post; *charge*: 9
HM 40892/2

177. Dorothy Adey to William Repton[877]

Harestreet, Thursday 24th [March 1814]

My dearest William

I take it for granted you was at Southwold when my last letter reach'd Aylsham or I am sure you wou'd have said if any thing was to be written to Black before you arrivd. your dear Father talk'd of it much at first, but another subject took possession of him afterwards.

the second morning after I arriv'd at Harestreet he sent for me into his room to tell me he felt so Giddy his bed turn'd round. I persuaded him to

---

875 The following two postscripts were written upside down at the top of the first page.
876 The Society of Antiquaries.
877 One letter written on three different days on the same sheet of paper.

get up and gave him Camphor and he was better, but as when stooping to put his head into the Basin of water he wou'd have fall'n if Sally had not prevented. we sent for Andrews, who said it proceeded from the stomach, and was of no consequence and he gave him salvolatile Litharge,[878] and by degrees the giddiness was forgotten. he had been at home and from bad weather unable to take exercise but was wanted at Wanstead[879] and at Earl Cambdens and fix'd yesterday to go to the former, and so to Town and Ld Cambdens and home next Monday, John to be with him. but ever since it has been thus setled he has thought of this said dizziness, and like all nervous people dreaded its return so that this I think accounts in some measure for his having enough of <it> *his giddiness* in a walk he took with John and me to the turnpike to alarm him, and he certainly was very queer all the day following and did not get his things about him as usual, and was shut up at Quadrille,[880] and not like himself, and we had all our fears of his not leaving home tho all were persuaded he wou'd be better for doing so.

fortunately Edward came down the night before and went with him and John, and he was better yesterday morning, and tho he did not leave us in comfortable spirits, yet he was not out of sorts as the day before, and a letter is come this morning to say he perform'd his journey vastly well, and stood the fag of between 3 and 4 hours walking at Wanstead. he rather flag'd when he came in but Mrs Edwards Relation Mrs Danvers (who took care of Georgina[sic] whilst her Father was at Wanstead) gave him a Glass of Wine & as soon made him himself again, and Edward said he was arriv'd at Robertsons[881] and quite comfortable and well. he found a letter there from Ld Cambden which Edward thinks when he sees his Lordsh'p this morning will postpone his journey for the present, and if so he will be at home tonight. Perhaps its as well it shou'd be so, and this time he will not mind the setting out from home, but upon my word it did [fb] did appear such an event I was sadly afraid it wou'd have been given up

---

878 Presumably a compound of smelling salts and litharge (protoxide of lead) to treat giddiness.

879 Wanstead House, the property of William Tylney Long Pole Wellesley. Repton had visited the property in 1813. (Daniels, *Repton*, p. 259, citing a letter in the Beineke Library, Yale University.) See also *Repton in London*, pp. 21–30; on p. 23 this particular letter is cited as evidence for Repton visiting Wanstead in June 1813; however, from its contents it is clear this letter falls within the sequence of letters written in March 1814, i.e. Repton was making one of several return visits.

880 Quadrille was a card game for 4 people.

881 i.e. Roberson's Hotel.

I hope you have got tho[*sic*] the fair Bustle[882] for I think you must want your Old Woman to take all idleers[*sic*] away from you. I wonder if you had the Ansons or if you have seen them for I promis'd Mr Charles I wou'd write to him when I had been here a fortnight, but I am in the dark as to where to direct. Mama has just call'd to say she is going down to breakfast, so God love you —

Sunday morning 27th

Your dear Father came home on <Wednesday> Thursday as Earl Cambden says he had rather see him after Easter.[883] He was the better for his out[ing] and came home in good spirits. once or twice when he thinks of it he talks of feeling dizzy, but not like what alarm'd us before. Dr Badderley (who visits old Page[884] every three days for water in the Chest) when your Mother in your Fathers absence on Wednesday said, what had hapned, told us he shou'd lose blood by Cupping if he was not against it, or leaches, or any how he lik'd, however you may be sure whilst he is free from fear he will not hear a word of bleeding. it seems he is very subject to bleeding at the Nose, and all say, they dont recollect any thing of the kind for a very long time. He goes to Wanstead to morrow, and Mrs William Wallenger and young Arnold[885] are coming hither for a week, the Girls go to their Friend Emma[886] on Wednesday, and your Father with Mr Wildman to some place that Gent[lema]n has purchas'd near Ongar;[887] I think Wildman is the man that is our Walkers brother in Law.[888] Somebody out of Dorsetshire wrote today for your Fathers Terms and if he cou'd go directly. he has said, yes, if he agrees to give him 100 G[uinea]s

---

882 One of Aylsham's two annual fairs was held on 23 March; the other was held on the last Tuesday in September. (*Aylsham Directories*, p. 1.)

883 Easter Sunday 1814 was 10 April.

884 Dr Badderley was presumably a local physician; Page is also mentioned in Letter 45.

885 Wallinger; the following letter says that they have arrived. Mrs William Wallinger was the wife of William, second son of John Arnold Wallinger (d.1792) and thus 'young Arnold' was William's son. (Searle and Brazier, *History of Hare Hall*, p. 11.) For Arnold see Letter 194 and the section on Repton's will in the Introduction.

886 Emma Potts, whose family lived near Hackney. (See Letter 179.)

887 Letter 178 confirms that the property in question was at 'the Rodings' in Essex. Henry Wildman (1733–1816) had property in Berners Roding and Margaret Roding, near Ongar, Essex. (ERO, D/DHt T223/8, dated 26 February 1802, Surrender of William Mills, of Bisterne, Hants., esq. to use of Henry Wildman, of London esq., of properties in Margaret Roding, near Ongar, Essex; ERO, D/DHf P5, Draft plans of Wildman's property in Berners Roding and Margaret Roding (in poor condition) (1807).)

888 Henry Wildman married Frances Walker in 1772. In 1791 they settled at The Knotts, Leyton. Henry had been an exporter to Jamaica in the 1770s. Frances died in February 1811, and Henry at Leyton in January 1816. (Information from John Phibbs.)

which is the sum he had a fortnight since from a Gent[lema]n in the same County[889] he will be with him next Monday.

can you read all this little account of what we are all about. thank you for telling what you are after. we all talk'd of you, and your two black Coats last night and agree'd you were all at Tradrille.[890] I am so beaten at Whist that I like our penny a fish pool of Quadrille best, but I am oblig'd to play Whist if Whist Gentry come to us. Mr James had sent a present of a delightful Stilton Cheese, but you must not eat it as we do at home, for your dear Mother has such a dread of Bile, that she begs and prays we will eat very little, for fear of being ill. I have heard of a variety of things hurting bilious people, but Stilton Cheese is not of the number, and tho we all eat what we like, we none of us eat near as much as Duff with all his Bile and his stomach Complaints.

I have been writing to Pearce and Dayrell this morning, and the latter I have by your Father & Mothers desire invited to Harestreet and to bring Martin with him,[891] and Harry Botham tells me he has also ask'd him to meet Mary and me at Haselwood.[892] He says there is no nearer way for me to get to him than through London, so I have written this morning to say, I shall defer my visit till the end of April because if we must go to London one journey thither had best do all. Edward has most kindly invited me to take a bed in Croford [Crawford] street, but I understand if I do so, I shall turn him and his Wife out of their room, and even for a Couple of nights I shou'd be sorry to do so. Mrs W. Wallenger has a spare room, and your Mother says, she may probably give me that, and she is quite in Edwards neighbourhood, but all this is at a distance, only that I like prating to you of all that is uppermost.

See also TNA, PROB 11/1576/494, will of Henry Wildman of Layton, Essex, dated 14 and 15 January 1816; proved 31 January 1816.

889 One of these gentlemen was probably Nicholas Gould of Stafford House, Frome Bilet, Dorset. Fragment XXI is 'From a report concerning Frome House, Dorsetshire, a seat of Nicholas Gould, esq.'. (*Fragments*, pp. 101–5, plus two illustrations.)

890 Tradrille was card game for 3 people.

891 Suggesting that she has written to John Dayrell of Lamport and asked him to bring John Dayrell Martin with him.

892 'In 1812 Henry Botham arrived at Hazelwood (in Abbots Langley, Herts) determined to build an impressive country seat for himself. The local estate he purchased was originally 43 acres. He and his wife built a very fine house and created an eventual estate of 72 acres with further purchases of adjoining land from the Earl of Essex.' Botham married Lydia Payne Mathew in 1788; he died in 1825; she died in 1838. (S. Hastie, *Abbots Langley: A Hertfordshire Village* (Abbots Langley, 1993), p. 45.) This *may* be a previously unknown Repton site but here only Mary and Dorothy would be visiting Botham.

I shou'd suppose you can have no better way of getting to Shugborough than from London, but I may be mistaken. If you pass thro Litchfield I trust you will remember poor Mrs Sneyd. I think if you had met with a Horse at the Fair or any where else you wou'd have said so, that is one of the things I shall be heartily glad to hear of. poor Flower, as one of the many that are sincerely attatch'd to you, I have a great regard for him and I by no means like to hear of his legs swelling, pray say how he does when you write.[893] I reach'd Romford yesterday for the first time and purchas'd Lambs wool [*fb*] to knit you a cap of your own, for it has often been on my conscience that I took mine away when you possibly wou'd have been glad of it. the half hour bell has gone and I shall go down and tomorrow before Mrs Wallenger comes I shall send you this full sheet. your dear Mother always likes to read my nonsense to you, I think this scrawl will vexe her a bit. Mrs Cookes letter was to enquire if I did not intend to visit Essex this Spring, and to hope they shou'd have the pleasure to see both you and me, but here I am in Essex, so God love you farewell till to morrow

Monday 4 oclock.

I have put on my things for dinner and before I go down I shall say a little more, but as I am afraid the <u>flaps</u> wont hold all I have to say on necessary matters, I shall begin here and finish as I find time. Your Mothers Peggy bottled her currant wine on Saturday, and mine must be done before the weather gets warm, and before you set out for Town, because tho you need not have any trouble as to bottling and corking, Betty Barnes will do all that, but you had best have it lock'd up in the Wine Cellar before you leave home, and the great Cask, and the small Cask, shou'd be kept separate, and the Elder and the mead be also drawn off. Jonathan I dare say will not forget to buy a Gross of corks when he goes for Eliza, and tho that will not do for all I hope, yet what more than 12 doz'n are wanted may be bought at Clovers, tho as his are just as dear, if Mrs John falls in your way before Eliza is sent for Jonathan may as well bring ½ a Gross more, she has sent another Hare which I beg of you to thank her for. we have not seen Edward since the Turkeys travell'd towards him —

I saw the Unicorn &c to be sold in last Norwich paper,[894] and that reminded me that ½ a years rent is due to Wade from the Widow Gray,

---

893 Unclear whether this is referring to Cook Flower, or a horse named 'Flower' (given the previous sentence).

894 The sale by auction of the Unicorn Inn, Aylsham, would take place on 5 April. The sale was with or without the four cottages in the yard, presently occupied by William Sayer, William Colman, the Widow Gray and Vincent Smith. The proprietor was Edmund Wade;

the half year is 2£ 5s but Stonham[895] is to pay a part and if you send Izzy or Mary he will give it to them and they may take a rec[eip]t for the whole half year to Mrs Gray. the Account of the Maidens wages is in the sideboard drawer, and I suppose they will be glad of their money at Lady Day. Pye & Riches[896] except they ask for it can wait till Mids[umme]r, they us'd always to send their Bill at the Quarter, but they get on in the world I suppose, for they have not done so lately. William Ulph[897] too may wait till I come home, but Booth[898] perhaps you had best call upon when ever you go to Norwich.

this is the time of year that a little Orange marmalade shou'd be put up. I generally put up a dozen but as sugar is dear eight will be sufficient, and four Lemons to add to the juice of the orange. Izzy knows how they shou'd be done but she must not forget to peel them thin as she did *forget* one year. I think the sugar here is much cheaper than ours, and I suppose in London it might be worth buying a few loaves. Best Tea is a great deal better than Mama has from Twining[899] and I should have lik'd to have orderd a Couple of [ƒ℔] pounds from our men, but Mary says it wou'd be very foolish to leave a man they have long dealt with, and so I have said no more of the matter. I am afraid by this time you stand in need of a fresh supply, if you order any it shou'd be 15 lb Sochong 6 lb of Mysore and I suppose 3 lb of Coffee will be enough, except you have had a great demand for it since I left you. the last account is ty'd up with others of Walkers & Mundy[900] in the marble drawer. there, now I think I wont plague you any more but you see I was right in fancying the flaps wou'd not be sufficient.

the auctioneer was James Roofe. (*The Norfolk Chronicle and Norwich Gazette*, Saturday, 26 March 1814, issue 2297, p. 2.)

895 Perhaps Thomas Stoneham, baker and confectioner, whose house/business was in the Market Place, Aylsham, in 1822. (*Aylsham Directories*, p. 7.)

896 Pye and Riches, haberdashers, London Lane, Norwich (*Norwich Directory for 1811*, p. 117.)

897 In 1821 William Ulph was living with his family in a house in Bond's Yard, Aylsham. (*Aylsham in 1821*, p. 17.) He was not listed in the 1822 edition of Pigot's *Directory*; in White's *Directory* (1836) a William Ulph was listed as a hairdresser living in Hungate Street. (*Aylsham Directories*, p. 22.)

898 Probably William Booth, bookseller and printer, Market Place, Norwich. (*Norwich Directory for 1811*, p. 79.)

899 In 1706 Thomas Twining began selling tea in a coffee house in the Strand. By 1717 he had acquired three adjacent houses and converted them to a shop, now 216 Strand, London. (https://www.twinings.co.uk/about-twinings/history-of-twinings.)

900 Munday and Walker, tea dealers, 73 Old Broad Street, London. (*Universal Directory* (1790), p. 236.)

Your Father and John are gone to Wanstead,[901] the Girls have been walking up to Mrs Heatons. Mrs William [Wallinger] and young Arnold are arriv'd. I expected from the Girls account to have seen a grubb of a school boy, but he is a tall gentlemanly looking young man, and eer long will be as tall as Leonard.[902] remember me to him, and I have no doubt but he will very soon be much pleas'd with his junior Clerk. Mrs William has brought a Turbot which we are to have to morrow.[903] Dont you wish to be of our party, if you dont I do for I shall be very very glad to see you again. a whole month to day my dear William since I left you. God bless you & all send love

ever yours most truly and affectionately   D Adey

Pray remember me to all the Maidens.   I dont mean to exclude old Izzy and young E[liz]a

Address: William Repton Esqr, Aylsham, Norfolk
B st: RUMFORD 12; Cross Post; *charge*: 9
HM 40892/3

178. Dorothy Adey to William Repton; Humphry Repton to William Repton; postscript from John Adey Repton

Harestreet, Tuesday 29 [March 1814][904]

My dearest William

Your dearest Father did not know of my sending you a letter yesterday & wants to know when I shall write again and wishes to say somthing in my letter, but does not seem inclin'd to begin and end one himself, and therefore as I have made a beginning it rests with him to add as much or as little as he pleases, and as the dinner & hour bell rings if he leaves me ever so much blank paper I shall not take any account of it *before* tomorrow,

---

901 'In 1814 it was said that [Long-Wellesley] was setting up Wanstead House to surpass Carlton House and that the interior was being transformed into a "uniform blaze of burnished gold". At the same time he was altering the park in preparation for a fête to celebrate his son's baptism and the return from the war of his uncle the duke of Wellington.' (*VCH Essex*, vol. 6, p. 326, citing H. Stead, 'Materials for the History of Wanstead House', pp. 71–2.)

902 Leonard Shelford.

903 See the following letter.

904 This letter was catalogued out of sequence among the letters written by Humphry Repton himself. It can be dated to March 1814 both because of the links with previous and following letters and because 29 March 1814 was a Tuesday.

11. First page of a letter from Dorothy Adey, with postscript from John Adey
Repton, HM 40881

but as he will be off directly after breakfast He shall have my letter tonight.
just as we were leaving the room below to adorn for Col Ferrier and Mr
James, who are invited to partake the Turbot, dear George step'd out of
a coach, but he talks of being off again tomorrow, all the good Boys save

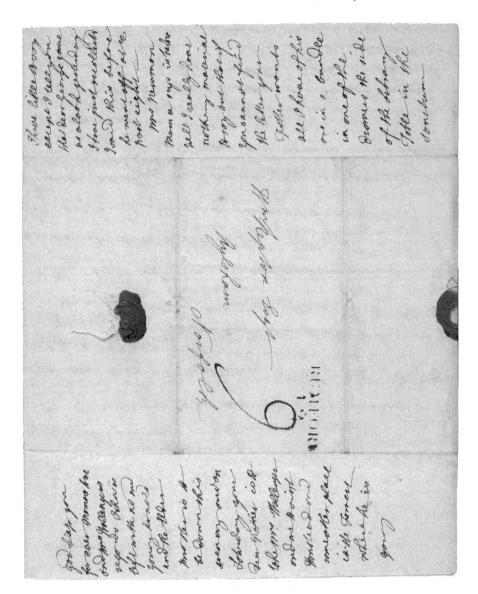

12. final page of a letter from Dorothy Adey showing address and flaps,
HM 40881

Duff (and he is in high good looks) are looking thin, and without rosy
cheeks. Edward improved upon me the second day, and when George has
shaked [*fb*] off his stage coach squeeze[*sic*] perhaps he will look more like
what I have been in the habit of seeing him, he puts me in mind of you

when you have fagg'd more than you ought – he says he wish'd he cou'd
have been with you during my absence. d: [Elizabeth] is astonish'd I shou'd
also wish it but I am sure I do for I think it wou'd have been comfortable
to both.

[*Repton*] What I wanted to say is – I wish you could find the Letter I wrote
about the first interview with HRH at Brighton because it would recall
to my memory much which I shall want for that Chapter[905] – & I have
nearly compleated my task – only that is wanting – & I am loth to trust to
recollection if any written document can be obtained written at the time –
so now Dee may tie on again & proceed with her knotting & splicing – I
am off to the Rodings a Wild part of Essex where I am going with a Mr
Wildman – – so God bless you – we are made very happy by having old Dee
& Young D with us & only want, we want but you, we want but you[906] [*fb*]
Apropos de bottes, tell Basey[907] I want a nu par o beutes & I want them
immediately my old ones are holy – but let him make 'em both alike, one
of mine is now an inch Longer than l'other[908] so one shews my stocking &
l'other not – but they are [?]puie large & easy to my feet – I wish I could say
as much of my Chest – but either wind or water eternally torment me & I
cannot describe what I feel – but I am determind to try a reduced system of
feeding & begin it to day – Dr James (our Mr James from the Barracks)[909]
says if I never eat but of one dish – I shall never eat too much – but I think
I eat too much of Mrs Wallingers Turbot yesterday – I eat it all up. Pray
thank Mrs John for a hare – it is the most acceptable of all game & the girls
take it with them to Potts's – who say they never get game from any body
but us so d & Mary are gone to make game of them for a week & wail over
Emma's virginity –[910]

[*fb*] [*Dorothy Adey*] God bless you for ever. Mamas love and Mrs Wallengers
regards. John is left with no one. Young Arnold and the Elder Brother is

905 This request to William refers to the section in Repton's memoirs about his various
visits to Brighton. William must have found a copy of the letter because the memoirs
include a transcript of a letter written by Repton following his first meeting with the Prince
Regent at Brighton. (*Memoirs*, pp. 145–54, letter on pp. 146–7.)
906 Perhaps this rather strange repetition is referring to a song?
907 Robert Basey/Beasey the Aylsham cordwainer and mail cart contractor.
908 Definitely 'l'other', not 't'other', i.e. pseudo French, as elsewhere in Repton's section of
this letter.
909 In 1795, during the Revolutionary War with France, barracks for six troops of cavalry
were built in London Road, Romford. They were demolished *c*.1825. (*VCH Essex*, vol. 7,
p. 63.)
910 Emma Potts was shortly to be married. (See Letter 179.)

to be down this evening and on Saturday your dear Father is to take Mrs Wallenger and me to visit Wanstead and some other place in the Forrest where he is going.

I have little to say except I tell you that dear George gave us a look yesterday. I have just recollected I said this before, he went off at ½ past eight –

Mrs Newman Mama says is below. Well I really have nothing material to say but that if you cannot find the letter your Father wants all I have of his are in a bundle in one of the drawers the side of the Library Table in the sanctum

[*John Adey Repton*][911] Dear William

I wish you could borrow the letters of Oliver Cromwell from Mr Sewell[912] to shew to the Society of Antiquaries – I will take great care of them & return them by you –

Your affectionate Brother John

Address: Wm Repton Esqr, Aylsham, Norfolk
B st: RUMFORD 12; *charge*: 9
HM 40881

179. Dorothy Adey to William Repton; Mary (Clarke) Repton to William Repton

[Hare Street], Tuesday April 5th [1814][913]

My dearest William

I want to hear from you, it is a very long time since you last wrote to us, a fortnight within two days, and your father wants to know if you have found the letter he has wrote about, and I want to tell you that in this place like all small ones there are tittle tattlers, and tho there is very probably not a word of truth in the nonsense Mrs Mott came over with yesterday, and which by the way we wou'd not tell to your Father, yet, I am very anxious to have the

---

911 Upside down, at the top of the first page.

912 NRO, AYL 1223, Index made by William Repton [n.d. *c*.1811] of clients and landholders includes William Sewell. These letters of Oliver Cromwell have not been identified.

913 This letter was catalogued out of sequence. Letters under the reference HM 40886 were written in 1808, apart from this and one other that were written in 1814. Tuesday 5 April occurred in 1814 (and in 1803). The postscript by Mary (Clarke) Repton refers to the fall of France (see footnote 920).

agreement with old Black setled. she came on Sunday to tell your Mother, that she hoped Mr Repton wou'd not lay out a great deal of money on the place for she was afraid he wou'd not have it as he expected "for I saw Mr Sterry Yesterday, and I told him how glad I was to hear Mr Repton was to continue at Harestreet, and Mr Sterry said, aye a little while, o! says I, Mr Repton told me he was to have a 12[914] years lease, he will be mistaken in that I fancy says Mr Sterry".[915] Your mother said very little to her, I believe only said it wou'd be all understood when her son William came, and so you may be sure we are [fb] fidgetty for fear this old man shoud go from his word.

we did not look for the Girls to be home till tomorrow night, but this morning's post has brought one from Mary to say, Emma Potts will be married next week,[916] and they feel themselves in the way of her engagements, and desire to have a Chaise sent for them to be at Hackney at 12 oclock on Monday, and today is Tuesday, and the doubt is if a Chaise is to go or not. your Father thinks not finding one sent yesterday they will take one from Hackney this morning and there will be two Chaises to pay for, how it is to be determin'd I dont know, but the letter was intended to be here on Sunday morning, dated Saturday, and either too late or was neglected to be sent, so they will be in a fine mess.

Your dear Father is expecting Mr Greenwood to take him to Sudbury today,[917] which I am heartily glad of for He is by no means what I like, and yet I hope there is nothing materially amiss, but with such an oportunity of consulting with Dr MacLean I am sure we were right in preventing Andrews putting Leaches on his neck Yesterday, he scarcely ceases complaining either of Giddiness, oppression on the Chest or old pains and achs.

Wednesday morning[918]

[*Mary (Clarke) Repton*] You will be surprized my dear William to see my hand writing but your Dear Aunt Adey is off for Sudbury with your Father,

914 The number in the reported speech is '12'; 'a fourteen years Lease' is discussed above in Letter 176.

915 Sterrys and Tweed were attorneys, based in Hornchurch Lane, Romford. (Pigot's *Directory* (1823), p. 63.) Benjamin Wasey Sterry was born 9 April 1767 at Shenfield, Essex; died 28 May 1830, buried in family vault, St Edward's Romford, 3 June 1830. (ERO, T/G 52/5 Pedigree of Sterry of Eastbury House, Barking, Essex and Poltimore Rectory, Devon.)

916 Emma married Henry Warburton at St John's, Hackney, on 14 April 1814. (LMA, P79/JN1/054.)

917 A return visit to Charles Greenwood's property of Auberies at Bulmer.

918 Written by Dorothy.

[*fb*] Mr Greenwood has just been here to fix his going to him tonight or to-morrow morning, and he said he thought he shoud set out to night but how he shoud go he coud not determine, whether by a Coach or take a Chaise; I did not like his going in a Chaise by himself, and John did not seem to like going, as he had no Cushin or any thing to sit upon, and many objections, I proposed Aunt to go with him, and she jumpt at it and said she should like it of all things, for she shoud see her old friends, Sir La and his Lady[919] – so they have eat cold meat, and are gone – as I said before – poor John is a little ashamed at his refusal, the girls are gone to Town with Mrs W. Wallinger and come back at night – to bag in a Carpet – as we are nothing but shags and tatters. Aunt A is rather disappointed at not hearing from you today, but we trust and hope all is well; let us hear, and tell us when we are likely to see you – come as soon as you can, and stay as long as you <u>possibly</u> can with us, as you may be assured of will make your affectionate Mother happy.

Your affectionate Mother   M Repton

[*fb*] Good news from Town: the Allies *are* <have France> are in possession of France. The Empress and her son are fled – and gone[920]

Address: W. Repton Esqr, Aylsham, Norfolk
B st: RUMFORD 12; Cross Post; *charge*: 9
HM 40886/14

180. Dorothy Adey to William Repton

Harestreet, [Saturday] April 9th [1814][921]

My dearest William

Your dear Mothers letter will have told you of my journeying 50 Miles nearer to Old Aylsham than I now am. what Dr Mac'lean says of your dear Father I will communicate when we meet. the purport of this present letter is to beg you to give me a line of where you are for all the way from Sudbury I travell'd with the hope of reading a letter from you when I arriv'd as it is three days more than a fortnight since I have heard. we fancy you may

---

919 Dr Lachlan MacLean and his wife.
920 Marie Louise, Archduchess of Austria, (1791–1847) and her son Napoleon Francis Joseph Charles (1811–1832) fled France following the unconditional abdication of Napoleon on 6 April. Alexander I of Russia and Frederick William III of Prussia had entered Paris on 31 March.
921 Just after Dorothy's visit to Sudbury mentioned in the previous letter.

have perhaps taken your journey into [fb] Staffordshire but except you went with the Ansons I say you wou'd not go till you come from thence to Town, however if you are at home when this arrives write if it is but ten words to let us know if all is well. Your Mothers letter ought to have been at Aylsham on Thursday and this morning we might have heard but not having a letter and knowing you will be engag'd in Parish matters the begining of the next week I am almost sure this will find you at home

Your Father and I slept at the Inn at Sudbury Wednesday and Thursday, drank Tea at Mac'leans that evening and breakfasted with them next morning and when Your Father went to Mr [fb] Greenwoods I took Horses and the doctor's <eldest> *second* daughter, a very pretty good temper'd Girl, went to Mr Cookes at Semer (eleven miles) dind there and returnd and met my dear Brother at M'Leans in thevening.[922] Yesterday morning I accompany'd him to Mr Greenwoods and whilst He was engag'd with the Laborours[923] I went to Church with Mr Greenwood and his neice[sic][924] a very agreeable and well bre<a>d Woman of four or five & twenty, who knew the <Lilfords> Powis's[925] and had seen Mrs Doughty there. At two Mr Greenwood orderd what he call'd a hot Luncheon for your father and me but which I call'd a very excellent dinner of Soup Salt Fish *hot* Chicken Cold Beef and Tarts. we came off about three and got home at nine in the evening, your dear Father pleas'd with my company and I happy to go with him.

a letter found at home from you wou'd have been an additional *pleasure* but I trust and hope all is going well, and will be content till I get one. Duff is with us. George comes to morrow & goes with John on Monday to Ld Darnleys.[926] Edward and his Wife were to have come down on Monday by a Coach for the week, but your Father has written to day to say he will go in a Chaise on Monday if Edward will go on with [fb] him to Ld Cambdens

---

922 Dr MacLean and Mr Cooke of Semer had married sisters. (See Letter 97.)

923 Indicating that Repton was advising on work in progress at Mr Greenwood's property in April 1814.

924 'Yesterday' was Good Friday, hence they went to church. Charles Greenwood's sister was Ann Hammersley; her daughters included Frances b.1788 and Charlotte b.1789.

925 Thomas Powys, second baron Lilford of Lilford (1775–1825), resided at Lilford Hall (Northants). (www.thepeerage.com/p3652.htm#i36513); brother of Ann Doughty.

926 Humphry Repton's work for Lord Darnley (q.v.) at Cobham Hall lasted from 1790 to 1816. In 1816 he wrote 'Whether we consider its extent, its magnificence, or is comfort, there are few places which can vie with Cobham ... and none which I can mention, where so much has been done, both to the house and grounds, under my direction, for so long a series of years'. (*Fragments*, p. 10.)

for a few days,[927] and Mrs Edward and Mr Hoskens[928] may return in the Chaise to Harestreet and if I chose I might go up and return but I do not, so Mary and d [Elizabeth] will one of them go with him, and so knowing what we are all about, I will say fare well

I shall write to Eliza today, that is I shall finish a letter I have began and I mean to direct it to Aylsham as I dare say on Sunday some one will be up from Oxnead. God love you. To hear you are well and to find Dr Mc'Leans directions <u>follow'd</u> by your Father are alone working to make completely happy

Yours ever affectionately   D Adey

Address: William Repton Esqr, Aylsham, Norfolk
B st: RUMFORD 12; Cross Post; *charge*: 9
HM 40892/4

181. Humphry Repton junior to William Repton; Dorothy Adey to William

2nd Edition <u>Star Office</u>   <u>April 9</u>[929]
Two Deputies are arrived from Dunkirk
Buonaparte has abdicated the Throne —[930]
The Bourbons proclaimed –
Louis 18th King – [931]
All prisoners immediately to be liberated

<u>3rd Edition</u> – 4 o'clock
Dispatches from Ld Castlereagh at Paris stating that B[uonaparte] had

---

927 In April 1814 in a letter to Lord Camden, apparently written after his visit to Bayham, Repton explained that following his carriage accident he was 'no longer able to "scramble thro' the thickets" but in truth he could see no need for such exertions: re-reading this Red Book, he found no changes to make and could "only repeat and confirm what he had written fifteen years ago"'. (*Repton in Kent*, p. 94, quoting from Repton's letter of April 1814, no reference given.) In November 1814 Repton did, however, submit a new hand-written, loose-leaved unillustrated report written while at Bayham in April. (*Repton in Kent*, p. 94.)

928 Not identified.

929 These notes taken from newspapers have been written by Humphry junior.

930 Repton published a 'sermon' which was prompted by the abdication of Napoleon on 6 April 1814 and which he suggested could be preached on 'Sunday, the 17th of April, being the first Sunday after Easter, 1814'. (*The Work of Twenty Years*, p. iii.)

931 Louis de Bourbon (1755–1824); he had spent twenty-three years in exile (1791–1814); proclaimed King Louis XVIII on 6 April 1814.

consented to abdicate the Throne of France & to retire to the Island of Elba –

The Messenger came direct from Paris to Calais – B was at Fontainbleau & placed under a strong guard to protect him from the rage of the populace –

[*fb*] Caulincourt[932] & Hulin[933] the murderers of the Duc D'Enghien[934] have been imprisoned in the Castle of Vincennes by order of Alexander[935] to await the pleasure of Louis 18th – Victor[936] & all the other Generals near Paris have offered their services to the new Government –

[Hare Street], Sunday [Easter Day, 10 April 1814]

Dear William

I am now at this moment writing you a <u>long letter</u>[937] in which I shall enclose the thing you sent to me to sign and George will take it tomorrow for Ld Darnley and you will find it at home when you return from Southwold but the News is so good this morning that we all think you will be glad to get it, and Duff as the paper belongs to Balls[938] has been so good as to coppy it. so God bless you and thank you for the letter we have had this morning and which I am thanking you for in the letter from Ld Darnleys. all well

yours ever   DA

Address: William Repton Esqr, Aylsham, Norfolk
B st: RUMFORD 12; Cross Post; *charge*: 9
HM 40928

---

932 Arnaud-Augustin-Louis de Caulaincourt (1773–1827), soldier, diplomat, and loyal aide to Napoleon.

933 Pierre Auguste Hulin (1758–1841), Bonapartist general who presided over the commission which found duc d'Enghien guilty of treason and ordered his execution.

934 Louis Antonie, duc d'Enghien (1772–1804), Bourbon prince, whose execution shocked European opinion.

935 Alexander I, tsar of Russia (1777–1825).

936 Victor Claude Victor-Perrin, duc de Belluno, (1764–1841), marshal of France under Napoleon, but who had switched his allegiance to the Bourbon dynasty.

937 See next letter.

938 A resident of Hare Street; by May 1816 the Ball family had left the village. (See Letter 200.)

182. Dorothy Adey to William Repton

Hare Street, Sunday 10th [April 1814]

My ever dear William

George join'd our fireside yesterday and is going with John to Ld Darnleys tomorrow from whom (he says) he can get a frank, and as I suppose you wish to have the enclos'd by the time you get home from Southwould I have accepted his offer of sending it to you from <thence > *Ld Darnley's*

I am afraid you will be angry with me for writing to you so directly after the letter your good Mother sent off in my absence, but you know when I am at home if I am a little unreasonable sometimes, I have nobody to encourage my nonsense, and here the case is different. you are a person of such consequence with the whole of the family party that a letter from you is as anxiously expected by every one as by myself, and, "any letters from Norfolk Sally" I have heard from the Girls in the Trel<l>iss room, and the room of your Mother morning after morning for some time, and your Father who is more fidgetty than ever thought you were gone into Staffordshire, and I declare when a second Coach stop'd yesterday (just after George came) and a [fb] smart looking Man jump'd from the Box, my heart too jump'd, and I turnd from the window to welcome <u>my own William</u>, but the coach <u>not</u> going on, I stop'd and saw a smart miss in a Buff satin pelisse get out of the Coach and budge down the Hornchurch Lane, so I sat me down content and went on with the letter I sent off by last nights post, and if we had had patience to have waited one day more, I need not *have* troubld you to read my nonsense.

I shou'd suppose E: Bulwers confinement is the happiest thing that can befall Miss Bulwer, but of course she does not think so, I wonder what he has done with his Children, left them with her I suppose.[939]

I shoud hope that foolish Bar[one]t will not have it in his power to do you any real Mischief, but it is not pleasant to meet with obstacles of any kind, surely he can have but little property to be affected but the enclosure *but* when a fool is at enmity with anyone <u>to oppose</u> the wishes of the person he is displeas'd with is an object, and perhaps the dislike S[i]r Thomas has to Billy Lubbock is the ground work of his opposition.[940]

---

939 Not identified: there were various people named Bulwer in the Aylsham area and the Bulwers were the major landed family at Heydon.

940 A reference to the enclosure bill on which William was currently working: Skeyton, Burgh and Tuttington. William Lubbock (q.v.) had been one of John Repton's executors and lived at Lamas. 'Sir Thomas' is Sir Thomas Durrant (1775–1829), second baronet, of

We shou'd like to know if you go to Town before you come hither or if we are to see you first because Mary has an invitation to pass a week or 10 days with Mrs Jederee,[941] and she wou'd like to manage so as to <be> *end her visit* there at the time I pass thro London to go to Harry Botham, and she cannot write to her friend, or I to Harry till we know somthing of your motions for we both determine to be at Harestreet <u>when you are</u>, you may be sure, and we shou'd like to know if you approve of our being in Town for two or three days whilst you are there, and if you do like it, whether you have any objection to our taking a couple of rooms, which all say is less expensive than a Hotel. I rather hop'd Mrs William Wallenger might have given Mary and me a Bed but it seems she is expecting Mr & Mrs Joseph [Wallinger] up from [fb] Gainsborough and of course reserves it for them. Dear Edward and his Wife are very anxious for my taking their bed, but it is literally <u>their bed</u> for they woud sleep uncomfortably if I accepted the offer, and tho I feel their kindness, I cannot think of it, beside, all tell me it is a prodigious way from shops &c I want to go to, and also so out of your way, that we shou'd stand no chance of seeing you. I am dispos'd if you like it to get Duff look out for somthing in the neighbourhood of the Adelphi, or in some of the streets on the left hand side the Strand that go down to the water. it cannot be as expensive as in any of the streets in the grander part of the Town, and I want nobody to call upon me the day or two I am there, and as I must take it they say for a week three days in that week I can go and make my visit in Herts.[942] so tell <you> *us* how you like we shou'd settle all this, and when you are to be here, or to be in London, and we shall write our letters accordingly —

Our Sudbury Trip was so totally unexpected by me, that I was quite hurried to put what was necessary together in time to be ready for your Father, and hurried down a peice of Cold Meat as quick as I cou'd, S[i]r Lh Maclean was out when the note went to say we wou'd take Tea with them. Lady M'Lean receiv'd us with her usual coldness, but in <u>her way</u> was I have no doubt realy glad to see me, and when the Dr came home he three times repeated his request, that she wou'd consider we shou'd be glad of

---

Scottow. (See Letter 184.) There are many papers about this dispute in NRO, AYL 547. See also NRO, AYL 483, letters of William Repton concerning Skeyton, Burgh and Tuttington, 1813–1815.

941 This name is unclear. Here it looks like 'Mrs Jederee'; it is the same surname as that which occurs as 'the Jedderes' in Letter 183, written by both Repton and Elizabeth. In 1811 John Jeddre esq. was residing at 31 Park Street, Grosvenor Square. (*London & County Directory* (1811).)

942 To Harry Botham's house.

somthing <u>substantial</u> for our supper, and as she took herself out of the room, we expected at least, a mutton Chop, or Veal Cutlet but an untidy looking servant brought in a tray upon a Dirty Cloth, a Stilton Cheese so high your Father order'd it out of the room, and four Eggs boil'd in the shell nearly hard enough for a sallad, and this with a bit of old dry bread was [fb] our <u>substantial</u> supper. We had good beds at the Inn and a shy[943] breakfast of Cocoa and bad Tea at the Drs next morning, a most wonderful difference in the houses of the two sisters.[944] When I arrived at Semer, Mr Cooke was rode to Hadleigh, and Mrs Cooke and Mary walk'd out, Mary Mac'Lean went with me and the servants told her where their mistress was gone, so we walked to meet her, and nothing on Earth cou'd be more happy than she appear'd *to seem* and He at his return equally so, and so very pressing for my stay it was with difficulty I cou'd persuade them my Brother wou'd be uncomfortable not to see me, if I wou'd send back the post Horses they wou'd send theirs next morning with me to Sudbury in time for breakfast; but I wou'd not have sufferd your Father to have been at the Inn alone on any account. Their dinner hour was five, but the Cook was order'd to have it ready as much sooner as she cou'd, and we sat down to it exactly as <u>we do</u>, if any one came in without alteration or bustle all clean and neat, the house like New and the Garden without a weed. he has he says on his late acquisition taken a Gardener into the House, which he has long wanted. I find from MacLean that He is left joint Exe[cutor] and Residuary legatee with a Neice of Mrs Brand's,[945] and that his share will not amount to less than 15,000 £. The old Lady left S[i]r Lacland 300£ as a present for his kind attention beside paying liberally every time he went to her, in her long and painful illness.

The Cookes gave me a Quarter of Pork to bring home to your Mother, and beg'd of me to assure you the pleasure it wou'd give them if you cou'd ever make it convenient to visit Semer, and I am very sure they mean what they say. if any pork is to be had at Aylsham I wish they wou'd send some small *pork* hither, and if the man I have <chickens> *pigeons* of has any ready we shou'd be very glad of them or in short of any[946] you can find to make up a basket. Mary says she willingly pays carriage for any thing she has given her, for all saves butchers bills and I am sure Butchers

943 The word here is 'shy', presumably meaning 'meagre, poor quality'. The *OED* gives a definition of 'shy' as 'doubtful in amount or quality', but the first mention is dated 1821.
944 i.e. Lady MacLean and Mrs Cooke.
945 Not identified.
946 Remainder written upside-down at the top of the first page.

Bills must be enormous here. are Mrs <u>Planes</u>[947] Turkeys all gone, or are there Chickens to be had and if there is a chance of a basket coming let the Cook if she can get one hash a Calves head and put into a Bladder the night before the basket comes and pack it up. d: [Elizabeth] <u>longs</u> for hash calves head. You must give her a Glass of Wine to add to the sauces and spice.[948]

HM 40892/5

Dear Duff is just come in and has seen what I have said. he says you know he has a large bed and he is sure it is the very thing in the world for us, in short he is so good to say he will not have me <u>think</u> of lodgings and he will give us his bed and can as a single man take care of himself. this is monstrous kind and good and an offer that if you have no objection I am sure I shall most gladly accept. so write and tell me that you approve and the thing is setled at once. the Girls are gone to Church with George.

Your Father and John, who is as you may suppose all alive about the hams, are writing in the study,[949] and your Mother & Duff here with me and join their love with that of
   yours affectionately D Adey

Address: Rochester April twelve 1814,[950] Wm Repton Esqr, Aylsham, Norfolk, Clifton[951]
B st: ROCHESTER [?]23; *r st*: FREE 13 AP 13 1814
HM 40891

---

947 Edward Plane lived near Pound Lane, Aylsham. (*Aylsham in 1821*, p. 19.)

948 Dorothy's letter, which is number 5 in the sequence of the 8 letters that have been catalogued under the reference HM 40892, ends here. There is no valediction or recipient's address. This unfinished letter was written on a folded sheet of paper of the usual size. She completed the letter in the document catalogued as HM 40891, which comprises a torn sheet of paper (half the usual size); the recipient's address is on the reverse.

949 In the next letter Elizabeth says that her father was working on his book, i.e. *Fragments on the Theory and Practice of Landscape Gardening (including some Remarks on Grecian and Gothic Architecture)* (London, 1816).

950 Posted from Lord Darnley's, as anticipated in the first part of this letter.

951 Lord Darnley had the title baron Clifton; he had provided a free frank.

183. Humphry Repton to William Repton; Elizabeth Repton to William Repton

[Hare Street, undated; late April 1814]⁹⁵²

The Case of Sally —
Sarah Gibbs the widow of James Gibbs – who died leaving two sons by a former marriage – one 11 – the other 9 years old, a house decently furnished, some Cloaths, but no Money nor securities *& made no Will* – His Mother claims all the furniture for the two boys – Qu[ery]: has not the Widow a right to her thirds of the same for herself & Little girl – or has she a right to any thing more – & by what means can she best secure what is her right. Would a letter from you as her attorney be of use. as we all wish that she should have justice done we should be glad of your advice & opinion as soon as you can conveniently send it, to prevent these people from taking what may be her due –

Sally says he gave her a watch – which they claim. must she give it up? —

We go on much as usual – times bad – health not worse – Mary gone to town with Jedderes for a few days which we hope will give her pleasure. Dee returned saucy as ever & too idle to add P.S. so I shall save half a sheet of a paper

God bless you   HR

[*fb*]⁹⁵³ D is not "too idle my dearest William to write a postscript" for I certainly shall not suffer this to go without my thanks for the very pretty *gown* which I find on my return from London, they will be most useful and pretty dresses for us, and just the sort of thing we were in want of. I shall make it according to the last new fashion, but not too fine for your taste, as I know you are an admirer of plain dressing – what would you say to the London ladies? their finery and furbelows perfectly astonished my weak nerves. I have had a most delightful visit in Town and am very glad dear Mary has also an opportunity to join in its gaieties. Her inducement to return with the Jedderes was a Fair to be held to day in Mr Ruckers park at Wandsworth.⁹⁵⁴ I fancy it will consist of ladies performances which are

---

952 This letter has been assigned to late April 1814 because both Repton and Elizabeth mention Mary going to town with the Jedderes as proposed in Letter 182.

953 Elizabeth's letter has been written in several blocks around the address panel.

954 Daniels (*Repton*, p. 268) states that Repton had been consulted by 'David Rucker', the German owner of West Hill, Wandsworth, before 1803, when a drawing was published in the *Polite Repository*. Repton also recalled meeting 'David Rucker' in his *Memoirs* (pp. 130–1). However, the section in *Repton in London* on West Hill (pp. 66–8) notes that the owner who commissioned Repton was Johann Anton Rucker (1719–1804). Indeed the

to be sold for the benefit for some charity. They expect a public breakfast and perhaps dancing so that it will be a gay thing and she will meet all her old friends, but I doubt this rain will destroy much of their pleasure. I hope you will be able to give us some consolation for Poor Sally as she is in sad distress and I am interested in securing the rights of my little God daughter.

Dear Papa seems upon the whole better than when I left home but it is sad work to see him wandering about the garden all day without employment or amusement except his book, which will not last for ever.[955] Mama is quite herself and still busy about her patchwork –

Give my love to Aunt Adey and tell her I will answer her entertaining long letter soon, and give my love to the Churchills if any are with you. Bessy Wilson[956] is kindly come to fill Mary's place and she desires to be kindly rememberd at Aylsham

Ever dearest William your most Affectionate D

P.S. Have you any objection to our new gowns being made like Mary Wyatts as hers is quite the thing, 6 rows of flounces just above the calf, the back an inche and half in depth and sleeves about 3 yards wide – an early answer to these queries will oblige as I am impatient to begin my gown.

Address: To Wm Repton Esq or Mrs Adey &c &c &c, Aylsham, Norfolk
B st: RUMFORD 12; Cross Post; *charge*: 9
HM 40880

184. Dorothy Adey to William Repton

Harestreet, April 29th [1814]

My dearest William

I am mortify'd that things do not go on smoothly in your Enclosure business as I had hope'd, and untill we meet and I hear all about it I can have no idea how enclosing Skeyton and Burgh, <u>can possibly affect Scottow</u>, but we shall know all in time, and I only hope and pray that after my long sojourn from home you will not have to fetch me without some one to pay the Piper.

---

caption of the drawing in the *Polite Repostory* says 'Westhill, Surrey, Seat of J. A. Rucker Esq'. As Repton described 'David Rucker' as 'a venerable bachelor of nearly 80 years old', it seems likely that he and Johann Anton Rucker were the same person. By the time that Mary visited in 1814 the owner was Daniel Henry Rucker, the previous owner's nephew. A survey of 1809 shows the house, 5 acres of garden and 25 acres of parkland.

955 That is, the manuscript of *Fragments on the Theory and Practice of Landscape Gardening*.

956 Not identified.

and before I go any farther with my letter, your dear Mother is looking forward to the anniversary of her Wedding day next Thursday the 5th, she will have been married 40 years[957] and Black is written to for a Plum and a sweetmeat Cake, and I am to be sure to tell you without you as well as the Cakes with us, half our joy will be lost, so be here on the 5th without fail and give me a line on the day you get this to say what morning [fb] a bed is to be prepard for you and it shall be ready, and come within and not withoutside a Coach these cold nights.

I say that you will if your Bill goes on be oblig'd to be in Town I think before the 4th as I have an idea of that being the day to finish Enclosure business in parliam[en]t.[958] How yours has been going on all this time without you I cannot conceive, but I suppose Mr somthing beginning with a:d: settles it all.[959] Mary Bulwer[960] says S[i]r Jacob[961] has been very ill. what has this to do with you, Mama will say, when she reads my letter but it is a concatenation of ideas which I must explain to her.

I shou'd like to have been with you in Mr Mays Green house. Florists make no scruple of beging. I hope you carried a rose plant or two home with you —[962] Your dear Father has been making a new basket or two of flowers on his Grass and no wheels have touch'd them yet. I have said nothing positively to H: Botham yet, but I have said enough on first coming hither, to make it necessary for me to go there for two days before I return, whether you have business in Town or not, and therefore I shall let writing alone till I hear what is to be.

[fb] On the rec[eip]t of your letter a fortnight ago, Mary fixd her London visit, and it ends tomorrow, and your Father and d: [Elizabeth] are to go for her. I had the offer, but having given dear Edward the trouble of feasting me one day, as I was right glad to have a look at them all, I dont think it is right to repeat my visit too often. they were very kind and good and still wou'd fain persuade me to accept *of* their apartment <but> I feel their kindness but have refused –

---

957 Humphry Repton and Mary Clarke married on 5 May 1773; Dorothy states the wrong anniversary year. See the next letter, where Mary (Clarke) Repton says that it is their 41st anniversary. In 1814 5 May was a Thursday, so this letter was definitely written in 1814.

958 Local and Personal Act, 54 George III, c. 37. See note to Letter 175 for details.

959 Mr Ad…..; or, something beginning with a D.

960 Mary Bulwer (1759–1821), sister of Augustine (q.v.).

961 Sir Jacob Astley (q.v.).

962 Mr May has not been identified; he might have been someone the family knew who had a greenhouse, or he might have had a commercial nursery. There is likely no candidate in the *Universal Directory* (1790) or in the *Post Office Annual Directory* (1808).

the Cooks din'd here on Monday in their way to town, they have taken a House in Maddox Street, Hanover Square, have their own carriage and three servants, and have engag'd it for three weeks, and they were very pressing for Mary and me to have a bed that they, by putting their own Mary into a smaller one <they> coud give us without the least inconvenience, and were very desirous we shou'd accept, but I thank'd them too and refus'd. I had rather go to Duffs lodgings than any where, and you must take care of him where you may be, poor fellow he was far from well last week, and tho he went away <u>better</u> than he came he was not at all the thing when he left us, and I shall be glad to see him come home well to morrow.

Your dear Father is on the whole I think better, but he is far from right. You will be delighted with a letter he has had from <u>his</u> good doctor and the rules he has given as to regimen <u>I mean to follow myself</u>, so you may be prepar'd to be plagued with me for the next score years at least. Duff never saw Mr Cooke before and is excessively pleas'd with him, so much so that after they had left us he said 'you may depend Mrs Adey I pay a visit to that Gentleman as soon as ever I get [*fb*] to Town. His manners are most Gentlemanly.'

Duff had been so good to get a friend engage places at the house above a month ago for the 3ᵈ of May and the 26ᵗʰ and till he heard from you wou'd not determine which to give up or if either.[963] there is no chance for the Cooks getting a Box to see Keen during the <month> three weeks they stay, and Duff is to do a handsome thing and let them have the 3ᵈ of May places instead of giving them to any body else.[964]

d went to Marshall[965] on <Wednesday> *Tuesday* and is to be home to dinner to day, so we old folks with the exception of John have been the fireside party of late, and play Tradrille every night. papa & mama did not win but bamboozled me out six fish on Wednesday, so last night I made them remember it by winning 3s 6d of the Gentlefolk. God bless you

Yours affectionately D Adey

---

963 Referring to obtaining seats for performances at Drury Lane Theatre. In 1807 Claude Scott had made over to Duff perpetual admission to that theatre. (See Letter 9.)

964 Referring to a performance by the actor Edmund Kean (*c.*1787–1833). 'In 1814 Kean astonished fellow actors and audience with a performance more powerful, Hazlitt wrote, "than any we have almost ever witnessed". Kean's unprecedented popularity saved the ailing Drury Lane from bankruptcy. His performances were celebrated for their frenzied, tempestuous emotion and for sudden, unexpected transitions between contrasting moods. In Richard III, perhaps his finest role, Kean was full of ironic contempt and sardonic humour …'. (Biography of Kean in *Oxford Companion to Theatre and Performance*, current online version: 2010 eISBN: 9780191727917.)

965 Not identified.

Address: William Repton Esqr, Aylsham, Norfolk
B st: RUMFORD 12; Cross Post; *charge*: 9
HM 40892/6

185. Dorothy Adey to William Repton; Mary (Clarke) Repton to William

[Hare Street], Tuesday 3ᵈ May [1814]

My dearest William

I write but little because probably you may not be at home to get my letter and probably your business may oblige you to go to Town before we see you and as Mary says Mrs W Wallenger she thought appear'd to be very anxious for your arrival & I have some fears that without your knowing this you may very likely postpone seeing her till you make a longer stay there. I think it is not amiss to write on purpose that you may give her a call.

Mr & Mrs Joseph [Wallinger] Mary says are expected to day. [*fb*] The Boys all know of the 5ᵗʰ but how many or if any are to be with us there is no saying. we shall be glad to see all that can join us. I hope poor old Sally will think of her loss as it really is <one> for unhealthy as the young man was his life must ever have been a precarious one and his death is what you say, a happy release.⁹⁶⁶

What a Goose you are to talk of Mead not having sugar enough, who ever thought of putting one atom into mead.⁹⁶⁷ thank you for your letter and your inclination to be with us, kindness to the Cookes, and H:B:⁹⁶⁸ and I am

ever Yours affectionately D A

Pray tell Izzy I shall send a Basket of Linnen (that I do not want *to be sent* here again on Sunday) directed to her, and she may let Mrs [*fb*] *Bell*⁹⁶⁹ Wash them. Dinner is going on & the Letters will be call'd for

[*Mary (Clarke) Repton*] You will be surprized, my dearest William, when I tell you what a hearty old Woman I am grown lately, and that I expect to be

---

966 See Letter 183.
967 Mead was made by adding honey to water, together with spices other ingredients, and then leaving it to ferment. See, for example, Elizabeth Raffald, *The Experienced English Housekeeper* (1769; reprinted 1997), pp. 171–2.
968 Harry Botham.
969 See note to Letter 152.

as gay and young as I was <thir> – 41 – years <back> ago. I have invited a party for next Thursday, and shall feel compleatly happy if you *are* able to join us. I am sure all of us will be delighted. I need not say dear Aunt Adey amongst the rest. God bless you says

your affectionate Mother M Repton

Adress: William Repton Esqr, Aylsham, Norfolk
B st: RUMFORD 12; Cross Post; *charge*: 9
HM 40892/7

186. Dorothy Adey to William Repton

Harestreet, May 9th Monday [1814]

My dearest William

Before I left home I had made up my mind to being absent from you for two Months but from the little smattering of law (Enclosure Law I mean) that I have I thought longer you cou'd not avoid attending to have the Bill pass'd, and when you wrote me word you shou'd be in Town about the 20th of April I hop'd all was going on well. the provoking business of the Ideot Bar[one]t[970] has all along annoyd us and we are afraid will in the end <will> knock up the Enclosure intirely, but to be told this at once, will ease our fidgets, and prevent the constantly listening to morning Mails and watching five o'clock dinner Coaches [*fb*] day after day, therefore if you are not on the road when this arrives at Aylsham write directly and on Thursday we shall know what we have to expect.

Bring Monday and Walkers last Tea bill with you. I had three lb of Tea from them since <they> *I* have been here and at the bottom of their letter they say no Tea has been sent to Aylsham since August. I had no idea it cou'd have been so long but what you can have substituted for Tea is my wonder, for I am sure two pounds was the utmost I left you.

Old Black has buried his housekeeper and it what people calls, "takes upon him", and the sooner we take him at his word the better, so that is another reason why we want to know when our Lawyer comes to us, and before you come thank Mrs John for a pike a very excellent one and at the same time say I will bring home the baskets.

One happiness I trust has attended the delay of your arrival, you will find your dear father comparatively better than I found him on Thursday

---

970 Sir Thomas Durrant (q.v.).

(the anniversary). He certainly fed luxuriously and to that I hope may be attributed [*fb*] a Giddiness that cou'd not fail to alarm, it was momentary and on the whole perhaps has been of use, for he has ever since been cautious and eat[en] sparingly, has consented to have leaches apply'd to his Temples, and, when he goes to Town next Thursday says he will be cupped but his spirits are very much better, and he is not from morning to night talking of various complaints

Duff has just said farewell and is off in the early Romford [coach]. it was He I believe that prevented my putting a line to you into the basket of Linnen I sent by a Coach Yesterday to Izzy, but he thought, tho he had heard nothing of you before he left London on Saturday, you probably had arriv'd early that morning, and engag'd at the House all day and we shou'd certainly see you yesterday to dinner, false hopes however, and therefore you will pay 9d for what if written yesterday wou'd have been basket free –

Breakfast is call'd for, perhaps a letter by the post this morning may render this unnecessary. I wish it may, and shall be glad to commit it to the flames but if that is not to be its fate, let it convey to you the love of all and of no-one more truly than

your ever Affectionate DA

Address: William Repton Esqr, Aylsham, Norfolk
B st: TOO LATE; *b st*: RUMFORD 12; *hand*: Cross Post; *charge*: 9
HM 40892/8

187. Humphry Repton to William Repton; Dorothy Adey to William[971]

H[are] S[treet], Tuesday [10 May 1814]

Dear William

<u>We</u> have been very fidgetty about you & are all glad to hear you are there where I hope to be on Thursday P[er] Romford Coach – <u>wind permitting</u> – so secure me a bed at Robersons –

I hope to return <u>with you</u> on Friday – <u>weather permitting</u> – for I depend on Wind & weather more than I like – the old watch does not go so well as it used to do – I was remarkable for doing my business regularly & daily – but now I am a stop watch – they tax my income & my outgoings – go out hardly – more noise than business – but I am alive &

ever most affectionately Yours. HR

---

971 This has been catalogued as being from Mary (Clarke) Repton, but the writer is definitely Dorothy Adey.

May 10th

Dearest William

I am glad you are so near us and shall be happy to see you whenever your business will allow. when John told me a fortnight ago he saw <u>Snow</u> in Town I did not like it but setled it his journey cou'd have nothing to do with your business as he had, you told us, given up the point. <get some one> put the note to H. B. in a <u>Cover</u> and get S[i]r Jacob or someone to direct it to Hasel Wood: Kings Langly Herts.⁹⁷² Papa is going to write, so God love you
    your D A.⁹⁷³

As dear H has left this side I think as Mary says I had better tell you what pass'd with Mrs Anson,⁹⁷⁴ according to custom she was excessively kind and hoped I wou'd contrive to let her see as much of me as I cou'd (she knows Mary is to [be] with me in Town). I said Duff had been so good to give up his apartments to us and that if she wou'd give me leave I wou'd take an opportunity of breakfasting with her as soon as I came to London. I had a letter from her last week desiring I wou'd come when it best suited me and at a ½ past ten breakfast was always upon the table, and when she had me to breakfast she hoped I wou'd contrive to give her a day for dinner & she cou'd assure me there were more than herself wou'd be glad to see me. I think she means Henry and Sambroke but as I said when I saw her I shou'd hope Lady Anson⁹⁷⁵ wou'd allow me to see Miss Anson.⁹⁷⁶ I think it is possible she may have said I am to be in town and we may be asked to St James's Square and if any thing of the sort shou'd be said to you dont say no, for Mary will like the thing. and my love to Bro Martin⁹⁷⁷ and we will dine with him any day you and he fix upon. tell *him* we look'd for him and his good uncle during the Easter hollidays in vain. I wrote to ask them down but have not heard from Dayrel since. perhaps you will fix with Duff what day we are likely to accept his kind offer and be sure to bespeak him a bed at Robertsons when we take possession of his.

Dear Mama rec*k*ons upon seeing you and bids me say she has it in remembrance that you have promised her a <u>week</u> at Harestreet and that week shall be when best suits you, so that she has you but she cares not

---

972 The home of Harry Botham; actually in Abbots Langley.
973 Repton's short letter was written on the first side of the paper.
974 This pasge was also written by Dorothy. Mrs Anson is Mrs Mary Anson (1739–1821).
975 Lady Anne Anson (q.v.), Mary Anson's daughter-in-law.
976 Hon. Anne Margaret Anson (1796–1882), eldest daughter of Lady Anne.
977 John Dayrell Martin (q.v.).

when. it will be impossible for me to go to Fulham but after I have seen you I shall write to Harriet.[978]

Address: To William Repton Esqre   At Roberson's Hotel   St Martins Lane London
B st: RUMFORD 12; *r st*: D 11 MY 11 1814; *charge*: 4
Endorsed: [*mathematical calculations*]
HM 40874

188. Humphry Repton to William Repton; Mary (Clarke) Repton to Dorothy Adey

[Hare Street], Sunday June [*recte* July] 3 1814[979]

Dearest William

In consequence of Aunt Adeys Letter I sent a very civil note to Black – to say I am going into Kent tomorrow & immediately afterwards into Norfolk[980] when I would take the Lease if Mr B. would be so good as to send it – his answer I will copy – 'W Black acquaints Mr Repton the draught of the Lease lies with W Sterry[981] who is so ill he cannot attend to it. So far as Mr B. can judge it is defective – no mention is made of the brick wall & in other respects not in the usual way his Leases are drawn by W. S. – Gidea Hall July 3. 1814' so there we stick – but I have taken care of his Letters & he can't turn me out you say – but we must wait his pleasure I suppose – & now for my projects –

I go tomorrow with my friend Shaw[982] to visit a job near Crayford[983] & return next day *by Woolwich[984] & Wanstead* – I shall see how I bear the effort – I am more free from pain – it is as often but not so severe & I think I am thinner – W. Adam says he cannot go to Devonshire till the 20th or later[985] – so I have told him the later the better as I mean to visit Norfolk

---

978 Harriet Kent, who had previously invited Dorothy to Fulham.
979 Dated 'Sunday June 3 1814', but 3 June 1814 was a Friday, whereas 3 July 1814 was a Sunday; also 3 July fits with two items/events mentioned herein.
980 Repton's will was dated 14 July 1814 and was most likely written at Aylsham during his proposed visit. (See Introduction.)
981 Benjamin Wasey Sterry (q.v.).
982 Probably the architect John Shaw. (See Letter 198.)
983 Perhaps a visit to Blendon Hall, Blendon, near Bexley, owned by John Smith. Fragment VIII is an account of Blenden[*sic*] Hall. (*Fragments*, pp. 24–8, plus illustration.)
984 i.e. via the Woolwich ferry.
985 William Adam, the duke of Bedford's steward. (Daniels, *Repton*, p. 170.) See Daniels, *Repton*, p. 186, for a discussion of this letter.

first – & then instead [*fb*] of hurrying down with him & his Clerk & Jeffry Wyatt[986] *in 2 hack Chaises* – I mean to travel as I always do with a son or Daughter in my own Carriage – which I suppose I can do for ab't 60 G[uinea]s & I am to have 200 G[uinea]s for the Visit – so if I am able to bear it perhaps I may vary the Scene to myself & Mary & not make a bad fortnights work – for I am to have 30 G[uinea]s from a man for a day near Bristol[987] en passant – thus we count our Chickens before they are hatched & if you have read the wonderful acc't of a Young man of 16 having died with an infant in his belly[988] – perhaps after all that may be my Complaint & I will come & lie in at Aylsham the end of this week & eat Strawberry Caudle –[989]

I have some thoughts of going by the <u>Ippy bue</u>[*sic*] to Ipswich[990] – & then I will calculate which will be cheapest (setting time out of the question which is now of no value to me) whether I must go P[er] post Chaise to Norwich – or P[er] Coach to Bungay – or to Yarmouth – & from thence to Norwich. I should wonderfully like the Steamboat[991] – & perhaps You my dear William [*fb*] may have some scheme in which I could join you for I am quite determin'd to forget that I am an invalid but I forget I must leave room for the women to Scribble

God bless you

[*Mary (Clarke) Repton*] the girls are all gone to drink tea with Mrs Newman. dear Humphry and my self are left, I <be> *am* rejoiced that he is able to go into Norfolk, though I do not accompany him now, he says we shall go in the Autumn, <u>that</u> my dear Dee I do not expect to do – a journey into Norfolk on purpose will never answer.

---

986 Jeffrey Wyatt, later Wyattville (1766–1840), architect and garden designer, with whom Repton had recently collaborated at Ashridge (Herts).

987 In July 1814 Repton visited Abbots Leigh near Bristol, on the southern bank of the Avon, an estate recently purchased by the Bristol banker Philip John Miles. (Daniels, *Repton*, p. 239.) Repton subsequently produced a 'Report concerning Abbot-Leigh, near Bristol'. (Rogger, *Landscapes*, p. 210.)

988 Reported in the *Morning Chronicle*, 1 July 1814, p. 3, col. 4. The female foetus was thought to have been present in the young man's stomach since his own birth and was moving inside him until he died; the foetus was reported to be in the possession of Mr Carpue, lecturer in Anatomy in Dean Street, London. This was James Constantine Carpue (bapt. 1764, d.1846), surgeon and anatomist. (*ODNB*)

989 A thick, sweet hot drink for invalids.

990 The 'Ippy Blue' was a coach to Ipswich.

991 On 26 July 1813 the 'Steam Boat' had arrived at Great Yarmouth from Hull. 'She is to be employed upon the river to Norwich, for which purpose she seems well adapted: she makes about seven miles an hour in smooth water, without either sails or oars.' (*Norfolk Chronicle*, 31 July 1813, p. 2)

Duff is just come in, 6 oclock – he has been walking by himself into the Forest to see the remains of Fairlop Fair[992] and he lost himself, and found <some> some difficulty to find his way out, but here he is safe and sound – I do not like Mr Blacks answer to Humphrys note. I have been, and still am, uncomfortable till the business is properly settled. Fanny and Caroline[993] desired their regards to you and William, they are clever entertaining Women, and amuses[sic] us very much indeed [fb] The letter Boy is waiting therefore I must say God bless you, let us hear from you soon

Yours most affectionately M R

Address: To Wm Repton Esqr (or Mrs Adey), Aylsham, Norfolk
B st: RUMFORD 12; Cross Post; *charge*: 8
HM 40875

189. George Repton to William Repton

Dover Street, March 3 1815

My dear William

You will read with deepest regret, the enclosed letter from Dr McLean, which Edward gave to me last night[994] – I am going to Harestreet today, and will write to you again either tomorrow from thence, or on Monday upon my return to Town – and will freely tell you if I think it desirable you should immediately come up – at any rate the latter part of McLeans letter should be attended to, and if you do come, it would perhaps be better that you should pretend some other business brought you to Town than the desire of seeing our dearest father – and also not come upon him unprepared – between ourselves I think it desirable that Mrs A should not accompany you unless My father (of his own accord) expresses a wish to see her – he must not now be flurried in any way – adieu my dear William – I will write to you again –

ever your affectionate GSR

PS I think Edward said he would also write to you to day – as he left Harestreet yesterday morning –

---

992 Held on 1 July. (See note to Letter 161.)
993 Not identified.
994 The letter from Dr MacLean given to George by Edward has not survived in this archive: in Letter 191 George instructs William to take it with him to London to show Duff.

Address: London fourth March 1815   To William Repton Esq Aylsham
Norfolk   From Macclesfield[995]
R st: FREE 4 MR 4 1815
HM 40921/1

190. Edward Repton to William Repton

1 Crawford Street, Saturday February [*recte* March] 4th [1815][996]

Dear William

George took S[i]r Lacland's answer to my letter, requesting his candid opinion of our dear Fathers case – this he said he would forward to you – and by it, you will learn but too clear a confirmation of all our fears – I requested S[i]r L. to say whether his disorder had arrived at <that> *such a* stage, as to lead us to expect a <u>speedy</u> issue – and I think you will agree with me, that his opinion of him seems to be as bad as it can be – He says [*fb*] the disease will *<u>not</u>* be stationary but progressive – and he is certainly considerably worse than when he was at Sudbury[997] – and he himself says – that He cannot last long – Whether he really feels that he is so rapidly declining, or not – I cannot say – but as his strength diminishes – the dangers of which Macleane speaks evidently become greater. – Under all these circumstances – I hardly know whether to advise your coming up or not – George is gone to Hare Street to day and will probably give you a later account than this – but indeed, I [*fb*] fear we must not look forward to many more weeks – I shall go on Tuesday *unless sent for sooner* and stay there on the Wednesday – Still there is another difficulty respecting your coming – especially – if you bring Aunt Adey with you – that it will cause that alarm – which Macleane seems to say we should guard against.

However, you must be guided by your own opinion – and either shew this to Mrs Adey or not as you think proper – I would willingly spare increasing

---

995 The address is wholly in the hand of George Parker, fourth earl of Macclesfield (1755–1842), who had provided George with a frank. Parker's main residence was Shirburn Castle, Pyrton (Oxon). According to Historic England, the early nineteenth-century gothic, two-storey, stucco South Lodge at Shirburn was possibly designed by John Nash. (https://historicengland.org.uk/listing/the-list/list-entry/1001105)

996 Both 4 February and 4 March were Saturdays in 1815. This letter relates closely to George's letter dated 3 March 1815 and posted on 4 March. The date stamp on Edward's letter is partly illegible, but 'MR' for March is visible; perhaps he had forgotten that the month had changed to March.

997 Repton had visited Dr MacLean at Sudbury in April 1814. (See Letter 182.)

her pain – where she can administer no relief – for which reason – I will get my friend Hellyar⁹⁹⁸ to direct this – Ever my dear William

your affectionate Brother   ER

Address: Wm Repton Esqr, Aylsham, Norfolk
B st: MR 4 8[*illeg*]
HM 40914/2

191. George Repton to William Repton

Dover Street, Monday March 6 1815

My dear William

I came this Morning from Hare Street and no longer hesitate to give it as my opinion (in which also Duff joins) that you should take the very first opportunity you can command to come to Town – I will state what passed yesterday. My Mother stated to me that my Father had said to her when we were all out walking "that he should like to see his Boy William once again", that is all that passed at the time – after dinner when alone with him and Duff, I took the opportunity of bringing on the subject and asked him if he would like me to write to you – he said no he should not wish you to come on purpose – unless Andrews had said he thought it was necessary – both Humphrey[*sic*] and myself then said, that from letters we had recently received from you, we thought there was every probability of business bringing you to Town very soon – perhaps in a few days – he then said "he should like to see him, but my Sister must not come" – I do not wish her to come". he then added much more that it is unnecessary to repeat at present – upon that subject therefore we are all unanimous, and how it is to be managed you best know – I should be sorry that it should give pain – yet the wishes of our dear father in his present state must be our first consideration, indeed any sudden surprize or distress of any kind, might I am inclined to think at this time be attended with the same effect as any sudden bodily exertion – and you should I think by all means not stop at Hare Street, but come on to Town as if you had been transacting business here – <per> and I will accompany you to Hare Street – let me therefore see you as soon as you arrive in Town – as I have an intention of going down again about Thursday – before which time I shall probably either see or hear from you –

---

998 Perhaps a fellow clergyman, but no one listed in the clergy database (including spelling variants) fits with the date.

My Father was asleep when we came away this morning but his Cough is very distressing – and he no longer reads for any length of time and appears to be uninterested in almost every thing – [*fb*] how long or how short a time our dear Father may remain in this state I can form no opinion upon, but I was glad to find that our poor Mother & Sisters appeard to be prepared for that event which the late gradual increase of the several symptoms of his complaint must naturally make them view as being (probably) not very distant –

we are all aware how much difficulty you will have in coming up <u>alone</u> – and scarcely know how you will contrive it, yet we are anxious it should be so – and equally anxious that our good Aunt should not be made uncomfortable – it must therefore remain with you to manage in the best way you can – I think my Father said something last night about writing to Aylsham, I believe to you – he may perhaps therefore do so – at any rate if I do not see you on <u>Thursday</u> Mor[nin]g, let me hear from you by that mornings post – if you come we will call upon Duff in our way out of Town – ever my dear William

your affectionate GSR

do not forget to bring or send Macleans letter which I sent you on Saturday as Duff has not seen it and wishes very much to do so – he also wishes you to make the enquiries he says that he requested of you –

Address: William Repton Esqre, &c &c &c, <u>Private</u>
HM 40921/2

192. Mary Claridge[999] to Dorothy Adey

Jervaux Abbey,[1000] March 13th 1815

My dear Madam

The Receipt of your kind letter gave me much pleasure, and my Father[1001] and myself were delighted to hear so good an account of your

---

999 Mary Claridge (d.1851), only daughter of John Claridge, married in 1820 Thomas Kitchingman Staveley (d. 1860), of Old Sleningford, Yorkshire, at St James (Piccadilly).
1000 At this time the Jervaulx estate was in the hands of the earl of Ailesbury.
1001 John Claridge, (fl.1750–1825?), land agent and surveyor (since 1772), with business premises in Pall Mall, acting for several aristocratic landowners, including here as steward for the earl of Ailesbury. He had taken charge of clearing the ruins at Jervaulx Abbey in 1805–7 (with careful records made) and building a 'neat residence' nearby for the earl which he occupied. The park had been laid out by Robert Menzies. Claridge had some Norfolk links but his wide agricultural interests led to a peripatetic existence; author of *General*

Norfolk festivities. We, indeed were not less gay, for my Father danced a whole evening, during the Christmas [period], with all the activity of youth, to the surprised[*sic*] of a young Friend of mine, whose lungs are not very strong – He often talks of his Friends in Norfolk, and of the Juvenile days he passed in your neighbourhood, with much pleasure. He has been [*fb*] in London for the last six weeks, much occupied with the Corn Bill, and the new regulations, relative to the Corn Laws,[1002] but I am in daily expectation of his return, as he is coming down, accompanied by my Brother,[1003] to spend the Easter [break] when he has a Colt to run for a Produce Stakes,[1004] in which we are all much interested. I hope it will be successful, as it has been one of his great <u>pets</u> for the last three years.

After the Spring attractions, which will be over early in May, I shall accompany my Father to London to see our Friends there, for a Month, or six weeks, and when I shall have great pleasure in meeting you. I [*fb*] hope by that time, these unpleasant disturbances in London will have abated, as I should think it far from agreeable in the present state of confusion.[1005]

My Father says you are fond of plants. I have a very nice collection, and have in blossom now, some new Narcissus, which are very beautiful indeed – But every thing is much later here, than in the South. I should have great pleasure in shewing you this country, and think you would be repaid for the length of the Journey, by the beauty of our Mountain scenery, and I am sure my Father would have great pleasure in entertaining you at Jervaux Abbey.

[*fb*] I beg my best compliments to Miss, & Mr W. Repton, and in the hope of hearing from you soon again, I remain, dear Madam

Yours sincerely obliged Mary Claridge

Miss Tiler begs her compliments.

View of the Agriculture of Dorset (1792), when of Craig's Court, London. As noted above he was for some time in partnership with Nathaniel Kent and William Pearce. (See Horn, 'An eighteenth-century land agent'; *Dictionary of land surveyors*, vol. 2, p. 97, entry C209.)

1002 The Corn Law of 1815 notoriously introduced protection for British agriculture, hoping to sustain prices and domestic supply in peacetime. Resolutions to this effect were introduced on 17 February and passed the Lords on 20 March, with royal assent on 23 March. John Claridge had given evidence, supporting protection, to the Commons Select Committee on Petitions on the Corn Laws in June 1814. (B. Hilton, *Corn, cash, commerce: the economic policies of the Tory governments 1815–1830*, (Oxford, 1977), pp. 5–30, D. G. Barnes, *History of the English Corn Laws* (1930), pp. 134–9.)

1003 Probably Henry, later (1838) listed as gentleman, of Jervaulx. (TNA, IR29/42/36.)

1004 Produce stakes: in horse racing, a race in which the runners must be the offspring of horses named and described at the time of entry. (*OED*)

1005 Anti-Corn Law riots in London. See, for example, J. Bonar, 'The disposition of troops in London, March 1815', *The English Historical Review*, 16, no. 62 (April 1901), pp. 348–54.

Address: Mrs Adey, Aylsham, Norfolk
B st: Bedale 219; *charge*: 11
Endorsed: 13 March 1815   Miss Claridge to Mrs Adey
HM 40898

193. Edward Repton to William Repton

1 Crawford Street, [24 March or May 1815][1006]

Dear William

Do you know the Dowager Lady Suffield[1007] – or how she is to be got at? – Some time ago, she sent for Mr Stephens a Preacher, whom she much liked in London – and told him that <the> a Living in Lancashire was at his Service (valued at £1,000 pa)[1008] upon the death of the present Incumbent – who is not expected to live many months[1009] – Stephens of course accepted the offer with pleasure – since, however, he has the promise of the Chaplainship of the H[ouse] of Commons[1010] – and has declined the Living – which is now [*fb*] to be disposed of to some worthy person – now as I have no small share of Vanity – I wan't her Ladyship be acquainted with my Merits – – at all events the thing is worth a little trouble – and that I would readily take if I knew how to set about it – Ask Mrs Adey if she knows any clue which may reach the Dowager.

You know from Harestreet that My Wife and young ones are all at Brighton – they are quite well – and I think of going for them on Tuesday

---

1006 This letter is undated. The unclear postmark is 'M[*illeg*] 24 815', indicating that the letter was posted on 24 March or May 1815.

1007 On 7 October 1760 Mary, daughter and coheiress of Sir Ralph Assheton, third baronet, of Middleton (Lancs) married Sir Harbord Harbord (who became Lord Suffield in 1786 and had died in 1810); she died on 1 June 1823. (*Hist. Parl.* for Harbord Harbord.)

1008 The living was that of Middleton. The patron was Lord Suffield but the patronage came through the Dowager, who clearly had influence over presentation. Rectors were presented by Lord Suffield in 1801, 1818, 1829, 1832 and 1835. (*VCH Lancashire*, vol. 5, p. 159.)

1009 The 'present incumbent' was Robert Walker, who, in fact, did not die until 1818. (CCEd Person ID: 170800.)

1010 The Chaplain to the Speaker of the House of Commons served for no more than three years. Robert Stevens was the 49th Chaplain, serving from 1815 until 1818. Eventually Edward himself was Chaplain, but only for a year from 1832 to 1833. The manner of the chaplain's appointment and subsequent preferment changed in 1835 in the wake of the Reform Act of 1832. See Donald Gray, *Chaplain to Mr Speaker: the religious life of the House of Commons* (London, 1991), pp. 18–21; the second part of the book comprises biographies of Speaker's Chaplains 1660–1991.

– and bring them back on Saturday following – It is rather a gloomy sort of Life I [*fb*] have been leading for the last fortnight – and should like to have you here to help to cheer me – Duff dined with me on Monday – and amused me with that inimitable composition of our accomplished Cousin – What fools her Parents must be to allow her to deal in such balderdash – Pray, Guardian, protect your Ward from such unintelligible jargon – for she bears the name of Repton.[1011] – My Kindest Love to her and Mrs Adey – and believe me Dear William

Ever your affectionate Brother Edward

Address: Wm Repton Esq, Aylsham, Norfolk
B *st*: M[*illeg*] 24 815 [i.e. 24 March or May 1815]
HM 40914/3

194. Arnold Wallinger[1012] to William Repton

Montague Sq[uare], Tuesday April 11th [1815][1013]

My dear Sir

When I left Aylsham, you were kind enough to say, that I might take my own time as to staying in Town – I have now been here above a fortnight and am almost ashamed to take so much advantage of your kindness as to ask permission to stop over Tuesday if (without <u>presumption</u> on my part) I am not particularly wanted – I trust and hope you would not in the least hesitate in saying so if I am – Did I think otherwise I would not ask it – My sole reason for naming Tuesday is, that there are two or three parties on that and preceding days, made, I have every reason to suppose, partly on my account, and I should consequently rather like to <bet> be at them – but by no means, unless I can be conveniently spared as I should & shall have <the> equal delight in returning to Aylsham after the kind reception & treatment, I so invariably met with, both from Mrs Adey & yourself, & which will I trust ever be remembered [*fb*] by me with deserved gratitude –

1011 Eliza, daughter of John Repton.
1012 By articles of agreement, dated 25 June 1814, Arnold, son of Elizabeth Wallinger (widow), of Montague Square, was apprenticed to William Repton. John Bird and Leonard Shelford were witnesses to the articles, sworn before Robert Copeman (q.v.) on 23 July 1814 and subsequently entered in the records of the court of King's Bench. (TNA, KB 105, Piece 25.) Arnold Wallinger and Leonard Shelford were two of the witnesses to Humphry Repton's will made on 14 July 1814.
1013 11 April 1815 was a Tuesday; the previous year when 11 April fell on a Tuesday was 1780.

I was rejoiced to find that Mr Repton was well enough to come up yesterday to Crawford Street to consult Dr Bailey[1014] – I did not hear what his opinion was, as he had not been, when I called there – I made a sad blunder in one of the commissions Mrs Adey favor'd me with – I mean in sending 3 lb of Candles instead of 6 lb – which I presume she has by this time received – I sent the largest they had, which were not so big as were requested – I inquired for the £30,000, but Mrs Adey's sixteenth was not drawn. The number of it is 5874[1015] – – My Mother is at present out, but has desired me to give her kindest regards to Mrs Adey & yourself, with those of, My dear Sir

Your ever most sincerely obliged A. Wallinger

PS I trust I need not say what pleasure I shall feel in performing any other Commissions which either you or Mrs Adey may have thought of since I left Aylsham –

Address [in pencil]: To Wm Repton Esqr, Aylsham
HM 40946

195. Humphry Repton to William Repton[1016]

[?Hare Street], 22 May 1815

Dear William

This frank[1017] will not cover your Book which I bought in London price 3s/- & 1/- porter to get it for me, being unable to walk any where – It will never pay carriage to Aylsham – I will quote you a specimen

With pretended submission the tyrant could deign
To make his entre, and to give me fresh pain
For he'd marry Miss North and have his own will
"Then", said I, "You have usd me excessively ill".[1018]
47 pages of such Stuff as I never read before –

1014 Not identified.

1015 Referring to tickets for the state lottery. On p. 1 of *The Morning Chronicle*, 28 March 1815 (issue 14,320), there were several advertisments from lottery contractors announcing that the next draw would be held on 5 April, in which there would be three prizes of £30,000.

1016 This letter features heavily in Daniels, 'Cankerous blossom'.

1017 There is no sign of a frank on this letter: it is a single sheet folded in half.

1018 *The Rivals; or The General Investigation*, by Miss Wassell (London, 1815); the quotation here is from p. 14. In this versified novel, the rivals for the affections of Mr Pinfold are Mary Ann Wassell and Kitty North.

apropos of Stuff – what can dear D. mean by comparing the fustian affected labourd Epistle she sent, to any thing of Anna Sewards[1019] (except in the hand writing) – I thought her Clever, but this letter overturns all my hopes – Duff was reading a New novel (*Varieties of Life*)[1020] when he suddenly burst out – 'here is the original of the Letter from Norwich', & he read a purposely affected performance so like the style that we laughed immoderately – that's more than you will do at Miss Mary Anne Wassel & Kitty North, which shall come by the first possible conveyance.

These two subjects being got over – the next two are my health – & my prospects – they say I look better – I do not feel so – my pains return & my difficulty of breathing increases – then I eat & sleep most heartily – & have no heart to do anything else – I am told to eat as I please & what I please [*fb*] but if times do not mend – We shall have nothing to eat – then I am told to do no business – & luckily I have none to do – We are to have more income tax[1021] – but I have no income – so I shall avoid that as well as hair powder tax having no hair to powder[1022] – Life seems gradually drawing to a Close – & from the tugs I feel at my heart – I think I cannot have long to bear its pains – its fears – or disappointments. I have experienced so many & been so often unexpectedly deliverd from impending evils that I will yet put my trust for myself & all that are dear to me – in that power which has hitherto preserved & cheerd me – but I am tired of admiring my flowers & my Kittens & my pigeons & my Young Canaries & my greatest beauties remaining are my Boys & dear Girls – their affection grows with my necessity for it – & my infirmities give them more trouble & anxiety than I can reconcile to my own feelings – but that & all we dread, will soon terminate & you will see me at Aylsham – whether I see you or not – Have you secured my retreat.[1023]

My task is all performd – I have revised [*fb*] & considered all my MSS. – & trust they will redound to my honor – to the praise of my Maker &

1019 Anna Seward, called the Swan of Lichfield (1742–1809), poet and correspondent. (*ODNB*) She was known to the Repton family. She maintained a long friendship with John Adey (Repton's brother-in-law) and corresponded with Dorothy. (*Aylsham*, p. 169.) She also contributed essays 25 and 26 published in H. Repton, *Variety or a Collection of Essays written in the Year 1787* (London, 1788). (See Carter et al., *Repton*, p. 172.)

1020 *Varieties of life; or, Conduct and consequences*, by the author of 'Sketches of character' (London, 1815, 3 vols).

1021 Despite Repton's fears, income tax was not renewed in 1816 and was only re-introduced in 1842.

1022 35 George III, c. XLIX (1795), An Act for granting to His Majesty A Duty on Certificates issued for using Hair Powder; repealed in June 1869.

1023 Referring to his plans to be buried in Aylsham churchyard, about which he had written to the vicar, Charles Norris, in January 1815. (Daniels, *Repton*, p. 101.)

to the profit of those for whom I have toiled many years in vain – When I reflect on the thousands of Miles I have traveld – the hundreds of Sketches – & Rheams of paper I have blotted – how every hour of a long life has been filled up – & now view myself crawling from one chair to another in the Garden I say – thy will be done! – I was not made for that in which others succeed – in this life. My hopes are fixed on another, which might not have been the Case had I prosperd (as it is called) in this worlds pursuits. Let Claude Scott increase & Nash dissipate, they cannot have had half the Satisfaction that I have experienced in earning & eating my daily bread – & sure it will last a very little longer – if it must be without Cheese in future so let it be – the Bourbons[1024] do the same –

Apropos of Claude Scott – have you thought of my annual tribute & will you do so – [*fb*] how am I ever to obtain from poor <Mrs Burrughs> Mrs Burroughes the £147 – she promised to pay[1025] is she alive & well – & can I ask for it? –

Our hopes from Lord Nelson are blown over[1026] tis all for the best – if we had built our Column on the Sand – we might have faild in our foundations & great would have been the fall. I see an Architect in the North has had £10,000 to pay for deficiency of skill – I don't think they could have made me pay that Sum, whatever deficiency they might have discoverd. – in the mean time ask Francis[1027] for our Drawings & keep them till we meet – they will not pay Carriage & the sight of hopes disappointed, is like the blossoms on our Apple trees – the Canker has destroyed them all – and a grub nips every rose bud – while cold winds nip me, but we go grubbing on & tho I verily beleive some great & portentous change will soon happen in the World it will last my time & You may live to see it but while you live – Let it be so that we may hope to Live & meet again

God bless you HR

HM 40876

1024 A reference to the restoration of the French Bourbon monarchy.

1025 Mrs Christobelle Burroughes of Hoveton Hall. This sum of £147 indicates a considerable amount of time devoted to the property by Repton. As noted above he had produced plans in 1809. The chapter on Hoveton Hall in *Repton in Norfolk* (p. 141) states that Mrs Burroughes was billed for £147 in 1812, citing this letter as evidence, but it is clearly dated 1815. The editors speculate that this work related in part to the glasshouse which still survives.

1026 In 1814 Standlynch Park, near Salisbury, was purchased as the estate for William, Lord Nelson. It was renamed Trafalgar Park. It is now in private ownership. See http://trafalgarpark.com/history/.

1027 Not identified.

196. Claude Scott to William Repton

Bruton Street, June 13th 1815

Dear Sir

I am just return'd from Dorsetshire[1028] and find here your Letter of the 6th covering your Draft for £31.10. on Messrs Hoare & Co on account of your Father, which shall be so placed accordingly by, Dear Sir
    Your obedient humble Servant Claude Scott

Address: To Wm Repton Esqre, Aylsham, Norfolk
B st: A JU 13 1815
HM 40953/20

197. Humphry Repton to William Repton

Harestreet near Rumford, 3 Oct 1815

Dearest William

Duff tells me that Unthank[1029] had told you Mrs. Burroughs's money was paid – I wish it was so as I am sadly harrass'd by the claims on me & those I have on others – good for £147:0:0[1030]

Long Wellesley saw Duff yesterday <&> as he rode by on horse back – when he bid him tell me he was going into Suffolk & could not call on me but would see me in his way back £120 –[1031]

Mr Andrews has quite done himself up at Newmarket & wants to sell or let Harlestone Park – but we come to no settlement & I expect there is from 2 to 300 due on P[e]rCentage.[1032]

[*fb*] Major Woodgate had been repeatedly written to for the balance of self & 2 Brothers – £119:5:0. He was a partner in the Tunbridge Bank which faild. it is said the Estates when sold will pay all – but mine is a private debt

---

1028 From his house, Sans Souci, at Lytchett Minster.
1029 Forster and Unthank, attorneys, Queen Street, Norwich. (*Norwich Directory for 1811*, p. 95.)
1030 See Letter 195.
1031 William Tylney Long Pole Wellesley of Wanstead House. See Daniels, *Repton*, pp. 250–4, for an account of the estate and Repton's work there, including this promise of an instalment of £120.
1032 Suggesting that Robert Andrew had made losses connected to horse-racing and had still not paid for Repton's work at Harlestone Park (Northants) in 1808. See Letter 47, written from Harlestone Park. In 1824–5 Andrew conveyed his estate to his brother-in-law, Henry Packe, to clear his debts, estimated at over £85,000.

– & now Mr. Allnut[1033] writes me that his Brother in Law (Major Woodgate) has had all my Letters but thinks there is nothing due to me – I have written 21 Sept. to have this explaind & in the mean time you must do something to get the debt acknowledged if not paid – before the 6 years expire –[1034]

From the Duke of Bedford's agent Mr Adam I have daily been expecting a balance of £200 –

now all these together would put me at ease with my Creditors, but in the mean time what can I do – Let me know what I may draw for on Mrs Burroughes' Acc[oun]t & on whom – whether on you or your Banker, at Norwich or London – [fb] & if hard push'd how I shall proceed – my heart is not in a Condition to contend with difficulties – but I am not as I was at Aylsham – so nearly dead. I am alive & have just sent my Coat to be taken in to fit me – you would see me shrunk but looking better in health – I bear walking half way to the bridge & am the better for such exertion – tho painful.

My Dear Dees Letter gave me some pleasure tho I do not suppose I shall ever avail myself of your proposal – there was a time when I thought the latter days of dear John Adey & of old Izzy – seem'd to point the Asylum for mine – but I pray such tedious gradual decay may be spared & my symptoms the less frequent – seem to promise a more decided Crisis – I rub on with some few concerns having lately been to one at Mickleham in Surry & got 25 G[uinea]s[1035] & my attention to my Fragments to fill up some of those Chasms in my Time & Johns[1036] – which but for that would hang [fb] miserably on our hands. – His affectionate regard & attention is delightful to my feelings – poor fellow he wheels me out in my Chair when the Sun shines, for I have no Footman & no foot to stand on – my ankles very weak, but I am alive, eat moderately – sleep most comfortably & am thankful

God bless you   HR

1033 Richard Allnutt (1772–1827), London wine merchant, had married Frances Woodgate in 1793; he built South Park, Penshurst (Kent) in 1809.

1034 See Letter 169. '6 years' refers to the Statute of Limitations. If, as surmised, Repton's first visit had been in 1810, then five years had already expired. It is likely that the phrase 'for the balance of self & 2 Brothers' refers to Repton and two of his sons, rather than Woodgate and his two brothers.

1035 Previously no one has identified this property in Mickleham, or its owner, but apart from this letter, it is known about from two letters from Repton to Sir Harry Fetherstonhaugh at Uppark, dated 3 & 8 October 1815, i.e. concurrent with this one. (Daniels, *Repton*, p. 267.) It is possible that the client was Richard Sharp, former M.P. for Castle Rising, whose property was Fredley Farm, Mickleham. See the Introduction for a discussion of this identification.

1036 The book published by Repton in July 1816.

Address: To William Repton Esqre, Aylsham, Norfolk
B st: RUMFORD 12; Cross Post; *charge*: 9
HM 40877

198. Humphry Repton to William Repton

Harestreet, 31 March 1816

Dear William

I have at last got my dear boy George at my Elbow – but now I feel I want Courage to pour into his bosom – a portion of that bitter Cup which I cannot pass from me – Ruin in its most aweful shape is pressing upon me – & my only hope arises from the reflection that for 60 years it has always been the Same – and now I have the consolation to see half mankind as bad as myself in Circumstances & the Satisfaction to know that my Life cannot long continue under my present state of Fortune – both in Body and Mind – When I look back on past events, I cannot see a single instance in which by my own [*fb*] by my own efforts – or my own endeavors, I ever extricated myself from difficulties – further than by resolutely seizing every opportunity to use my best endeavors –

In the schemes which I thought most beneficial, such as the P[rince] of Wales – Long Wellesley – Evans – &c &c I met only with disappointment[1037] & others produced me fame & profit where I least expected it – is this Chance – or Accident – or the Ordination of that Higher power to whom I have ever bowd gratefully. & *from whom I have ever most* humbly solicited assistance – but now the Time is come – & I must resolve on something – not knowing how long I may be doomd to bear this Life of Pain & Anxiety – & most earnestly hoping & expecting that every night may be my last – for indeed I am unfit to be trusted with the settlement of [*fb*] my own affairs – & wish you could bring them to such a Crisis – that I might retire to an Arm Chair with bread & Water and a Mind at ease – & free from Duns

You hint something in your Letter of retreating to Taylors House at Aylsham – this would be incumbring you & Dee as much as living with

---

1037 Repton's suggestions for the Royal Pavilion, Brighton, were not taken up. Long Wellesley had not paid him in full. Repton's surviving correspondence with George Freke Evans of Laxton Hall (Northants) comprises 50 letters written over the years 1806 to 1808: the correspondence 'became increasingly acrimonious and, in the end, Repton was never paid for his work'. (Daniels, *Repton*, p. 38; photocopies of letters at Northamptonshire RO, Freke-Evans (Laxton collection).)

you – & burying me before I am dead – <While> *so Long as I am* here – I can sometimes fancy myself yet alive & able to contend with pain & difficulty while I pick up a little to pay for my Bread & the repairs of my pump – as for My Beer – the Brewer faild last week & thank heaven I do not owe him a farthing –

Sir Thomas Neave sends his Car[ria]ge for me & lets me give him my advice for 2 or 3 hours – then for 3 such Visits gives me Twenty Guineas[1038] – and Sir Thomas Plummer – Vice Chancellor has proposed to give me 30 Gui[ne]as for going ten miles from London one day this week & making him a Map[1039] – so I mean to try the East wind on Wednesday & Thursday next [fb] and if I survive – I will eat – if it kills me, the worms may eat me – *tho'* they <you> will find me miserably lean.

If you could see your dear Mother – you would feel as I do thankful that with all our afflictions, like myself she keeps up her spirits & we never see her without a smile on her Countenance, as if anticipating happier times here or hereafter

Do not blame me dear William for the terrible scrape I have been drawn into by Paynes Bankruptcy[1040] – I am a fool, an idiot & a child in Matters of Acc't – & sadly wish I could lay all mine before you – or take them to the Vice Chancellor – they distract me.

God bless you   HR

Our Mary is still at Mr Shaws No 28 Gower Street,[1041] I have told her

---

1038 Sir Thomas Neave, second baronet (1761–1848), owned Dagnams, South Weald (Essex). It was illustrated in the *Polite Repository* in 1802. In Fragment XXXI, 'Of water fences', Repton discussed, and provided a 'slide' (before and after illustration), of a submerged fence. He explained that 'The following expedient occurred to me very recently, on considering the view from the windows at Dagenham in Essex, a seat of Sir Thomas Neave, Bart. ...'. (*Fragments*, pp. 188–90.)

1039 Sir Thomas Plummer (1753–1824), of Canons Park, Stanmore (Middx). (*Hist. Parl.*) He was a barrister, as well as an M.P. He rose through the ranks of the law to be appointed solicitor-general in 1807; attorney-general in 1812; vice-chancellor in 1813; and master of rolls in 1818. This letter is the only evidence of Repton's work at Canons. It is not discussed in *Repton in London* but is listed in the Gazetteer on p. 113 of that book.

1040 Probably the bankruptcy of an individual, rather than the failure of a bank. There is no bank called Payne's listed in *British Banking*, or *Country Banks and Bankers*. Fourteen years earlier, in 1802, Repton had produced a drawing for William Payne, merchant of Bristol, of his property of Brentry Hill. (Daniels, *Repton*, p. 236.) The distance in time makes this person an unlikely identification, unless he had not paid Repton for his work.

1041 28 Gower Street was the home of the architect John Shaw (1776–1832), and his wife, Elizabeth Hester, née Whitfield (bap. 1776, d. 1864). The youngest of their nine children, Thomas Budd Shaw (1813–1862), translator and literary scholar, was born there on 12 October 1813. (*ODNB*, Thomas Budd Shaw.)

my plan of going to Town <on Wednesday> – sleeping at Edward's[1042] – & visiting S[i]r T Plummer at Cannons on <Thursday> *Friday* – perhaps bring her home on <Friday> *Saturday* –

Address: To William Repton Esqre, Aylsham, Norfolk
B st: RUMFORD 12; *charge*: 9
HM 40878

199. William Repton to Baxter & Bowler[1043] (draft)

Letter to Baxter & Bowler, 13 April 1816

Have rec[eiv]ed letter from Wilkinson who complains of taxation – Debt was paid to Joyners[1044] as desired before action – this exorbit[an]t demand how I answered Wilkinson – Money was paid to Joyners I believe 7 January last – my father perhaps sho'd have given notice of it. Action appears to have been going on in February & March

Holditch's Claim for hire of Chariot 1809 £7.16. *Stating hire for Yorkshire Itinerary &c at p[er] w[ee]k with option to p[ur]chase*[1045] Father [?]enter'd to purchase. [?]Sent for it but carr[ia]ge [?]subed[1046] either for Client <or> in execution. doubtful if can prove this – may confound this case with some other Coachmaker as was continually hiring Ca[rria]ges from diff' p[er]sons in Longacre.[1047] Memory bad under present infirmities –

Pray say what has been done in the above two Cases – & what recommend to be done bearing in mind lawyer not fond of going to law – do not wish my [?]father unless on those ground[s]. Stat[ute] of Lim[itatio]ns wo[ul]d serve in Holditchs Case if we can neither find Rec[eip]t for money among my fa[ther]'s papers nor prove his narrative to be correct.

HM 40954/6

1042 The house in Crawford Street.
1043 A legal partnership, perhaps successor to the Baxter partnerships mentioned in earlier letters.
1044 Wilkinson and Joyners not identified.
1045 Holditch not identified. See Letter 110, in which Edward mentions Repton's visit to Yorkshire in 1809, accompanied by several of his sons. See also *Repton in Yorkshire*.
1046 Very unclear: means something like 'substandard' or 'substituted'.
1047 According to *The London Encyclopaedia* (p. 480) in the middle of the seventeenth century Long Acre became a centre of coachbuilding and in the eighteenth century it was a centre for cabinet-making and furniture designers, but it is clear from this letter that in the early nineteenth century there were still a number of coachmakers there.

200. Humphry Repton to William Repton; Mary (Clarke) Repton to William

for Leisure perusal

Hare Street, Tuesday 23 [April] 1816[1048]

Thank you dearest William for the kind note you squeezd into D's [Dorothy's] letter & so bilkd the post – between you &c & the post – it came free – & was most welcome. For some how I had thought of late that the Change in my prospects & the trouble I had given you – had produc'd a silence – which I never should have broken if you had not done it by entering into a discussion of this Law Subject. I p[ai]d Wilkinson[1049] & glad – fearing he might even run up another 20£ if I delayd a day – so perfectly ignorant am I in all Law, or indeed all that relates to property in any shape – that I feel totally incompetent to the management of any Money transaction what ever – & if I could receive with one hand & pay with the other as I have always done – I should rub on as happy as a king – but alas! how is this to be done –

Dee [Dorothy] talks of *my* going long journeys – & accepting all business as formerly – but there is no business – except the Vice Chancellors 30 G[uinea]s[1050] I have not earned one Shilling since Christmass – nor have I rec[eive]d any thing of what I had earned before that time – all my d[ra]fts being refused acceptance to Lubbock tho they do not write Urgently or uncivilly[1051] – my debt there is £250. – it has often been 500 to 600 – but I suspect Bankers may be hard run – Ours at Romford had stood his ground tho' he p[ai]d 10,000 last Wednesday from a Run brought on by the failure of 4 other Essex Banks – viz Epping Ongar Rochfort & Billericay[1052] – but if Corn only sells for half what it did – there can only be half as much money pass thro Bankers hands & the other half may go whistle –

Of Duff we see weekly as usual, he saws the Bass Viol every Sunday – Edward is too busy with his good Wife & Naughty Women at the

---

1048 Later in the letter, Repton says that it is St George's Day.

1049 See Letter 199.

1050 Sir Thomas Plummer; payment as described in Letter 198.

1051 This bank was established in the City of London in 1772 as Sir William Lemon, Buller, Furley, Lubbock & Co.; by 1814 it was known as Sir John Lubbock, Lubbock & Co; its principal was Sir John Lubbock, elder brother of William Lubbock (q.v.).

1052 This was one bank which failed that had branches in Epping, Ongar, Rochford and Billericay. A bank was established in Epping in 1812, first known as Benjamin Fincham, William Fincham & Benjamin Fincham junior, and also recorded in 1812 as 'Epping & Ongar Bank'. It had a branch at Billericay and an office at Chipping Ongar. In 1814 it was known as Fincham & Sons, which had branches at Billericay in 1814 and Rochford in 1815. It was bankrupt in 1816. (*Country Banks and Bankers*, vol. 2, p. 216 and notes thereto.)

Magdelen[1053] – & pupils great & Small, & his 5 Children to think of his poor Father & Mother – so we neither see him nor hear from him as we could wish –

Dear George is supposed to be so engaged with Nash that we seldom see him & I fear his absence is affected – either by his vexation to feel that he cannot help me or that [*fb*] his own Views are not so pleasant as they were – Nash has contrived to abridge his former Salary in Consideration of sharing the profits of his business, which he will do as he did with me, reducing one O into [*a diagram of 11 small zeros in 4 rows*] Thus suppose the Sum earned jointly nothing – deduct the expenses & there remains Nothing which divided equally leaves nothing to each – & that is poor George's share[1054] but he is hard at work for Nash – who is making numerous plans for the Waterloo Competition[1055] – a sign he has not more profitable work to do. John and I have of late been so employd & he has this day taken *to Town* the result of his last Months Labours – in 3 large beautiful designs to be submitted to the Committee of Taste[1056] in that Busy Month of May – when I was born – & married – when Exhibitions open & Chimney Sweepers dance – & when Oxnead Bullocks used to be turned into Beef – How many May months of Promise – Joy – hope – & happiness have I remembered – but it seems sad work to begin it all over again.

1053 Indicating that Edward was chaplain to the Magdalen Hospital for penitent prostitutes in Blackfriars Road, London. (*London Encyclopaedia*, p. 69, entry for Blackfriars Road.)

1054 By 1816 Nash had recognised George's abilities by giving him a share in the profits of the business, but at the same time cut his salary.

1055 Parliament had launched a prestigious architectural competition to commemorate Wellington's victory at Waterloo; it was agreed in the House of Commons on 29 June 1815; Trafalgar was added on 5 February 1816. The monuments would be dedicated to all the fallen of these two key battles and were to stand in for all the battles of the French Wars. Plans were submitted by various people, including Sir John Soane and John Martin, plus as is obvious here, John Nash and George Repton, and Humphry and John Adey Repton. In the end no national monument was ever built. Nash designed Marble Arch in 1825 (built 1827–33) as a celebration of Napoleonic victories and a gateway to Buckingham Palace. (In 1850–1, the arch was rebuilt at the northern entrance to Hyde Park.) (H. Hoock, *Empires of the imagination: politics, war and the arts in the British world, 1750–1850* (London, 2010), pp. 361, 367.)

1056 In 1802, the Treasury had set up regular administrative procedures regarding commemorative monuments. A committee for national monuments, popularly known as 'The Committee of Taste', of initially seven leading connoisseurs and collectors chaired by Charles Long, was appointed to supervise competitions, select designs, award commissions, and supervise the progress and erection of monuments. The government wanted national monuments to 'be the best Testimonies of Taste of the age in which such works are executed'. (Hoock, *Empires of the imagination*, p. 141.)

My MSS. employ some of my time in revising, transcribing & Correcting the press – it gives me pleasure to see how much mind my little D [Elizabeth] displays in her comments on my Labours – but what avails Mind when I look at Miss Bayley with her £60,000 & Miss Severn with nothing but ignorance & Vulgarity – & a rotten reed in her Uncle's hand – who will make a pretty hand of it by Marrying Mr Mason after all[1057] – !! so much for wealth & folly –The depression which it is impossible always to avoid, from the Consideration of Disappointed hopes & painful deprivations – added to much indisposition & Torture – would be too much for my Sensitive Mind to bear – but from that reliance on the Aid of Providence, which has so wonderfully supported me above 60 years – during the whole of which time I never had £100 to spare – nor ever wanted so much, this has often appear'd to me as a standing Miracle – I never rec[eive]d from my [*fb*] Property of any kind – Rent – Interest – or benifit – I earn'd & I rec[eive]d & I spent daily – my daily bread – & if at last it must be dry – or only moisten'd with water – I will bear it as the good pleasure of that Being who knows what is best for me. – I shall by this means from mere compulsion – leave some works which may perpetuate my Name – & perhaps contribute to my support, & remove the dreadful – most dreadful of all Calamities – becoming a burthen to my Children – humbly intreating the Author of my being to remove me from this world of trouble, when I can bear it no longer as I ought – Sick – Sick – I am sick of it. Yet when I see your Mother & Sisters smile & feel that they share without complaining in the Change we experience in our daily Comforts – it is sometimes enough to try all my Philosophy & [Chris]tian fortitude – It is a pleasure to me thus to expand my soul before you & Dee – May the God of Mercy bless us all & preserve us for some good End.

Here the warmth & beauty of the day – & my breathing somewhat easier I resolved to try a long walk by my self – John being gone to his Anniversary of the A.S.S. Society on St Georges day[1058] – when they cook a turtle or a dragon or something that John talks of all the rest of the year, as the best dinner he ever gets *for 5/-* – & he poor fellow obliges me to talk so loud – that I was glad to enjoy a Walk by myself to day – moving too slow for my dear skipping girls – so I have been sauntering half way to the bridge – sitting & sunning against Blacks pales – then walking into the Unicorn Yard & viewing all the premises – empty – untenanted & dilapidated – No Chaises

---

1057 Local residents, not identified.
1058 The Society of Antiquaries. 'In 1751 the Society was granted a Royal Charter and took on its present form. ... The basic structure of the governance of the Society, with the annual election of Officers and Council on St George's Day (23 April) was also put in place at this time'. (https://www.sal.org.uk/about-us/our-history/.)

or Stage Coaches which used to enliven our scene – now all a blank. Such are the Changes growing out of Property – Poor Woollands house is let on Lease 21 years for £20 P[er] ann[u]m often long standing empty & refusing that poor industrious wheelwrights offer of £30 – requiring 40 & not taking half – so it will be with the Unicorn which nobody Can live in these hard times

[fb] [Mary (Clarke) Repton] You complain My dearest William that you never see my hand writing, a pretty stick it is, but you must not suppose that I love you the less, for my not writing but I know that you have so much better Correspondance from Harestreet that I ever can be, that I leave it to them to say how much we all love you and dear Aunt *Adey*. Though I am such a poor Creature, and can but just coast about, I am allways employd, with work, what with making gowns, patch work, and mending old Rags, which is the only thing I am good for, still I flatter myself I am of some use in the family, though God *only* knows how long that may last, and how long we may be in this place, my best love to dear Aunt Adey, and tell her, the girls *are* much better Correspondants <and> *than* I can be to <them> you, and tell her I am <fine> finishing my last Curtain of my Bed – which I think will rather surprize her – kiss her for me and tell her I wish we were not so far from each other, you cannot imagine unless you were to see it how very Beautiful my Bed will be it is the admiration of every one who see it, theres vanity for you

Your affectionate Mother M Repton

Remember me [space] to Mrs John. We understood Basey talkd of coming to see Maria,[1059] her husband has been very ill, poor thing, I doubt they have not much to live on as Balls have left Harestreet, and Marias husband get but little posting now. She has the care of Sallys little girl which is only 4[1060] shillings a week. Perhaps if you mention this they will send her somthing

Mrs G has got a Cook[1061]

Address: To Wm Repton Esqre, Aylsham, Norfolk, or Mrs Adey, Single Sheet
B st: RUMFORD 12; charge: 9
HM 40879

1059 Probably Maria Basey, daughter of Robert and Sarah, who was born at Aylsham in 1794. (Information from M. Vaughan-Lewis.)
1060 Figure unclear.
1061 Written in pencil at the beginning of the letter in a hand contemporary; Mrs G not identified.

Further items in the Repton papers at the Huntington Library

1. Undated letters from John Repton of Oxnead

HM 40929/3,[1] John Repton to Dorothy Adey

I am in hopes you and Dear John Adey will now often change your Air for that of Oxnead

We performed our Journey to Yarmouth well thank God and the Child as happy as the Day – Jonathan sees our Wine home safe by the Craft and William must give me a Dr[a]ft for 23=15=0 prompt payment and the Pipe of Wine will [be] the property of our Good M[r] Kent[2] and ourselves and I Trust and hope safe brickd up in my Vaults to be bottled at any time agreed by the partys. the immediate payment saves [fb] us Five Pounds and having agreed for it when we did, save us us[sic] now also Five Pounds. thus stands the Case or I sho'd not trouble him for the Dr[a]ft for <26> 23=15=0

With best love to all your party I am

Yours Affectionately J Repton

[fb] We have 4 Doz'n Porter wine by the Craft (is that our usual quantity) I am sure I am much obliged to Mr Meux for that but if you think the Watermen have detain'd one [?]Hamper we sho'd write about it.

Address: Mrs Adey, Aylsham
Endorsed: John Repton Esqr Dra' for Port Wine

---

1 The other two letters filed under this number, which can be dated, are Letters 44 (April 1808) and 59 (9 or 10 January 1809).
2 Nathaniel Kent (q.v.).

HM 40930, John Repton to Humphry Repton[3]

My Dear HR

Mr Kent gave me your Note. He is a Man that is always the the[*sic*] same to me & my Wife <in obl> *pleases*. He proposed to us to join his family to a sea side frolic to Day but its to cold – Lubbock wo'd have wishd us to have gone to the Norwich Ball with his party in Basseys Coach and return the same Even'g but that I refused – Mr Marsh sent us a kind note to meet you all on Wednesday but that I declined. so my dear Girl you see has Friends in this County – so every blessing attend you <u>my</u> good Friends
    Yours affectionately   J Repton

I must be at Norwich on Thursday dinner

Address: Hy Repton Esqr
Endorsed: Uncle John Repton to my father   Rather off because Mrs John is not treated with proper Respect

HM 40931[4]

HM 40931/1, John Repton to William Repton

I thank you very much and Jonathan speaks highly of your Kindness – I have sent him to say as I want something from Norwich he may <and> *as* well go in the Morning with your Case to our Friend Plumbtree[5] – and if he is at home he may see him and ask any Questions (or be askd any) that they may wish – and if from Home leave the Case seald up for his Mr Plumbtree return. God bless you, in haste
Yours affectionately   J R

Address: Mr W Repton
Endorsed: John Repton Esqr   About Jonathan Knights Case[6]

---

   3 Written on a torn sheet of paper. It is likely that the other half was something that had been sent to John, i.e. he used the blank half of the sheet for this letter.

   4 The cataloguer suggested that the five letters filed under this number were written by John Adey Repton; however, only one of them is from him (Letter 113, dated 17 February 1810). The others are by John Repton of Oxnead and must have been written before that date because he died in June 1809; they have therefore been numbered 40931/1 to /4.

   5 Robert Plumptre, esquire, barrister in Pottergate Street, Norwich. (*Norwich Directory* (1811), p. 117.)

   6 Jonathan Knight was probably a relative of John Repton's wife, whose maiden name

HM 40931/2, John Repton to William Repton

Oxnead, Sunday Mor[nin]g[7]

My Dear William

I have sent Mr Knight with Mr Plumptres Opinion which I am much please with, and as he had also some conversation with Jonathan I wishd much you sho'd see him before the meeting on Tuesday, Upon this ground we shall be bold to stand against *any* order that may be made upon us (I promise you) so I shall follow your directions, and am again determined (situated as I am) not to attend unless as Constable they oblige me, but I hope from the kind temper they were in with you at the last meeting all will go off handsomly – but I cannot now I am upon this subject (but *again* say) your kind attention to it requires, and you have my best thanks, and I am my

Dear William   yours most truly   John Repton

Address: Mr W Repton
Endorsed: John Repton Esqr   As to Jonathan Knights drawn for the Militia

HM 40931/3, John Repton to William Repton

My Dear William

As Mr Knight wish's to hear something about his cause I have sent him up. Lubbock yesterd'y meet Lord Chief Justice Cooke of Blickling who said (between ourselves) the party ag[ain]st us co'd make nothing of it. pleasd to say what passd Yesterday the Noble Coun[c] of Blicking is against us –

I hope we shall see you every Day or as often as your Courts and the Assembly Day will allow you – I am sorry in this jumble of change of Courts that we shall not see my Sister & Dear John Adey. It is most singular that my good sister sho'd write me word and I suppose the same to Mr Ansons that she sho'd be [fb] happy to meet them at Oxnead and the more so its being assembly Week and then (God love her changebleness) to say to my wife she wo'd come the *week* before our Friends came *for she like us

---

was Knight. (*Aylsham*, p. 177.) As the endorsement to HM 40931/2 indicates, the 'case' referred to is Knight's selection for the militia, suggesting that he had been called up and John Repton was trying to prevent it. Perhaps 'Jonathan' at Oxnead.

7 Written after the valediction.

best alone*. this in the preparations of a house (I suppose) was inconvenient but my Lady had not boldness enough to say so – In short the visit being made that of convenience hurt my feelings – So I doubt I may have offended and you must procure my Pardon see them I cannot now expect as they have made their appointments for the Wednesd'y with the Windhams & Wyndhams those with a (Y) I have askd to extend their visit the Day after the Assembly and have over [*fb*] some of own old [?]Storeys if they come or not I cannot say; We shall give you a party from my Table to your Ball, on the Wednesday, but do not allow my good Sister to be in a Fright, for it will not in the least interfere with her party there;

This I promise you, that I shall not dance <if> there but will do so with the party that remains with me (if they like it)

Our little Eliza is languid and not well which her Aunnt will be hurt for so God love her & Dear John Adey

Yours affectionately   John Repton

Jonathan had rather not show himself and will leave everything to you so I have sent a Boy to hear all about it

Address: Mr Will'm Repton, Aylsham
Endorsed: John Repton Esqr   As to Jon'n Knights liable to serve in the Militia

HM 40931/4, John Repton to William Repton[8]

Let us see my Dear William before the Post arrive and put me in confusion what I have cooly to say for I am all upon the tremble – can our dear Mr Adey join us in any way[?] good God what a state are we both in (go I will) – Therefore send me all my Title Deeds for the Litchfield *Estate* – send my Tenants name and Street, say something about Rents I conceive them received by some body on my Acco[un]t and I shall say stand in their Acco[un]t with me what would I give that these Votes at Norwich and Litchfield stood as clear as my Sloley Estate[9] – sad work – Somthing if I live shall be done about the rec[eip]ts of these Rents. I like to look <blod> boldly in all these questions at the Hustings its the only value the Estates are off to give us votes and then we feel at the moment we want *them* something wrong – May I ask at Litchfield my Tenant when she paid them or will she be bro[ugh]t in Evidence against me[?] when wear[*sic*] this Lease

---

8 Written before death of John Adey on 4 May 1809; John Repton was ill at the time of writing.
9 The village of Sloley is about 5 miles from Oxnead.

Granted and for how long term to the Tenant give me full Acco[un]t before I go my good fellow

Your affectionate   J Repton

Love to my sister if we have orders we shall be off in the Morn'g to Cambridge How we shall have Horses God knows   I wish Adey was well enough to go   My Love to him. Child cannot go.

[*fb*] Lett us see. If I should not be back for the Archd[eaco]n and Mr Steward you must receive them for me [?]home &c all left out – The[y] must not be disappointed remember a Dinner at Aylsham will not do for I know from Jewell his Burrough Church[10] is at 7 o'Clock and all his arrangem[en]ts attend in consequence of my invitation if you are not at home I shall not know what to do I will then have dinner for them and they shall live in momentary hopes of my return to them – by the way I shall be back shall I not

Post *in* and Mr Lubbock[11] the Express must therefore come to Lyng, on to you at Aylsham. send an immediate Answer, if you have heard any more.

Address: Mr Adey, Aylsham   Send an Answer and Title Deeds
Endorsed: John Repton Esqr   Lichfield Vote   for Title Deeds &c

2. Letters from Mary Sneyd[12]

HM 40943, Mary Sneyd to John Adey

Cheltenham, October the 18th 1807

My dear Brother

I write a few <u>hasty</u> lines from this place to tell you I am <u>better</u>. – It requires <u>no small</u> Exertion on <u>my</u> part to [?]attend Mrs [?]J [?]only at half past seven – but I Receive great benefit from her [?]Salutory Springs which have in some degree got the better of my lameness – The weather is still chilly but [?]fine with Cheltenham full of Company The Music played at The Well till after Michaelmas [*fb*] which I desired play that favourite Scots Tune every [?]March "The last time I went oer the Moor – or <u>Came</u> oer the Moor I forget which –

So ask some one to play it for you with the <u>Variations</u> – It will remind you of me –

---

10 William Jewell (1749–1829), rector of Burgh. (CCEd Person ID: 113685.)
11 William Lubbock.
12 She was John Adey's half-sister. See Letter 4. Her writing is virtually illegible.

Mr Sneyd went to the first play without me as I was I̲l̲l̲ – but we have been together since the [?]Bearer of [?]Vencie allowed me – Little Miss [?] Ballers a Child of Eight years of age has had her Concerto
[*On the third folio text has been written both horizontally and vertically across the page, each set of text obscuring the other.*]
[*fb*] shall be at Bath next soon after the 5th of November to have a Letter will send
    Your affectionate Sister
    Mary Sneyd
    with Nov Coming up want four fine Horses to Bath. I am well and God bless you
    Mr and Mrs Granville and the Parkers are our near Neighbours. There are u̲n̲d̲e̲r̲ people of Titles and Splendour & [?]Nobol

Address: John Adey Esqr, Aylsham, Norfolk
R st.: A Oct 19 [*illeg*]; *b st*: CHELTENHAM [*illeg*]; *charge*: <8> 10
Endorsed: 18 Octo' 1807, Mrs Sneyd to Mr Adey

HM 40944/1 and 40944/2, Mary Sneyd to William Repton

Both in poor handwriting and over written as described above.
40944/1, endorsed by William: 9 May 1809, Mrs Sneyds L[ett]re on Mr Adey's death
40944/1, endorsed by William: 6 June 1809, Mrs Sneyd

3. Other items

HM 40952, Cheques written by, or to, William Repton, relating to his business, dated 1806–1812

The bank which he used principally was Messrs Ketts & Back – Bankers – Norwich.

Some cheques from Sir Roger Kerrison & Son, Bankers, Norwich; some papers are regarding payments made through Kerrison's bank, perhaps following its failure.

Also blank cheques on:
    Messrs Williams, Son, Drury, Moffat & Burgess, no. 20 Birchin Lane, London
    Sir Roger Kerrison & Son, Bankers, Norwich

HM 40953/21–30, papers and receipts to William Repton from various bankers.

HM 40955, Paston family pedigree

HM 40956, John Adey's marriage settlement with Dorothy Repton, dated 23 June 1770 (copy)

HM 40957, John Adey's marriage settlement with Dorothy Repton, dated 23 June 1770 (second copy)

HM 40958, Articles regarding the marriage of John Adey with Dorothy Repton, dated 29 July 1769

HM 40959, John Botham, settlement of Brook House, dated 3 June 1746

Concordance of HM references
and the letter numbers assigned in this edition

Entries in the Comments column provide details of additional correspondents under the given reference number.

Abbreviations used in final column:

DA	Dorothy Adey	JAR	John Adey Repton
ElizR	Elizabeth Repton	M(C)R	Mary (Clarke) Repton
ER	Edward Repton	MR	Mary Repton
GR	George Repton	PS	postscript
HR	Humphry Repton	WR	William Repton
HRjr	Humphry Repton junior		

HM ref	No.	Writer	Addressee	Date	Comments
40834	47	H Repton	D Adey	24 Aug 1808	
40835	48	H Repton	D Adey	5 Sept 1808	PS by ElizR
40836	123	H Repton	D Adey	27 Mar 1810	
40837	168	H Repton	D Adey	11 Dec 1812	HR to WR
40838	84	H Repton	C Repington	8 May 1809	
40839	11	H Repton	J A Repton	26 July 1807	
40840	67	H Repton	M (C) Repton	4 April 1809	
40841	158	H Repton	M Repton	28 Sept 1811	
40842	68	H Repton	M Repton	5 April 1809	
40843	159	H Repton	M Repton	23 Oct 1811	
40844	6	H Repton	W Repton	14 Dec 1806	
40845	9	H Repton	W Repton	12 & 13 Mar 1807	Ld Chancellor to HR (11 Mar)

HM ref	No.	Writer	Addressee	Date	Comments
40846	17	H Repton	W Repton	30 Aug 1807	
40847	23	H Repton	W Repton	24 Dec 1807	
40848	24	H Repton	W Repton	10 Jan 1808	
40849	26	H Repton	W Repton	25 Feb 1808	
40850	28	H Repton	W Repton	11 Mar 1808	
40851	43	H Repton	W Repton	13 April 1808	
40852	46	H Repton	W Repton	13 July 1808	PS by M(C)R
40853	54	H Repton	W Repton	5 Dec 1808	
40854	57	H Repton	W Repton	29 Dec 1808	PS by ER, JAR and M(C)R
40855	101	H Repton	W Repton	after 14 June 1809	
40856	89	J Repton	(changes to will)	15 May 1809	notes by HR
40857	60	H Repton	W Repton	21 Jan 1809	C Abbott to HR
40858	60	H Repton	W Repton	22 Jan 1809	
40859	66	H Repton	W Repton	April 1809	
40860	20	H Repton	W Repton	25 Sept 1807	
40861	61	H Repton	W Repton	early 1809	
40862	117	H Repton	W Repton	7 Mar 1810	M(C)R to DA
40863	112	H Repton	W Repton	9 Feb 1810	
40864	118	H Repton	W Repton	12 Mar 1810	
40865	119	H Repton	W Repton	16 Mar 1810	
40866	127	H Repton	W Repton	4 April 1810	
40867	134	H Repton	W Repton	1 May 1810	
40868	149	H Repton	W Repton	21 Jan 1811	
40869	153	D Adey	W Repton	24 Feb 1811	PS by HR
40870	160	H Repton	W Repton	21 April 1812	
40871	163	H Repton	W Repton	27 Sept 1812	PS by ElizR
40872	164	H Repton	W Repton	16 Nov 1812	MR to DA
40873	169	H Repton	W Repton	15 Dec 1812	
40874	187	H Repton	W Repton	10 May 1814	PS by DA
40875	188	H Repton	W Repton	3 July 1814	M(C)R to DA

HM ref	No.	Writer	Addressee	Date	Comments
40876	195	H Repton	W Repton	22 May 1815	
40877	197	H Repton	W Repton	3 Oct 1815	
40878	198	H Repton	W Repton	31 Mar 1816	
40879	200	H Repton	W Repton	23 April 1816	PS by M(C)R
40880	183	H Repton	W Repton	late April 1814	PS by ElizR
40881	178	D Adey	W Repton	29 Mar 1814	PS by HR; PS by JAR
40882	125	H Repton	Stevenson	1 April 1810	
40883	81	H Repton	J Wodehouse	6 May 1809	HR to W Windham
40884	39	D Adey	M (C) Repton	7 April 1808	
40885	69	D Adey	M (C) Repton	12 April 1809	
40886/1	29	D Adey	W Repton	18 Mar 1808	
40886/2	30	D Adey	W Repton	19 Mar 1808	
40886/3	31	D Adey	W Repton	20 Mar 1808	
40886/4	32	D Adey	W Repton	21 Mar 1808	
40886/5	33	D Adey	W Repton	23 Mar 1808	
40886/6	34	D Adey	W Repton	24 Mar 1808	
40886/7	35	D Adey	W Repton	26 Mar 1808	
40886/8	36	D Adey	W Repton	27 Mar 1808	
40886/9	37	D Adey	W Repton	29 Mar 1808	
40886/10	38	D Adey	W Repton	5 April 1808	
40886/11	40	D Adey	W Repton	9 April 1808	
40886/12	41	D Adey	W Repton	11 April 1808	
40886/13	175	D Adey	W Repton	10 Mar 1814	PS by ElizR
40886/14	179	D Adey	W Repton	5 April 1814	PS by M(C)R
40887/1	62	D Adey	W Repton	26 Jan 1809	
40887/2	70	D Adey	W Repton	14 April 1809	
40887/3	71	D Adey	W Repton	21 April 1809	
40887/4	72	D Adey	W Repton	22 April 1809	
40887/5	73	D Adey	W Repton	28 April 1809	
40887/6	74	D Adey	W Repton	28 April 1809	
40887/7	75	D Adey	W Repton	29 April 1809	
40887/8	76	D Adey	W Repton	2 May 1809	

HM ref	No.	Writer	Addressee	Date	Comments
40887/9	77	D Adey	W Repton	3 May 1809	
40887/10	78	D Adey	W Repton	4 May 1809	
40887/11	79	D Adey	W Repton	4 May 1809	
40887/12	93	D Adey	W Repton	17 May 1809	
40888	141	D Adey	W Repton	2 Aug 1810	
40889/1	152	D Adey	W Repton	19 Feb 1811	PS by ElizR and GR
40889/2	155	D Adey	W Repton	10 Mar 1811	
40889/3	156	D Adey	W Repton	8 April 1811	PS by MR
40890/1	161	D Adey	W Repton	29 June 1812	
40890/2	162	D Adey	W Repton	6 July 1812	PS by ElizR
40891	182	D Adey	W Repton	10 April 1814	end of Letter 182
40892/1	174	D Adey	W Repton	4 Mar 1814	
40892/2	176	D Adey	W Repton	17 Mar 1814	PS by HR, ElizR and M(C)R
40892/3	177	D Adey	W Repton	24, 27 & 28 Mar 1814	
40892/4	180	D Adey	W Repton	9 April 1814	
40892/5	182	D Adey	W Repton	10 April 1814	main body of Letter 182
40892/6	184	D Adey	W Repton	29 April 1814	
40892/7	185	D Adey	W Repton	3 May 1814	PS by M(C)R
40892/8	186	D Adey	W Repton	9 May 1814	
40893	8	D Adey		4 Jan 1807	instructions on will
40894	86	M Anson	W Repton	13 May 1809	
40895	91	C Anson	W Repton	16 May 1809	
40896	151	C Anson	W Repton	21 Jan 1811	
40897	172	E Boyd	Eliz Repton	17 Sept 1813	
40898	192	M Claridge	D Adey	13 Mar 1815	
40899	97	C Cooke	H Repton	24 May 1809	
40900	139	A Disney	W Repton	17 July 1810	
40901	88	A Doughty	D Adey	May 1809	

HM ref	No.	Writer	Addressee	Date	Comments
40902	98	J Dugmore	W Repton	2 June 1809	
40903	108	J J Gay	W Repton	12 Dec 1809	
40904	130	J Marsh	W Repton	11 April 1810	
40905	142	J T Mott	W Repton	2 Aug 1810	
40906	7	J T Mott	H Repton	Jan 1807	
40907	51	Ed Repton	H Repton	27 Oct 1808	
40908	1	Ed Repton	W Repton	6 June 1805	
40909	10	Ed Repton	W Repton	11 July 1807	
40910/1	27	Ed Repton	W Repton	5 Mar 1808	
40910/2	56	Ed Repton	W Repton	20 Dec 1808	
40911	110	Ed Repton	W Repton	27 Dec 1809	
40912/1	111	Ed Repton	W Repton	12 Jan 1810	
40912/2	133	Ed Repton	W Repton	25 April 1810	
40913	150	Ed Repton	W Repton	Jan 1811	
40914/1	170	Ed Repton	W Repton	4 Jan 1813	
40914/2	190	Ed Repton	W Repton	4 Mar 1815	
40914/3	193	Ed Repton	W Repton	24 Mar [or May] 1815	
40915/1	104	G Repton	D Adey	1 Aug 1809	
40915/2	105	G Repton	D Adey	28 Aug 1809	
40916	58	G Repton	J A Repton	Jan 1809	HR to DA
40917	12	G Repton	W Repton	31 July 1807	
40918/1	80	G Repton	W Repton	4 May 1809	
40918/2	83	G Repton	W Repton	8 May 1809	
40918/3	90	G Repton	W Repton	15 May 1809	
40918/4	103	G Repton	W Repton	20 July 1809	
40918/5	109	G Repton	W Repton	18 Dec 1809	
40919/1	116	G Repton	W Repton	7 Mar 1810	
40919/2	122	G Repton	W Repton	22 Mar 1810	
40919/3	128	G Repton	W Repton	5 April 1810	
40919/4	132	G Repton	W Repton	13 April 1810	
40919/5	135	G Repton	W Repton	31 May 1810	
40919/6	146	G Repton	W Repton	14 Dec 1810	
40920	147	G Repton	W Repton	1 Jan 1811	

HM ref	No.	Writer	Addressee	Date	Comments
40921/1	189	G Repton	W Repton	3 Mar 1815	
40921/2	191	G Repton	W Repton	6 Mar 1815	
40922/1	143	H Repton jr	D Adey	10 Aug 1810	
40922/2	144	H Repton jr	D Adey	11 Sept 1810	
40922/3	145	H Repton jr	D Adey	15 Oct 1810	
40923	3	H Repton jr	W Repton	24 Oct 1806	
40924	22	H Repton jr	W Repton	31 Oct 1807	
40925/1	50	H Repton jr	W Repton	13 Oct 1808	
40925/2	52	H Repton jr	W Repton	29 Oct 1808	
40925/3	53	H Repton jr	W Repton	27 Nov 1808	
40925/4	55	H Repton jr	W Repton	15 Dec 1808	
40926/1	126	G Repton	W Repton	2 April 1810	HRjr to WR, 4 April
40926/2	131	H Repton jr	W Repton	11 April 1810	PS by GR
40927	148	H Repton jr	W Repton	2 Jan 1811	
40928	181	H Repton jr	W Repton	10 April 1814	PS by DA
40929/1	44	J Repton	D Adey	April 1808	
40929/2	59	J Repton	D Adey	9 or 10 Jan 1809	
40929/3	App 1	J Repton	D Adey	1808	
40929/4	99	J Repton	D Adey	7 June 1809	S Brett to DA
40930	App 1	J Repton	H Repton	1808	
40931/1	App 1	J Repton	W Repton	undated	
40931/2	App 1	J Repton	W Repton	undated	
40931/3	App 1	J Repton	W Repton	undated	
40931/4	App 1	J Repton	W Repton	undated	
40931/5	113	J A Repton	W Repton	17 Feb 1810	
40932/1	154	M Repton	W Repton	Mar 1811	PS by ElizR and HR
40932/2	157	M Repton	W Repton	?Spring 1811	
40933/1	5	M (C) Repton	D Adey	8 Dec 1806	
40933/2	19	M (C) Repton	D Adey	16 Sept 1807	
40933/3	102	M (C) Repton	D Adey	late June 1809	
40934	45	M (C) Repton	W Repton	26 May 1808	

HM ref	No.	Writer	Addressee	Date	Comments
40935	173	M (H) Repton	W Repton	1 Mar 1814	ER to WR; ER to DA
40936	96	W Repton	C Anson	23 May 1809	
40937	92	W Repton	M Anson	16 May 1809	
40938	100	W Repton	H Anson	15 June 1809	
40939	49	W Repton	Ed Repton	Sept 1808	
40940	165	W Repton	H Repton	17 Nov 1812	
40941	87	W Repton	K Walpole	14 May 1809	
40942/1	65	G Walpole	D Adey	20 Mar 1809	
40942/2	95	W Repton	W Windham	21 May 1809	
40943	App 1	M Sneyd	J Adey	18 Oct 1807	
40944/1	App 1	M Sneyd	W Repton	9 May 1809	not transcribed
40944/2	App 1	M Sneyd	W Repton	6 June 1809	not transcribed
40945	42	J Stadler	H Repton	13 April 1808	
40946	194	A Wallinger	W Repton	11 April 1815	
40947	64	G Walpole	W Repton	27 Feb 1809	
40948	140	H Walpole	W Repton	18 July 1810	
40949	85	K Walpole	W Repton	11 May 1809	
40950	94	W Windham	H Repton	18 May 1809	HR's draft reply
40951	82	J Wodehouse	H Repton	8 May 1809	
40952	App 1	W Repton		1806–1812	cheques to or from
40953/1	4	R Robinson	J Adey	30 Oct 1806	
40953/2	13	H Smith	W Repton	1 Aug 1807	
40953/3	14	J D Martin	W Repton	7 Aug 1807	note from S Baxter
40953/4	15	H Botham	Adey & Repton	18 Aug 1807	
40953/5	16	H Smith	Adey & Repton	20 Aug 1807	
40953/6	18	Pipe & Blair	J Adey	16 Sept 1807	WR's reply
40953/7	21	H Repton jr	W Repton	25 Sept 1807	(printed item)
40953/8	25	R Buckeridge	W Repton	24 Jan 1808	S Simpson to Buckeridge (23 Jan)

HM ref	No.	Writer	Addressee	Date	Comments
40953/9	63	T Blake	W Repton	2 Feb 1809	
40953/10	107	W Harbord	W Repton	11 Sept 1809	
40953/11	114	J Marsh	W Repton	1 Mar 1810	WR's reply
40953/12	115	G Phipps	W Repton	3 Mar 1810	
40953/13	120	C Scott	W Repton	20 Mar 1810	
40953/14	121	C Scott	W Repton	24 Mar 1810	
40953/15	124	C Flower	W Repton	31 Mar 1810	
40953/16	136	J Steward	W Repton	12 June 1810	WR's reply
40953/17	138	T Coke	W Repton	7 July 1810	
40953/18	166	C Norris	W Repton	23 Nov 1812	
40953/19	171	C Scott	W Repton	14 June 1813	
40953/20	196	C Scott	W Repton	13 June 1815	
40953/ 21–30	App 1	Bankers	W Repton	1812–14	listed only
40954/1	2	W Repton	Dr MacLean	6 July 1805	2 draft letters
40954/2	106	W Repton	W Harbord	9 Sept 1809	
40954/3	129	W Repton	N Kent	11 April 1810	
40954/4	137	W Repton	T Coke	4 July 1810	
40954/5	167	W Repton	T Erskine	4 Dec 1812	
40954/6	199	W Repton	Baxter & Bowler	13 April 1816	
40955	App 1	Paston	family pedigree	undated	listed only
40956	App 1	J Adey	marriage settlement	23 June 1770	listed only
40957	App 1	J Adey	marriage settlement	23 June 1770	listed only
40958	App 1	J Adey	re. marriage	29 July 1769	listed only
40959	App 1	J Botham	re. Brook House	3 June 1746	listed only

Select Bibliography

Manuscript sources

Huntington Library, California
HM 40834–40959

Norfolk Record Office
ANW, Records of the Archdeaconry of Norwich
AYL 80, Repton family pedigree
AYL 125/7, abstracts of property in Horsford (18th century–early 19th century)
AYL 250, correspondence between the Fishmongers' Company and Adey & Repton
AYL 420, correspondence with Fishmongers' Company re. Holt enclosure
AYL 440, Tivetshall enclosure act (1808) statement of claims, commissioners' minute book, 1808–1809
AYL 495, papers relating to the enclosure of Swanton Abbott, Buxton and Lamas
AYL 835, copy conveyance Marsh and Repton to Shalders of property in parish of St George Colegate, Norwich, 1814
AYL 847, probate copy of the will of Elizabeth D. Repton
AYL 940, Sheringham enclosure commissioners' minutes, 1809–1810
AYL 1019, deeds of Adey property and Repton property in Hanbury, Lichfield, Aylsham, Stoke-by-Clare etc
AYL 1025, East Dereham enclosure act
AYL 1157, papers relating to will of William Repton, will dated 26 February 1855
AYL 1215, various letters addressed to William Repton
AYL 1223, index made by William Repton [n.d. c.1811] of clients or landholders
C/Sca 2/284, Swanton Abbott, Lammas and Buxton enclosure award 1824

MC 3/61(a), 466X3, account between Hon. Colonel Harbord and Robert
    Copeman, 1802–1808
MC 3/589, 516X9, letters from J. Dugmore to Lord Suffield
MC 185/1, presentation copy of a resolution, dated 1826, passed by the
    Governor, Deputy Governor, Assistants, and Guardians of the Poor of
    the City of Norwich to William Simpson Esq.
MC 253/3-5, 678X7, Letter from Sewell & Blake, Norwich, 1815
MC 2403, Day of Horsford papers
MC 2689, Spurrell Plumbly's letter of commission as Ensign in the
    Southrepps Volunteer Corps of Infantry, 4 September 1804
NCC will register Bloss
NRS 23537, 82X2, abstract of Tttle of George Grimmer to the manor of
    Haddiscoe
PD 192/3, St Giles, Norwich, baptisms
PD 393, Sustead Archdeacon's transcript, Easter 1784 to Easter 1785
PD 393/3, Sustead parish register, 1783–1808
WGN 1/4/121, William Stokes, Fakenham, to William Gunn, Irstead,
    30 November 1802
Y/D 51/1401-1402, includes a 60-year lease from Thomas Anson to William
    Palgrave for property in Great Yarmouth, 1770

Essex Record Office

D/DHf P5, draft plans of Wildman's property in Berners Roding and
    Margaret Roding (1807)
D/DHt T223/8, surrender of William Mills, of Bisterne, Hants., esq. to use
    of Henry Wildman, of London esq., of properties in Margaret Roding,
    near Ongar, Essex (26 February 1802)
D/P 115/1/12, St Andrew, Hornchurch, burials 1813–1848
D/P 346/1/3, St Edward the Confessor, Romford, parish registers

Suffolk Record Office (Bury)

613/747, Printed sale particulars of 'Auberies', Bulmer, Essex &c.
HA 516/8/1-4 and HA 516/9/1-9, relating to property in Clare formerly
    owned by the MacLean family

The National Archives

ADM 9/3/575, appointment of Clement Sneyd to rank of Post Captain,
    3 April 1811
MP 1/105/69, pp. 342–342a, movements of HMS Myrtle in 1812, under
    Captain Sneyd
PROB 8/211, Probate Act Book, 1818

PROB 11/1507/69, will of Sir Philip Stephens of Saint Faiths, probate
    5 January 1810
PROB 11/1609/222, will of Humphry Repton of Harestreet, probate
    16 October 1818

Works by Humphry Repton

Repton, Humphry, *Variety or a Collection of Essays written in the Year 1787*
    (London, 1788)
Repton, Humphry, *Observations on the Theory and Practice of Landscape
    Gardening* (London, 1803)
Repton, Humphry, *An Enquiry into the Changes of Taste in Landscape
    Gardening* (London, 1806)
Repton, Humphry, *Designs for the Pavillon[sic] at Brighton* (London, 1808)
Repton, Humphry, *The Work of Twenty Years Brought to a Crisis in Twenty
    Days! Addressed to the Fashionable World, at the West End of the Town*
    (Romford, 1814)
Repton, Humphry, *Fragments on the Theory and Practice of Landscape
    Gardening (including some Remarks on Grecian and Gothic Architecture)*
    (London, 1816)

Printed primary sources

*A concise history and directory of the City of Norwich for 1811: containing besides
    the lists, a variety of local information, useful and interesting to residents
    and strangers Norwich* (printed by C.Berry, jun. Dove-lane, 1810)
Anon., *Varieties of life; or, Conduct and consequences*, 3 vols (London, 1815)
A to Z of Regency London (Richard Horwood's Map, 3rd edn. 1813),
    introduction by P. Laxton (London, 1985)
Bloxam, J. R., *A register of the presidents, fellows, demies, instructors in grammar
    and in music, chaplains, clerks, choristers, and other members of Saint Mary
    Magdalen College in the University of Oxford, from the foundation of the
    College to the present time* 8 vols (Oxford 1853–85), vol. 7 (1881)
Gale, G. and Mollard, T., eds., *Aylsham Directories, 1793 to 1937 (extracted
    from the directories for Aylsham Norfolk …)* (Aylsham, 2004)
Gentleman's Magazine, various issues
Hasted, E., *The History and Topographical Survey of the County of Kent*, vol. 5
    (Canterbury, 1798)
Hawkins, L. M., *The Countess and Gertrude; or, Modes of Discipline*, 4 vols
    (London, 1811)

Hindry Mason, R., *The history of Norfolk: from original records and other authorities preserved in public and private collections* (London, 1884)

Kent, N., *General view of the agriculture of the county of Norfolk. With observations on the means of improvement, Drawn up for the consideration of the Board of Agriculture and Internal Improvement* (London, 1794) (his preliminary view; the 1796 edition is the final publication)

Kent, N., *Hints to gentlemen of landed property. To which are now first added, supplementary hints* (London, 1793 edition)

Lincoln's Inn Admission Register: 1420–1893, vol. 1, *Admissions from AD 1420 to AD 1799* (Records of the Honorable Society of Lincoln's Inn; Lincoln's Inn, 1896)

Long Fox, E., 'An account of the establishment of an asylum for lunatics, lately erected near Bristol', in R. Reid, *Observations on the Structure of Hospitals for the Treatment of Lunatics* (Edinburgh, 1809), pp. 71–7

Loudon, J. C., *The Landscape Gardening and Landscape Architecture of the Late Humphry Repton Esq.* (London, 1840)

Mackie, C., *Norfolk Annals: A chronological record of remarkable events in the nineteenth century (Compiled from the files of the 'Norfolk Chronicle')*, vol. I, *1801–1850* (Norwich, 1901)

Mollard, T., ed., *Aylsham in 1821. The population of the parish of Aylsham recorded by William Morris in May, 1821* (Aylsham, 1997)

Norfolk and Norwich Chronicle, various issues

Ogborne, Elizabeth, *The History of Essex, from the earliest period to the present time, illustrated with … engravings of churches, monuments … With biographical notices of the most distinguished … natives.* (London, 1814)

Peacock, W., *Polite Repository* (London, 1790 onwards) (annual publication)

Pecke, T., *The Norwich directory: containing an alphabetical list of the principal inhabitants, their address, profession, or trade: a concise history of Norwich: pointing out the most remarkable places in it worthy the attention of strangers* (Norwich, 1802)

Pigot, *Directory of Middlesex and the towns and villages within 12 miles of London* (1823)

Porter, J., *The Scottish Chiefs*, 5 vols (London, 1810)

Price, F. G. H., *A handbook of London bankers: with some account of their predecessors the early goldsmiths, together with lists of bankers, from the earliest one printed in 1677 to that of the London post-office directory of 1876.* (London, 1890–91)

Repton, E., *The Works of Creation, A Series of Discourses for Boyle's lecture, No. 1. Being the First Sermon of the series delivered at St. Mary Le Bow Church, Cheapside, On Monday 5th of September, 1808* (London, 1808)

*Select Committee on Regulations to control Branches of the Public Expenditure in
Great Britain & Ireland, Fifth report, Part II (Audit of Public Accounts)*
PP 1810 II (371), presented to the House 20 June 1810
Sotheby & Co., *Catalogue of Valuable Printed Books, Autograph Letters
and Historical Documents comprising The Property of Sir Christopher
Chancellor, the Property of Lady Pooley, The Property of P. J. McKie, esq.,
The Property of P. W. Ford, esq., the Property of the Jewish Museum and
other properties* (Day of Sale: Monday, 25th March, 1974, at 10.30 a.m.
precisely) (London, 1974)
Wassell, Miss, *The Rivals; or The General Investigation* (London, 1815)

Secondary sources

Adams, W. D., *Dictionary of English Literature* (London, 1880)
Alcock, R. C., and Holland, F. C., *British Postmarks: A Short History and
Guide* (revised edn.,1977)
Baker, T. F. T. and Pugh, R. B., eds., *A History of the County of Middlesex,*
vol. 5, *Hendon, Kingsbury, Great Stanmore, Little Stanmore, Edmonton
Enfield, Monken Hadley, South Mimms, Tottenham* (London, 1976)
Bald, M. A., *Women-writers of the nineteenth century* (Cambridge, 1923)
Barnes, D. G., *History of the English Corn Laws, from 1660 to 1846* (London,
1930)
Bate, S., Savage, R., and Williamson, Tom, eds., *Humphry Repton in Norfolk*
(Aylsham, 2018)
Batty, S., ed., *Humphry Repton in Sussex* (Sussex, 2018)
Bendall, S., ed., *Dictionary of land surveyors and local map-makers of Great
Britain and Ireland, 1530–1850* (2nd edn., 2 vols., London, 1997)
Birkbeck, R., *Notes on the history and genealogy of the family of Lubbock*
(London, 1891)
Bonar, J., 'The disposition of troops in London, March 1815', *The English
Historical Review*, vol. 16, no. 62 (April 1901), p. 348–54
Campbell-Smith, D., *Masters of the Post: the authorized history of the Royal
Mail* (London, 2011)
Carter, G., Good, P., and Laurie, K., *Humphry Repton: Landscape Gardener
1752–1818* (Norwich & London, 1982)
Cattermole, P., ed., *Wymondham Abbey: a history of the monastery and parish
church* (Wymondham, 2007)
Cheney, C. R., ed., *Handbook of Dates for Students of English History* (London,
1991)
Cherry, S., *Mental Health Care in Modern England: the Norfolk Lunatic
Asylum/St Andrews Hospital, c. 1810–1988* (Woodbridge, 2003)

Cutmore, J. B., *Contributors to The Quarterly Review: a history, 1809–25* (London, 2008)

Damiano, S. T., 'Agents at home: wives, lawyers, and financial competence in eighteenth-century New England port cities', *Early American Studies*, 13 (2015), pp. 808–35

Daniels, S., 'Cankerous blossom: troubles in the later career of Humphry Repton documented in the Repton correspondence in the Huntington Library', *Journal of Garden History*, 6 (1986), pp. 146–61

Daniels, S., *Humphry Repton: Landscape Gardening and the Geography of Georgian England* (Yale University Press, New Haven and London, 1999)

Daniels, S., 'View from Westminster', *Landscapes of Memory: Landscapes of Humphry Repton*, special edition of *Garden Museum Journal*, 36 (Winter 2018/19), pp. 26–30

Daniels, S., 'Voices from the grave', *Landscapes of Memory: Landscapes of Humphry Repton*, special edition of *Garden Museum Journal*, 36 (Winter 2018/19), pp. 12–25

Davidoff, L., and Hall, C., *Family Fortunes: Men and Women of the English Middle Class 1780–1850* (London, 2nd edn., 2002)

Dawes, M., and Ward-Perkins, C. N., *Country Banks and Bankers 1688–1953*, vol. 2, *Register of Towns with their Banks* (Canterbury, 2000)

Eyres, P., and Lynch, K., *On The Spot: The Yorkshire Red Books of Humphry Repton, Landscape Gardener* (Huddersfield, 2018)

Farrer, W. and Brownbill, J., eds., *A History of the County of Lancaster*, vol. 5, *Part of Salford hundred* (London, 1911)

Feldman, H., *Letter receivers of London, 1652–1857: a history of their offices and handstamps within the general, penny and twopenny posts* (Bristol, 1998), vol. 2

Flood, S., and Williamson, T., eds., *Humphry Repton in Hertfordshire* (Hatfield, 2018)

Foster, J., *Alumni Oxonienses: The Members of the University of Oxford, 1715–1886*, (London, 1887–8)

Gee, A., *The British Volunteer Movement, 1794–1814* (Oxford, 2003)

Gore, A., and Carter, G., eds., *Humphry Repton's Memoirs* (Norwich, 2005)

Gray, D., *Chaplain to Mr Speaker: the religious life of the House of Commons* (London, 1991)

Harling, P., *The Waning of 'Old Corruption'* (Oxford, 1996)

Harvey, A. D., *Britain in the early nineteenth century* (London, 1978,

Hastie, S., *Abbots Langley: A Hertfordshire Village* (Abbots Langley, 1993)

Hilton, B., *Corn, cash, commerce: the economic policies of the Tory governments 1815–1830*, (Oxford, 1977)

Hoock, H., *Empires of the imagination: politics, war and the arts in the British world, 1750–1850* (London, 2010)

Horn, P., 'An eighteenth century land agent: the career of Nathaniel Kent (1737–1810)', *Agricultural History Review*, 30:1 (1982), pp. 1–16

(Kent Gardens Trust), *Humphry Repton in Kent* (Eynsford, 2018)

Knapman, D. J., *Conversation Sharp: the biography of a London Gentleman Richard Sharp (1759–1835) in letters, prose and verse* (Dorchester, 2003)

(London Parks and Gardens Trust), *Repton in London: The gardens and landscapes of Humphry Repton (1752–1818) in the London Boroughs* (London, 2018)

Meade-Fetherstonhaugh, M., and Warner, O., *Uppark and its people* (2nd edn., London, 1995)

Neve, A. H., *The Tonbridge of Yesterday* (Tonbridge, 1933)

Orbell, J., and Turton, A., eds, *British Banking: a guide to historical records* (Aldershot, 2001)

Page, W., ed., *A History of the County of Bedford*, vol. 3 (London, 1912)

Powell, W. R., *A History of the County of Essex*, vol. 5, *including accounts of Barking, Ilford, Dagenham and other areas of Essex now within greater London* (London, 1966)

Powell, W. R., ed., *A History of the County of Essex*, vol. 6, *Parishes of Becontree hundred now within the London boroughs of Newham, Waltham Forest and Redbridge* (London, 1973)

Powell, W. R., ed., *A History of the County of Essex*, vol. 7, *The ancient parishes ... now within the London borough of Havering, and those in Chafford hundred in western Essex* (London, 1978)

Robson, R., *The attorney in eighteenth-century England* (Cambridge, 1959)

Rogger, A., *Landscapes of Taste, The Art of Humphry Repton's Red Books* (Oxford, 2007)

Rutherford, S., ed., *Humphry Repton in Buckinghamshire and beyond* (Buckinghamshire, 2018)

Sanford, O. R., and Salt, D., *British postal rates, 1635 to 1839* (Beckenham, 1990)

Sapwell, J., *A History of Aylsham* (Norwich, 1960)

Schmidt, A. J., 'Lawyer professionalism in rural England: changes in routine and rewards in the early nineteenth century', *Lincolnshire History and Archaeology*, 32 (1997), pp. 25–39

Schmidt, A. J., 'The country attorney in late eighteenth-century England: Benjamin Smith of Horbling', *Law and History Review*, 8 (1990), pp. 237–71

Schmidt, A. J., 'The Smiths of Horbling: country attorneys', *Huntington Library Quarterly*, 54 (1991), pp. 143–76

Searle, A., and Brazier, C., *A History of Hare Hall* (n.p., 1960)

Smith, L., 'A gentleman's mad-doctor in Georgian England: Edward Long Fox and Brislington House', *History of Psychiatry*, 19 (2008), pp. 163–84

Spooner, S., ed., *Sail and Storm: The Aylsham Navigation* (Aylsham, 2012)

Staff, F., *The Penny Post, 1680–1918* (Cambridge, 1993)

Stroud, D., *Humphry Repton* (London, 1962)

Tarver, A., *Church Court Records: an introduction for family and local historians* (Chichester, 1995)

Temple, N., 'Humphry Repton, Illustrator, and William Peacock's "Polite Repository" 1790–1811', *Garden History*, 16:2 (Autumn 1988), pp. 161–73

Vaughan-Lewis, M., ed., *A New History of Aylsham Public Houses* (Aylsham, 2018)

Vaughan-Lewis, W., and Vaughan-Lewis, M., *Aylsham: A Nest of Norfolk Lawyers* (Itteringham, 2014)

Walpole, N., *The Walpoles of Wolterton* (Lewes, 1986)

Weinreb, B., and Hibbert, C., eds., *The London Encyclopaedia* (London, 1983)

Whitehead, D., and Bradney, J., 'In the enemy's quarters': Humphry Repton in the West Midlands* (Hereford, 2018)

Williamson, T., *Polite Landscapes: Gardens and Society in Eighteenth-Century England* (Stroud, 1995)

Wright, A. P. M., ed., *A History of the County of Cambridge and the Isle of Ely, vol. 8, Armingford and Thriplow hundreds* (London, 1982)

Wyndham H. S., *The Annals of Covent Garden Theatre from 1732 to 1897*, 2 vols. (London, 1906)

Unpublished theses

Hales, M. R., 'Civilian soldiers in Staffordshire, 1793–1823' (PhD thesis, Sheffield Hallam University, 1995)

Online sources

British Newspapers online – *Norfolk and Norwich Chronicle, Morning Chronicle, London Gazette*

Bulmer history http://www.bulmerhistory.co.uk/page49.html

Clergy of the Church of England database www.theclergydatabase.org.uk

Complete Peerage, vol. V, online www.thepeerage.com/p1327.htm#i13261

Ducal house of Leinster from http://www.angelfire.com/realm/gotha/gotha/leinster.html, accessed 15/09/19

English Heritage https://www.english-heritage.org.uk/visit/places/witley-court-and-gardens/things-to-do

Hansard, Governor Of Curacoa https://api.parliament.uk/historic-hansard/commons/1807/apr/22/governor-of-curacoa

Historic England website: https://historicengland.org.uk/listing/the-list/
list-entry/1061187 (Sandgate)

History of Parliament https://www.historyofparliamentonline.org/research/
members/members-1790-1820

HMRC https://web.archive.org/web/20100724033906/http://www.hmrc.gov.
uk/history/taxhis1.htm

Landed Families of Britain and Ireland, the family of Thomas Anson https://
landedfamilies.blogspot.com/search?q=anson%2Cthomas

London Gardens online http://londongardensonline.org.uk/gardens-online-
record.php?ID=BAR019

London street views https://londonstreetviews.wordpress.com/2014/02/10/
george-halfhide-seal-engraver/

Maid's Head, Norwich https://www.maidsheadhotel.co.uk/about/our-history/

Oxford Dictionary of National Biography

Oxford English Dictionary

Ranelagh family http://www.cracroftspeerage.co.uk/online/content/
ranelagh1628.htm

Shugborough estate http://www.shugborough.org.uk/theshugboroughestate/
EstateHistory.aspx

Times online

Index of persons

Index of places

Note: The county names used in this index refer to the old counties.

Index of subjects